BTEC Level 3

edexcel
advancing learning, changing lives

INFORMATION TECHNOLOGY LEVEL 3

Book 2 BTEC National

Karen Anderson | David Atkinson-Beaumont | Allen Kaye
Jenny Lawson | Richard McGill | Jenny Phillips | Daniel Richardson

A PEARSON COMPANY

Published by Pearson Education Limited, a company incorporated in England and Wales, having its registered office at Edinburgh Gate, Harlow, Essex, CM20 2JE. Registered company number: 872828

www.pearsonschoolsandfecolleges.co.uk

Edexcel is a registered trademark of Edexcel Limited

Text © Pearson Education Limited 2011

First published 2011

14 13 12 11
10 9 8 7 6 5 4 3 2

British Library Cataloguing in Publication Data
A catalogue record for this book is available from the British Library.

ISBN 978 1 846909 29 0

Edited by Carol Usher and Melanie Birdsall
Designed by Wooden Ark
Typeset by Tek-Art
Original illustrations © Pearson Education Limited 2010
Cover design by Visual Philosophy, created by eMC Design
Picture research by Cath Bevan
Cover photo © Shutterstock.com: Bliznetsov
Back cover photos © Getty Images: PhotoDisc tr; Pearson Education Ltd: Steve Shott tc, Studio 8, Clark Wiseman c
Printed in Spain by Grafos

Disclaimer
This material has been published on behalf of Edexcel and offers high-quality support for the delivery of Edexcel qualifications.

This does not mean that the material is essential to achieve any Edexcel qualification, nor does it mean that it is the only suitable material available to support any Edexcel qualification. Edexcel material will not be used verbatim in setting any Edexcel examination or assessment. Any resource lists produced by Edexcel shall include this and other appropriate resources.

Copies of official specifications for all Edexcel qualifications may be found on the Edexcel website: www.edexcel.com

Contents

Credits

The publisher would like to thank the following for their kind permission to reproduce their photographs:

(Key: b-bottom; c-centre; l-left; r-right; t-top)

Alamy Images: Charles Bowman 1, David J. Green 119, 127r, 254r, Eric Nathan 251br, Lenscap 251t, Mary Evans Picture Library 246, Ralf Mohr 55, Sho Shan 91; **Commodore Media:** 125; **Corbis:** Bettman 251cr, Hulton Deutsche Collection 254l; **Getty Images:** Aurora 121, PhotoDisc 97, 198; **image courtesy of NASA Earth Observatory:** Jet Propulsion Laboratory (JPL) 127l; **iStockphoto:** Andrey Prokhorov 25, NuStock 187, Vikram Raghuvanshi Photography 185; **Kobal Collection Ltd:** Focus Features 241, Touchstone / Amblin 253; **Kodak Media:** 220; **Media Pictures:** 147, 224bl; **Pearson Education Ltd:** Gareth Boden 123, 195, 239, Martin Beddall 189, Steve Shott 99, 100, Studio 8, Clark Wiseman 3, 93, 157, 243; **Photolibrary.com:** age fotostock 135, HillCreek Pictures BV 213, imagebroker.net 57, 219l, Oxford Scientific (OSF) 141; **Science & Society Picture Library:** 245, 247t, 247bl, 247br; **Science Photo Library Ltd:** Peter Menzel 129b; **Shutterstock.com:** 169t, 169b, Adisa 131, Aga Rafi 129t, Anton Andronov 222t, Auremar 311, Chepko Danil Vitalevich 155, Denis Vrubleuski 59, Dmitry Strizhakov 103, Geanina Becheu 153, Karin Hildebrand Lau 27, Khwi 211, Lepus 275, Monkey Business Images 273, NatUlrich 219r, Stocklite 23, 89, Tracy Whiteside 277, Yuri Arcurs 18, 215; **Summa, Inc.:** 224t; **Tungsten:** 224cl; **Wacom Technology Corporation:** 222b

Cover images: *Front:* **Shutterstock.com:** Bliznetsov; *Back:* **Getty Images:** PhotoDisc tr; **Pearson Education Ltd:** Steve Shott tc, Studio 8, Clark Wiseman c

All other images © Pearson Education

The authors and publishers would like to thank the following individuals and organisations for permission to reproduce material:

pp. 110, 113, 116 Material from gamemaker8.com is used by kind permission of YOYO Games at yoyogames.com.

p. 179 Quote from Obscene Publications Act (1959) © Crown Copyright 1959.

p. 225 CorelDRAW screen shot is reprinted with permission from Corel UK Limited.

p. 225 Screen shot from Autodesk AutoCAD is used by permission.

pp. 225, 226 Corel Paint Shop Pro screen shots are reprinted with permission from Corel UK Limited.

p. 257 Data on Windows® usage is used by kind permission of the Microsoft Corporation.

p. 257 Data on Mac® usage is used by permission of MacNN.com.

Adobe product screen shot(s) reprinted with permission from Adobe Systems Incoporated.

Microsoft product screen shot(s) reprinted with permission from Microsoft Corporation.

Every effort has been made to trace the copyright holders and we apologise in advance for any unintentional omissions. We would be pleased to insert the appropriate acknowledgement in any subsequent edition of this publication.

About your BTEC Level 3 National Information Technology

Choosing to study for a BTEC Level 3 National Information Technology qualification is a great decision to make for lots of reasons. This qualification is a further step towards a career in the IT industry. The IT industry is an exciting and constantly changing one with a wide range of opportunities – from working in computer games development to working with robotic systems or supporting scientists in combating global warming. The opportunities are endless.

Your BTEC Level 3 National in Information Technology is a **vocational** or **work-related** qualification. This doesn't mean that it will give you all the skills you need to do a job, but it does mean that you'll have the opportunity to gain specific knowledge, understanding and skills that are relevant to your future career.

What will you be doing?

The qualification is structured into **mandatory units** (ones that you must do) and your choice of **optional units**. *BTEC Level 3 National Information Technology Student Book 1* (ISBN: 9781846909283) contains mandatory 12 units (with a further 2 mandatory units on the Pearson Education Website – www.pearsonschoolandfecolleges. co.uk/btecnationalit). This book covers a number of optional units. How many units you do and which ones you cover depend on the type of qualification you are working towards.

- BTEC Level 3 National Certificate in Information Technology: two mandatory units plus optional units to provide a total of 30 credits (no more than 10 credits can come from optional specialist or vendor units)
- BTEC Level 3 National Subsidiary Diploma in Information Technology: two mandatory units optional units to provide a total of 60 credits (no more than 20 credits can come from optional specialist or vendor units)
- BTEC Level 3 National Diploma in Information Technology: three mandatory units plus optional units to provide a total of 120 credits (no more than 30 credits can come from optional specialist units and no more than 40 credits can come from optional vendor units)
- BTEC Level 3 National Diploma in Information Technology (Business – **B**): four mandatory units plus optional units to provide a total of 120 credits (no more than 30 credits can come from optional specialist units and no more than 40 credits can come from optional vendor units)
- BTEC Level 3 National Diploma in Information Technology (Networking and System Support – **NSS**): seven mandatory units plus optional units to provide a total of 120 credits (no more than 30 credits can come from optional specialist units and no more than 40 credits can come from optional vendor units)
- BTEC Level 3 National Diploma in Information Technology (Software Development – **SD**): four mandatory units plus optional units to provide a total of 120 credits (no more than 30 credits can come from optional specialist units and no more than 40 credits can come from optional vendor units)
- BTEC Level 3 National Extended Diploma in Information Technology: three mandatory units plus optional units to provide a total of 180 credits (no more than 40 credits can come from optional specialist units and no more than 60 credits can come from optional vendor units)
- BTEC Level 3 National Extended Diploma in Information Technology (Business – **B**): six mandatory units plus optional units to provide a total of 180 credits (no more than 40 credits can come from optional specialist units and no more than 60 credits can come from optional vendor units)
- BTEC Level 3 National Extended Diploma in Information Technology (Networking and System Support – **NSS**): eight mandatory units plus optional units to provide a total of 180 credits (no more than 40 credits can come from optional specialist units and no more than 60 credits can come from optional vendor units)
- BTEC Level 3 National Extended Diploma in Information Technology (Software Development – **SD**): six mandatory units plus optional units to provide a total of 180 credits (no more than 40 credits can come from optional specialist units and no more than 60 credits can come from optional vendor units)

The table below shows how the units covered by the books in this series cover the different types of BTEC qualifications.

Unit number	Credit value	Unit name	Cert	Sub Dip	Dip	Dip (B)	Dip (NSS)	Dip (SD)	Ext Dip	Ext Dip (B)	Ext Dip (NSS)	Ext Dip (SD)
1	10	Communication and employability skills for IT	M	M	M	M	M	M	M	M	M	M
2	10	Computer systems	M	M	M	M	M	M	M	M	M	M
3	10	Information systems	O	O	M	M	M	M	M	M	M	M
4	10	Impact of the use of IT on business systems	O	O	O	M	O	O	O	M	O	O
5	10	Managing networks	O	O	O	O	M	O	O	O	M	O
6	10	Software design and development	O	O	O	O	O	M	O	O	O	M
7	10	Organisational systems security	O	O	O	O	O	O	O	M	O	O
8	10	e-Commerce	O	O	O	O	O	O	O	M	O	O
9	10	Computer networks	O	O	O	O	M	O	O	O	M	O
10	10	Communication technologies	O	O	O	O	M	O	O	O	M	O
11	10	Systems analysis and design	O	O	O	O	O	O	O	O	O	M
12	10	IT technical support	O	O	O	O	M	O	O	O	M	O
13	10	IT systems troubleshooting and repair	O	O	O	O	O	O	O	O	M	O
14	10	Event driven programming	O	O	O	O	O	O	O	O	O	M
17	10	Project planning with IT	O	O	O	O	O	O	O	O	O	O
18	10	Database design	O	O	O	O	O	O	O	O	O	O
20	10	Client side customisation of web pages	O	O	O	O	O	O	O	O	O	O
22	10	Developing computer games	O	O	O	O	O	O	O	O	O	O
23	10	Human computer interaction	O	O	O	O	O	O	O	O	O	O
28	10	Website production	O	O	O	O	O	O	O	O	O	O
29	10	Installing and upgrading software	O	O	O	O	O	O	O	O	O	O
30	10	Digital graphics	O	O	O	O	O	O	O	O	O	O
31	10	Computer animation	O	O	O	O	O	O	O	O	O	O
42	10	Spreadsheet modelling	OS	OS	OS	OS	OS	OS	OS	OS	OS	OS

M = Mandatory   O = Optional   OS = Optional Specialist

How to use this book

This book is designed to help you through your BTEC Level 3 National Information Technology course. It contains many features that will help you develop and apply your skills and knowledge in work-related situations and assist you in getting the most from your course.

Introduction

These introductions give you a snapshot of what to expect from each unit – and what you should be aiming for by the time you finish it!

Assessment and grading criteria

This table explains what you must do to achieve each of the assessment criteria for each of the mandatory and optional units. For each assessment criterion, shown by the grade buttons **P1**, **M1**, **D1**, etc. there is an assessment activity.

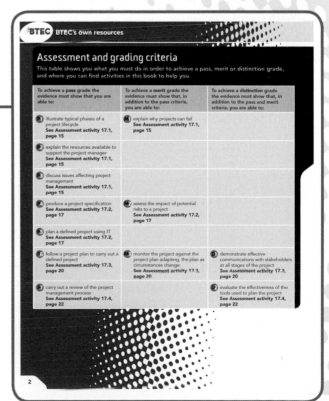

Assessment

Your tutor will set **assignments** throughout your course for you to complete. These may take a variety of forms. The important thing is that you evidence your skills and knowledge to date.

Stuck for ideas? Daunted by your first assignment? These learners have all been through it before…

Activities

There are different types of activities for you to do: **Assessment activities** are suggestions for tasks that you might do as part of your assignment and will help you develop your knowledge, skills and understanding. **Grading tips** clearly explain what you need to do in order to achieve a pass, merit or distinction grade.

There are also suggestions for **activities** that will give you a broader grasp of the world of IT, stretch your understanding and develop your skills.

Activity: Planning a project

Your workplace hopes to convert an existing room into a training room including audio-visual aids and computers for trainees. Working in pairs, carry out the following steps.

1 Consider the stages in the project lifecycle. Create a document listing these stages with bullet points for what actions would be needed for each stage.

2 Write a short note next to each of the actions that will be needed in the implementation stage explaining why each is needed.

3 How long do you think the project would take?

How to… activities

These activities run through the steps involved in software and hardware processes, as well that you will need to carry out successfully to complete the assessment activities in this book and in your career in IT.

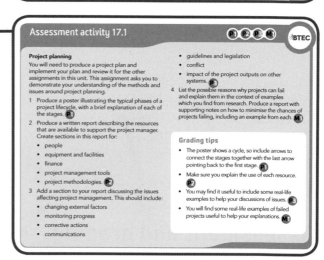

Unit 17 Project planning with IT

How you will be assessed

This unit will be assessed by internal assignments that will be designed and marked by the staff at your centre. It may be subject to sampling by your centre's Lead Internal Verifier or an Edexcel Standards Verifier as part of Edexcel's on going quality assurance procedures. Assignments are designed to allow you to show your understanding of the unit outcomes. These relate to what you should be able to do after completing this unit.

Your assessment could be in the form of:
- presentations
- case studies
- practical tasks
- written assignments

Loren, BTEC National IT learner

This unit provided me with good knowledge about analysing different situations and how to put different methods into practice. It's helped me to become more independent, as I've needed to understand how projects are managed and to plan projects myself. I've had to follow project plans, which has enhanced my skills and given me valuable experience for the future.

The assignments were quite easy and covered many planning skills and techniques. I had never seen a Gantt chart before and it was interesting to create my own and see how a wall chart like this can benefit project management. PERT charts were fascinating. They taught me about the time it takes to complete a project and how to allocate more resources to the slowest critical tasks.

I noticed a Gantt chart at work and asked my supervisor about it. She showed me the PERT chart that related to it and I could understand both of the charts, following them whilst I worked. I could see then how they fit together and how they provide benefits for time management.

I have used the Gantt idea to help me plan my assignment work – it shows me where I am with the work and what's still needed. It has helped me prioritise different assignments so that I am able to meet the deadlines.

I am glad I studied this unit, as it has opened my eyes to some powerful techniques and has provided me with knowledge that could be used in a future career. I feel that the techniques that are learnt in this unit can be used in different areas and will always bring benefits.

Over to you
- Can you find out how a PERT chart can be used to identify how long a project should take to complete?
- Loren mentions allocating more resources to the slowest critical tasks. What is a critical task in a PERT chart?
- Can you find and explain an example of a Gantt chart from the Internet?

3

Assessment activity 17.1   P1 P2 P3 M1   BTEC

Project planning

You will need to produce a project plan and implement your plan and review it for the other assignments in this unit. This assignment asks you to demonstrate your understanding of the methods and issues around project planning.

1 Produce a poster illustrating the typical phases of a project lifecycle, with a brief explanation of each of the stages. **P1**

2 Produce a written report describing the resources that are available to support the project manager. Create sections in this report for:
- people
- equipment and facilities
- finance
- project management tools
- project methodologies. **P2**

3 Add a section to your report discussing the issues affecting project management. This should include:
- changing external factors
- monitoring progress
- corrective actions
- communications

- guidelines and legislation
- conflict
- impact of the project outputs on other systems. **P3**

4 List the possible reasons why projects can fail and explain them in the context of examples which you find from research. Produce a report with supporting notes on how to minimise the chances of projects failing, including an example from each. **M1**

Grading tips

- The poster shows a cycle, so include arrows to connect the stages together with the last arrow pointing back to the first stage. **P1**
- Make sure you explain the use of each resource. **P2**
- You may find it useful to include some real-life examples to help your discussions of issues. **P3**
- You will find some real-life examples of failed projects useful to help your explanations. **M1**

How to… import data into Access™

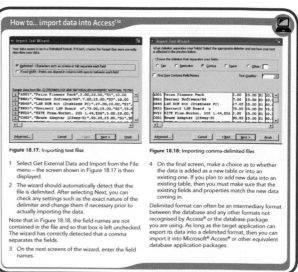

Figure 18.17: Importing text files

Figure 18.18: Importing comma-delimited files

1 Select Get External Data and Import from the File menu – the screen shown in Figure 18.17 is then displayed.

2 The wizard should automatically detect that the file is delimited. After selecting Next, you can check any settings such as the exact nature of the delimiter and change them if necessary prior to actually importing the data.

Note that in Figure 18.18, the field names are not contained in the file and so that box is left unchecked. The wizard has correctly detected that a comma separates the fields.

3 On the next screens of the wizard, enter the field names.

4 On the final screen, make a choice as to whether the data is added as a new table or into an existing one. If you plan to add new data into an existing table, then you must make sure that the existing fields and properties match the new data coming in.

Delimited format can often be an intermediary format between the database and any other formats not recognised by Access® or the database package you are using. As long as the target application can export its data into a delimited format, then you can import it into Microsoft® Access® or other equivalent database application packages.

Personal, learning and thinking skills

Throughout your BTEC Level 3 National Information Technology course there are lots of opportunities to develop your personal, learning and thinking skills. These will help you work in a team, manage yourself effectively and develop your all-important interpersonal skills. Look out for these as you progress.

PLTS

When you produce your project specification, you will identify questions to answer and problems to resolve showing that you are an **independent enquirer**.

When you produce your project specification, you will need to ask questions to extend your thinking showing that you are a **creative thinker**.

By assessing the impact of potential risks to your project, you will explore issues, events or problems from different perspectives showing that you are an **independent enquirer**.

Functional skills

It's important that you have good English, Mathematics and ICT skills – you never know when you'll need them, and employers will be looking for evidence that you've got these skills too.

Functional skills

You will practise using **ICT** functional skills to plan solutions to complex tasks by analysing the necessary stages when you plan your project.

Key terms

Technical words and phrases are easy to spot. The terms and definitions are also in the glossary at the back of the book.

Key term

Project methodology – a standard, documented way of tackling a business project.

WorkSpace

Case studies provide snapshots of real workplace issues, and show how the skills and knowledge you develop during your course can help you in your career.

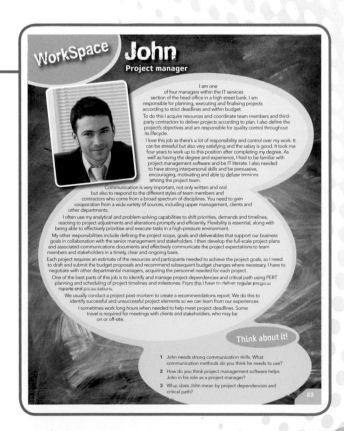

WorkSpace **John** Project manager

I am one of four managers within the IT services section of the head office in a high street bank. I am responsible for planning, executing and finalising projects according to strict deadlines and within budget.

To do this I acquire resources and coordinate team members and third-party contractors to deliver projects according to plan. I also define the project's objectives and am responsible for quality control throughout its lifecycle.

I love this job as there's a lot of responsibility and control over my work. It can be stressful but also very satisfying and the salary is good. It took me four years to work up to this position after completing my degree. As well as having the degree and experience, I had to be familiar with project management software and be IT literate. I also needed to have strong interpersonal skills and be persuasive, encouraging, motivating and able to defuse tensions among the project team.

Communication is very important, not only written and oral but also to respond to the different styles of team members and contractors who come from a broad spectrum of disciplines. You need to gain cooperation from a wide variety of sources, including upper management, clients and other departments.

I often use my analytical and problem-solving capabilities to shift priorities, demands and timelines, reacting to project adjustments and alterations promptly and efficiently. Flexibility is essential, along with being able to effectively prioritise and execute tasks in a high-pressure environment.

My other responsibilities include defining the project scope, goals and deliverables that support our business goals in collaboration with the senior management and stakeholders. I then develop the full-scale project plans and associated communications documents and effectively communicate the project expectations to team members and stakeholders in a timely, clear and ongoing basis.

Each project requires an estimate of the resources and participants needed to achieve the project goals, so I need to draft and submit the budget proposals and recommend subsequent budget changes where necessary. I have to negotiate with other departmental managers, acquiring the personnel needed for each project.

One of the best parts of this job is to identify and manage project dependencies and critical path using PERT planning and scheduling of project timelines and milestones. From this I have to deliver regular progress reports and presentations.

We usually conduct a project post-mortem to create a recommendations report. We do this to identify successful and unsuccessful project elements so we can learn from our experiences.

I sometimes work long hours when needed to help meet project deadlines. Some travel is required for meetings with clients and stakeholders, who may be on or off-site.

Think about it!

1 John needs strong communication skills. What communication methods do you think he needs to use?

2 How do you think project management software helps John in his role as a project manager?

3 What does John mean by project dependencies and critical path?

Just checking

When you see this sort of activity, take stock! These quick activities and questions are there to check your knowledge. You can use them to see how much progress you've made and to identify any areas where you need to refresh your knowledge.

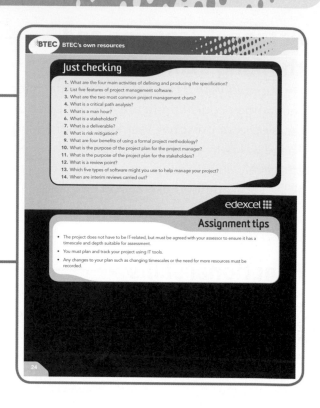

Edexcel's assignment tips

At the end of each unit, you'll find hints and tips to help you get the best mark you can, such as the best websites to go to, checklists to help you remember processes and useful reminders to avoid common mistakes. You might want to read this information before starting your assignment…

Don't miss out on these resources to help you!

Have you read your **BTEC Level 3 National Study Skills Guide**? It's full of advice on study skills, putting your assignments together and making the most of being a BTEC Information Technology learner.

 Ask your tutor about extra materials to help you through your course. We also provide **Student Book 1** which gives you even more units for study. The **Teaching Resource Pack** which accompanies this book contains interesting videos, activities, presentations and information about the world of IT.

Your book is just part of the exciting resources from Edexcel to help you succeed in your BTEC course. Visit www.edexcel.com/BTEC or www.pearsonfe.co.uk/BTEC2010 for more details.

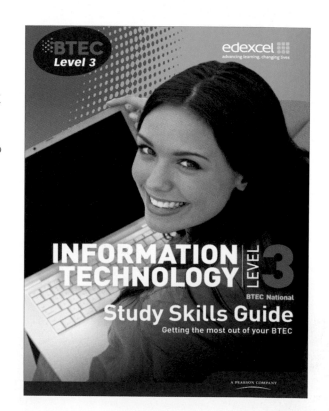

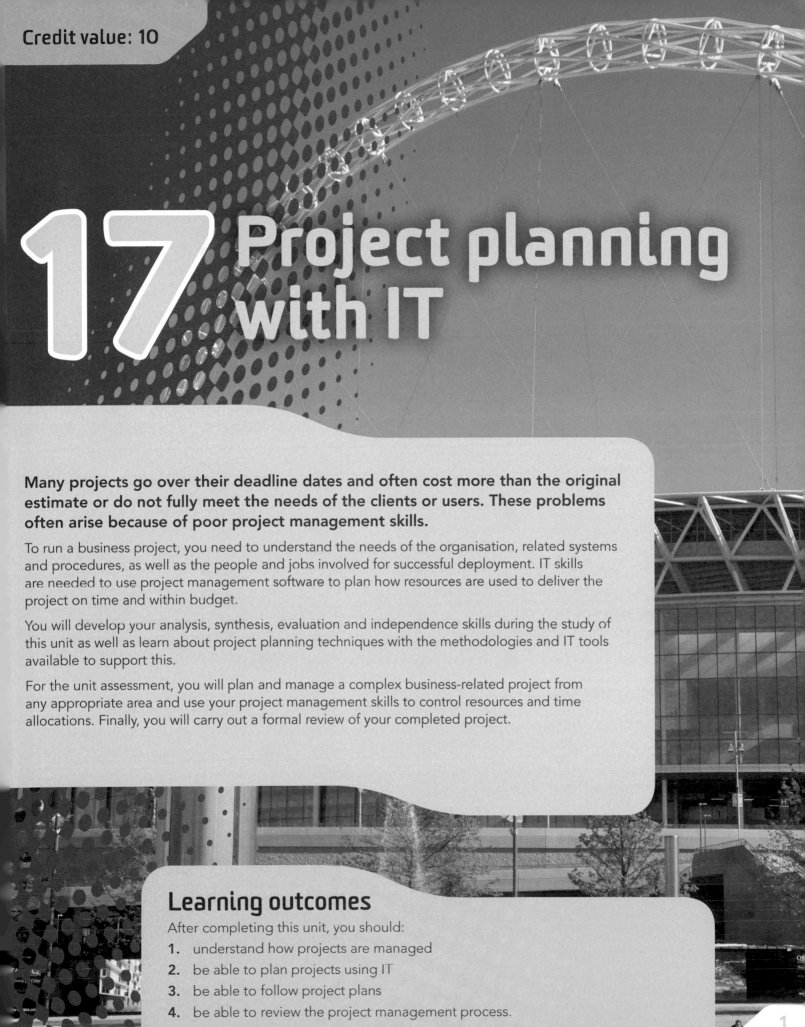

17 Project planning with IT

Many projects go over their deadline dates and often cost more than the original estimate or do not fully meet the needs of the clients or users. These problems often arise because of poor project management skills.

To run a business project, you need to understand the needs of the organisation, related systems and procedures, as well as the people and jobs involved for successful deployment. IT skills are needed to use project management software to plan how resources are used to deliver the project on time and within budget.

You will develop your analysis, synthesis, evaluation and independence skills during the study of this unit as well as learn about project planning techniques with the methodologies and IT tools available to support this.

For the unit assessment, you will plan and manage a complex business-related project from any appropriate area and use your project management skills to control resources and time allocations. Finally, you will carry out a formal review of your completed project.

Learning outcomes

After completing this unit, you should:

1. understand how projects are managed
2. be able to plan projects using IT
3. be able to follow project plans
4. be able to review the project management process.

Assessment and grading criteria

This table shows you what you must do in order to achieve a pass, merit or distinction grade, and where you can find activities in this book to help you.

To achieve a **pass** grade the evidence must show that you are able to:	To achieve a **merit** grade the evidence must show that, in addition to the pass criteria, you are able to:	To achieve a **distinction** grade the evidence must show that, in addition to the pass and merit criteria, you are able to:
P1 illustrate typical phases of a project lifecycle **See Assessment activity 17.1, page 15**	**M1** explain why projects can fail **See Assessment activity 17.1, page 15**	
P2 explain the resources available to support the project manager **See Assessment activity 17.1, page 15**		
P3 discuss issues affecting project management **See Assessment activity 17.1, page 15**		
P4 produce a project specification **See Assessment activity 17.2, page 17**	**M2** assess the impact of potential risks to a project **See Assessment activity 17.2, page 17**	
P5 plan a defined project using IT **See Assessment activity 17.2, page 17**		
P6 follow a project plan to carry out a defined project **See Assessment activity 17.3, page 20**	**M3** monitor the project against the project plan adapting, the plan as circumstances change **See Assessment activity 17.3, page 20**	**D1** demonstrate effective communications with stakeholders at all stages of the project **See Assessment activity 17.3, page 20**
P7 carry out a review of the project management process **See Assessment activity 17.4, page 22**		**D2** evaluate the effectiveness of the tools used to plan the project **See Assessment activity 17.4, page 22**

How you will be assessed

This unit will be assessed by internal assignments that will be designed and marked by the staff at your centre. It may be subject to sampling by your centre's Lead Internal Verifier or an Edexcel Standards Verifier as part of Edexcel's on-going quality assurance procedures. Assignments are designed to allow you to show your understanding of the unit outcomes. These relate to what you should be able to do after completing this unit.

Your assessment could be in the form of:

- presentations
- case studies
- practical tasks
- written assignments.

Loren, BTEC National IT learner

This unit provided me with good knowledge about analysing different situations and how to put different methods into practice. It's helped me to become more independent, as I've needed to understand how projects are managed and to plan projects myself. I've had to follow project plans, which has enhanced my skills and given me valuable experience for the future.

The assignments were quite easy and covered many planning skills and techniques. I had never seen a Gantt chart before and it was interesting to create my own and see how a wall chart like this can benefit project management. PERT charts were fascinating. They taught me about the time it takes to complete a project and how to allocate more resources to the slowest critical tasks.

I noticed a Gantt chart at work and asked my supervisor about it. She showed me the PERT chart that related to it and I could understand both of the charts, following them whilst I worked. I could see then how they fit together and how they provide benefits for time management.

I have used the Gantt idea to help me plan my assignment work – it shows me where I am with the work and what's still needed. It has helped me prioritise different assignments so that I am able to meet the deadlines.

I am glad I studied this unit, as it has opened my eyes to some powerful techniques and has provided me with knowledge that could be used in a future career. I feel that the techniques that are learnt in this unit can be used in different areas and will always bring benefits.

Over to you

- Can you find out how a PERT chart can be used to identify how long a project should take to complete?
- Loren mentions allocating more resources to the slowest critical tasks. What is a critical task in a PERT chart?
- Can you find and explain an example of a Gantt chart from the Internet?

1 Understand how projects are managed

Start up

How badly did that project go over budget?

There have been many large projects that have taken much longer than expected to complete and cost far more than the original estimate. These overruns don't just happen in the United Kingdom – they occur in most countries in the world.

- Work in pairs to find some examples of projects that have gone way over cost. A good starting point in this research is to Google the phrase 'cost overrun'.
- Research this for 20 minutes. If the cost is shown in another currency, convert it to pounds sterling (GBP).
- The pair finding the worst cost overrun can then describe the project they found to the rest of the group.

1.1 Project lifecycles

A project may be broken down into stages in a number of different ways. How you break it down is called a project lifecycle. This section describes one way to break a project down; there are other ways that are just as valid.

The following stages are commonly found in a project lifecycle (see Figure 17.1):

- define and produce specification
- plan and design
- collect information
- implement the plan
- complete and review.

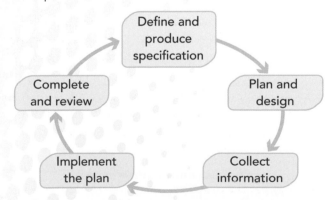

Figure 17.1: Project lifecycle

Define and produce a specification

This stage is about finding out what is actually wanted. It may include recording what is done now, what the customer wants to happen once the new system or

procedure is in place and any performance needs. The four main activities of this phase are:

- interview the customer
- analyse the customer's requirements
- produce the specification
- produce a business case.

The end result or **deliverables** of this phase are usually:

- a specification saying what the new system or procedure must do but not how it will do it
- a business case for going ahead with the new system or procedure, giving the potential costs and benefits.

Plan and design

The plan and design stage turns the customer's requirements into a potential solution with a plan on how to make it happen.

Collect information

The project plan requires you to collect information from the **stakeholders** to check the project is appropriate and will meet the customer needs. You will need to review and summarise that information and present it to the stakeholders.

Key terms

Deliverable – a product or service that a project aims to produce.

Stakeholder – a person or organisation that is actively involved in a project or whose interests the project may affect.

Implement the plan

The implementation stage includes:

- build the product or service
- test that the product meets the need
- provide documentation and possibly training
- hand the product over to the customer.

Complete and review

Completion involves the customer and the users using your product. It includes identifying the actual benefits and costs of building and running the product. It also includes a final project review, in which the stakeholders review how well you did in managing the project and product delivery.

Activity: Planning a project

Your workplace hopes to convert an existing room into a training room including audio-visual aids and computers for trainees. Working in pairs, carry out the following steps.

1 Consider the stages in the project lifecycle. Create a document listing these stages with bullet points for what actions would be needed for each stage.

2 Write a short note next to each of the actions that will be needed in the implementation stage explaining why each is needed.

3 How long do you think the project would take?

1.2 Resources

This section reviews the resources needed for a project: information, people, equipment or facilities, and finance.

Information

Very few business projects could exist without information. Some of the information that your project needs may already exist in other systems. In this case, your project will need to build feeds from these systems. Often your project will need to capture new information or add to or update existing information. Your project will need to include the functions to do this. Finally, your project may need to supply information to other existing systems.

People

In your project, there are a number of different skills that contribute towards success. In a small project, one person may possess all these skills. In a larger business project, each of these skills is likely to come from a different specialist. These specialists are likely to include:

- project managers – this unit teaches you all about this skill
- systems analysts – they talk to the customer and the users about their needs and then produce the specification of what computer systems should do
- product developers – either a general term for people who work on a business project or, more specifically, the people who turn the specification into a detailed design for the programmer on how to build the project
- programmers – the people who write or code the detailed instructions to the computer.

Activity: Specialist jobs

Search online for a job advert for each of these positions:

- project manager
- systems analyst
- product developer
- programmer.

Equipment or facilities

Most projects need equipment or facilities, such as furniture, machinery, hardware and software. Sometimes the equipment is already in place. If it isn't, you must decide on the equipment needs of your project. You must order it and install it early enough in the plan so as not to delay the project. If the equipment is specialised, your plan must allow for designing and building it.

Finance

In a learner project, you may not need to worry about money as a resource. You may have all your equipment for your project already, provided for free. Your own time is not chargeable but may be included as a cost to your project.

In a business project, however, all the resources have a cost. Management expect the project manager to keep the total cost within the overall budget. You have to pay to buy or capture the information your project needs. The people on your project will have to be paid. You may have to buy new hardware and software or other equipment. Even if these exist already, your project is likely to have to pay its share for using them.

1.3 Project management tools

This section considers a number of project management tools, ranging from simple to complex.

General planning and scheduling tools

Project management software helps you to manage the administration, planning and scheduling of your project. You can often use the software charting facilities included in this software to produce graphical versions of your plans.

Project management software has the following features:

- create a task
- store information about a task – eg who will do it, how long it will take, how it is to be done, how it depends on other tasks
- update task information as your project changes
- generate plans based on the tasks
- create charts and reports to help you manage the project and to present information to the stakeholders.

Two common charts are **Gantt charts**, used to see progress on the project, and **PERT charts**, used to plan when the resources are best used.

Critical path methods

Critical path methods identify the minimum time needed to complete a project. They show which tasks or activities are on the critical path. This lets you, as

project manager, prioritise these tasks to give the project the best chance of being finished on time. PERT charts (see below) are a powerful tool, often used to help identify the critical path.

Critical path analysis (CPA) works on the principle that some tasks cannot start until previous tasks are finished. For example, you cannot test a program until you have coded it. You must complete these dependent tasks in a sequence. Often, tasks are not dependent on other tasks starting or finishing, so you can do these tasks in parallel.

The critical path is the key to reducing project timescales. To bring forward the end-date, you would need to use more resources for tasks on the critical path.

PERT charts

Consider this series of tasks for setting up a new computer room. The project manager has worked out the dependencies and timescales.

	Tasks or activities	Dependencies	Timescales (days)
A	Detailed planning	-	2
B	Assemble furniture	A	1
C	Computer delivery time	A	5
D	Install mains and network cabling	A	3
E	Set up computers	B, C, D	2

So, in this example, task A needs to be completed first. Tasks B, C and D cannot be started before task A is completed, as they are the dependencies of task A. From this we can start a PERT chart (see Figure 17.2) with the lines representing tasks and the circle nodes showing where tasks begin and finish.

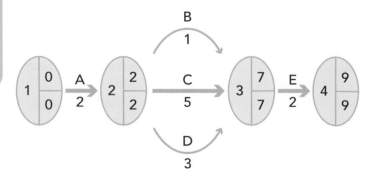

Figure 17.2: Beginning a PERT chart

The numbers in the left of each node are used to identify them, not to show sequence. The number in the top right of each node shows the earliest the next task could start. This is calculated by adding up the durations of the longest path of tasks before the node. The longest path of tasks through the PERT chart from beginning to end is the critical path.

The critical path is calculated by adding together the durations of the longest path through the PERT from beginning to end. This will amount to the total time expected to implement the project. In this example, the critical path is A C E, totalling nine days.

The number in the bottom right of each node shows the latest the next task could start without delaying the project, calculated by subtracting durations of tasks after the node from the end node. This bottom number will always be the same as the top number in the critical path.

The bottom number should be different for non-critical tasks, so the PERT chart needs a little more detail by adding some dummy activities to the non-critical tasks, as in Figure 17.3.

The dummy activities are shown as dashed lines with no duration and the bottom numbers are now different for the non-critical tasks.

Node 5 shows 6 in the bottom right, as this is one day less than the 7 in the bottom right of node 3. This means that node 5 could be started as late as day 6 of the project without delaying the end-date because one day on from day 6 is day 7, the same as the node where this activity joins the critical path.

Node 6 shows 4 in the bottom right, as this is three days less than the 7 in the bottom right of node 3. This means that node 6 could be started as late as day 4 of the project without delaying the end-date.

From this, the project manager can see the importance of non-critical tasks and schedule them appropriately

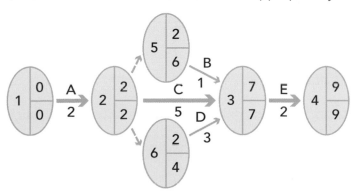

Figure 17.3: PERT chart with dummy activities

to spread out use of resources, such as staff, and to avoid expensive bunching of activities, where lots of tasks are needlessly happening at the same time.

In this example, the cabling (task D, node 6) could start on day 2. Then assembling the furniture (task B, node 5) could start on day 5.

Activity: PERT chart

A hotel is planning to install a new computer system and has identified these tasks, identified as A–X, with their durations in days, dependencies and descriptions:

A	4	N	Install mains cabling
B	1	A	Install network cabling
C	1	-	Place equipment orders
D	2	B, C	Receive equipment deliveries
E	2	D	Unpack equipment deliveries
F	2	E	Connect equipment
G	2	F	Install network
H	2	G	Test network
I	1	H, R	Install programs
J	1	H	Install office applications
K	1	J	Test office applications
L	5	H	Install WAN comms hardware
M	2	L	Test WAN comms hardware
N	5	-	Produce detailed floor plans
O	10	-	Produce detailed program specifications
P	5	O	Produce test data specifications
Q	40	P	Produce programs
R	20	Q, U	Initial programs testing
S	10	I	On-site programs testing
T	5	O	Transfer data from existing systems
U	25	T	Enter paper-based data into new systems
V	2	S	Train hotel staff to use Windows®
W	2	V	Train hotel staff to use network
X	2	W	Train hotel staff to use new system

Create a PERT chart for the hotel.

Gantt charts

A Gantt chart is used to show tasks and their progress in the project. It may be produced by the project management software or from other applications such as spreadsheets. There is a timescale across the top of the chart. Each task is shown as a horizontal bar, which is carefully placed so the start and end is lined up with the timescale at the top of chart. The length of each horizontal bar represents how long the task will take.

As the project progresses, the horizontal bars are often coloured in to show the progress that has been made. Thus, a vertical line can be drawn on today's date with the colouring showing whether tasks are on-schedule, behind or ahead of expected progress.

Many project managers use their Gantts as wall charts so they can easily check progress. Gantt charts are also a good communication tool for stakeholders, to show the current state of the project.

The Gantt chart shown here (Figure 17.4) is based on the PERT example in the previous section. If this chart is looked at towards the end of day 3 it shows good news. Task A was completed on time, task D is ahead of schedule – so the project looks good. Task C would not show any progress yet – it will be filled in when the new computers arrive.

If this chart is looked at at the end of day 5 it shows a little cause for concern. Task A was completed on time, but task D is a day behind schedule, so the project is slipping. There is no need to panic yet, as there are another two days to complete task D before

this has an impact on the project delivery time by delaying the start of task E from node 3. Task B can still start on schedule, as it is not a dependency of the delayed task D.

If viewed at the end of day 8 the chart shows a disaster, with the project delayed by at least two days (one day to complete tasks B and D plus one day to catch up with the delayed start of task E). The new computers have not arrived (task C) so the supplier will need chasing to obtain a realistic delivery date which could delay the project even more. At this point the stakeholders need to be informed urgently of delays and the project manager could be considering adding extra resources (more people) to complete the remaining tasks more quickly.

Activity: Gantt chart

Create a Gantt chart for the PERT chart activity (see page 7).

Specialised software packages

To help manage a project, there are many packages available. At the simplest, there are freeware or shareware packages available from the Internet. Microsoft® Project (see Figure 17.5) is a popular middle-of-the-range tool that can help manage a wide variety of projects.

There are many specialised project management software applications available with different levels of complexity and cost.

Day	1	2	3	4	5	6	7	8	9	10
A Detailed planning										
B Assemble furniture										
C Computer delivery time										
D Install mains and network cabling										
E Set up computers										

Figure 17.4: Gantt chart for the PERT chart shown in Figure 17.3

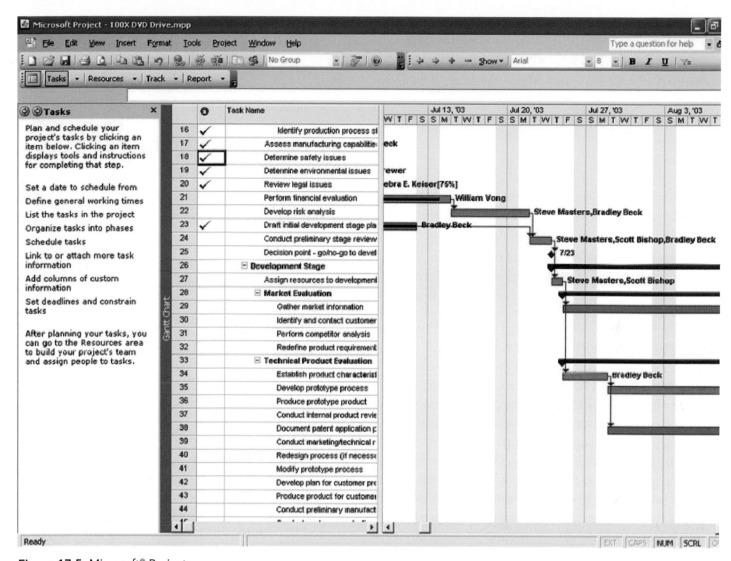

Figure 17.5: Microsoft® Project

1.4 Project methodologies

Most large organisations use a chosen **project methodology**.

> ### Key term
>
> **Project methodology** – a standard, documented way of tackling a business project.

Project methodology examples

There are many different project methodologies. Here are three examples of formal methodologies to give you an idea of what they do.

PRINCE2

The UK government's Central Computer and Telecommunications Agency (CCTA) released PRINCE2 in 1996 as a generic project management method. PRINCE stands for PRojects IN Controlled Environments. It was designed as a UK government standard. It is process-driven and divides up into the following eight processes:

1   starting up a project

2   planning

3   initiating a project

4   directing a project

5   controlling a stage

6   managing product delivery

7   managing stage boundaries

8   closing a project.

Six Sigma

Six Sigma provides a structured data-driven methodology using tools and techniques that measure performance both before and after projects. Management can measure the baseline performance of their processes to find the root causes of variations, then improve their processes to meet desired performance levels.

It has a solid control phase (DMAIC: Define-Measure-Analyse-Improve-Control) that makes specific measurements, identifies specific problems and provides specific solutions that can be measured.

Six Sigma encourages strategic and systematic application of its tools on targeted and important projects to bring about significant and lasting change to the whole organisation.

Company-specific methodology

Companies with a large in-house IT department often feel it is worthwhile to develop their own methodology. They usually do this by taking a standard methodology and removing large parts that they feel are not relevant to them. The rest they tailor to their organisation structure and to the type of projects that they run. For example, if they have outsourced their network, then they do not need a methodology for network projects. If they do not sell their software, then customer and user management and acceptance and product distribution is much easier.

Sometimes, when large software companies develop a project for a customer, they will use their own methodology for the project. While this offers benefits to that company, it sometimes produces pressure on the customer to adopt the methodology for other related projects. This incurs additional consultancy costs, training costs and a potentially much greater lock-in to the software company.

Benefits and drawbacks of formal methodologies

The benefits, particularly to a large organisation, of a formal methodology lie in the fact that everybody does things in the same way. This means that the organisation can:

- use set standards for managing projects
- transfer staff more easily between projects
- avoid spending time thinking about how to tackle each project individually.

The drawbacks of a formal methodology are that they:

- are often over-complex for a simple project
- may be inappropriate for an unusual project
- require an investment in training, time and product that might not be repaid.

1.5 Project management issues

Project management issues are any of the many ways a project can be disrupted or delayed.

Changing external factors

External factors, such as a supplier bankruptcy, may happen during the life of a project. While you cannot anticipate such changes when you write the project specification, they may mean that you need to change the specification once the project is under way.

Examples of external factors that could affect a project are:

- a change in legislation
- a prominent news story such as a safety scare
- significant changes in product prices
- supplier problems
- a new rival business starting up.

Monitoring progress

You need to monitor progress of your project (see also Section 3.1 on page 18). To do this, you should ask for reports from the people doing the work. They will tell you what they have done, what they still have left to do and any problems or delays they have had or are facing. In a formal project, for each task, they may report to you on **man hours** spent, man hours remaining, how much longer they think it will take to finish and percentage of task completed.

Key term

Man hour – the amount of work a person can be expected to do in one hour.

These reports may be produced daily, weekly or fortnightly.

The stakeholders will also want to know how things are going.

Corrective actions

When you find that things are not going to plan, you should immediately take corrective action to bring the project back towards the plan. Sometimes, the chosen action is within your control, such as changing who will do which task in the future. More often, you may need one or more of the stakeholders to take action or make decisions. You may even need to persuade senior management to accept a delay to the project or to reduce the scope of the project.

Communications

One of your responsibilities as project manager is to make sure there is good communication between everyone involved. This does not mean that all communication must go through you. However, you should organise meetings or reports to make sure everyone knows what is going on in those areas of the project that affect them. You should consider your audience when you communicate.

Guidelines and legislation

Although this may not be specifically mentioned in the specification, your project should comply with legislation and with the relevant guidelines. The pieces of legislation most likely to affect your project are the Data Protection Act and various Health and Safety laws. Your staff may be subject to other laws such as the Offices, Shops and Railway Premises Act.

Most large organisations have internal guidelines stating how they go about developing projects. They may, for example, describe a common look and feel for applications, or say where particular documents should be stored or how files should be named. Smaller organisations without their own guidelines can use external guidelines for good development practice, which are available on the Internet.

Dealing with conflict

As project manager, you will need to manage conflict between the stakeholders in order to make the project happen. There may be many causes of conflict – Figure 17.6 shows some of the more common ones.

In some cases, you may be able to make an executive decision to resolve the conflict, in others, you will have to use your persuasive skills to get the stakeholders to agree.

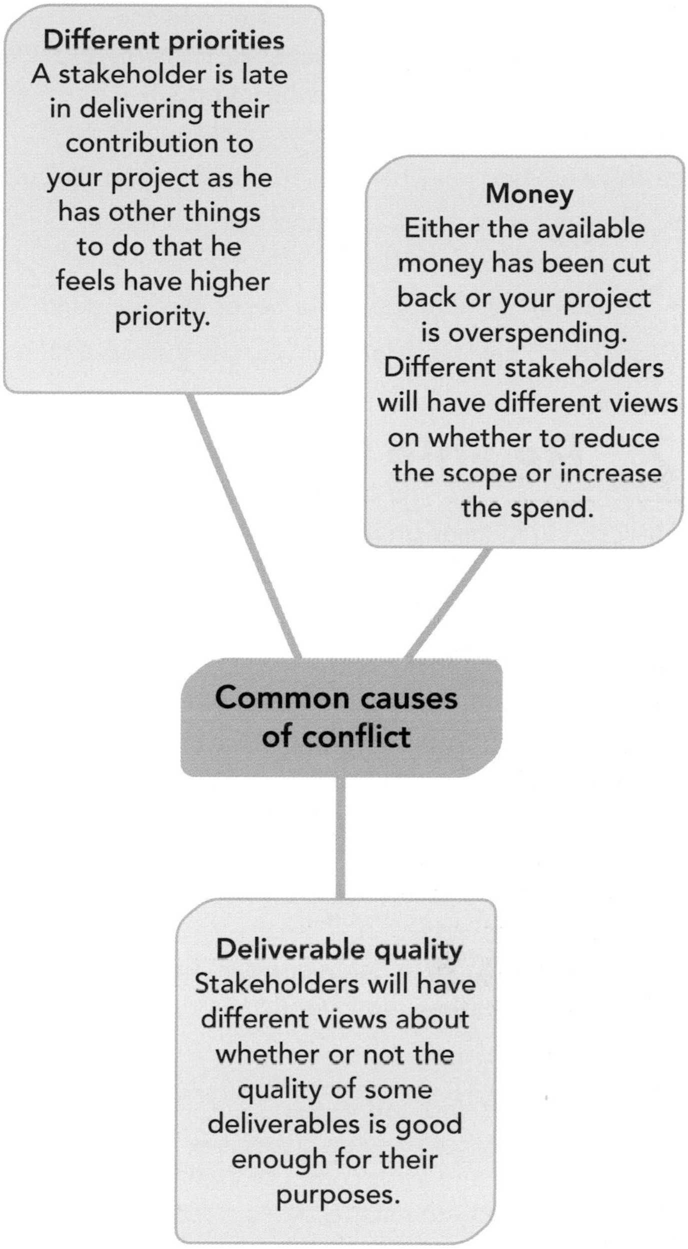

Different priorities A stakeholder is late in delivering their contribution to your project as he has other things to do that he feels have higher priority.

Money Either the available money has been cut back or your project is overspending. Different stakeholders will have different views on whether to reduce the scope or increase the spend.

Common causes of conflict

Deliverable quality Stakeholders will have different views about whether or not the quality of some deliverables is good enough for their purposes.

Figure 17.6: Some common causes of conflict

Impact on other systems

The project outputs will probably impact on other systems inside the organisation, which can affect existing staff roles and organisational structures.

If the project is to implement a new computer system then it will probably be more than simply automating some existing manual processes. When designing a new system, a good designer takes the opportunity to exploit the strengths of a computer compared with a clerk doing a similar task. The designer should also integrate the new system with other existing computer systems.

The management, therefore, will often take the opportunity to change organisational structures and existing working practices with the introduction of a new computer system. This could affect staff in these ways:

- the work becomes harder and therefore too difficult
- the work becomes easier and hence there is pressure to reduce pay
- skills built up over the years become redundant
- staff need training to learn how to use the new system.

In extreme cases, the new system may reduce the workload so much that some staff are no longer required. This may mean redundancy, retraining or redeployment.

Activity: Project impacts

The government is planning to abolish statutory retirement ages. What do you think will be the impacts of this project?

2 Be able to plan projects using IT

This section focuses on the planning aspects of a project: the plan itself and the activities involved.

2.1 Project specification

The project specification is a statement, agreed by all stakeholders, on what the project will do. It does not say how it will be done.

Identification of stakeholders

Most business projects will have the following stakeholders:

- senior management – in control of the project's overall direction
- customer/client – the person or part of the organisation that benefits most from the project
- users – those people who use or operate the new system
- project manager – runs the project on a day-to-day basis
- team members – those who do the technical work to make the project happen
- supplier – the company or person who supplies the necessary equipment.

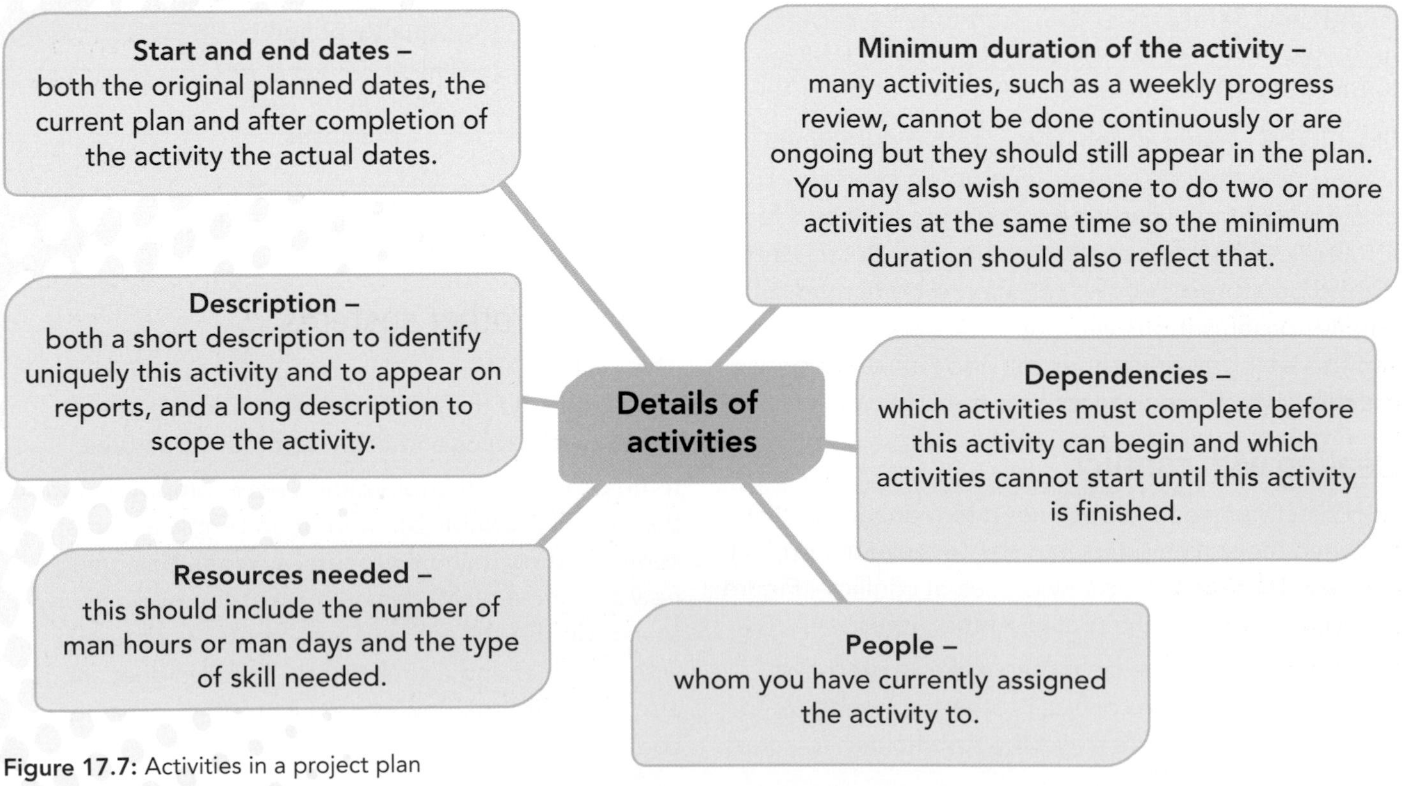

Start and end dates – both the original planned dates, the current plan and after completion of the activity the actual dates.

Minimum duration of the activity – many activities, such as a weekly progress review, cannot be done continuously or are ongoing but they should still appear in the plan. You may also wish someone to do two or more activities at the same time so the minimum duration should also reflect that.

Description – both a short description to identify uniquely this activity and to appear on reports, and a long description to scope the activity.

Details of activities

Dependencies – which activities must complete before this activity can begin and which activities cannot start until this activity is finished.

Resources needed – this should include the number of man hours or man days and the type of skill needed.

People – whom you have currently assigned the activity to.

Figure 17.7: Activities in a project plan

Business case requirements

The **business case** should state what the project should achieve in general terms. It should then state the one-off costs of the project and the ongoing costs of running the delivered system.

Typical cost items are:

- IT resources to specify, manage, design, build and implement
- customer resources to help specify, manage and implement
- user resources for training and implementation
- equipment costs
- ongoing running costs
- possible costs of moving from an old system to the new one.

The business case should also state the expected benefits. Most projects are an investment, which should repay after the **payback period**.

> ### Key terms
>
> **Business case** – a proposal stating the objectives, costs and benefits of a project.
>
> **Payback period** – during a project, this is the length of time taken before the cash benefits exceed the cost.

Specific objectives or deliverables

Specific, measurable objectives are very important to the success of a project. Many stakeholders judge the success of a project on how closely it has met its objectives.

One objective is that a project should be delivered on time. A specific objective may be that the project produces all its deliverables by July. This statement removes all doubt as to what 'on time' means.

Another objective is that a project should be delivered within budget. A specific objective could be that, up to the time that a project is delivered to the customers, it will cost less than £200,000. This objective makes it clear what the budget is. It also makes it clear that the budget does not include any ongoing support costs or any later additional features.

A deliverable is a product or service that a project aims to produce.

Benefits and success factors

At the start of your project, you should define the expected benefits and what success should look like. Success may include any of the factors that are important to the stakeholders (the people involved in the project).

The benefits of a new system could include one or more of the following:

- better customer service
- lower costs
- increased revenue
- greater staff productivity
- better management decision making
- compliance with legislation
- better safety and security.

These benefits may be measurable in cash terms, such as lower costs or higher revenue. Other benefits are intangible and cannot be costed, such as better security.

In order to identify whether a project has been successful, you need to measure the project against pre-defined criteria. Success criteria may be of the following types:

- **Functional**: These state what functions the project must have.
- **Timescale**: This gives the date by which the project must be complete, such as a sales project that must be ready before a Christmas selling peak.
- **Resources**: A project's resources include people, their effort and money. For any project, there may be a limit on how many people can be involved, how much effort they can put in and a fixed cost which the project must not exceed.
- **Ease of use**: Systems or software that full-time, trained users will operate should be full of features; powerful functions should be available with just a few clicks or key presses. Software intended for casual users, perhaps customers of a business using the Internet, should be easy to use; the functions should be very simple and there should be a lot of user guidance.
- **Performance**: Systems should meet minimum performance standards that depend upon the user's needs. For example, the software functions in a game may need to work in much less than a second, while the time to run a large organisation's monthly payroll could be several hours.

Case study: System benefits

A new sales order system has been designed to improve customer service through:

- faster order processing time
- better stock checking
- better features for customers to view the status of their orders.

Identify another type of new computer system. List the benefits that this could bring to its stakeholders.

Project boundaries or scope

The boundaries or scope of a project are what the project aims to achieve. The project should be no more and no less than what is defined in the scope. If a feature is in the scope, then it should be delivered as part of the project. If it is not in the scope, then it should not be built, as building unnecessary features will incur extra costs. The scope of a project is recorded in the written project specification, which should contain the:

- reason for undertaking the project
- expected benefits
- objectives
- success criteria
- constraints and risks
- project roadmap
- resource requirements
- stakeholders
- deliverables
- review points
- target completion date.

Constraints

These are obstacles that may make the project difficult to achieve. These constraints might be:

- financial (eg no major investment might be allowed until the next year)
- staff (eg the skills needed for this project might not be available; the necessary staff would have to be trained or recruited)
- equipment (eg the project might require specialised hardware or software; this might have to be developed, bought in or installed before the project could proceed very far)

- business (eg the project might be needed to support the launch of a new product or service; it would therefore need to be complete in some form in time for that launch)
- legislation (eg the project might be required for the organisation to conform to new laws; work on the project would therefore need to finish in time for these laws)
- competition (eg the project might provide a competitive advantage or respond to a competitive threat, so a part or phased solution delivered quickly would be preferable to no solution at all)
- user resources (eg the users might be unavailable for training during the peak business season).

Consideration of options

There is usually more than one solution to a business problem. One option may be cheap and quick to produce with limited benefits. Another option may meet every possible need very well, but may be very costly with benefits that may never exceed the build and running costs. The chosen option is often somewhere between these two extremes. You should record briefly in the project definition any options that were rejected and why.

Other issues

The project specification should highlight any issues that the stakeholders need to decide on to make the project a success. Examples of these include the following:

- **Ethical**: Will this project change business terms and conditions to make them unreasonable?
- **Sustainable**: Can the organisation still function effectively once the changes brought in by the project happen?
- **Effect of failure**: What would happen to the organisation if the project failed to hit its deadlines or did not produce a working product?

Risks and risk mitigation

All projects face **risks**, which you need to consider. You should also plan for **risk mitigation** – what you might reasonably do both to prevent them happening and if they do happen.

There are many types of risk, including business, IT and implementation risks.

A business risk is that the nature of the business may change during the life of a project.

Typical IT risks include:

- the reliability of any new hardware or software
- the availability of staff with the right business and technical skills at the right time
- the integration of different technologies.

A project implementation risk is, for example, introducing a new system just prior to an expected peak in business activity. This is because relatively minor problems within the project could lead to major risks for the business.

Key terms

Risk – any event, foreseen or not, that may happen and that puts the success of the project in jeopardy.

Risk mitigation – the actions taken to reduce the effect of a risk if it should happen.

Activity: Risks

An organisation is undertaking a major project to relocate to larger premises. What do you think are the potential risks from such a project?

Assessment activity 17.1

Project planning

You will need to produce a project plan and implement your plan and review it for the other assignments in this unit. This assignment asks you to demonstrate your understanding of the methods and issues around project planning.

1 Produce a poster illustrating the typical phases of a project lifecycle, with a brief explanation of each of the stages. **P1**

2 Produce a written report describing the resources that are available to support the project manager. Create sections in this report for:
   - people
   - equipment and facilities
   - finance
   - project management tools
   - project methodologies. **P2**

3 Add a section to your report discussing the issues affecting project management. This should include:
   - changing external factors
   - monitoring progress
   - corrective actions
   - communications

   - guidelines and legislation
   - conflict
   - impact of the project outputs on other systems. **P3**

4 List the possible reasons why projects can fail and explain them in the context of examples which you find from research. Produce a report with supporting notes on how to minimise the chances of projects failing, including an example from each. **M1**

Grading tips

- The poster shows a cycle, so include arrows to connect the stages together with the last arrow pointing back to the first stage. **P1**

- Make sure you explain the use of each resource. **P2**

- You may find it useful to include some real-life examples to help your discussions of issues. **P3**

- You will find some real-life examples of failed projects useful to help your explanations. **M1**

PLTS

You can show yourself to be an **independent enquirer** when you assess risks by listing the possible reasons why projects can fail.

Functional skills

Your report will use a **writing** functional skill when you use language, format and structure suitable for purpose and audience.

2.2 Project plan

Every business project should have a plan. A good plan is both easy to understand and easy to maintain. For a very simple project you may produce the plan with word processing or spreadsheet software. For larger projects you should use project management software to help produce detailed plans.

Purpose

The project plan has two purposes. For you, it is a tool to monitor progress, manage the project and help you evaluate options and make decisions on how to make the project a success. This means that it should be easy to maintain. For your stakeholders, it is a good way for you to communicate how the project is proceeding. This means that it should be easy for them to read and understand.

Content

Your plan should show:

- phases – where your project is split up into stages or sections
- activities – the detailed tasks that need to be completed within the project phases
- dependencies and the potential for **parallel** or **sequential processes**
- resources needed for each activity
- timescales – the start and end date for each activity
- **review points** – the dates of key **milestones**, **checkpoints** and deadlines.

Use of software

There are several types of software that you can use to help manage and plan your project, including the following.

- **Project management packages**: are the most powerful aid to managing a project but they may be too complex for simple projects.

Key terms

Parallel processes – processes that can run side by side, at the same time.

Sequential processes – processes that need to run in sequence, ie the next process cannot start before the previous process has completed.

Review points – points where the project manager and others meet to review the progress of the project.

Milestones – major points in the project where a number of activities should have been completed.

Checkpoints – points between milestones where progress can be checked.

- **Spreadsheets**: can be used to record activities, help with calculations as well as presenting plan tracking and other results graphically.
- **Drawing and graphics packages**: can present the results of your planning to your stakeholders in ways that are easier for them to understand.
- **Databases**: can be used to record activities in the plan.
- **Word processors**: can be used to document projects and support other software.

Activity: Project software

1 Identify a product from each of these software categories:
   - project management package
   - spreadsheet
   - drawing or graphics package
   - database
   - word processor.

2 Produce a document showing a screenshot for each of the products, including the supplier name and a UK price.

Assessment activity 17.2

Starting your project

Unit 17 focuses on your skills as a project manager in running a project using IT for planning and tracking the project.

Your project needs to be substantial, based upon anything that interests you, and will need to be agreed with your tutor to confirm there is sufficient scope in it for meeting the needs of your project plan.

1 Produce a project specification. This will be a structured document that identifies the:
   - stakeholders in your project
   - specific objectives and deliverables
   - benefits and success factors
   - project boundaries or scope
   - constraints
   - consequences of failure to hit deadlines or produce the product
   - risks and risk mitigation. **P4**

2 Produce a plan for your project using suitable software. The plan will include:
   - a word-processed document explaining the purpose of your project
   - PERT and Gantt charts identifying your activities, potential for parallel or sequential processes, resources needed for each activity, timescales and review points. **P5**

3 Assess the impact of potential risks to your project. You will need to consider each of the risks you identified in your project specification to explain the impact of each if they were to occur. **M2**

Grading tips

- The project specification should be a structured document with a contents page and section headings. **P4**

- The project must use IT for the planning, preferably project management software, but you can also use other software such as a spreadsheet and graphics package to help this planning. **P5**

- Make sure you include the impact of what would happen if the risks you identified were to actually happen. **M2**

PLTS

When you produce your project specification, you will identify questions to answer and problems to resolve showing that you are an **independent enquirer**.

When you produce your project specification, you will need to ask questions to extend your thinking showing that you are a **creative thinker**.

By assessing the impact of potential risks to your project, you will explore issues, events or problems from different perspectives showing that you are an **independent enquirer**.

Functional skills

You will practise using **ICT** functional skills to plan solutions to complex tasks by analysing the necessary stages when you plan your project.

3 Be able to follow project plans

A lot of managers who produce project plans are not very good at actually implementing their plans to produce the end result at the right time and inside budget.

This section looks at the issues around following project plans and making them work.

3.1 Monitoring

Regular monitoring is essential to ensure that progress is being made, to identify when to bring in extra resources and to keep everyone informed on progress and any delays that may be likely.

Communications with stakeholders

A stakeholder is anyone who has an interest or role in the project. There should always be routine communications with stakeholders so they know how the project progresses.

If there are no problems and everything is going well then the stakeholders will be pleased to know this.

If there are problems with the project then the stakeholders will want to know so they understand what's happening and when they can expect completion. This helps them adjust their own plans, if needed.

It may be useful to have regular meetings with stakeholders to keep them informed.

> **Activity: Stakeholders**
>
> A company is planning a reorganisation to merge two functional areas into one. Who do you think the stakeholders would be in this project?

Nobody likes surprises. It's far better to keep people informed than to wait until the expected completion day to inform there is no end product or, even worse, failing to deliver with no communication at all!

Interim reviews

Interim reviews are a useful way of checking progress on the project and should be carried out regularly and then communicated to any project stakeholders not present at the review.

Use of logbooks

A logbook can be useful for recording progress and problems as they are encountered. It can also be a helpful reference if there is a need to justify anything to do with the project, such as bringing in extra resources to keep the project delivery date on track.

Routine updating of plan where necessary

The project plan is the starting point but often there are changes that have to be made due to unforeseen problems, better progress than expected or external events such as new products entering the marketplace.

The project plan should be routinely updated, to keep it realistic and to respond to events as they occur.

Other actions

Other actions may be needed to keep the project plan end-date realistic. For example, if the project is running late it may be necessary to access additional resources to complete some tasks in the project more quickly and therefore catch up on any delays.

You may have to react to unforeseen circumstances such as a change in personnel in the project team, a change in the marketplace or something else that could affect the project's effectiveness.

3.2 Functional testing of product or service

Before developers release any product or service to the client, they need to test the product to make sure that it does what it should. They also have to test it to make sure that it doesn't break or behave in an unexpected way. This is particularly important for projects involving the creation and implemention of new software.

Test data

Test data may not be needed for some business projects but it is essential for software-orientated projects.

Test data is designed to meet four sorts of conditions:

- normal – valid data that the program should handle correctly
- extreme – also valid data but at the limit in terms of size, range or other constraint that the program should handle
- just wrong – invalid data that is just beyond the limit that the program should handle
- wrong – invalid data that is clearly wrong.

An example is given in Table 17.1.

Test data type	Typical value of a date
Normal	15th January
Extreme	29th February 2008 (in a leap year)
Just wrong	29th February 2009 (not a leap year)
Wrong	38th September

Table 17.1: Examples of the four types of value that need to be tested

Walk-through

The first part of testing might be a **structured walk-through**. Its main benefit is to pick up any major logic flaws in the design or coding of a program or system. It is also sometimes used where an important bug is particularly difficult to find and fix. Structured

walk-throughs can be expensive in terms of time and resources and so are not often used.

Test plan

The first step in preparing a test plan or schedule is for the tester to specify what tests they want to do on which functions. The tests will involve a mixture of valid and invalid input. This reflects how the product will be used, with all users making some errors at some point. The next step is for the tester to generate the right test data to cause each test to happen. Finally all the tests are put together in the right sequence to test all aspects of the program and capture what happens to each test.

The tester then runs this test plan on the software. The results are captured. The tester compares the actual results against the expected results. Often, on early tests, there are big differences. These differences may be caused by wrong test data, but more usually they are caused by bugs in the program.

The tester records all the bugs found and gives these to the developer to be fixed. When a significant number have apparently been fixed, the tester reruns the test plan and compares results. They record where bugs have actually been fixed and also any new bugs that are found. Testing is complete when either all the actual results match the expected results, or only a few insignificant bugs remain that are hard to find and fix.

Activity: Test plan

A company is writing new software to track orders placed through to their production, delivery and payment. Produce an outline test plan for this software, describing what will need to be tested and why.

Assessment activity 17.3

Implementing your project

Your IT project will be substantial, based upon anything that interests you. It will need to be agreed with your tutor, who can confirm there is sufficient scope in it for meeting the needs of your project plan.

1 Create a log book to record how you follow your project plan and keep it up to date. **P6**

2 Create a document to monitor the project against the project plan, adapting the plan as circumstances change. Record in this document your project plan reviews at each of your milestones and checkpoints. **M3**

3 Demonstrate effective communications with stakeholders at all stages of the project by writing minutes from regular meetings with them,

reporting the progress that has been made on your project. **D1**

Grading tips

- You need to produce evidence that you actually followed your project plan. **P6**

- The plan must both be monitored and adapted to respond to any changes that are needed. **M3**

- You must provide evidence that you have regularly communicated with everyone involved in your project. **D1**

PLTS

When you follow your project plan to carry it out, you will respond positively to change, seek advice and support when needed, showing that you are a **self-manager**.

As you monitor your project against plan, adapting it as circumstances change, you will adapt your ideas to show that you are a **creative thinker**.

Monitoring your project against plan, adapting it as circumstances change, you will communicate your learning in relevant ways for different audiences, showing that you are a **reflective learner**.

When you demonstrate effective communications with stakeholders at all stages of the project, you will discuss issues of concern, seeking resolution where needed, showing that you are an **effective participator**.

If you demonstrate effective communications with stakeholders at all stages of the project, you will collaborate with others to work towards common goals, showing that you are a **team worker**.

Functional skills

You will use the **ICT** developing, presenting and communication information functional skill to combine and present information in ways that are fit for purpose and audience when you demonstrate effective communication with stakeholders.

4   Be able to review the project management process

This section covers the final parts of your business-related project. It includes completion of the outcome of your project, as well as other important supporting activities.

4.1 Review

Against specification

The specification agreed before the development of a project normally states what the project is to achieve. It does not say how it does it. It is therefore important to review the project outcomes and compare them against the specification.

It is unusual for developers not to deliver on functionality, as set out in the specification – these are referred to as quantitative aspects of the project and it should be clear to everyone what is meant by them. However, a specification might also refer to qualitative features such as ease of use, high security or fast response time – these are more open to personal opinion, so a developer and a user might have different views on what they mean.

Identification of potential additional development

Often when the customer or the user sees the finished product, they see further opportunities for improvement. They may even have expected these features to be in the delivered product but did not spell this out in the specification. A functional review identifies and records these features. This will provide the input to any future developments.

4.2 Review of project management

This type of review may be called a post-implementation review. Its purpose is to identify and document the successes of the project. It also records those things that did not go so well in order to help you make sure that they do not happen on your next project. Either you or an independent reviewer may set up and run this meeting.

The organiser of this meeting should make sure that:

- all stakeholders or their representatives come to the meeting so there is a balance of views
- all attendees voice their opinions
- the meeting covers all aspects of the project
- someone takes accurate notes to minute the discussion
- there is a written summary of the main points.

You should use this opportunity to gather information about your own performance and identify further development needs. You should make a list of the lessons learnt.

This meeting usually covers the topics of dates, resources, external factors and tools.

Actual dates versus planned dates

The most common cause of project failure is missing the planned dates. The reviewer often starts by finding out which parts of the project were on time or late. If parts were late, then the reviewer may try to identify why they were late and what impact the delays had on project success. They may also consider whether the project manager could have done anything about the delays.

The project plan should be regularly reviewed and updated with the actual dates achieved for milestones compared to planned dates and the reasons for differences.

Actual use of resources versus planned resources needed

This part of the review is similar in principle to the review of dates. The reviewer will identify which parts of the project used much more or less of the resources than planned. If more of the resources were used than planned, the reviewer may try to identify why and what the impact on project success was. They may also consider whether the project manager could have done anything about any overspend.

External factors

Sometimes unanticipated external factors will affect the project. For example, the customer's priorities may change; expected resources may not appear on time or not be there at all or there may be major changes to the specification. The reviewer should consider what impact this had on the project and how well the project manager managed the change to the project.

Validity and effectiveness of the tools used

The choice of tools may have a major impact on the success of a project. For example, was the project management tool powerful enough to help the project manager manage the project effectively? Was it too powerful and was time wasted in learning and using unnecessary features?

The review scope may also include the validity of tools used to design, build and test the project. These again may have either been too simple or too powerful and complex for use on the project.

Activity: External factors

Have a race with other members of your group to list as many external factors as you can find in ten minutes. The longest list of sensible external factors is the winner!

Assessment activity 17.4   P7 D2 BTEC

Reviewing your project

Now the project is completed, you need to produce a formal review of your project plan and how you implemented it.

1 Produce a report reviewing the project management process and how it helped you to achieve the planned outcomes of your project. This document will need to focus on activities and timescales you identified with how effective this plan was. **P7**

2 Add a section to your report evaluating the effectiveness of the tools you used to plan your project. **D2**

Grading tips

- The review is of the process, so make sure you include the stages you completed in creating and implementing the project plan. **P7**

- This distinction criteria asks you to review the tools you used such as PERT, Gantt, logbooks and so on. **D2**

PLTS

You will be an **effective participator** when you discuss issues with key stakeholders.

Functional skills

You will use the **ICT** developing, presenting and communicating information functional skill to evaluate the selection, use and effectiveness of ICT tools and facilities used to present information when you evaluate the effectiveness of the tools used to plan your project.

John
Project manager

I am one of four managers within the IT services section of the head office in a high street bank. I am responsible for planning, executing and finalising projects according to strict deadlines and within budget.

To do this I acquire resources and coordinate team members and third-party contractors to deliver projects according to plan. I also define the project's objectives and am responsible for quality control throughout its lifecycle.

I love this job as there's a lot of responsibility and control over my work. It can be stressful but also very satisfying and the salary is good. It took me four years to work up to this position after completing my degree. As well as having the degree and experience, I had to be familiar with project management software and be IT literate. I also needed to have strong interpersonal skills and be persuasive, encouraging, motivating and able to defuse tensions among the project team.

Communication is very important, not only written and oral but also to respond to the different styles of team members and contractors who come from a broad spectrum of disciplines. You need to gain cooperation from a wide variety of sources, including upper management, clients and other departments.

I often use my analytical and problem-solving capabilities to shift priorities, demands and timelines, reacting to project adjustments and alterations promptly and efficiently. Flexibility is essential, along with being able to effectively prioritise and execute tasks in a high-pressure environment.

My other responsibilities include defining the project scope, goals and deliverables that support our business goals in collaboration with the senior management and stakeholders. I then develop the full-scale project plans and associated communications documents and effectively communicate the project expectations to team members and stakeholders in a timely, clear and ongoing basis.

Each project requires an estimate of the resources and participants needed to achieve the project goals, so I need to draft and submit the budget proposals and recommend subsequent budget changes where necessary. I have to negotiate with other departmental managers, acquiring the personnel needed for each project.

One of the best parts of this job is to identify and manage project dependencies and critical path using PERT planning and scheduling of project timelines and milestones. From this I have to deliver regular progress reports and presentations.

We usually conduct a project post-mortem to create a recommendations report. We do this to identify successful and unsuccessful project elements so we can learn from our experiences.

I sometimes work long hours when needed to help meet project deadlines. Some travel is required for meetings with clients and stakeholders, who may be on or off-site.

Think about it!

1 John needs strong communication skills. What communication methods do you think he needs to use?

2 How do you think project management software helps John in his role as a project manager?

3 What does John mean by project dependencies and critical path?

Just checking

1. What are the four main activities of defining and producing the specification?
2. List five features of project management software.
3. What are the two most common project management charts?
4. What is a critical path analysis?
5. What is a man hour?
6. What is a stakeholder?
7. What is a deliverable?
8. What is risk mitigation?
9. What are four benefits of using a formal project methodology?
10. What is the purpose of the project plan for the project manager?
11. What is the purpose of the project plan for the stakeholders?
12. What is a review point?
13. Which five types of software might you use to help manage your project?
14. When are interim reviews carried out?

Assignment tips

- The project does not have to be IT-related, but must be agreed with your assessor to ensure it has a timescale and depth suitable for assessment.

- You must plan and track your project using IT tools.

- Any changes to your plan such as changing timescales or the need for more resources must be recorded.

18 Database design

Most people who use computers as part of their work will routinely use one or more databases.

Simple databases such as an address list for your Christmas cards can consist of one table and be stored using a spreadsheet application. Many other databases contain large numbers of tables of related information and require a specialist database application package. The ability to handle and manipulate larger and more complex volumes of information adds complexity to the database systems and tools used, but the consequent benefits are overwhelming.

In most commercial situations, users will be interacting with an existing database – perhaps adding records, amending records, searching for information or producing reports. Some users, however, will need to be able to design and create databases – this unit covers the knowledge and skills required to do this.

Learning outcomes

After completing this unit, you should:

1. understand the features of relational databases
2. be able to design, create and populate a relational database
3. be able to test a relational database.

Assessment and grading criteria

This table shows you what you must do in order to achieve a pass, merit or distinction grade, and where you can find activities in this book to help you.

To achieve a **pass** grade the evidence must show that you are able to:	To achieve a **merit** grade the evidence must show that, in addition to the pass criteria, you are able to:	To achieve a **distinction** grade the evidence must show that, in addition to the pass and merit criteria, you are able to:
P1 explain the features of a relational database **See Assessment activity 18.1, page 36**	**M1** explain referential integrity and the purpose of primary keys in building the relationships between tables **See Assessment activity 18.1, page 36**	**D1** discuss how potential errors in the design and construction of a database can be avoided **See Assessment activity 18.2, page 51**
P2 design a relational database for a specified user need **See Assessment activity 18.2, page 51**		
P3 create and populate a database **See Assessment activity 18.2, page 51**	**M2** import data from an external source **See Assessment activity 18.2, page 51**	
P4 create features in data entry forms to ensure validity and integrity of data **See Assessment activity 18.2, page 51**		
P5 perform queries using multiple tables and multiple criteria **See Assessment activity 18.2, page 51**	**M3** export data to an external source **See Assessment activity 18.2, page 51**	
P6 include an advanced feature in a database design **See Assessment activity 18.2, page 51**	**M4** implement an automated function **See Assessment activity 18.2, page 51**	
P7 test a relational database **See Assessment activity 18.3, page 54**		**D2** evaluate a database against the specified user need **See Assessment activity 18.3, page 54**

How you will be assessed

As with all BTEC units, in general, evidence can be presented in a variety of different forms, including written reports, graphs and posters but also projects, performance observation and time-constrained assessments.

In the case of this unit, however, apart from the first task, most of the evidence you will be presenting will be based upon the database that you will be asked to design and create. The evidence should be generated naturally as you respond to the questions in the assignment but you would be advised to check against the criteria to be sure that it matches.

Your tutor will advise in the detail of how the evidence can be captured – in some cases it could be the actual database provided in electronic format that your tutor assesses directly. You may also be asked some questions about the objects in it and also asked to explain or demonstrate some aspects of it.

Michael, 20 year old former BTEC learner

Michael took a BTEC National in IT and is now taking a gap year before going to university.

'This unit has helped me connect some of my real life experiences and situations with my studies. When I talk to people on the phone about such things as car insurance, credit card accounts, mobile phone records and similar, I am more aware now that they are using a database. I understand that the size and complexity of the databases they are using are much greater than the ones I have developed on the course but the principles are the same.

'Connected with that, I have learnt how important it is for the database to contain accurate information – especially when the users of the database are disconnected from the people who enter the data. When I did a short spell in a call centre last year I was arranging insurance for people and we had an induction that emphasised the importance of capturing the information without mistakes from callers – the manager gave some examples of where operators had not captured the information correctly and what problems it could cause. I have learnt that there are techniques that can be used to validate data being entered but it is still possible to make mistakes.'

Over to you

- **How experienced are you in using databases?**
- **What might you do to prepare for this unit?**

1 Understand the features of relational databases

The case for rejecting spreadsheets

The job functions of many people depend on easy access to reliable databases and the accuracy of the data they use is often key to the effectiveness of their job and the company they work for. Compared to database application packages, spreadsheets are used extensively and most computer literate people have some confidence and skills in their use. For these reasons, when asked to create a database of information, many individuals will naturally reach to a spreadsheet.

Tasks

1. A supermarket has a special offer that allows individuals to buy up to four mobile phone tokens at half price each week for a year. Discuss this situation in groups and decide whether a spreadsheet or a database will be suitable for managing the claims made by customers, giving reasons why.

2. A small country surgery currently not using IT at all for patient information wants to store patient details. The practice manager wants to use Excel® because she is already familiar with spreadsheets. She is aware of the importance of verifying and validating the information stored. However, another colleague has suggested that a database application program would be more suitable. What do you think would be more suitable and how would you present your argument to the practice manager and her colleagues?

1.1 Features

There are three core features of relational databases that underpin their design and operation. These are entities, relationships and attributes and all relate to the concept that any information required can be described in terms of a number of discrete entities that are based on things in the real world and that each of these entities can be described in detail using a set of attributes. A few attributes are made common to different entities and it is through these common attributes (called primary keys and foreign keys) that relationships are built that link the entities together into a coherent database. The consistent application of these simple features through a relational database system brings significant benefits to the user.

1.2 Entities

An entity is a thing or object of importance about which data must be captured. Examples of entities in commercial contexts are customer, stock, order or supplier. Other examples in educational contexts are learner, course, results, staff, etc. In relational databases each entity is usually stored in a separate table.

STOCK	ORDER
Stock reference	Order reference
Stock name	Stock reference
Stock level	Customer reference
Minimum stock level	Order date
Supplier reference	
Price	

Table 18.1: Example Stock and Order entities with some field names that show what information is stored within each entity.

An actual Stock or Order table will contain many individual records, one for each of the items of stock or orders that are being stored in the database. The ordering of records or fields is not significant. When data is added to tables, it should be possible to interchange records and fields without changing the information content.

Each record (row) must be distinct; no two rows can be the same to reduce confusion about which record you are accessing or updating. This requires a unique attribute (field) called the **primary key**. Sometimes the primary key is a single field but in other situations you might need a combination of fields to always uniquely identify each record. In many situations there will be a natural choice for the primary key, but where this is not the case, designers often choose a new attribute and set it to **auto-increment** so that each new record gets a primary key which is just the next one in a sequence.

If an organisation already uses a particular combination of letters or numbers to uniquely identify records, such as a product code, then it makes sense to use this as the primary key. It will already be understood by other people or systems in the organisation and possibly outside the organisation.

Key terms

Primary key – aims to uniquely identify every record preferably using only one attribute. Sometimes more than one field in a record could act as a primary key.

Auto-increment – means adding a value (normally one) automatically and is used to describe the process of automatically assigning a value to the primary key of a new record which is the last primary key plus one. It is used where no naturally occurring primary key is available.

Activity: Attributes

1   Two of the attributes that might be part of a CAR entity used to store information for a second-hand car sales company are colour and manufacturer. Identify others.

2   Identify which of the attributes of a CAR table should be the primary key.

Composite (Combination) primary keys

In some circumstances, one field is not enough to uniquely identify each record. In the example shown in Table 18.2, the table stores the details of appointments in a doctor's surgery. The patient reference looks like it might work as a primary key field – however, the patient may have many appointments and so it cannot be a primary key field on its own. To identify each record uniquely you need both Patient reference and Appointment date together as the composite primary key field – and even this assumes that a patient will not have more than one appointment on the same day.

Patient reference
Appointment date
Telephone
Appointment time
Patient name
Doctor reference

Table 18.2: Appointments table

Foreign keys and referential integrity

Often the primary key of one table is found in another table when it is used to link the tables together. In this situation, in the other table it is called a foreign key. It is important that the tables related in this way are kept consistent and it should not be possible to add a record to the second table that does not exist as a primary key in the first table. When all the tables are consistent in this way, the database is said to have referential integrity.

Activity: Keys and integrity

1   In the two tables shown in Table 18.3 identify the probable key fields and foreign keys.

2   Identify whether the tables have referential integrity and explain your reasoning.

Table STOCK

Stock reference	Stock name	Stock level	Min stock level	Supplier reference	Price
GH2	Monitor	34	20	S3	£120.00
JK7	Mouse	56	20	S4	£7.00
NJ8	Keyboard	87	20	S4	£9.00
KL9	Hard Drive	23	20	S3	£56.00
BG6	Speakers 15W	17	10	S8	£34.00
BG5	Speakers 40W	33	10	S8	£70.00

Table ORDER

Order reference	Stock reference	Customer reference	Order date
OR3	NJ8	C127	03/07/2010
OR4	KL8	C345	03/07/2010
OR5	KL9	C563	03/07/2010
OR6	BG6	C781	03/07/2010
OR7	BG6	C999	03/07/2010
OR8	GH2	C1217	03/07/2010

Table 18.3: Stock and Order tables with example records

Data redundancy

Data redundancy describes a situation where information is duplicated in more than one table. It wastes space and can cause problems if all copies of the duplicated data are not updated at the same time, resulting in inconsistency within the database. In some cases, however, duplication can be acceptable if it speeds up processing.

Activity: Converting tables

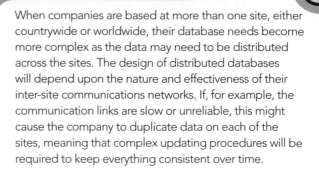

1 Convert the information in the two tables STOCK and ORDER into just one table.

2 Identify and explain if the new single table has any data redundancy.

Did you know?

When companies are based at more than one site, either countrywide or worldwide, their database needs become more complex as the data may need to be distributed across the sites. The design of distributed databases will depend upon the nature and effectiveness of their inter-site communications networks. If, for example, the communication links are slow or unreliable, this might cause the company to duplicate data on each of the sites, meaning that complex updating procedures will be required to keep everything consistent over time.

1.3 Attributes

The attributes of each entity show its internal structure. Attributes are often called fields. Each attribute needs to have properties defined according to the nature of the data that it will store. The first key property is the data type.

Data types

The data types available in Microsoft® Access® are shown in Table 18.4. When entering new fields into a table, apart from choosing a field name and data type, there is also an opportunity to add an optional description that can be used to give some additional information that will help to explain some background or give a justification for the choices made.

Data type	Description	Comment
Text	Text or combinations of text and numbers	Up to 255 characters. Microsoft® Access® only stores the characters entered in a field. Examples are names or addresses. You can control the maximum number of characters that can be entered using the FieldSize property.
Number	Numeric data	Can be used for calculations but calculations involving money normally use currency type.
Date/time	Dates and times	Uses 8 bytes only. Different formats can be chosen.
Currency	Currency value	Use the currency data type to prevent rounding off during calculations. Accurate to 15 digits to the left of the decimal point and 4 digits to the right.
AutoNumber	Unique number incrementing by 1 each time	Automatically inserted when a record is added. Uses 4 bytes only. Can also choose random numbering instead of sequential.
Yes/No	Field to contain only one of two values	Appropriate for fields storing Yes/No, True/False or On/Off. Only uses 1 bit.

Data type	Description	Comment
OLE object	Objects	Examples might be such as documents, spreadsheets, pictures or sounds. Can use up to 1 gigabyte but may be limited by disk space.
Hyperlink	Field that will store a hyperlink	Can store up to 64,000 characters.
Lookup Wizard	A field that allows you to choose from another table or from a list of values	The same size as the field that is also the Lookup field. Choosing this option in the data type list starts a wizard to define the lookup table for you.

Table 18.4: Descriptions of data types available in Access®

Other field properties

The screenshot shown below (Figure18.1) shows some of the additional properties that can be set in Microsoft® Access®. The exact set shown will depend upon the particular data type of the current field selected.

The input data should always be **validated**, as otherwise you cannot rely on the database. One way that the input data can be validated is to use an Input Mask. The example in the screenshot below, for example, means that the user can only enter two alphabetic characters followed by two numeric characters. This will avoid the substitution of 0 for O, or 1 for I.

Activity: Data types

Explore and describe the potential of the other properties of different data types to help validate data entry.

Key term

Validation – the process of checking that data entered into a system is reasonable and in the correct format.

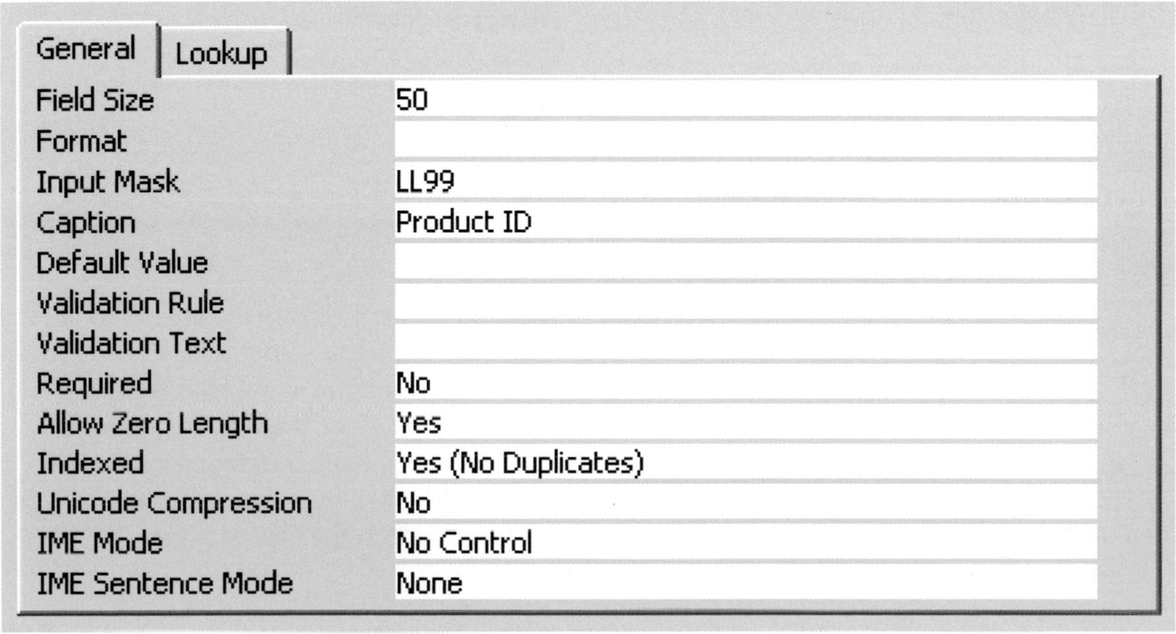

General	Lookup
Field Size	50
Format	
Input Mask	LL99
Caption	Product ID
Default Value	
Validation Rule	
Validation Text	
Required	No
Allow Zero Length	Yes
Indexed	Yes (No Duplicates)
Unicode Compression	No
IME Mode	No Control
IME Sentence Mode	None

Figure 18.1: Field properties

A particularly useful pair of additional properties in this respect is the validation rule and validation text. The validation rule property allows the table designer to set rules that control the data to be input. The validation text is displayed in a window if the validation rule is contradicted.

Example use of validation text and validation rule

If one of the fields is for an email address, you can check that the user has entered a string of characters that includes the @ character. This uses the 'Like' operator which can match a pattern using the wildcards ? (any one character) or * (any number of characters). This does not of course really check that the character string is a valid email address – only that it has an @ character somewhere in the middle of it! An example is shown below.

A full set of operators and examples can be found on the Microsoft® website. To access, go to www.office.microsoft.com and search for 'table of operators'.

General	Lookup	
Field Size	50	▲
Format		
Input Mask		
Caption		
Default Value		
Validation Rule	Like "*@*"	
Validation Text	"You must enter a valid email address"	
Required	No	
Allow Zero Length	No	
Indexed	No	

Figure 18.2: The validation rule

Did you know?

When using field naming conventions, fields must be carefully and uniquely named. One convention when referring to fields in a number of tables is to prefix the field name with the table name. This means that a Stock reference field within a table called Stock would be more completely named as Stock.Stock reference (in the Stock table) and when this field is used in an Order table as Order.Stock reference.

1.4 Relationships

The main feature of **relational databases** that distinguishes them from other types of databases is the use of simple named tables (each based on an entity) to store the information. These tables are created separately and then linked.

Two such tables are shown below.

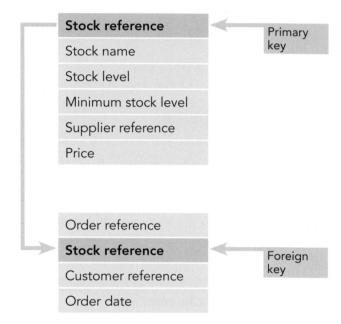

Figure 18.3: Two tables (Stock and Order) related by Stock reference

Key terms

Relational database – contains a set of tables which are linked together by the relationships between the tables. It is for this reason such a database is called relational.

Entity – a real world object of importance about which data must be captured in a system under investigation. Examples are employees, learners, stock, orders, and so on.

The field that will enable the linking to take place is Stock reference. It is usual to use exactly the same field name when the same field is included in different tables, though not essential. It is essential that the properties of the Stock reference field in the Stock table are identical to the properties of the Stock reference field in the Order table.

Figure 18.3 shows which fields are involved but not everything we need to know about the nature of the relationship.

One-to-many, one-to-one and many-to-many relationships

Each item in the Stock table can be ordered by many customers, so for every record in the Stock table, there may be more than one record in the Order table. For this reason it is described as a one-to-many relationship.

The tables actually relate to **entities**. The relationship can be shown using an entity relationship diagram (ERD) as in Figure 18.4.

Figure 18.4: Two entities showing a one-to-many relationship

In many situations, however, the relationship is many-to-many. For example, if a number of products could be put in any order, then the relationship becomes a many-to-many relationship. Many-to-many relationships are difficult to implement in a database and so, to deal with this type of relationship, another intermediate table is created that breaks the many-to-many relationship into two one-to-many relationships.

In some situations, the relationship is one-to-one. For example, between the Patient details table and the Patient medical details table shown in Tables 18.5 and 18.6. In both cases Patient reference is the primary key.

Patient reference
Patient first name
Patient address
Patient phone number
Patient next of kin
Patient date of birth

Table 18.5: Patient details table

Patient reference
Blood group
GP
Gender

Table 18.6: Patient medical details table

Figure 18.5: A one-to-one ERD that describes their relationship

One-to-one relationships are not good practice and can be quite inefficient. Figure 18.5 shows this one-to-one relationship.

Normalisation

Normalisation is the process by which complex real world information used by an organisation is analysed and rearranged to be represented efficiently in a number of simple tables that can then be implemented using relational database software such as Microsoft® Access®.

Over time a series of guidelines linked to a procedure have been developed. Stages in the procedure are referred to as normal forms and are numbered from one to five, although it is usual to only consider the first three. They are only guidelines and sometimes it is necessary to ignore them.

First normal form

The first series of checks involves three tasks:

1. Identify and remove calculated fields – a calculated field is one that can be derived from other fields. For example, if age and date of birth are two fields then age is a calculated field because you can always work out someone's age given today's date.

2. Make sure each item of data is atomic – an atomic item is a single item of information. Someone's name (eg Mr John Brown) is non-atomic because it should be broken down into at least three fields – title, first name and last name. Breaking fields down in this way gives more flexibility as to how the data can be used.

3. Identify and remove repeating items and show them in a separate table – make a link so as not to lose the relationship.

Table 18.7 on the following page shows an example of a set of fields in a table that will be used to log faults in machines. Each machine may have many faults over time.

| Machine description |
| Machine code |
| Machine purchase date |
| Machine location |
| Machine date of fault |
| Fault description |
| Machine repairman |
| Fault report |

Table 18.7: Machine faults table

If we were looking to normalise the table to first normal form, we would find that there are no issues with atomic attributes or calculated fields but there is a repeating group – there are lots of faults for each machine. Two tables are needed, one for the machines themselves and one for the faults – linked by the machine code field.

| Machine description |
| **Machine code** |
| Machine purchase date |
| Machine location |

Table 18.8: Machine table

| **Fault reference** |
| Machine date of fault |
| Fault description |
| Machine repairman |
| Fault report |
| Machine code |

Table 18.9: Fault table

Note that a new key field has been created for the Fault table (Fault reference).

Second normal form

Assuming that the table is in first normal form (1NF) and the table has a composite primary key, then check that every field that is not part of the composite primary key (ie the non-key fields) depends on the whole of the primary key.

If an attribute depends on just part of the primary key, then it can be removed, with its key field (create one if

needed), into another table. This will convert the table into second normal form (2NF)

The following shows an example of second normal form.

A learner does many courses and gets a grade for each. This information is recorded in a table but needs to be normalised into second normal terms.

| **Course ref** |
| **Learner ref** |
| Learner name |
| Learner address |
| Grade gained |

Table 18.10: Learner course details

Prior to checking for second normal form, it is always necessary to also check that the table is in first normal form. In this case, the only first normal form issue is that some of the fields (name, address) are not atomic. There are no calculated fields or repeating groups. For the purpose of this exercise we will ignore the atomic fields issue.

The key field is a compound key – both Course ref and Learner ref are needed to uniquely identify each record.

It is then important to check that every field that is not part of the composite primary key (ie the non-key fields) depends on the whole of the composite primary key. We find that Learner name and address, however, depend only on the Learner ref part of the key, so this is not in second normal form. The solution (as is so often the case) is to break the table up into two tables – and leave a foreign key (Learner ref) behind.

| **Course ref** |
| **Learner ref** |
| Grade gained |

Table 18.11: Courses and results

| **Learner ref** |
| Learner name |
| Learner address |

Table 18.12: Learner

Third normal form

Check if any of the non-primary key fields depend on any other non-primary key fields and if so, move to 3NF by removing them to a separate table, leaving one of the fields (the primary key of the new table) behind in the original table.

In the example table below, assuming that a GP only works at one surgery, checks will show that the table has a key field of GP reference and is already in first and second normal form.

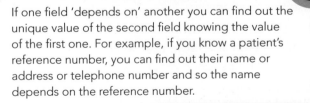

Did you know?

If one field 'depends on' another you can find out the unique value of the second field knowing the value of the first one. For example, if you know a patient's reference number, you can find out their name or address or telephone number and so the name depends on the reference number.

| GP name |
| GP ref |
| Surgery reference |
| Surgery name |
| Surgery postcode |
| Surgery phone |
| Surgery manager |

Table 18.13: The GP surgery

A check for third normal form will, however, show that the last four fields all depend upon the surgery name and so these fields, with a copy of the Surgery ref field, need to be extracted into their own surgery table leaving behind a smaller GP table consisting of GP ref, GP name and Surgery reference.

1.5 Benefits

There are a number of benefits of the relational model for databases.

1. Efficiency of storage and updating – minimising unnecessary data redundancy.

2. Simplicity of design.

3. Ease of modification – new tables can be added without putting the whole database out of action.

4. Can represent complex relationships between objects in the real world (entities).

5. Different 'views' of the database can be created for different users and this can aid the production of reports to meet specific needs. The different views required are achieved in Microsoft® Access® using queries.

Assessment activity scenario

BTEC

The assessment tasks in this unit are based on the following scenario.

A large department store wishes to improve its customer service. It decides that it needs a database to capture and store information relating to customer complaints in order to be better informed about the problems. The database must be easily available to staff in different locations within the same store and also at different stores. You will be working on the project as a database designer.

A systems analyst has been asked to undertake a feasibility study – this resulted in the following outline specification requirements for the database.

Data stores

Complaints details – This should include an open text box to allow the customer the opportunity to describe the complaint, but there should also be some yes/no fields that relate to different categories of complaints (eg product malfunction, rude staff, late delivery, overcharging, etc). The customer contact details will be needed as well as information about the product/department that the complaint related to, the date of the complaint and the store where the complaint was made. It must be possible to add progress details – this might involve an additional table.

Store details – This should include at least the contact details and store manager's name.

Product details – This data store is likely to have already been developed for stock control purposes. However, in the development of this system, a limited product database should be developed.

Manufacturer details – This stores the manufacturers of the products. Again, this is likely to be already available in the company but a limited version should be developed for use in the development stages.

Customer details – The company already holds a database of all customers who use a store card; however, the system must be able to cope with customers who do not and perhaps have bought from the store by cash purchase.

Input requirements

These are limited to the need for the customer service department to take the details of the complaint, document subsequent actions and log them onto their system. It is very important that the details are captured accurately and that good use is made of validation and verification procedures. The screen must also be able to capture ongoing progress comments as the investigation into the complaints is undertaken. It must be able to store the date the complaint was finally resolved so that analysis of the time taken can be made.

Assessment activity scenario continued...

Output requirements

A variety of on-screen and printed reports will be necessary. As an on-screen minimum, anyone should be able to view the records and query the complaints by category of complaint or by store or by product. There should be a facility for outputting appropriate fields for mail merging letters to customers.

Processing

Some processing of the data held will be required, but it is probable that the inbuilt routines for

searching, sorting, etc, will be sufficient. No additional routines will be required, except for ones that might be used to automate some of the tasks involved.

A consistency of styling must be employed – both to provide a professional image and also to help users interact with the system effectively. This consistency of styling should extend to the layout, use of logos, etc, of the forms and reports, as well as such things as naming conventions for the tables and fields.

Assessment activity 18.1

As part of the initial information gathering, the systems analyst encounters a senior member of staff who has never experienced a relational database before – the individual is influential within the company and it is seen as important that he understands them and will thus be able to contribute to the project.

You are asked to prepare a presentation with supporting notes that can be used to explain:

- how business information can be represented using entities and attributes
- how entities are related to each other using primary keys and foreign keys
- referential integrity.

You will be asked to take part in verbal discussions using prepared examples with your tutor and demonstrate practically the features using examples. Be prepared to answer questions. **P1** **M1**

Grading tips

- Note the use of the verb 'explain' in both P1 and M1. Explain means that you need to go beyond a simple description and provide more complete information – perhaps giving reasons for why the item is what it is or does what it does. **P1** **M1**

- Keep the number of bullet points limited on the actual slides and put the additional information into the notes facility of each slide. **P1** **M1**

- It would be useful to include real-life examples within your presentation to help support your explanations and these can be the prepared examples that will be needed in the verbal discussions. **P1** **M1**

PLTS

In your explanations there is scope for you to show that you are an **independent enquirer**, **creative thinker** and **reflective learner** in the selection of appropriate examples within the presentation. Referential integrity in particular is a difficult concept and will take some considered thought in how this will be expressed.

Functional skills

There are opportunities to use some of the evidence developed to support that required for both **English** reading and writing skills.

2 Be able to design, create and populate a relational database

2.1 Design

As with all creative activity, every database needs to be designed on the basis of a full analysis of the requirements. In addition, databases are always part of wider systems and as such, database design activity should be seen and be part of a systems analysis process.

In practical terms, a database consists of a number of the following objects:

- **Tables** – to store raw data. Even small commercial databases may need dozens of related tables.
- **Queries** – often described as virtual tables or views. They are designed to represent a specific view of the data as needed for a particular user or requirement. Queries can be developed from single tables or a series of related tables.
- **Data entry forms** – a mechanism by which data can be entered into the tables and often utilise a series of validation and verification techniques to ensure that the entered data is as accurate as possible.
- **Reports** – the printed outputs.

Design documentation

Although the requirements for documentation may vary between companies and projects, the core set of elements will be entity relationship diagrams (ERDs) and data dictionaries. In addition, you may have to provide what data entry screens and output screens and reports are needed with outline designs or report layouts.

When providing design documentation, data flow diagrams (DFDs) are also used frequently to show how processes and data stores work together. They, together with ways of documenting the processes themselves including flow charts, decision tables and structured English, are comprehensively covered in Unit 11 Business systems analysis.

Data dictionaries

In large or complex systems, it can be very difficult to keep track of all of the different tables and data items. If different tables are constructed over time or by different people then inconsistent naming conventions can cause errors and confusion. A data dictionary is a central store of information about all of the data in a database. Expectations by particular employers and

methodologies are likely to vary but below are a core set of detail that will always be necessary.

- Table names and descriptions.
- Relationships between tables (ie entities) – often shown using ERDs.
- Field names (attributes) and the table(s) in which they appear.
- Field definitions including field types and lengths and meanings if not self evident.
- Additional properties for each field including format and validation controls.
- Aliases or alternative names for the same field as used in different tables.

2.2 Creating relationships

Normalisation

The theoretical normalisation process has been described in section 1.4. In this section the theory is translated into practical activity.

Activity: Converting to first normal form

1 Make appropriate changes to the Order table shown in Table 18.14 to turn it into first normal form. Create new table(s) as needed.

2 Make appropriate changes to the Supplier table shown in Table 18.15 on the following page to turn it into first normal form. Create new table(s) as needed.

Order reference
Customer reference
Customer telephone
Products and quantities ordered
Date of order
Estimated date of delivery
Number of days to delivery date

Table 18.14: An un normalised Order table

Activity: Converting to first normal form continued...

Supplier reference
Supplier name
Supplier address
Supplier telephone
Product name
Qty in stock
Price
Price + VAT

Table 18.15: An un-normalised Supplier table

Activity: Converting to second normal form

Look at the list of fields in the Appointments table shown in Table 18.16. Make appropriate changes to turn it into second normal form. The primary key is a composite primary key (shown in bold). Create new table(s) as needed.

Patient ref
Date of appointment
Patient name
Patient address
Patient phone
Doctor name

Table 18.16: Appointments table

Activity: Dealing with complexity in table design

What would be the impact on your answer to the last activity if you considered that people often have two phone numbers?

Third normal form

To be in third normal form, the table must already be in first and second normal forms.

Activity: Converting to third normal form

Look at the list of field names in Table 18.17. Make appropriate changes to the table to turn it into third normal form. The Holiday type field states whether it is a beach holiday, cruise, etc. Do not assume that it is already in 1NF or 2NF.

Holiday reference
Destination
Holiday type
Hotel reference
Hotel name
Hotel address

Table 18.17: Holiday table

Remember that every time you regroup a set of field names and create additional (often smaller) tables, you have to start again and test for first normal form, then second and then third. Once you are sure that the design of the tables is in first, second and third normal forms, you can start to actually create the tables.

It is also important to note that the design of the database must be finalised before you begin to implement it. Later changes made to the underpinning design, structure of tables or field properties could mean that you may have to start again from scratch.

An ideal table:

- has a field (or pair of fields) that uniquely identifies each row (the primary key)
- does not contain unnecessary duplicate fields
- has no repetition of the same type of value
- has no fields that belong in other tables.

An ideal field:

- represents a characteristic of a table subject
- contains a single value
- is atomic (ie not multi-part)
- is not calculated
- is unique throughout the database structure
- has an appropriate name.

Activity: Normal form questions

1   Summarise what is meant by first normal, second normal and third normal forms.

2   How would you check that a table is fully normalised?

Modifying databases

Modifying relationships can be done once a database has been constructed, but this should only be undertaken with care. Once information has been added to tables and a variety of other forms, queries and reports have been designed and created, changing one of the relationships can cause significant problems. It may be necessary to first delete a relationship and then create all of them again.

Modifying a table design has the greatest potential for causing additional work as all of the relationships, queries and reports that depend upon the table may need revisiting.

Cascading updates and deletes

In Microsoft® Access®, with a relationship in which referential integrity is enforced, you can specify whether you want to automatically cascade update or cascade delete related records. If you set these options, delete and update operations that would normally be prevented by referential integrity rules are allowed. When you delete records or change primary key values in a primary table, Access® will make the necessary changes to related tables to preserve referential integrity.

If you select the Cascade Update Related Fields check box when you define a relationship, each time the primary key in a primary table is changed, Microsoft® Access® automatically updates the primary key to the new value in all related records. For example, if you change the Supplier reference field in a table called Suppliers, the Supplier reference field in the Products table will update automatically for every one of the products supplied by that supplier – this ensures that the relationship is not broken. (See Figure 18.6.)

If you select the Cascade Delete Related Records check box when you define a relationship, any time that you delete records in one table, Access® will automatically delete related records in the related table. For example, if you delete a Supplier record from the Suppliers table, all the products produced by that Supplier would be deleted in the Products table.

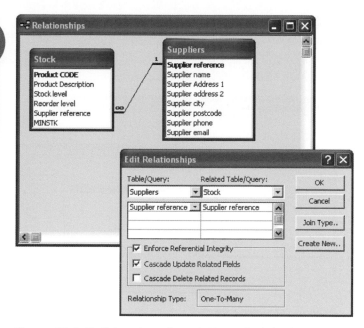

Figure 18.6: Defining the referential integrity rules between two tables

As shown in Figure 18.6, the relationship between the two tables using the Supplier reference field is defined as one in which referential integrity is enforced. The system will 'cascade update' related fields but not 'cascade delete' related records.

In practical terms, this means that if the Supplier reference is changed from, say, S2 to S002 in the Supplier table, then all S2 supplier references of the records in the Stock table will automatically change to S002. So this would be a useful setting to make.

Not checking the cascade delete option means that if the Supplier table record for S2 was deleted because the company went out of business, the related records in the Stock table would not be deleted. This is also a useful setting.

2.3 Query design

Queries represent a very powerful method of allowing users to see different views of the information in a database. Once a query has been created, it acts as if it is a real table – however, the underlying information is not duplicated. Queries can be created based on a number of tables that are linked together. The default type of query is the **select query**.

Key term

Select query – a query that selects the data from the fields that you specify and with the criteria that you set for those fields.

Creating a query

How to... create a query

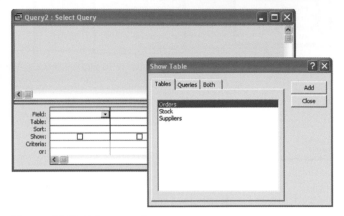

Figure 18.7: Select queries

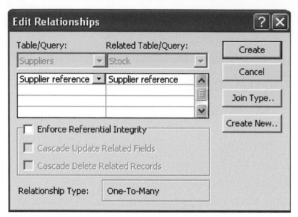

Figure 18.9: A simple select query

1 Open a database and select Design Query. The dialogue box shown in Figure 18.7 appears.

2 In the Show Table dialogue box, choose the tables that you wish to work with. Note that it is possible to select existing queries as well as tables.

3 The selected tables from your database will be displayed at the top of the screen (see Figure 18.8) – note that the one-to-many relationship between the tables is displayed visually as 1-∞.

4 The query is created in the lower part of this screen. Drag field names down as needed. Make sure that the Show box is checked for all the fields you wish to display when you run your query.

The query shown in Figure 18.9 will select and display the three fields indicated of all records in the Stock table, as well as the Supplier name field of all records in the Supplier table.

5 You can also set criteria for your query. For example, the query shown in Figure 18.10 (bottom half of screen only in the screenshot) will select the three fields indicated from the Stock record, but only for those records which have a Stock level less than 20.

Figure 18.10: A select query with one criterion set

6 You can set multiple criteria for your query. For example, the query shown in Figure 18.11 will select the fields indicated, but only for those records which have a Stock level less than 20 and that are supplied by supplier S2.

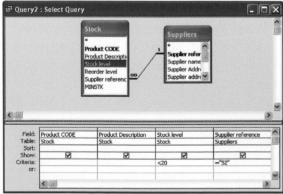

Figure 18.11: A select query with multiple criteria

7 Click on the Run button on the toolbar (with the red exclamation mark) to run the query and check that it selects the correct fields.

This shows the relationship between the tables.

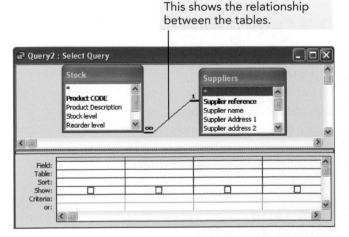

Figure 18.8: Adding the tables to be used in the query

Activity: Designing queries

1 Design a query to show all details of the products in the Stock table except for the Supplier reference.
2 Design a query to show the Product Description and Product Code of all products supplied by suppliers based in Bristol.

Use of logical operators

The method used by Microsoft® Access® to create queries is called Query by Example. In this method, an example is given of what the output will be (eg the query shown in Figure 18.11 specifies that the Supplier reference must be "S2" and the Stock level must be less than 20). The system uses the normal set of operators as given below.

Operator	Meaning
=	Equal to
Not	Not equal to
<	Less than
<=	Less than or equal to
>	Greater than
>=	Greater than or equal to
Like	Matches a prescribed character pattern. The * symbol is used as a wildcard.

Table 18.18: Operators that can be used in query criteria

In other systems, other logical operators such as AND and OR are also employed to develop complex queries. However, in Query by Example systems AND and OR are implemented through the design of the query itself – there is no need for the user to enter them.

For example, the query shown in Figure 18.11 has both the criteria on the same line. So, the query means:

(Stock level <20) AND (Supplier reference ="S2")

If the criteria are on separate lines as seen on Figure 18.12 the meaning will be:

(Stock level <20) OR (Supplier reference ="S2")

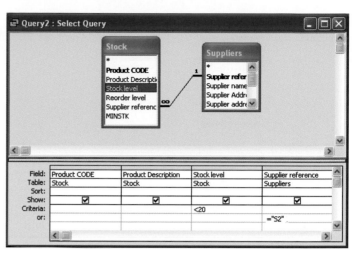

Figure 18.12: Query showing Stock level <20 OR Supplier reference = "S2"

Activity: Basic queries

1 What is a select query?
2 Give five examples of operators that can be used in query design.

Special queries

Parameter queries

A query could be written to select the names of suppliers based in London only. To select a series of different towns then a number of queries – one for each possible town – would need to be created. This is time consuming and tedious to do.

A **parameter query** overcomes this problem and allows the user to choose the town as the query is run – this makes it a lot more flexible. The query is set up in the same way but instead of putting a specific town into the Criteria row a question is used as shown in Figure 18.13.

Key term

Parameter query – a query that prompts the user of a database to set specific criteria for the fields selected for that query by the database designer.

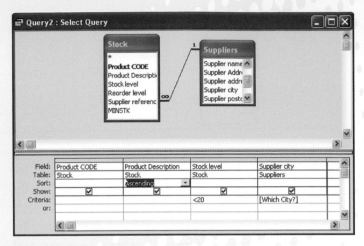

Figure 18.13: Parameter query

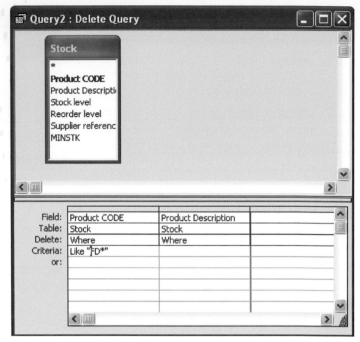

Figure 18.15: Delete Query

When the query is opened or run, the question given in square brackets is displayed and the user types in whatever town is required. The user enters the required town and the query runs accordingly. This is a much more flexible way of managing queries.

When the query is run, the dialogue box shown in Figure 18.14 opens. Once the city is entered, the query runs as before.

Delete queries

The default type of query already described is a Select Query. Another type of query that can prove useful is the Delete Query – as shown in Figure 18.15. The query is built in the usual way but the type of query is changed to Delete using the options in the Query pull down menu.

The query shown in Figure 18.15 will, when run by clicking in the Run button (red ! in the toolbar), delete all records where the Product CODE starts with the letters "FD".

Other special queries

Other special queries such as Update or Append can be selected in the same way as the Delete Query.

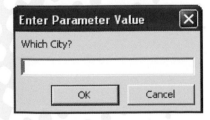

Figure18.14: Dialogue box for parameter query

Activity: Special queries

Find out how the other types of queries operate and experiment with them to be sure you understand how they operate. **Tip:** experiment on a backup copy of your database.

2.4 Data entry forms

Creating forms

Typically, forms are initially generated using the Forms wizard. A number of basic design choices are provided by the wizard and the final form is then produced automatically. The forms produced can then be modified using the toolbox if necessary.

Verification and validation

Microsoft® Access® offers a number of techniques to enable **verification**. One technique used is shown in

Key terms

Verification – a method of checking that the data entered on to the system is correct and the same as that on the original source.

Input mask – used to control what users are allowed to enter in as input in a text box. The key purpose is to improve the quality of input data.

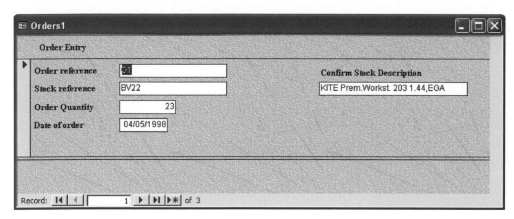

Figure 18.16: Order entry form

Figure 18.16. A simple form is used for entering order details over the phone. To avoid an incorrect Stock reference being entered, a query (new virtual table) has been created that uses the relationship between the Order table and the Stock table. This allows the Stock description to be displayed as the Stock reference is entered in order to confirm that the correct product is being ordered.

The data entry clerk can then confirm this by looking at the source document and checking that it matches. If the clerk has miskeyed the code, they will notice their mistake during this verification check and can re-enter the code.

Activity: Special queries

1 Explain the difference between verification and validation of data.

2 How can the use of forms help with the validation of data?

Validation routines

Input masking

One very useful validation technique is to set up an **input mask** for a particular field, as shown in the table below.

Input mask character	Description of control
0	Number (0 through 9, entry required; plus [+] and minus [-] signs not allowed).
9	Number or space (entry not required; plus and minus signs not allowed).
#	Number or space (entry not required; blank positions converted to spaces, plus and minus signs allowed).
L	Letter (A through Z, entry required).
?	Letter (A through Z, entry optional).
A	Letter or number (entry required).
a	Letter or number (entry optional).
&	Any character or a space (entry required).
C	Any character or a space (entry optional).
. , : ; - /	Decimal placeholder and thousands, date, and time separators. (The actual character used depends on the regional settings specified in Microsoft Windows® Control Panel.)
<	Causes all characters that follow to be converted to lowercase.
>	Causes all characters that follow to be converted to uppercase.
\	Causes the character that follows to be displayed as a literal character. Used to display any of the characters listed in this table as literal characters (for example, \A is displayed as just A).
Password	Setting the InputMask property to the word Password creates a password entry text box. Any character typed in the text box is stored as the character but is displayed as an asterisk (*).

Table 18.19: Input mask characters

Data redundancy and consistency

Users would not normally be expected to enter information more than once unless it is required to double-check an important item, eg a password for consistency. If appropriately normalised, the database will store items only once.

Visual prompts

Visual prompts, eg leaving gaps at key places or pre-inserting special characters that structure the data entry, can be very useful. It is also sometimes valuable to put explanatory text onto the form next to a field that could be misunderstood. For example, if a form asks a user to enter the check digit for a credit card, you might want to add text explaining where the check digit is found and how many characters it needs.

Drop down and combo boxes

These techniques are widely seen in all Windows® applications and are used to assist users in their interactions with the system. In Figure 18.13 (page 42), for example, the word 'ascending' is highlighted and this is because only a few choices are available to the user in this situation (no sort, descending or ascending) and rather than presenting an open text box, the system gives you the choices in a drop down box so that errors are minimised and the entry process is more user-friendly. Combo boxes work in a similar way and techniques for creating them using the toolbox are described in the Advanced features later on in this chapter.

2.5 Populate

In many situations, tables are populated by direct data entry – ideally through a purpose-built form that has appropriate validation and verification controls built in. This process is sensible where, for example, the data is being captured through a phone conversation and the speed of entry is controlled more by the human interaction rather than the speed by which the computer can accumulate information.

If the data already exists in electronic format then attempts should be made to import the data directly into the tables. This is quicker and much more reliable.

Importing data

If data that is to be used in a database is already available in another form, it makes sense to import the data electronically, thus avoiding the possibility of errors made when re-entering the data.

However, it may be complex to do so. Importing can be a dangerous and sometimes time-consuming job. Things can go wrong and, if the file is large, it will not be possible to check the accuracy of every single entry. It is recommended that small tests are done on a limited number of records to make sure that the technique chosen is working.

Some common formats of files that can be imported are explained in this section.

Delimited files

Some files are stored as text but with a **delimiter** to separate the fields and a hard return to separate records. In the example shown below, the delimiter is a comma.

Key term

Delimiter – a character used to separate fields when data is stored as plain text. The delimiter most often used is the comma, hence the term comma-delimited file.

```
"AS01","Psion Finance
Pack",3.00,25.00,"S1",10.00
"BH61","Usernet Software/86",7.00,25.00,
"S3",10.00
"BR45","LAN ROM kit (Diskless
PC)",27.00,25.00,"S1",50.00
"BR51","Usernet2 LAN Board
u",75.00,25.00,"S2",75.00
"BV22","AST Prem.Workst. 203
1.44,EGA",3.00,25.00,"S1",10.00
"CS03","Mouse Adapter (25way-
9)",90.00,25.00,"S1",90.00
"CX31","AST Premium 286 FastRAM
2000",5.00,25.00,"S1",10.00
```

```
"DF61","Psion Oxford Dictionary",8.00,25
.00,"S2",10.00
"DS12","AST Premium 286 Model
90",53.00,25.00,"S1",50.00
"DW01","Floor stand
(800)",9.00,25.00,"S1",10.00
"EW22","AST Premium White
Monitor",53.00,25.00,"S1",60.00
"FD03","AST Premium 286 Model
85",90.00,25.00,"S1",50.00
"FD31","AST Premium/386 390
90MB",0.00,25.00,"S2",10.00
```

Note that text fields are always contained within inverted commas.

How to... import data into Access™

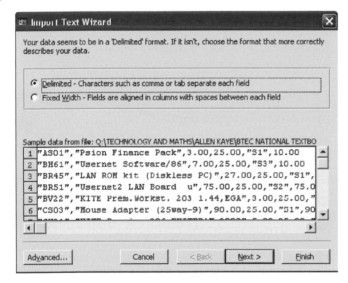

Figure 18.17: Importing text files

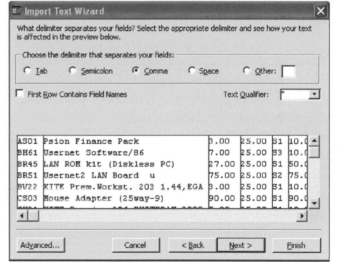

Figure 18.18: Importing comma-delimited files

1 Select Get External Data and Import from the File menu – the screen shown in Figure 18.17 is then displayed.

2 The wizard should automatically detect that the file is delimited. After selecting Next, you can check any settings such as the exact nature of the delimiter and change them if necessary prior to actually importing the data.

Note that in Figure 18.18, the field names are not contained in the file and so that box is left unchecked. The wizard has correctly detected that a comma separates the fields.

3 On the next screens of the wizard, enter the field names.

4 On the final screen, make a choice as to whether the data is added as a new table or into an existing one. If you plan to add new data into an existing table, then you must make sure that the existing fields and properties match the new data coming in.

Delimited format can often be an intermediary format between the database and any other formats not recognised by Access® or the database package you are using. As long as the target application can export its data into a delimited format, then you can import it into Microsoft® Access® or other equivalent database application packages.

Spreadsheet input

If data is already held in spreadsheet format you can import the data directly into the database. When you make the choice to import a file, change the file filter to see spreadsheet files and navigate to the appropriate directory – this will allow you to select the appropriate file.

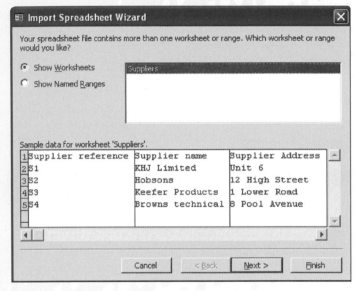

Figure 18.19: Importing spreadsheets

If the spreadsheet has named ranges then you can select from these, as seen in Figure 18.19. This is particularly useful if the spreadsheet layout is complex and the data you wish to import is only in part of a sheet.

It is important that the spreadsheet is in a simple format, without additional rows or columns of cells that do not form part of the actual data to be imported. The top row is normally interpreted as a heading line with field names in each column.

Subsequent screens in the wizard allow you to add a new auto primary key field as needed and decide whether the imported data should go into a new table or an existing one.

As an alternative to importing the data, it is possible to link tables in appropriate formats to an existing database. This has the advantage that the data is stored only once if another application also needs to use the data in its original format.

2.6 Exporting data

Data can be exported from Microsoft® Access® into a variety of formats. Sometimes the data can be exported directly into a format that is understood by another application package or system, for example Excel®, Word or an HTML document. At other times it is necessary to export to a low level file, such as a simple text file, to allow transference of the data to the widest set of systems. However, it may also mean that much of the extra information in terms of field attributes will be lost. A number of types of objects can be exported apart from tables; these include reports and queries, although the types of formats allowable may be restricted.

How to... export data

1 Select a table or query in your database.
2 Select Export data from the File menu. You will be prompted to choose a file name and a file type.

2.7 Advanced features

As with all application packages, there are a range of advanced features that are available to the user. The features that are needed will depend upon the particular nature of the application but will be particularly related to ensuring and maintaining integrity.

Styles

As with all applications, there are a number of advantages in imposing particular styles on various aspects of the finished product.

- A style can help to provide or reflect an image of the organisation or company.

- Users will find it easier to navigate the system if there are similar ways of interacting with screens or if there is a consistency about where items are placed on the screen or how they are named. This may reduce errors and also increase speed of interactions.

- Whole systems are easier and quicker to develop if styles are reused.

As database application packages are opened, it is usual for the user to be given choices as to which overall style or template should be used.

There are a number of standard built in styles for reports and screens and these can provide an easy way of imposing consistent styling. However, in most situations, developers design and generate special new styles for forms and reports that relate directly to the user and system needs.

Creating special forms and reports using toolbox

A form is designed to be viewed on-screen and a report is designed to provide a printed output. Wizards can be used to design basic forms and reports in a limited number of styles and can be modified to suit a particular need. It is possible to create forms and reports from scratch, but often people choose to let the wizard create a basic object and then use the toolbox to modify it.

The Access® Toolbox is a toolbar. Choosing one of the buttons that appear in the Toolbox adds or influences a control, represented by that tool's symbol.

When you create a report, the Toolbox serves the same purpose as when it is used with forms, although tools that require user input, such as combo boxes, are seldom used in reports. It is useful to understand about the different objects that are found on forms and reports.

Control object categories

There are three types of control objects in forms and reports.

- **Bound controls** are associated with a field in the table or query for the form or subform. Text boxes are the most common bound control. You can also show the content of graphic objects or play a waveform audio file with a bound OLE (object linking and embedding) object. You can bind toggles, check boxes, and option buttons to Yes/No fields. All bound controls have associated labels that display the Caption property of the field; you can edit or delete these labels without affecting the bound control.

- **Unbound controls** display data you provide that is independent of any data in the database. You can use the unbound OLE object to add a drawing or bit-mapped image to a form. You can use lines and rectangles to divide a form into logical groups, or simulate boxes used on the paper form. Unbound text boxes are used to enter data that is not intended to update a field.

- **Calculated controls** use expressions derived from normal mathematical operations. Usually, the expression includes the value of a field.

Figure 18.20 shows the Access® Toolbox and the name of each control. Table 18.20 gives details of what each of the controls is and what it does.

Select Objects	Control Wizard	
Label	Text Box	Option Group
Toggle Button	Option Button	Check Box
Combo Box	List Box	Command Button
Image	Unbound Object	Bound Object
Page Break	Tab Control	Subform/Subreport
Line	Rectangle	Advanced Controls

Figure 18.20: The toolbox in outline

Control wizard	Activates wizards for all controls. It is normally left on.
Label	Control that displays descriptive text, such as a title, a caption or instructions.
Text box	Use to display, enter, or amend data in the underlying record source of a form. Also, a text box can be used to display the results of a calculation or accept input from a user.
Option group	Use along with check boxes, option buttons or toggle buttons to display a set of alternative values – valuable to help control user input.
Toggle button	Use as a stand-alone control bound to a Yes/No field in a Microsoft® Access® database.
Option button	Use as a stand-alone control bound to a Yes/No field in a Microsoft® Access® database.
Check box	Use as a stand-alone control bound to a Yes/No field in a Microsoft® Access® database.
Combo box	Use to control data entry. You can type in the text box or select an entry in the list box to add a value to an underlying field.
List box	Displays a scrollable list of values.
Command button	Use to create buttons with actions attached, such as via macros.
Image	Use to display a static picture on a form.
Unbound object frame	Use to display an unbound OLE object, such as a Microsoft® Excel® spreadsheet, on a form.
Bound object frame	Use to display OLE objects, such as a series of pictures on a form. This control is for objects stored in a field in the form's or report's underlying record source.
Page break	Starts a new screen on a form or a new page in a printed form.
Tab control	Creates a tabbed form with several pages or tabbed dialog box.
Subform/subreport	Use to display data from more than one form or table.
Line	Adds a graphic line to help visual layout.
Rectangle	Adds a graphic box to help visual layout.

Table 18.20: The parts of the Access® Toolbox explained

The Commands buttons can be used to create bespoke systems that provide more limited options to the end user. Navigation buttons on blank forms can be used to create a friendly front end to systems (See figure 18.21).

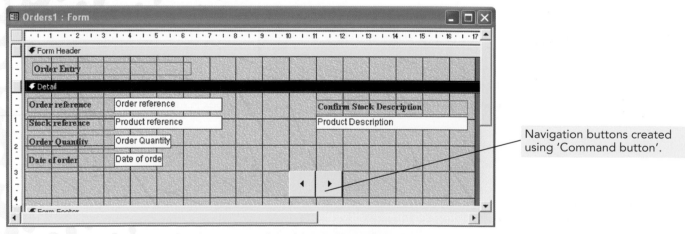

Figure 18.21: Form with navigation buttons produced using the toolbox

Figure 18.22: Form with controlled data entry combo box produced using the toolbox

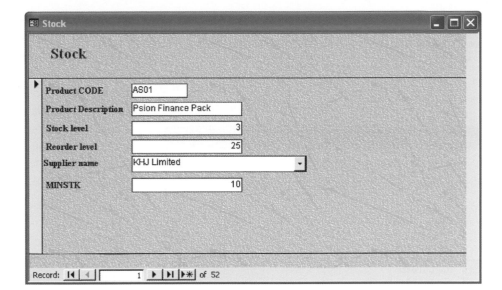

In Figure 18.22, the entry into the Supplier name field is controlled by a drop-down combo box.

Remember

Make sure the wizard button is activated in the toolbox before you add the combo box and then the wizard will take you through the options.

Using Toolbox for reports

Only a limited number of the tools available in the toolbox are normally used when generating reports. Particularly useful are the page break and unbound object frame, the latter allowing a graphic image to be added to the report layout.

Customising

Most database application packages are generic and are designed to be used in any and all situations. When a particular application is designed for a specific purpose, it can be very useful to customise it in order to remove unnecessary options or provide specific front ends to support the intended users.

Apart from only providing to the user the tools that are appropriate to their work, it can also be useful to remove some tools that might be used deliberately or accidentally to do unacceptable actions, eg delete such things as table fields or change relationships.

Customising toolbars

In general, all of the options available on toolbars are also available within the menu choices, and the sets chosen on each particular toolbar are grouped because they relate to a similar area or function. It is however, possible to build a new toolbar.

The next exercise relates to Microsoft® Access®, although similar facilities are available in other application packages.

Select Tools and Customise from the menu and then ensure that the Toolbars tab is chosen. A screen is displayed as shown in Figure 18.23. Select New and provide an appropriate name for your new toolbar.

When this new toolbar is initially created, it is empty. Switching to the Commands tab gives access to all of the commands on all of the toolbars so that individual ones can be highlighted and then dragged onto the new toolbar. In this example a very limited toolbar is created with, for example, no access to the New command.

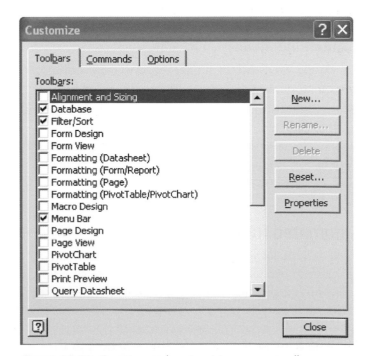

Figure 18.23: Creating and customising a new toolbar

Note that all new toolbars have an additional command, which allows further customisation.

Figure 18.24: Screenshot showing the new customised toolbar

Figure 18.25: New toolbar created and displayed called 'Unit 5 example'

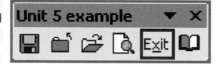

This can then be selected using Toolbars within the View pull down menu, the final result as shown in Figure 18.24.

Customising menus

In a similar way, and for similar reasons, new menus can also be created and then customised.

Select Customise, as you did for creating new toolbars, but then select the Commands tab and choose new menu. The new menu can be held and dragged up to the existing menus at the top of the screen. Initially it will again be empty but individual commands can be held and dragged onto this new toolbar.

Automated functions

Database packages such as Microsoft® Access® are designed to be used in the widest variety of situations – they are application packages rather than bespoke solutions. This makes them very powerful. Database systems created using these application packages are generally much easier, quicker and cheaper to develop. In addition, the final solution tends to be

more reliable as it is built using a tried and tested underpinning application package.

Database solutions can be created from scratch using a programming language and in some respects this allows for the production of a very focused product, but it would be unusual for companies to adopt this approach unless it was really necessary. Apart from the advantages of database application packages already noted, the skills needed to develop databases with them are much more readily available than specialist programmers.

There are some disadvantages, however, of using a generic database package. Many of the options and features available will not be needed in any one given database and allowing users access to all of them could generate problems. In addition, there may be some actions or complex combinations of keystrokes that are used time and time again and designers of systems will want ways of providing special interfaces or automated routines. In some cases an apparently bespoke system can be designed and created using buttons on forms that trigger macros that carry out predefined tasks. This approach combines the advantages of using a generic package with the flexibility of bespoke systems.

Automated functions can be created using:

1. macros   2. scripts

3. programming languages such as Visual Basic® for Applications (VBA).

Note: *VBA programs can be attached to a menu button, a macro, a keyboard shortcut, or an OLE/COM event, such as the opening of a document in the application. The language also provides a user interface in the form of UserForms for added functionality.*

2.8 Errors

Reasons

It is common for problems to arise in the use of databases. Some are caused by the underpinning design, while others are caused by insufficient control of the entry of information into the records. Organisations come to rely on the detail and the reports they obtain from databases, so it can be crucial that these reports are based on reliable information.

Activity: Errors

1 Describe one problem not mentioned in Table 18.21 that might occur in a database.

2 Suggest a possible solution for this problem.

Symptom	Possible error	Solution
Tables will not link at all.	Properties of the two fields (particularly the data types) that create the relationship are different.	Check that the data types of each of the two fields are the same. Fix as necessary and check implications on other objects, such as forms, queries or reports.
Tables appear to link but the information in the related table does not appear.	The range of values in the tables are not consistent, eg G010 and GO1O.	Add validation controls to stop alpha letters being entered instead of numbers.
Information relating to the same thing in different tables is different.	The database has not been designed or normalised properly allowing for data redundancy.	Back up the data. Redesign, reconstruct and repopulate the database.
It is not possible to enforce referential integrity rules when a relationship is being created.	There are some values of one of the linked fields for which there are no equivalent values in the other table.	Inspect the data in the tables and add or amend as necessary.

Table 18.21: Typical database errors and their solutions

Assessment activity 18.2

1 Consider the information provided in Assessment activity 18.1 and decide what entities you intend to implement and normalise them. You are expected to need five related entities.

Document the relationships, table structures, fields and properties.

Check with your tutor or client and get this signed off before proceeding to the next task. Modify as necessary and implement your design. **P2**

2 Using the information provided, design and implement suitable data entry forms for the capturing of the information incorporating features to ensure the validity and integrity of data.

You must include at least three of the following techniques within the set of data entry forms:

- validation routine
- verification routine
- input masking
- check for completeness
- visual prompts
- data consistency
- check for data redundancy
- drop-down/combo boxes.

Enter sufficient data into the system. At least some of the data should be imported from an external source. **P3 P4 M2**

3 Devise queries that respond to the requirements identified using multiple tables and multiple criteria. Export appropriate customer data to a file that can be used for a mail merge as noted in the scenario requirements. **P5 M3**

4 Select and implement one advanced feature in the database that is appropriate to the scenario. Check the Advanced features content in the specification or with your tutor if you are unsure.

Select and implement one automated function that is appropriate for the scenario. One example that would be suitable is the creation of a form and objects with associated macros that act as a menu, allowing the objects to be easily chosen by the user. **P6 M4**

5 Using the experiences gained and using any appropriate examples from this activity, prepare a set of notes that describe and explain how errors in the design and construction of databases can best be avoided. Prepare to engage with your tutor in a discussion about this task and be ready to both respond to questions and initiate dialogue to make sure you cover everything necessary. You will be expected to hand in your prepared notes. **D1**

Grading tips

- Present your theoretical design to your tutor or client and consider any feedback before you start implementing it. In this way, you will ensure that there are no flaws in the core design developed. **P2**

Assessment activity 18.2 continued (P2) (P3) (P4) (P5) (P6) (M2) (M3) (M4) (D1) BTEC

- Sufficient data probably means at least 100 records; most of this can be imported from a file that may be provided by your tutor although the file may need additional work to ensure it is compatible with your structures. Make sure the values in each of the fields are realistic and not just nonsense text. (P3) (P4) (M2)

- For D1, you should record ideas that could be used from the beginning of your work in this assignment. Look at the whole activity objectively and try to identify where errors might be introduced and how you can avoid them. (D1)

PLTS

Careful planning and management will provide good opportunities to develop your skills as a **self-manager**.

Generating ideas, exploring possibilities, choosing and deciding on the design and structure of your database will help you develop skills as a **creative thinker**.

Task 5 in particular provides opportunities to practise and develop your skills as an **independent enquirer** as you explore and consider potential errors and how they can best be avoided.

Functional skills

These activities allow you to use your **ICT** skills when you select, interact with and use ICT systems independently for a complex task to meet a variety of needs.

The designing, developing and use of queries in task 5 involves **ICT** skills in developing, presenting and communicating of information, and provides opportunities to generate appropriate evidence.

It is important to ensure that the evidence produced for these tasks is written at the appropriate level of detail and takes account of the intended audience. Both the written reports and any records of verbal discussions could very well contribute to the evidence you may be putting together for **English** functional skills.

3   Be able to test a relational database

3.1 Testing

Test Plan

Test planning seeks to identify the list of tests which, if performed, will identify whether the system meets the business and technical requirements that guided its design and development and works as expected.

The test plan documents the overall approach to the test. It shows how the tests will be organised,

and outlines all of the tests that are needed. When developing the series of tests, the tester must take full account of the original set of user requirements, as this will connect it to the fundamental purpose of the wider developmental activity. Furthermore, the user should be given some access to the test results and testing could be a stage that requires formal customer acceptance and sign off.

The test plan should be discussed and agreed with the wider development team.

A typical test case includes:

1. A unique name and number
2. A description of what is being tested
3. Preconditions which describe the state of the software before the test case
4. Steps that describe the specific steps which make up the interaction
5. Expected results which describe the expected state of the software after the test case is executed
6. Actual results
7. Comments.

Test cases must be repeatable.

There are typically several iterations of test execution and issues being identified, resolved and retested.

Test automation is a practice in which testers employ a software tool to reduce or eliminate repetitive tasks. This can save a lot of time, but the development of automated tests can be expensive.

3.2 Evaluation criteria

The primary criterion that should be used when evaluating a finished database system is whether it meets the user need. There is an emphasis on capturing the requirements of a system fully and formally – without such a requirements specification, it is impossible to test and evaluate properly.

Finally, it is necessary to confirm that the system is fit for purpose by asking the client to formally sign off the finished system. Fit for purpose should be based on a simple mechanistic check that everything in the requirements specification has been fulfilled. However, in some cases there will be aspects of look and feel and considerations of the compromises that have been made during the development process that will make the checking of fit for purpose less mechanistic and more qualitative judgement calls. It is to be hoped that the client is not taken by surprise at this stage by significant deviations, limitations or other unexpected changes – any such should have been brought to the attention of the client as they arose and ways forward agreed at the time.

Note that being fit for purpose does not only mean that it fulfils all of the requirements. If, for example, the system is extremely costly or over-engineered then this might give cause to describe it as not fit for purpose.

Although not normally required by the customer, it would be good practice on the part of the developers to reflect on the development, consider and justify the database features that were used – this will help the developer build expertise and consolidate experience ready for the next project. The developers may also choose on the basis of their by now deep knowledge of the system and its context, to identify further improvements to the system – this they would most likely share with the customer giving added value and possible further business opportunity.

The act of asking a customer to sign off will encourage a more detailed check than would otherwise be made. Once the customer has signed off the system, it means that they accept it as it is.

Other units detail test strategies that could be used but to summarise:

1. The detailed functionality of the components of the system is tested using **white box testing** – this is typically undertaken by someone who understands the detail of the system.

2. The less detailed check on user requirements is typically done using **black box testing**, perhaps using a formal requirements specification that was produced during the design phase.

Key terms

White box testing – tests internal structures or workings of an application. It uncovers coding errors and other software problems but cannot identify if the overall system meets the requirements specification.

Black box testing – focuses on the testing of functional requirements. The test designer develops a series of valid and invalid inputs and checks for each combination to see if the output is as expected.

Assessment activity 18.3

BTEC

1 Using any appropriate testing regimes, design and document a test plan. Execute the test plan, fixing problems if needed. Record the results and any subsequent iterations of tests and fixing.

Ensure you test both the detailed functionality and the overall user requirements.

Engage with the user or check with the detailed user requirements to confirm that the system is fit for purpose. Present your final system with documentation for sign off. **P7**

2 Reflect on the development process and justify the features used, making suggestions for improvements. The evidence for this final part can either be through a written report or through a suitably recorded discussion with your tutor. **D2**

Grading tips

- Make sure you check against the original user requirements as the specification focuses on black box testing. It will also be good practice to check the key internal queries, input screens and reports function as required. Allow the customer to check the completed system and sign off that it meets the requirements. Leave enough time to fix any problems identified. **P7**

- The test plans should show at least the test data, expected results and the actual results. For D2, you will build upon the black box testing aspects of P7 but also provide justifications for the tools and techniques used and a list of potential improvements. **D2**

PLTS

This task requires the production of a comprehensive test plan and in doing so offers opportunities to develop your skills as a **self-manager**.

In addition, there will be an opportunity through the final activities to reflect both on the specific tools and techniques used in the activities, but also on the way you approached the tasks and whether if done again, you might do things differently. This will show that you are a **reflective learner**.

Functional skills

The second part of this task will use either your **English** speaking or writing skills, depending on how you choose to approach this reflective section.

My name is Max and I own a high street printing shop. I have one employee and we manage the whole business, but we do have some sales assistants that work for us at busy times. It is a franchise and most of the systems and procedures were provided to us when we set up the business. We have each focused on different aspects of the business and one of my roles is to manage the IT work – particularly the databases. We were given some blank databases at the start and some training to help us come to terms with them. However, over time I have developed some new ones and also adapted the standard ones to give us more functionality and better reports.

In respect of my work with databases, the vast majority of my time is spent as a user – simply entering data or running reports. Occasionally, however, when I know the shop will not be busy, I take the time to look for improvements and added functionality – mostly by designing new queries and reports that we think will help us understand the business better. I also added an extra field to the customer database that identified the poor payers – it is quite useful now and seemed easy to do, but in the end it was a lot of work to chase down all of the changes that needed doing to other objects to actually make it work!

The change that I am most proud of is when I added a menu system to the main database – this was done using a series of standard macros and made a huge difference to how easy it was to use the database. One additional benefit that I only realised later was that it restricted my employee's access to the underlying queries and reports – he had a tendency to 'tinker' with them and sometimes caused problems.

Think about it!

1 Max seems to only occasionally work with the database as a designer – most of the time he is just a user. What problems might Max encounter when he does want to change the database or add functionality? How might they best be alleviated?

2 What databases do you think the printing shop might need?

3 Do you think that Max was sensible to add a menu system? What are the advantages and disadvantages in his situation?

Just checking

1. Explain how one field can both be a primary key and a foreign key.
2. Explain one-to-many relationships and many-to-many relationships. Give an example of each.
3. What does referential integrity mean?
4. Atomic fields. Fix the entries in the order table shown below to make sure that each entry represents a single item. Hint: You will need to add two more rows.

Name	Stock reference	Order date	Order quantity
HN56	JKY34, JKL46	3/7/2006	4 of each stock item
HN57	KNL13, KNM78	14/6/2006	234 of KNL13 and 45 of KNM78
HN87	JRD01	5/9/2006	78

5. What is a composite primary key?
6. Explain the quickest way of identifying whether a table might not have an issue being in second normal form.

Assignment tips

- Remember that you cannot be awarded a merit or a distinction grade unless you have achieved every one of the pass criteria.
- The most common problem found when database queries do not work is that the attributes of the two fields that are used to link the tables have different properties.
- D1 involves a discussion – before you engage with your tutor make sure you have a series of prepared notes and comments. Rehearse the points that you will raise and anticipate some of the questions you might be asked.
- Choose which function you intend to automate carefully for M4. Check out the list contained in the content (eg macros, scripts, program code). It is not recommended to elect for scripts or program code unless you are already familiar with a scripting or other programming language.
- When completing the task for P7 and D2, it is suggested that you devise and document the test plan using familiar techniques that you may have learnt in another unit. It is likely that the customer in this situation will be your tutor and in order to gain acceptance you may be asked to demonstrate a working version of the database. Leave enough time to fix any problems identified.

20 Client side customisation of web pages

Increasingly, websites consist of sophisticated, interactive web pages. A key feature is that the code is stored on the user's computer rather than on the web server.

In this unit, you will learn about web page layout using cascading style sheets (CSS) and interactivity using a scripting language, such as JavaScript or VBScript.

The examples given throughout this unit for a scripting language are in JavaScript.

Learning outcomes

After completing this unit, you should:

1. understand the fundamentals of cascading syle sheets (CSS)

2. understand the fundamentals of scripting languages

3. be able to control the layout of web pages using CSS

4. be able to create interactive web pages.

Assessment and grading criteria

This table shows you what you must do in order to achieve a pass, merit or distinction grade, and where you can find activities in this book to help you.

To achieve a **pass** grade the evidence must show that you are able to:	To achieve a **merit** grade the evidence must show that, in addition to the pass criteria, you are able to:	To achieve a **distinction** grade the evidence must show that, in addition to the pass and merit criteria, you are able to:
P1 explain how HTML files access CSS **See Assessment activity 20.1, page 65**		
P2 explain the features of the box model for CSS **See Assessment activity 20.1, page 65**	**M1** assess different implementation styles of CSS **See Assessment activity 20.1, page 65**	
P3 explain the fundamentals of a scripting language **See Assessment activity 20.2, page 74**	**M2** discuss how a scripting language can improve functionality **See Assessment activity 20.2, page 74**	**D1** explore how web pages using scripts are implemented in different browsers **See Assessment activity 20.2, page 74**
P4 design web pages using CSS to control layout **See Assessment activity 20.3, page 81**		
P5 create interactive web pages using CSS and a scripting language **See Assessment activity 20.4, page 88**	**M3** employ good practice in the design and implementation of web pages. **See Assessment activity 20.4, page 88**	
P6 test interactive web pages. **See Assessment activity 20.4, page 88**		**D2** evaluate the web pages and discuss improvements **See Assessment activity 20.4, page 88**

How you will be assessed

The assessment for this unit is in three parts. For your first project, you will need to create a report about CSS, including how HTML files access it and the features of the box model. In the second project, you will create a presentation to describe the fundamentals of scripting languages and how they can be used. Finally, your third project is split into two parts. The first part is the design, where you will create plans for a website which uses CSS to control the layout. The second part is building the website, adding scripting to enhance functionality and make it interactive, and use good practice. Finally you will test and evaluate your site, suggesting future improvements.

Charlotte, BTEC National IT learner

Having done the previous unit on web design, I was really interested to find out more and learn about making websites interactive and more exciting.

The first two projects were really interesting as we learned about how CSS and JavaScript really worked and how we could include them in a website. We did lots of practice activities in class, making simple web pages or mini-elements to practise each bit.

The third project was the best part as I got to use all the theory and practice in a real website. It was challenging at times, especially when my first attempt at some script did not work, but I persevered and it felt brilliant when it did work correctly.

This is a great unit, especially if you want to be a web designer, because you get to learn in-depth. But I think anyone could be interested as it shows how the websites we use every day actually work.

Over to you

- Which areas do you think you will enjoy about this unit?
- What skills do you think will be important for this unit and are there any you think you will need to develop as you work through it?
- Look at existing websites and think about how the user can interact with them. What do you think this kind of functionality adds to their experience?

1 Understand the fundamentals of cascading style sheets (CSS)

Under the bonnet

Every single web page that you visit is controlled by code. You may be aware of HTML, but there are lots of other elements to it. They work like a car – the outside is seen and looks nice but lift the bonnet and you get to see how it actually works, although it might not be pretty.

- Visit five different websites and select one of its pages. For one page on each different website, open the source code (in Internet Explorer®, click Page/View Source). Print this code.

- Using coloured pens or highlighters, mark where you think different types of languages are being used. See if you can spot the words:

  (a) html   (b) script   (c) style.

- Compare your printouts to the websites on screen. Can you see where each visual part of the website occurs in the code?

It is good practice to use the same layout and styling throughout a website. This is known as the **house style**.

CSS allows you to create a standard layout and style which can be easily used on each web page in the site. Due to this standardisation, it is also easier to alter and maintain the site. For example, in normal HTML, to change the font colour of all the titles to white would involve changing each one individually. When using CSS, only one style value would need to be changed and it would be applied throughout the site.

1.1 Characteristics of CSS

CSS is made up of a series of **styles**, each of which is given a name so it can be recognised throughout the code.

The style is defined in the CSS and then used in the HTML. The style **tags** are placed around the content which is to be affected (see Figure 20.1).

```
<html>
<head>
<link rel=stylesheet type="text/css" href="styles.css">
</head>

<body>
<h1>Example of h1</h1>
<h2>Example of h2</h2>

</body>
</html>
```

Figure 20.1: CSS tags used around text in HTML code

Key terms

House style – a design theme carried throughout a website or even a business, eg letters, faxes, emails, web pages, etc.

CSS – stands for cascading style sheets. It is a form of web language which standardises the layout throughout a website.

Style – a group of formatting decisions to be applied together as defined in the CSS. For example, to have text display as red and centred could be a style.

Tags – elements of web page code, either in HTML or CSS. Usually they are written between angle brackets, < and >, to indicate that they are code words.

Head – the head of the web page, the part of the code where all the styling and other invisible parts are written.

Body – the part of the code where all the elements that are visible on the web page are coded.

Pixel perfect – a term used in the design field where graphics are accurate down to the very last pixel.

CSS frameworks

CSS can be written into the HTML in three ways: inline, header and external.

- **Inline**: the CSS is defined in the same area of the code as that to which it is to be applied.

```
<p style="background: red; colour: white;
font-family: Times New Roman;">An example
of inline CSS</p>
```

This code will produce:

An example of inline CSS

- **Header**: the CSS is defined in the **head** section of each web page and applied throughout the **body**:

```
<head>
 <style>
h1 {
background: red;
color: white;
font-family: times new roman;
}
</style>
</head>


<body>
 <h1>An example of header CSS</h1>
</body>
```

This code will produce:

An example of header CSS

- **External**: the CSS is defined in a separate file, which all web pages can reference (see Figure 20.2). This is a .css file, rather than an .html file. There are two lines which can be put in the head of the HTML to link to external CSS pages:

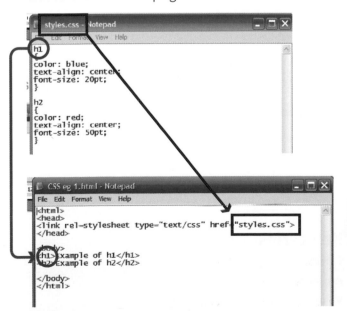

Figure 20.2: A .css file applied to an .html file

```
<link rel="stylesheet" type="text/css"
href="class.css" />
```

or:

```
<style type="text/css"
title="currentStyle" media="screen">
@import "style.css";
</style>
```

Both the header and external methods can also be called block methods. This is because the CSS is grouped together in a block, rather than distributed through the code.

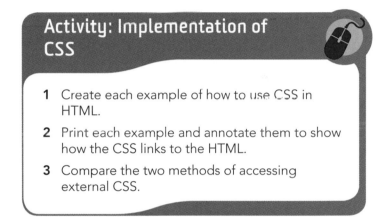

Activity: Implementation of CSS

1. Create each example of how to use CSS in HTML.
2. Print each example and annotate them to show how the CSS links to the HTML.
3. Compare the two methods of accessing external CSS.

Box model

CSS is used to create layouts on web pages. Using this method, the pages can be viewed in any browser or resolution and the integrity of the design should remain. This is because the layout is recalculated on each opening. The resulting web page can therefore be designed very accurately; in fact, it can be **pixel perfect**.

The CSS box model structures the web page in a similar way to a table. Margins, borders, padding and content are each defined (see Figure 20.3).

Figure 20.3: Layout of box elements

Four elements can be defined in the box model: content area, padding, border and margin.

- **Content area**: where the text and images which will be displayed on the web page should be placed. There can be more than one content area.
- **Padding**: the blank space around the content area so it is not displayed right up to the edges of the border.
- **Border**: the design surrounding the padding and content area.
- **Margin**: the blank space around everything so it is not displayed right up to the edges of the screen.

The padding, border and margin are optional and, if not defined, are set at a default value of zero. This would mean that the border would be invisible.

The height and width can be defined for each area. Different widths and heights can be set for top, bottom, left and right. It is even possible for margins to have negative values.

Setting the dimensions can be done using a variety of measurements, the most popular being pixels and percentages. Defining the layout by percentage of the screen is the most effective for maintaining layout consistency.

As with formatting statements, layout statements can be written inline or in a block method (header or external).

Selectors

Each style which is defined in CSS consists of a **selector**, a **property** and a **value**.

For example, `h1 {color:red}` will create the rule that wherever `h1` is used, the colour will be red.

Table 20.1 shows some of the selectors available and how they would be implemented into a web page.

Type of selector	CSS	HTML
Headings	h1 {color:red}	`<h1>A red heading</h1>`
Paragraph	p{color:red}	`<p>Some red text.</p>`
Anchor (as in 'a href')	a:hover{color:red}	This should 'overrule' the default settings for hyperlinks so these turn red when the cursor hovers over them.
class	.alert{color:red}	`<p class=alert>Some red text.</p>` `<span class=alert>Some red text.</span>`
id	#alert{color:red}	`<p id=alert>Some red text.</p>` `<span id=alert>Some red text.</span>`

Table 20.1: CSS selectors

Remember

For class and id selectors, any label can be applied after the dot. It is advisable to use sensible naming so it is recognisable.

A class can be used for formatting which needs to be used several times, whereas id is used for individual instances of formatting only.

Activity: Box model and selectors

1 Describe the four parts of the box model.
2 Describe the three parts of selectors.

Key terms

Selector – similar to the title of the style.
Property – what is being changed.
Value – the amount the property is being changed.

Accessing CSS from HTML

External CSS needs to be accessed from every web page in which it is to be used. There are two methods of connecting it:

```
<link rel="stylesheet" type="text/css"
href="class.css" />
```

or:

```
<style type="text/css"
title="currentStyle" media="screen">
@import "style.css";
</style>
```

The appropriate line would need to be inserted into the head section of each web page.

1.2   Uses of CSS

CSS can be used to alter the layout and formatting of any web page. Here are some examples of the hundreds of tags available (using the header method).

- Background colour:
```
<html>
<head>
<style>
body {background-color: yellow}
</style>
</head>

<body>
</body>
</html>
```

- Background images:
```
<html>
<head>
<style>
body {background-image: url('picture.
jpg')}
</style>
</head>

<body>
</body>
</html>
```

Remember

The image must be in the same folder as the web page, otherwise the whole file location must be included.

- Formatting text:
```
<html>
<head>
<style>
h1{
font-family: serif;
font-style: italic;
font-weight: bold;
font-size: 200px;
color: green;
}
</style>
</head>

<body>
<h1>Example text</h1>
</body>
</html>
```

- Applying borders:
```
<html>
<head>
<style>
.border1 {border-style: groove}
.border2 {border-style: double solid}
.border3 {border-style: double solid
groove}
</style>
</head>

<body>
<p class="border1">Example text</p>
<p class="border2">Example text</p>
<p class="border3">Example text</p>
</body>
</html>
```

- Applying padding:

```html
<html>
<head>
<style>
.padding1 {padding: 1cm}
.padding2 {padding: 0.5cm 1.5cm}
</style>
</head>

<body>
<table border="1">
<tr>
<td class="padding1">
Example text
</td>
</tr>
</table>

<br>
<table border="1">
<tr>
<td class="padding2">
Example text
</td>
</tr>
</table>
</body>
</html>
```

- Heading styles:

```html
<html>
<head>
<style>
h1 {
background: red;
color: white;
font-family: times new roman;
font-style: italic;
}
h2 {
text-align: center;
text-decoration: underline;
font-size: xx-large;
```

```html
font-weight: bold;
}
</style>
</head>

<body>
<h1>Example text</h1>
<br>
<h2>Example text</h2>
</body>
</html>
```

- Positioning elements:

```html
<html>
<head>
<style>
.position_relative
{
position:relative;
left:20px
}
.position_absolute
{
position:absolute;
left:200px;
top:200px
}
</style>
</head>

<body>
Example text
<p class=position_relative>Exampletext</p>
<p class=position_absolute>Exampletext</p>
</body>
</html>
```

- Creating columns:

```html
<html>
<head>
<style>
.nav {
        width: 220px;
```

```
        padding: 10px;
        float:left;
        }


.content {
        padding: 10px;
        margin-left: 230px;
        border-left: 1px solid #006;
        }


.footer {
        border-top: 1px solid #006;
        text-align: right;
        }
</style>
</head>

<body>
Example text
<div class='nav'>Example text</div>
<div class='content'>Example text</div>
<div class='footer'>Example text</div>
</body>
</html>
```

Activity: Uses of CSS

1 Create each of these examples and make notes on how they affect the formatting.
2 Try altering the values and make notes on how this alters the formatting.

Advantages

The key advantages of CSS are:

- controlling and editing the layout of web pages is faster
- house style is more reliable as all pages use the same style sheets, therefore the same font size, colour, etc
- file sizes are smaller, as all the formatting is in one CSS file rather than duplicated across several web pages
- accessibility for users with screen readers is improved.

Assessment activity 20.1
P1 P2 M1 BTEC

oink is a business selling piggy banks. They want to create a website which is easy to maintain and interesting and interactive for their users. They hope in the future to sell their products online.

oink have heard that it is best to have the website's structure and design built in CSS.

1 Write a short report explaining:
   (a) what CSS is P1
   (b) why it should be used P1
   (c) how HTML files access CSS. P1
2 Explain the features of the box model. P2
3 Assess the different implementation styles of CSS. M1

Note: *you are advised to research wherever possible and use correctly referenced sources.*

Grading tips

- This is a straightforward description. Make sure you include inline, header and external. P1
- You could expand your description with printouts from web pages you have created to demonstrate the box model. P2
- One of the methods might be through scripting, so you may wish to return to this and add to your report after you have completed Assessment activity 20.2. M1

PLTS

You can show you are a **reflective learner** by using your new knowledge to write your report. You can be an **independent enquirer** by assessing the different implementation styles.

Functional skills

Your report will highlight your **English** writing skills.

2 Understand the fundamentals of scripting languages

Scripting languages create **interactivity** on a web page. For example, this could involve a user filling in a form and the computer sending a message to say thank you. Another example could be a user typing a product name into a search bar and the computer displaying the relevant product from its catalogue. Essentially, it is a message from user to computer and vice versa.

Interactivity is not only useful but is now expected by customers. **Static websites** are seen as old-fashioned and useless.

Users on the whole prefer using **dynamic websites**, and they are also easier to maintain once they **'go live'** on the Internet.

There are a wide variety of scripting languages available. In order to provide consistency, all examples of scripting code in this unit are in JavaScript.

Key terms

Interactivity – two-way communication between user and computer.

Static website – one which has only fixed information on it. If it is to be altered, the designer needs to change the code and then upload the amended page to the web server; a laborious task.

Dynamic website – one which is updated live online. Usually, there are scripting languages and/or databases.

'Go live' – when a website is uploaded to be viewed on the Internet.

Interpret – to convert HTML, which the developer can understand, to a language the computer understands.

Object – a special type of data which has properties and methods.

Event – an action which can cause a reaction in the code.

Method – an action which can be performed by an object.

Data mining – the extraction of large amounts of information, often about customers of businesses.

2.1 Characteristics of scripting languages

Scripting languages are inserted into HTML between `<script>` and `</script>` tags. This is usually in the head of the HTML.

```
<head>
<script>
SCRIPTING LANGUAGE WOULD BE INSERTED HERE
</script>
</head>
```

The scripting language is put into the head section because an HTML page is **interpreted** as it is loaded into the browser – the browser loads each line as it encounters it. If the scripting language is below visible elements of the web page, it will run after all the elements have been loaded into the browser.

Nature of language

Scripting languages can be object oriented and event driven.

With object-oriented languages, the code is broken into **objects** (see Figure 20.4). Each object knows about itself and what it can do. Each object is a self-contained module. By knowing what it can do, an object knows with what it can interact.

With languages that are event driven, the code is broken into **events** (see Figure 20.5). An event is any action. It could be a click of a mouse, a press of a key, a movement or the transmission of data. The code is triggered into running when that particular action happens.

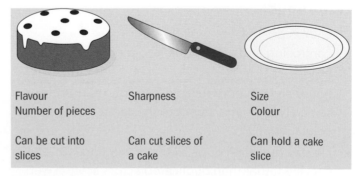

Flavour Number of pieces	Sharpness	Size Colour
Can be cut into slices	Can cut slices of a cake	Can hold a cake slice

Figure 20.4: In object-oriented languages, the code is broken into objects

When mouse is clicked Do these actions	When key is pressed Do these actions

Figure 20.5: In event-driven languages, the code is broken into events

Objects

An object is a type of data which knows things about itself (properties) and it knows how to do things (methods). There are many objects already existing in scripting languages and also it is possible to create new ones.

This is an example in JavaScript of the String object:

```
<script>
hw="Hello world"
document.write(hw.length)
</script>
```

The output on the screen would be **11**, as ten characters and a space make up the length of the String called **hw**. For more detail see Properties, page 74.

Methods

Each object knows which **methods** it can carry out.

This is an example in JavaScript of the String object:

```
<script>
hw="Hello world"
document.write(hw.toUpperCase())
</script>
```

The output on the screen would be **HELLO WORLD**, as the method **UpperCase** has forced the whole word to be in upper case. For more detail see Methods, page 72.

Handling events

As mentioned earlier, events are actions which are sensed by the script and to which a reaction occurs. Events can include a mouse button being clicked or a keyboard button being pressed. For more detail on this, see Handling events, page 72.

Hiding scripts from older browsers

Some older browsers do not support scripting languages or the activities they create. Therefore, to prevent confusion it is best to hide the scripting language from them. This can be done by putting the script within HTML comments (see Comments in the script, page 86). For example:

```
<script>
<!--
insert script here
//--!>
</script>
```

Browsers which can interpret script will see the **<script>** tags and interpret the code between them as such. Browsers which cannot interpret script will ignore the script tags and also the HTML comments, therefore preventing them becoming confused when trying to interpret script as HTML.

Security issues

When using client side scripting, there is an inevitable security implication. As code is being executed on the user's computer, that opens up a possible entry point for hackers. Reading from and writing to client files make both the website and the client's computer vulnerable. In addition, by using client side scripting it is possible for unscrupulous website owners to read the content of the client's computer. They can perform operations on the computer such as **data mining**, opening applications and reading other browser windows.

Including scripts inside HTML

Script can be placed anywhere within a web page, depending on what result is desired. Since HTML is interpreted, it is executed line by line. Script in the body is run at the point it occurs in the code. Functions can be placed anywhere as they are not run until they are called. Script needs to be placed between **<script>** **</script>** tags for the browser to know it is no longer interpreting HTML, but a scripting language.

2.2 Uses of a scripting language

Scripting languages provide interactivity, which is a vital part of modern web design. Table 20.2 shows some of the actions which can be performed.

Alerts	Pop-ups to alert the user to something
Confirming choices	Feedback to ensure the user has made the choices wanted
Prompting the user	A message to help the user or to ask for an action
Redirecting the user	To move the user to another page
Browser detection	When a user loads a website, it can detect which browser they are using and load the optimum viewing settings
Creating rollovers	To add more visual interactivity a web page can use **rollover buttons**
Checking/ validating input	Examining what a user has entered, eg if they have entered words in a search box, the script can read it and search its databases
Handling forms	Allows users to fill in forms and submit them, either for the website to process or to email to an inbox
Maintaining **cookies**	Deposits cookies on a user's computer, then reads them when they return to the site; it also can ensure that the user has the latest cookies for that site

Table 20.2: Scripting language uses

Key terms

Rollover buttons – work as normal buttons on a web page, but when the mouse hovers over them, the image or text changes.

Cookies – packets of data exchanged between the client computer and web server for authentication or personalisation of a website.

Syntax – the grammar of a programming language, prescribing the order in which words can be used.

Variable – used to store data and is given a name, eg the data 'Fred' might be stored in variable 'firstname'.

Array – a collection of variables that have a single name.

Operator – a mathematical symbol used in a calculation or comparison.

Loop – a piece of code which is executed over and over again until it fulfils a preset criterion.

2.3 Scripting language constructs

As with any code, scripting languages need to use the correct construction for it to work. This includes the **syntax**, which is its grammar and ensures the code words are in the right order. It is important for any programming language that the syntax is correct.

The dot operator is used to allow an object to use a method. For example, for the object String to use the method replace:

```
<script>
str="First message"
document.write(str.replace(/
First/,"Second"))
</script>
```

Programming languages use **variables** to store a variety of data including text and numbers.

Each variable must have a unique name within that script. Variables names cannot contain spaces or begin with a number. It is good practice for them to be meaningful, both to the initial developer and also others who may work on it in the future.

Variables can be assigned values, which is the initial data it will store. For example:

```
<script>
product_name="turnip"
quantity=50
</script>
```

Vegetables	turnip	carrot	spinach	celery	cabbage
	0	1	2	3	4

Figure 20.6: Variables in an array

A collection of variables can be stored in an **array**, where each variable can be called by its position in the list (see Figure 20.6). The array has a name, eg vegetables, and the items within are numbered from 0 onwards.

Quite often, within a script, a mathematical calculation will need to be performed, especially on eCommerce sites. An **operator** is used to carry out this task, eg + (plus), - (minus), * (multiply), / (divide), ++ (increment by 1), -- (decrement by 1).

For example:

```
<script>
price=200
quantity=50
total= price * quantity
</script>
```

Operators are used to assign values to variables. For example:

```
<script>
```

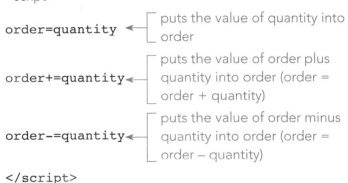

order=quantity ← puts the value of quantity into order

order+=quantity ← puts the value of order plus quantity into order (order = order + quantity)

order-=quantity ← puts the value of order minus quantity into order (order = order – quantity)

```
</script>
```

Also, operators can perform comparisons between values. For example:

```
<script>
```

order==quantity ← checks if they are equal and returns true or false

order!=quantity ← checks if they are not equal and returns true or false

order>quantity ← checks if order is greater than quantity and returns true or false

order>=quantity ← checks if order is greater than or equal to quantity and returns true or false

```
</script>
```

Activity: Syntax of a scripting language

1 Describe how a variable is defined and obtains an initial value.

2 Create syntactically correct scripts to:

  (a) add two numbers together

  (b) multiply two numbers together

  (c) check if an amount is greater than the other

  (d) check if two amounts are equal.

Loops

A **loop** (also known as an iteration) is a piece of code which is executed over and over again until it fulfils a preset criterion. There are different types of loops which produce different effects. The criterion for exiting the loop is defined either at the beginning or end of it, and the actions to be performed during the loop are within curly brackets { }.

The following **FOR** loop will be executed while **count** is less than or equal to five. Once **count** equals six the loop will be exited. This means the loop will run six times.

```
<script>
for (count = 0; count <= 5; count++)
{
document.write("The number is " + count)
document.write("<br>") // this uses HTML
within the script to put in a line break
}
</script>
```

The following FOR/IN loop will be executed through an array. This array will run through each of the three elements.

```
<script>
numbers = new Array()
numbers [0] = "zero"
numbers [1] = "one"
numbers [2] = "two"

for (x in numbers)
{
document.write("The number is" +
numbers[x])
document.write("<br>")
}
</script>
```

The following WHILE loop will be executed while count is less than or equal to five. Once count equals six the loop will be exited. This means the loop will run five times.

```
<script>
count = 0
while (count <= 5)
{
document.write("The number is " + count)
document.write("<br>")
count++
}
</script>
```

The following DO/WHILE loop will be executed while count is less than or equal to five. Once count equals six the loop will be exited. This means the loop will run five times.

```
<script>
count = 0
```

```
do
{
document.write("The number is " + count)
document.write("<br>")
count++
}
while (count <= 5)
</script>
```

Activity: Loops in a scripting language

1 Create each loop example.
2 Print each script and annotate to explain how it works.

Decision making

Decision making code has a criterion defined and actions to be executed whether it is met or not met (also known as a selection).

An IF/ELSE loop can take three forms: IF, IF/ELSE or IF/ELSE/IF. The latter version is where there are several conditions to be met with several different actions, so IF statements are nested inside each other. An example of an IF/ELSE loop:

```
<script>
name=prompt("Please enter your name","")
if (name!="")
{
document.write("Hello " + name + "! How
are you today?")
}
else
{
document.write("Hello anonymous! How are
you today?")
}
</script>
```

A SWITCH/CASE loop allows there to be a variety of conditions, each with an action. The same can be achieved with nested IF statements, but SWITCH/CASE is much neater therefore less likely to contain mistakes.

```
<script>
colour=prompt("Please enter a colour for
your t-shirt","")
switch (colour)
{
case "blue":
document.write("Good choice. Blue is
brilliant.")
break
case "red":
document.write("Nice! A bright, vibrant
colour.")
break
case "green":
document.write("Fabulous - a wonderful
colour.")
break
default:
document.write("Sorry, we don't stock that
colour")
}
</script>
```

Activity: Decision making in a scripting language

1 Create each decision example.
2 Print each script and annotate to explain how it works.

Functions

A function is a piece of code, written separately, which can be **called** and executed whenever needed.

Key terms

Call – to access a function from wherever it is stored and execute it.

Parameter – a value passed to or from a function to use in its execution.

A function will not be executed until it is called. They can be written anywhere in the web page or even in a different page, in a .js file. Below is an example of a function (could go in the head section or in a different page or even in the body section) and the function being called (within the body section of the page):

```
<script>
function hello() // this is where the
function is named
{
alert("Hello!")
}
</script>

…

<body>
<input type="button"
onclick="hello()" // this is where the
function is called
value="Click me!"
</body>
```

Notice the brackets beside the name of the function. This is so a **parameter** can be passed. This means either a value that is passed to the function and that the function uses while running, or a value that is passed back to the main code once the function has run.

```
<script>
function topping()
{
topp=prompt("Enter your favourite
topping.", "")
alert(topp + " " + food)
}
</script>

…

<body>
<script>
food="pizza"
topping(food)
</script>
</body>
```

Handling events

Events can be triggered by something gaining focus (onfocus), something losing focus (onblur), when a page is loaded (onload), and when the cursor moves over something (onmouseover). They are used within the HTML tags in the body.

The syntax for the onfocus event could be:

```
<form>
<input type="text" onfocus=" alert('An
onFocus event') "
</form>
```

Here is an example of the onmouseover event (NB: image1.gif must be in the same folder as the code file).

```
<img src="image1.gif"
onmouseover=alert('An onMouseOver event')"
```

The syntax for the onload event could be:

```
<body onload=alert("loaded")>
```

The text of the alert cannot contain spaces when it is part of the onload command. To be able to do more, a function should be called from the onload, eg:

```
<body onload="functionname()">
```

Methods

Methods can be applied to objects to create actions. There are several preset objects which have predefined methods.

The method `.write` can be used to display information on screen. It can be fixed text, eg `document.write ("Hello")`, or it could be the value of a variable, eg `document.write(x)`.

The method `.click` will simulate a click, such as a button being clicked or a check box being checked. In the following example clicking the button automatically clicks the check box:

```
<script>
function autoclick()
{
myform.box.click();
}
</script>
...
<body>
<form name="myform">
```

```
<input type="check box" name="box">check
box
<input type=button value="button"
onclick="autoclick()">
</form>
</body>
```

The method .value() will extract the value from an input, using the format formname.inputname. value. For example, on a form called "student" there is a text box called "firstname". The user enters "Fred" into the text box. The method student. firstname.value will extract the value "Fred" from this text box.

The method .open will load a page in a new browser window. The format of the command would be window.open("index.html").

The method .selectedIndex will show which option in a drop-down list has been selected, allocating the entry a number starting with 0. In the following example, clicking the button will find which entry has been selected.

```
<script>
function selected()
{
opt=document.getElementById("mylist")
alert(opt.selectedIndex);
}
</script>
...
<body>
<form name="myform">
<select id=mylist>
<option>option 0</option>
<option>option 1</option>
</select>
<input type=button value="button"
onclick="selected()">
</form>
</body>
```

Activity: Methods in a scripting language

1 Enter this code into a text editor such as Notepad:

```
<html>
<head>
<title>Methods Example Page</title>
<script>
function details()
{
// INSERT YOUR NEW CODE HERE
}
</script>
</head>

<body>
<b>Methods Example Page</b>
<br><br>
<form name="DetailsForm">
Enter full name  <input type="text"
name="fullname">
<br>
Gender:
<select id=gender>
<option>male</option>
<option>female</option>
</select>
<br>
<input type="button" value="Click
Me" onClick="details()">
</form>
</body>
</html>
```

2 Save the file as methodexample.html.

3 Amend the function using methods so the following things happen:

   (a) find out the value of name

   (b) find out which gender has been selected

   (c) write both to the page so they are displayed on screen.

Properties

Properties are characteristics of objects in code. For example, an input object has a type, name and value.

```
<input type="radio" name="gender"
value="male">
```

The type shows that it is a radio button; the name is how to refer to the radio button; the value is what the radio button means – the method `form.gender.value` would result in male if it had been selected.

Instead of the name property, id can also be used in the same way. Whereas there can be more than one element with the same name, the id must always be unique. The methods `getElementById(AnId)` will always return an individual element, whereas `getElementByName(AName)` can return a collection of elements.

The properties width and height can be used with visible items such as tables and images, to define their dimensions, for example: `<table width=200 height=200>`. It is also possible to define the size of new pages or pop-up windows with JavaScript. For example, `window.open("index.html", "","width=200, height=200")` will open index.html in a new window 200 pixels square. Notice the extra set of quotes between the page and the sizes – these can be used if a name is to be allocated to the window.

Assessment activity 20.2

oink have also heard that a scripting language can add extra functionality and interactivity.

1 Create a presentation to explain:

   (a) what a scripting language is, how it works in a web page and what types are available **P3**

   (b) what the main features of a scripting language are. **P3**

2 How can a scripting language improve functionality? **M2**

3 Explain in detail how web pages with scripts are implemented in different browsers. **D1**

***Note**: you are advised to research wherever possible and use correctly referenced sources.*

Grading tips

- Make sure you include all the features in this unit. You may also want to provide printouts from examples you have made. **P3**

- As well as describing the different ways, also include advantages and disadvantages to show why you would use each one in different situations. **M2**

- Use research to find more information on how different browsers interpret scripts. Make sure you use reputable sites and cite your sources in your presentation. **D1**

PLTS

You can demonstrate that you are a **creative thinker** by making your presentation attractive while making sure the information is clear.

Functional skills

Prove your **English** skills by writing your communicating information, ideas and opinions effectively and persuasively for developing, presenting and communicating information.

3   Be able to control the layout of web pages using CSS

By using CSS, the website can more easily use a house style; it is also easier to maintain. This section explains practical ways to implement CSS in a web page to control layout.

3.1   Design

The design of a website can be created in CSS and this makes it easier to control and maintain. All the formatting is done in the CSS and therefore the HTML web page itself only holds the content. Without the CSS it would just read like a normal text document.

Changes only need to be made to one entry in the CSS, rather than throughout the HTML – this saves a lot of time and helps prevent errors from occurring. CSS promotes standardised design throughout a website, which is good practice and promotes house style.

Layout planned using appropriate graphical or other tool

There are several methods which can be used to design the layout of a website in a graphical way. It is useful to do this to ensure that when coding begins there is a clear idea of how it should look and therefore the code which needs to be created.

A **screen design** should clearly show the precise layout of each page and include the fonts, sizes, colours, images and other elements to be included in the page (see Figure 20.7).

Where the screen designs show each individual page, a **navigation diagram** shows how these separate pages will be linked together (see Figure 20.8).

Key terms

Screen design – depicts the layout of a web page and should be drawn before starting to build it.

Navigation diagram – shows how the different parts of a project will combine. In web design, it shows how different pages will interrelate.

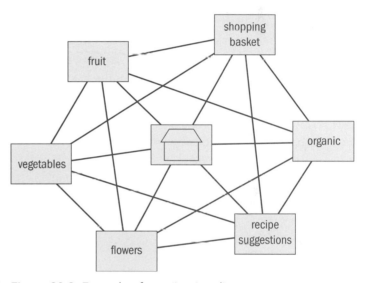

Figure 20.8: Example of a navigation diagram

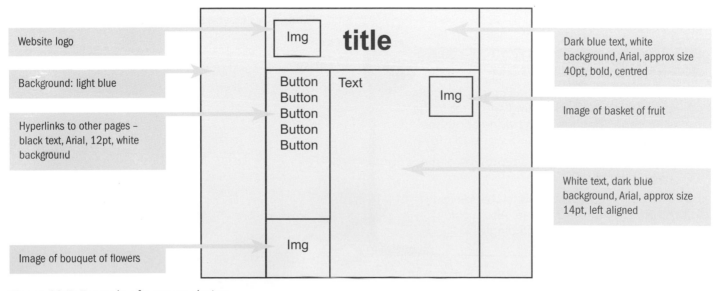

Figure 20.7: Example of a screen design

Choose an existing website with which you are familiar, such as your school or college site.

1 Create a screen design for the home page.
2 Create a navigation diagram for the whole website.

3.2 Headings

The first elements which must be created are the layout and formatting. This includes the structure of the page, both that which is only seen by the designer and also the visible version for the user, including borders and other decoration.

Styling

To implement the design defined beforehand in screen designs, CSS can create the styles of each font to be used. Also, it can establish an image for the background.

Here is an example of some of the CSS for the screen design in Figure 20.7:

```
body {background-color: #DDDDFF}
.title
{
color: #0000FF;
font-family: Arial;
font-size: 40pt;
font-weight: bold;
text-align: center;
}
```

Activity: Styling with CSS

1 Using the screen design in Figure 20.7, create the CSS for the background and fonts in the web page. (For now, don't worry about the layout.)
2 Test it works by creating a prototype of the page in HTML.
3 The business has decided to change its house style to a red theme. Alter your prototype web page accordingly.

Spacing

CSS can control the layout of a web page by dictating the borders, margins and padding. Margins are used on normal paragraph text, padding is used in table cells and borders can be used on both. For measurements, either length in centimetres, number of pixels or percentages can be used.

Here is an example of some of the CSS for the screen design in Figure 20.7:

```
<style>
.titleparagraph
{
border: red solid thin;
margin: 50%;
}
.titlecell
{
border: blue groove;
padding: 3cm 6cm; // the first number is
top and bottom, the second number is left
and right
}
</style>
```

This is how these would be implemented in HTML:

```
<body>
<span class="titleparagraph">Title</span>
<br>
<table border="0">
<tr>
<td class="titlecell">Title</td>
</tr>
</table>
</body>
```

Activity: Spacing with CSS

1 Using the screen design in Figure 20.7 on page 75 and prototype web page you created in the previous activity, create the CSS for the layout of the web page.

2 Test it works in the HTML.

3 The business has decided to change the design (see screen design below). Alter your prototype web page accordingly.

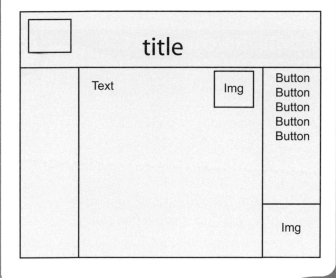

3.3 Lists

Most users prefer not to have to read huge paragraphs of text, so a developer should try to lay out the content in the easiest format for reading. By using lists, the content can be put in an orderly format which is easier for the user to read and so makes the website usable by more people.

There are two types of lists which can be created with CSS: ordered lists are numbered and unordered lists are bulleted. The style is defined in the CSS, then within the HTML using the <li> tag to identify each item in the list.

Ordered lists can be created with numbers, roman numerals or alphabetical letters:

```
<style>
.numbers {list-style-type: decimal}
.numerals {list-style-type: lower-roman}
.letters {list-style-type: lower-alpha}
</style>
```

The following code shows how it would be implemented in HTML:

```
<body>
<ol class="numbers">
<li>Pumpkin</li>
<li>Aubergine</li>
</ol>
<ol class="numerals">
<li>Pumpkin</li>
<li>Aubergine</li>
</ol>
<ol class="letters">
<li>Pumpkin</li>
<li>Aubergine</li>
</ol>
</body>
```

Unordered lists can be created with round filled bullets, round empty bullets, square bullets or invisible bullets:

```
<style>
.round_full {list-style-type: disc}
.round_empty {list-style-type: circle}
.square {list-style-type: square}
.invisible {list-style-type: none}
</style>
```

This is how it would be implemented in HTML:

```
<body>
<ul class="round_full">
<li>Daffodil</li>
<li>Sunflower</li>
</ul>
<ul class="round_empty">
<li>Daffodil</li>
<li>Sunflower</li>
</ul>
<ul class="square">
<li>Daffodil</li>
<li>Sunflower</li>
</ul>
<ul class="invisible">
<li>Daffodil</li>
<li>Sunflower</li>
</ul>
</body>
```

Styling tags and the hover effect

There are default settings for hyperlinks, such as blue and underlined turning to purple and underlined once clicked. These can be overridden by CSS so they can fit in with a design.

The anchor links must be written in the order shown below for them to work. Other formatting can be used instead of colour, using the same syntax.

`a:link`
`{color: red}` ← the original colour of the link, before it has been clicked

`a:visited`
`{color: blue}` ← the colour of the link once it has been visited

`a:hover`
`{color: green}` ← the colour of the link when the mouse hovers over it

`a:active`
`{color: yellow}` ← the colour of the link when it has been clicked and is active

Use for navigation

Using CSS, it is possible to create menus which simulate drop-down menus – these can look very impressive when implemented correctly. Below is an example of how this can be done:

```
<style>
ul {
  margin: 0;
  padding: 0;
  width: 150px;
  list-style: none;
  }
ul li {
  position: relative;
  float: left;
  }
```

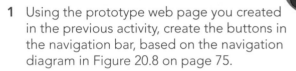

Activity: Styling with CSS

Using the prototype web page you created in the previous activity:

1 add an ordered list of your favourite five fruit and vegetables to the main body of text

2 add an unordered list of your three favourite flowers below the first list. Make sure there is at least one line break **
** between them.

Activity: Hovering with CSS

1 Using the prototype web page you created in the previous activity, create the buttons in the navigation bar, based on the navigation diagram in Figure 20.8 on page 75.

2 Using CSS, create the following:
   • for the unclicked link, the text should be black
   • when the user hovers over the link, it should become a larger font size
   • when the link is visited, it should become a different font
   • when the link is active, the background colour of the link should become yellow.

The ul style formats the whole list which is surrounded by a <ul> tag.

The ul li style formats the main list headers as they exist between both <ul> and <li> tags.

```
li ul {
  position: absolute;
  top: 0;
  left: 149px;
  display: none;
  }
ul li a {
  display: block;
  padding: 5px;
  border: 1px solid red;
  height: 1%;
  text-decoration: none;
  color: black;
  }
li:hover ul, li.over ul {display: block;}
</style>
```

The li ul style formats the list sub-headers as they exist between both <li> and <ul> tags.

The ul li a style formats the actual list elements as they exist between <ul>, <li> and <a> tags.

The hover and over commands control the appearing and disappearing of the list items.

This is implemented in HTML as follows.

Some browsers, including Internet Explorer®, do not support the hover command, so this script will allow it to work.

```
<script>
ie_patch = function() {
  if (document.all&&document.getElementById) {
    listitem = document.getElementById("nav");
    for (i=0; i<listitem.childNodes.length; i++) {
      ie_element= listitem.childNodes[i];
        if (ie_element.nodeName=="LI") {
          ie_element.onmouseover=function() {
          this.className+=" over";
        }
        ie_element.onmouseout=function() {
          this.className=this.className.replace(" over", "");
        }
      }
    }
  }
}
window.onload=ie_patch;
</script>
...
```

```
<body>
<ul id="nav">
  <li><a href="#">FRUIT</a></li>
    <ul>
       <li><a href="#">cherry</a></li>
       <li><a href="#">tangerine</a></li>
       <li><a href="#">peach</a></li>
    </ul>
  </li>
  <li><a href="#">VEGETABLES</a></li>
    <ul>
       <li><a href="#">celery</a></li>
       <li><a href="#">cucumber</a></li>
       <li><a href="#">lettuce</a></li>
    </ul>
  </li>
</ul>
</body>
```

This is the HTML where the content of the list is written. Notice the only formatting in this is the structure of the <ul> and <li> tags.

Activity: Navigation with CSS

1 Using the prototype web page you created in the previous activity, add the menus given in the code above.
2 Add three more menus for: flowers, nuts and herbs.

3.4 Links and pseudo classes

Hyperlinks are controlled by the <a> tag, which stands for anchor. They are one of the **pseudo classes** which can be controlled by CSS. There are others; however, they are not supported by all browsers therefore it is better not to use them. By ensuring a website is accessible by all browsers, a developer can increase traffic to their site.

Key term

Pseudo class – a section of CSS code which controls certain behaviours of the HTML, for example .

Setting pseudo class order

As we saw earlier (page 78), the default settings for hyperlinks can be overridden by CSS. However, they must be written in a specific order for them to work, ie hover must follow link and visited; active must follow hover.

Adding background images

The background colour of a web page can be changed by using the code:

```
body {background-color: #DDDDFF}
```

Alternatively, an image can be used as the background instead of a colour, using the following code:

```
body
{
background-image: url('picture.jpg')
background-position: center; // THIS WILL
CENTRE THE IMAGE ON THE WEB PAGE
}
```

Note: the image must be in the same folder as the web page; otherwise, the whole file location must be included.

By using this code, the image will appear behind all the web page elements. However, when it is scrolled, it will move up the page. To keep it in the same place, the following code can be used:

```
{
background-image: url('picture.jpg')
background-attachment: fixed; // THIS WILL
PREVENT IT MOVING WHEN THE PAGE IS SCROLLED
}
```

Styling

Underlining of text can sometimes be tricky in web pages, as it is not done in the same way as in other applications. For example, when using Dreamweaver® you might expect the Underline button to be beside the Bold and Italic buttons, but it is in a list all of its own. The same issue occurs when underlining using CSS. The property for it is **text-decoration** and can be used as follows:

```
.lineabove {text-decoration: overline}
.linethrough {text-decoration: line-through}
.underline {text-decoration: underline}
a {text-decoration: none} // THIS CODE
WILL REMOVE THE UNDERLINE FROM A HYPERLINK
```

Activity: Creating web pages with CSS

Keystone Zoo wants a website to advertise on the Internet. Their star attractions are the lions, the flamingos and the giant pandas.

1 On paper, design the layout and design of each page of the website (home page and one for each animal).
2 Using CSS, create the structure of the pages.
3 Using CSS, create the formatting for the pages.
4 Complete the website, including the content.
5 Write a brief evaluation of your website.

PLTS

You will demonstrate that you are a **creative thinker** in designing the website and a **self-manager** in making sure you control your use of time effectively.

It is possible to make the active link area larger on text hyperlinks. This could make it more accessible for those people with limited mobility. This code can have this affect:

```
a
{
 padding: 10px 0;
 position:relative;
 background: yellow; // this is to show
the new hyperlink area
}
```

Assessment activity 20.3

1 Design a website for *oink* using CSS. It must include at least five pages and at least three examples of interactivity. To create the design:
  (a) create a navigation diagram and explain how CSS will control the layout
  (b) describe the house style and explain how CSS will control the layout
  (c) produce screen designs for each page and explain how CSS will control the layout. **P4**

Note: you are advised to research wherever possible and use correctly referenced sources.

Grading tips
• Be methodical in your design and ensure you are thorough. You know you will be using CSS, so make sure you think about this from the start, rather than designing it then trying to add in the CSS later. **P4**

Functional skills

Finding relevant information from websites and bringing it together in your presentation could provide evidence for your functional **ICT** skills in finding and selecting information and developing, presenting and communicating information.

4   Be able to create interactive web pages

Scripting languages can provide a wide range of interactivity for a website. This section will look at some of the more commonly used. As with all programming languages, it is important to have a clear design of the script before beginning to code it.

4.1   Script requirements

It is important to define the inputs, processes and outputs of a script so as to understand exactly what is happening in the code.

Inputs

Inputs are the data which is entering the system. This could be from the user or another application. By defining the inputs before creating the code, a programmer can ensure that they make provision for the appearance of this data.

Outputs

Outputs are the information which is produced by the processes. This could be yielded in a variety of ways, such as on-screen or as a printout. The customary aim is to convert input data to output information that is meaningful and useful.

Processing

By identifying all the processes to be carried out in the script, code can be written more efficiently. For example, the programmer can decide if the processes are to be performed straight from the bulk of the code or in separate functions.

4.2   Design script

It is important to plan the script before beginning to implement it. There are several methods available – the best methods are flowcharts and pseudo code. Using both of these methods will provide the full picture of how the script should function and in what order.

Flowchart

A flowchart shows the order in which actions should be executed and can also model selections and loops (see Figure 20.9). There are certain symbols which can be used to represent certain activities which means any flowchart can be understood by all system designers (Table 20.3).

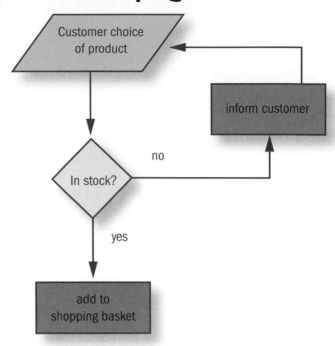

Figure 20.9: An example of a flowchart – this one models purchasing from an ecommerce site

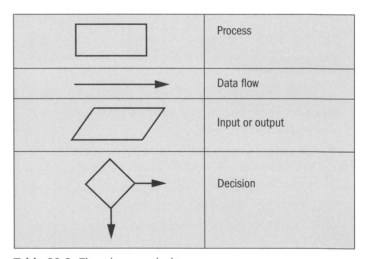

▭	Process
→	Data flow
▱	Input or output
◇	Decision

Table 20.3: Flowchart symbols

Activity: Flowcharts

1   Draw a systems flowchart for a user filling in a feedback form which is then emailed to the administrator. If any fields are left blank, it should loop back to allow the user to fill it in again.

2   Research to find what other symbols can be used in a systems flowchart and make notes for future reference.

Pseudo code

Pseudo code is a method of designing code, forming an intermediary step between an explanation in English and the coding language. (See Table 20.4.)

Pseudo code	JavaScript
age = input from user	age=prompt("Enter age","");
if age >= 18 then	if (age>=18)
print onscreen "i am an adult"	{document.write("I am an adult");}
else	else
print onscreen "i am x years old"	{document.write("I am " + age + " years old");}

Table 20.4: Example of pseudo code used to plan JavaScript

By using pseudo code, a designer can plan what the code will do, without having to worry about ensuring the correct words and syntax are used. It is also easier to convert from a flowchart into the full programming language by using this transitional step.

Activity: Pseudo code

Design the pseudo code for a feedback form on a website.

4.3 Implement script

Once you have designed the script, you can implement it into the web page. This section shows a few features that can be created with client side scripting.

Rollovers

A rollover is where a button displays a different formatting or image when the mouse hovers over it. Two separate images need to be prepared first to be used for both parts of the rollover.

This script can produce a rollover:

```
<script>
function over()
{
document.button1.src ="red.gif"
```

```
}
function out()
{
document. button1.src ="blue.gif"
}
</script>
```

...

```
<body>
<a href="index.html">
<img src="blue.gif" name=" button1"
onmouseover="over()" onmouseout="out()"
/></a>
</body>
```

Activity: Rollovers

Create an example rollover button.

Clocks and calendars

Time can be used in JavaScript with the setTimeout object. For example:

```
<script>
function timer()
{
setTimeout("alert('3 seconds')",3000)
}
</script>
...
<body>
<script>
function timer()
{
setTimeout("alert('3 seconds')",3000)
}
</script>
</body>
```

This will display the alert saying "3 seconds" once three seconds have elapsed. The measurement 3000 is in milliseconds.

In programming, it is usual to try to avoid infinite loops (loops that repeat forever). However, using an infinite loop is a way of creating a counter in JavaScript. The following code is an example of how to create a timer with two buttons, one to start and one to stop the timer.

```
<script>
count=0
function startCount()
{
document.getElementById('txt').value=count
count=count+1
t=setTimeout("startCount()",1000)
}
function stopCount()
{
clearTimeout(t)
}
</script>

...

<body>
<form>
<input type="button" value="Start"
onClick="startCount()">
<input type="text" id="txt">
<input type="button" value="Stop"
onClick="stopCount()">
</form>
</body>
```

It is possible to pull the time and date from the computer's system clock. This allows calculations to be done, such as calculating the age of a person from their date of birth. The following code will write today's date and time to the screen:

```
<script>
document.write(Date())
</script>
```

This example will calculate the separate parts of a date from the current date on the system clock:

It is now

```
<script>
now = new Date()
day = now.getDate()
month = now.getMonth() + 1
year = now.getFullYear()
document.write(day + "/" + month + "/" +
year)
</script>
```

Activity: Clocks and calendars

1 Create a counter that counts even seconds, eg 2, 4, 6, etc.

2 Write the code to calculate the user's age when they input their date of birth. Use today's date to calculate their age.

Client side processing of calculations

Calculations can be carried out with variables using operators (see 2.3 Scripting language constructs, page 68).

Remember

An operator is a mathematical symbol used in a calculation or comparison.

The following example will output 25 to the screen:

```
<script>
x=10
y=15
total=x+y
document.write(total)
</script>
```

There are also other mathematical objects available. The next example shows the use of the max() and min():

```
<script>
document.write(Math.max(5,7) + "<br />")
document.write(Math.min(7,5))
</script>
```

Both commands will also work for negative and decimal numbers.

Activity: Calculations

Using mathematical operators, find the min, max and total of 10, 837, 267, 94, 293, 2, 112, 398, 62, 928, 737, 918.

Forms validation

When users are inputting data into forms, there is a risk of them filling it in incorrectly which can cause problems later on. Therefore, it is useful to check their input as it is entered. This example will check that the name field is not null.

```html
<html>
<head>
<script>
function validate()
{
  namefield=myform.yourname.value;
  if (namefield==' ')
  {
    alert('you must enter your name.');
    event.returnValue=false;
  }
}
</script>
</head>
<body>
<form name="myform"
onsubmit="validate();">
<input type="text" name="yourname" >please
enter your name (required)
<br>
<input type="submit" value="enter name">
</form>
</body>
</html>
```

This example will check that a radio button has been selected.

```html
<html>
<head>
<script>
function validate()
{
  if (!(myform.mood[0].checked ))
  {
    if (!(myform.mood[1].checked))
    {
      alert('you must choose a mood.');
      event.returnValue=false;
    }
  }
}
</script>
</head>
<body>
<form name="myform"
onsubmit="validate();">
<input type="radio" name="mood"
value="happy">happy
<input type="radio" name="mood"
value="sad">sad
<br>
<input type="submit" value="enter mood">
</form>
</body>
</html>
```

The [0] checks the first radio button (happy) and the [1] checks the second radio button (sad).

The ! (exclamation mark) denotes a NOT, so this checks if it is not checked.

Activity: Forms validation

1 Create your own form to enter the title of a film and a set of check boxes to choose its genre (horror, sci-fi, comedy, etc).

2 Validate the form to check the film title has been entered.

3 Validate the form to check at least one check box has been selected.

Mouse movement followers

A mouse movement follower creates an image trail behind a cursor, as shown in Figure 20.10. This can add fun to a website and attract users. However, they must be used carefully as they can also annoy users and turn them away.

Figure 20.10: What a mouse trail looks like

4.4 Good practice

The original writer of the code may not be the person who maintains or updates it. Therefore, it is essential that a developer follows good practice in their programming. Good code should be understood by any programmer, even if they are not familiar with that specific language.

Comments in the script

Code needs to be converted from a language the programmer understands to one the computer understands. In HTML and client side scripting, code is interpreted one line at a time in the order in which it is stored. A **comment** is a line of code which is ignored by the interpreting software; comments can be used to explain what action each piece of code performs.

- To comment in HTML and CSS, use `<!-- Comment -->`
- To comment in JavaScript, use `//Comment`
- To comment in VBScript, use `'Comment`

Correct indentation

To ensure that code can be clearly understood, sections can be indented to show which tags affect it. For example:

```
<body>
  <script>
  if (time < 10)
    <b>document.write("<b>Good morning</b>")
  else
    <b>document.write("<b>Good day</b>")
  </script>
</body>
```

Naming variables

Variables should have meaningful names so that wherever they are used in the code their purpose is clear. Their aim is to store some data so it can be used later. The name should clearly reflect what the variable does and be easily understandable.

Variable names must begin with a letter, which can be followed by either letters or numbers. Spaces are not allowed but it is acceptable to use an underscore (_) as part of the name to make it more meaningful: eg product_ quantity.

Care must be taken not to use a **reserved word** as a variable.

Short, simple names are ideal. If variable names are long, complicated or easy to spell incorrectly, then it will become tiresome to rekey throughout and could cause problems if they are not keyed consistently.

Key terms

Comment – an uninterrupted line of code which describes what is happening and helps developers understand how it works.

Reserved word – a word which is already used in the programming language and therefore cannot be used as a variable name.

Activity: Creating web pages with a scripting language

1 Keystone Zoo wants to add more interactivity to their website. Using the site you made for them earlier (see page 81), add these features using a scripting language:

   (a) rollover buttons

   (b) a button which, when clicked, displays the current date and time

   (c) a calculation to multiply the cost of entry into the zoo by the number of visitors.

2 Create a form so customers can enter their details to book tickets. Validate the form to ensure all required fields are entered.

3 Comment and indent your code to make it easy to read by other developers.

4 Briefly evaluate each function you have created with regard to user needs.

4.5 Testing

Once the website is built, it must be tested to ensure there are no errors in the pages before they are uploaded to the web server and go live worldwide. It can be harmful to an organisation's reputation if its website contains errors, especially if it is an eCommerce site, as potential customers may lose faith in the business.

All the elements of the website should be tested. This includes the HTML, CSS and scripting language.

A test plan such as the one shown in Table 20.5 can be used.

Activity: Testing web pages with CSS and a scripting language

Using a test plan like the one shown in Table 20.5, test the website you built in CSS (on page 81) and JavaScript (left) for Keystone Zoo.

Check using different browsers

It is important to test whether the website also functions correctly in the variety of browsers available. The more browsers on which it runs successfully, the more potential users are available. This test will involve loading the web pages into different browsers such as Microsoft® Internet Explorer®, Mozilla Firefox® and others.

Activity: Scripts in different browsers

Explain how scripts are implemented differently in two browsers, such as Internet Explorer® and Firefox®.

Test Number	Test Element	On Page	Test Data	Expected Result	Actual Result	Success or Failure	Screenshot Reference
1	Title	Index.html	Load page	Font should be green	Font is green	Success	S1
2	Home rollover	Index.html	Hover	Should turn purple	Doesn't change	Failure	S2

Table 20.5: Example test plan

Assessment activity 20.4

1 Using the design you created in Assessment activity 20.3, build your website for *oink*. Use the CSS you have planned and also include a scripting language. You are advised to design your scripting before implementing it – add this to your design documentation. **P5**

2 *oink* want to be sure that you are providing a good service. Use good practice while you are creating the website and provide an accompanying short document describing how you have done this. **M3**

3 Once your website is complete, test it thoroughly and produce a report for *oink*. **P6**

4 Evaluate your web pages, stating good points, bad points and possible improvements. **D2**

Note: You are advised to research wherever possible and use correctly referenced sources.

Grading tips

- Make sure that the website you build matches your original design. You can make changes, whether aesthetic or practical (eg if you find you don't have time to implement an ambitious part of the script) as you build it, but make sure you add a note in your design of how you have changed it. Remember you must use CSS and a scripting language throughout your site. Also, ask your tutor to provide a witness statement of you building your website. **P5**

- As you test, you do not need to make changes, just document them. **P6**

- Remember, do not only write about what good practice is but demonstrate that you have used it, eg show examples of your script where you have sensibly named variables, correct indentation and comments. **M3**

- When suggesting possible improvements, use your testing as that will highlight areas where there are problems. Also consider the user's perspective: is there anything that could make the site more user-friendly or provide better functionality? Finally, consider aesthetics: would your colour scheme, layout and other visual features attract users or deter them from using your site again? **D2**

PLTS

Self-managers will successfully control this task, **creative thinkers** will use imagination to make a more interesting product and **reflective learners** will be able to test to find areas to improve.

Functional skills

Evidence for using **ICT** could be created when designing your interface as you use ICT in complex and non-routine tasks.

Damien
Web developer

There are two main areas of website production: designing and developing. Working as a web developer means that I am responsible for the coding of the site.

I work with languages such as HTML to create the basic structure of the site. I add CSS to control the formatting and to ensure that styling is consistent across all of the pages. By adding scripting like JavaScript I can create any sort of functionality to make the site interactive. I like the magic of the words I type actually creating something visual and physical on the pages.

I have to work very closely with the web designer who has created the artistic elements of the site and ensure that what I'm creating will work with their whole page layout.

The most important personal abilities in my job I think are patience and determination. Code won't always work the first time, but if you keep trying it is very rewarding when it is successful. I also think it is useful to remember that just because the user doesn't see the code, it still needs to be tidy and elegant. You should always aim to create the functionality you need using the fewest lines of code possible, which makes it run more efficiently.

Think about it!

1 Describe the difference between a designer and a developer.

2 Research and find out what skills are needed when applying for these types of jobs.

3 Take a screenshot of three websites' home pages and print them out. Label them in different colours to show which parts are the responsibility of the designer, which are of the developer and which are both. What does this tell you about the two roles?

Just checking

1. Describe the three methods of using CSS with HTML.
2. Describe the structure of the box model.
3. What is the main purpose of a scripting language?
4. Where is client side scripting processed?
5. What is the difference between object-oriented languages (like JavaScript®) and event-driven languages (like VBScript)?
6. What is the purpose of a function?
7. What two methods are most commonly used to design CSS?
8. What is the purpose of pseudo code?
9. Why should code be commented and indented?
10. What is the purpose of testing?

Assignment tips

- Always design before implementation. If you are creating a CSS layout, draw it on paper first so you know how your page will look once it is built. If you are creating a script, use pseudo code or a flowchart to plan it.

- Remember the user. You may create something which is amazing, works perfectly and is very impressive – but if it does not add to the user's experience, either visually or by giving them extra functionality, then it should not be included on the website.

- Persevere. Programming, writing CSS and scripts can be frustrating at times but you will get a real sense of satisfaction when it finally works. Do not give up!

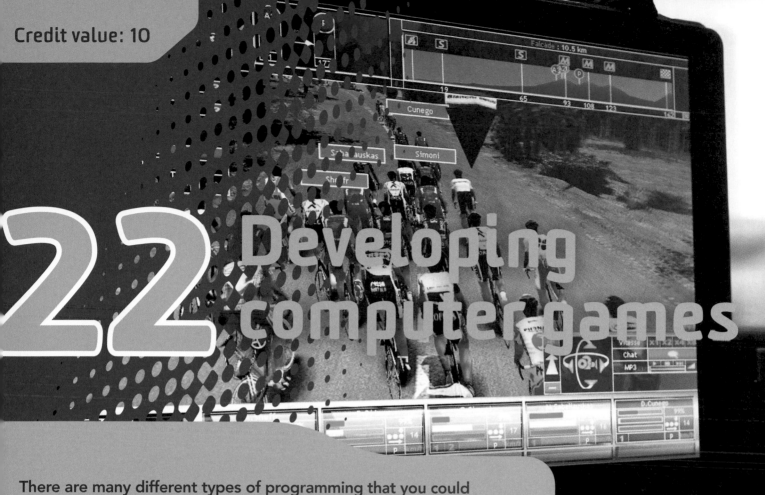

22 Developing computer games

There are many different types of programming that you could become involved with in the IT industry and one of the most complicated of these is computer games development. You may have played different computer games on consoles like Sony PlayStation®3, on your PC, on the Internet or even on your mobile phone. Whilst the development of such games varies according to the platform for which they are designed, the process and planning is the same.

Computer games development is hard work but it is rewarding. You get to create a program that is fun and exciting to play and, if successful, could be used by millions of people.

This unit is all about computer games development. You will learn about the different considerations involved when designing and planning a game and also the variety of games that are available.

Some people have very strong opinions about computer games, believing that they have a bad influence on those who play them. This unit helps you to understand how computer games have become more acceptable over the last few years and why attitudes are changing.

Learning outcomes

After completing this unit, you should:

1. understand the impact of the gaming revolution on society
2. know the different types of computer game
3. be able to design and develop computer games
4. be able to test and document computer games.

Assessment and grading criteria

This table shows you what you must do in order to achieve a pass, merit or distinction grade, and where you can find activities in this book to help you.

To achieve a **pass** grade the evidence must show that you are able to:	To achieve a **merit** grade the evidence must show that, in addition to the pass criteria, you are able to:	To achieve a **distinction** grade the evidence must show that, in addition to the pass and merit criteria, you are able to:
P1 explain the impact of computer games on society **See Assessment activity 22.1, page 101**		**D1** examine the psychological effects of computer gaming on individuals and society **See Assessment activity 22.1, page 101**
P2 describe different types of computer game **See Assessment activity 22.2, page 105**		
P3 produce a design for a computer game for a given specification **See Assessment activity 22.3, page 114**	**M1** determine appropriate data types for a computer game and show how they are declared **See Assessment activity 22.3, page 114**	**D2** explain how the structure and design of a game can assist in maintenance and capacity for extension **See Assessment activity 22.3, page 114**
P4 develop a computer game for a given specification **See Assessment activity 22.4, page 118**	**M2** use appropriate selection and iteration methods for a computer game **See Assessment activity 22.4, page 118**	
P5 follow a test strategy to test and debug a computer game **See Assessment activity 22.4, page 118**	**M3** use a variety of testing tools **See Assessment activity 22.4, page 118**	
P6 produce user documentation for a computer game **See Assessment activity 22.4, page 118**	**M4** suggest improvements to a computer game following user feedback **See Assessment activity 22.4, page 118**	
P7 produce technical documentation for a computer game **See Assessment activity 22.4, page 118**		

How you will be assessed

In order to achieve the assessment criteria for this unit, you will need to show that you understand the role that games play in society and the different types of games and genres that are available. You will also design and create your own game. To finish off you will create technical documentation that records the game development process and the testing that you completed.

Graham, BTEC National IT learner

I really enjoyed this unit. Not only did we get to play games that I knew about, but we also learnt about the differences between genres. I was surprised that there were so many different genres out there and it was interesting to see the common features between games of a certain genre.

It wasn't all playing games though! There has been a huge impact on society over the last thirty years and in my assignment I wrote about how young children in schools are able to learn by playing games. That didn't happen when I was in primary school and it shows how much things have changed.

I also made my own game for the assignment and designed a platform game where the player had to find their way out of a forest and rescue their friends. I wanted the game to have a high score table and different types of power-ups that helped the player move faster and dodge the enemies easier. I was able to add these features using some extra code that I had to write.

It wasn't too hard making the game because I designed it in advance both visually and technically. I drew images of the kinds of levels and mazes that I wanted to make and I also planned the objects and variables that would allow the game to play as designed.

It was important that I tested the game thoroughly after I had finished creating it. This wasn't a hardship and I really enjoyed making sure that my game worked perfectly.

Over to you!

- **How many different game genres are you aware of?**
- **What sort of variable would Graham have had to create for his game?**
- **Do you think you know any design tools that you have looked at in other units that could be used for designing a game?**

1 Understand the impact of the gaming revolution on society

Start up

Games are applications too

It's easy to forget sometimes that a computer game is built using a lot of the same tools and techniques as a more traditional software application such as a word processor or spreadsheet.

- List the similarities between a computer game that you are familiar with and a software application.
- Add to your list common types of storage media that both games and applications use.
- Finally, come up with some suggestions of how small games could be incorporated into a common application like a spreadsheet or a web browser.

After you have finished, get into small groups and compare what you have written.

Games are big business! They are associated with a broad range of creative industries, including film, television and music. A lot of money is spent making games and a lot of money is spent buying games. The games industry is one of the few industries to have grown during the 2008–2009 recession and, as high-street shops selling luxury items and designer clothes closed down, more and more games retailers opened their doors.

It is believed that a gaming revolution has taken place over the last few years – where something that was previously considered to be an unhealthy pastime is now embraced wholeheartedly by families. Today, games are considered to be an acceptable way of spending your free time. This is partly because of the advances that Nintendo® has made, expanding audiences and the types of people who play games. Games consoles are found in millions of households and game sales make millions every year. We've reached the stage where almost every big film that is released has a companion game released shortly after it, and any game that sells well has sequels released over the following few years. People get as excited about certain game releases as they do about new Apple® hardware or a new Harry Potter book, and shops will open at midnight for the release of really popular games.

Did you know?

Shops in London stayed open all night when the Sony PlayStation®3 was released and laid on food and entertainment for the customers who waited for hours in the queue.

1.1 Games in society

If there is one area of entertainment that people have a lot of opinions about, it is computer games. Since games first came onto the market in the late 1970s, concerns have been raised about people playing games. In more recent years, however, many benefits of playing games have also been brought to light.

Concerns

Parents, teachers and members of parliament have stated their concerns about people who play computer games for long periods of time each day over many years. Some of these concerns are valid and some are not – but in general, until games took off and became a mainstream form of entertainment (around 2005 onwards), a lot of presumptions were made about games without a great deal of research being undertaken.

An example of a game that has been misunderstood is Canis Canem Edit, by Rockstar. Rockstar are quite secretive about their new games in order to build up as much excitement as they can. When they announced a game called Bully, there was massive uproar all across the world and people were calling for the game to be banned without knowing anything about it. When it was released it became clear that the player does not take control of a school bully, as they had assumed, but has the role of a younger pupil who undertakes a series of tasks in order to survive school. The game was retitled Canis Canem Edit (Latin for 'dog eat dog') in Europe, and was rated a '15' by the British Board of Film Classification (BBFC). The game is described as an action comedy and the player has to foil the bullies in many different ways, including fighting the bullies themselves, which is regarded by some as harmless and by others as the player becoming the bully. The game has sold well, despite the calls to ban it and it has been compared to TV programmes such as Grange Hill or comics such as The Beano, in terms of its seriousness. Nonetheless, the game still makes some people feel uneasy.

The reason that computer games are often viewed negatively may be because older people have not grown up playing them. They are unfamiliar with the games and sometimes fearful of them. There are some valid criticisms but most of these are exaggerated by the media.

Excess playing time

A single-player game with a storyline will often take about 8-10 hours to complete, a casual online game will be designed to be played for about 5-10 minutes at a time and a **MMORPG** (massive multiplayer online role playing game) can be played for 100 hours upwards, if a player chooses to accept every quest they find.

Time is one of the concerns that people have about playing computer games and it is a genuine concern. Any kind of entertainment is distracting and this is why we enjoy it – it gives you time off from thinking about school, college or work worries and it helps you to relax. **Designers** have got many different ways of making games more **immersive** and gripping. It's not just single-player story-based games that have this allure – competitive online games are slightly addictive too, because people have a natural tendency to want to win or be the best.

One of the most successful MMORPGs is World of Warcraft (WOW). You will have probably heard of it even if you don't play games. WOW was released in 2004 and still remains very popular today, despite looking a bit old-fashioned in terms of graphics and game play. WOW has

been compared to Class A drugs in terms of its addictive potential. People have even been taken to hospital after playing it for over 20 hours without taking a break. This is 20 hours that they have spent staring at a computer monitor and sitting in a chair without sleeping. People have made themselves very ill over the years and even been sacked from their jobs because they couldn't leave the game alone.

Time is a real concern. As far as young people are concerned, parents should monitor the time their children spend playing computer games. Research has shown that a large proportion of the those who have made themselves ill playing games are young men who live by themselves and show signs of depression. It is worth bearing in mind that, for them, computer games may be taking the place of other potentially destructive habits. It is impossible to judge such cases on anything but an individual basis.

The Pan European Game Information (PEGI) site recommends that the player should take regular breaks and not play games for hours on end, no matter how compelling the games are.

Social isolation

Another concern that is often voiced about computer games is that they lead to social isolation. This concern is probably linked to an old-fashioned view that young people who play computer games tend to be 'geeks' or 'nerds' who have few friends and shy away from team games and social clubs.

Everybody is different – we are all individuals and we all learn at different rates. Some people are naturally shy as youngsters and find it hard to talk in front of people that they don't know. They may find it difficult to be involved in large social groups and might not be very good at popular sports. These kinds of children tend to seek out games and activities that they can

Key terms

MMORPG – stands for massive multiplayer online role-playing game. A game that many people play together across the Internet.

Designer – the person who decides how the game is going to play, what it is going to look like, how many levels it will have, etc.

Immersive – when a game gains your complete focus and you feel like you are part of it.

play on their own or with just one or two friends. For them, computer games have taken over the older role-playing board games (such as Dungeons and Dragons) or strategy card games. Computer games allow the shyer child an opportunity to be the best in a particular area and develop an interest in something that they can play without fear of being held back by their shyness.

Community gaming has gone a long way to address the issues of social isolation. People can now belong to large communities of online friends who share the same gaming interests. Sites where people play games such as WOW and other MMORPGs have chat systems that enable the players to talk to each other, either by typing or through microphones and speakers.

Similar chat systems are available on Xbox® and PlayStation® game sites. There are dangers attached to this kind of interaction (as discussed below) but at the same time it gives many people the chance to make friends with people that they would never be able to meet outside of the game. There are even stories of people meeting in a game and falling in love, then meeting in the real world and getting married.

Cost

Games can be expensive. Although costs have recently come down, a £300 games console is still a major purchase, particularly when you consider that it is purely for the purpose of entertainment. It is understandable that parents and teachers may be concerned when young people spend all of their available money on computer games. In fact this is often one of the main concerns that are voiced about computer games.

However, this concern isn't entirely justified if you compare the cost of playing games with the cost of other activities. If a cinema ticket to watch a two-hour film costs £5 then you could say that the film provides entertainment at the cost of £2.50 per hour. The Elder Scrolls IV: Oblivion cost £40 when it was first released (it is now a budget title that can be bought for as little as £15 new) and holds an average of 100 hours game-play. This makes a cost per hour of 40 pence. Not all games can claim 100 hours of game-play so even if a game only provided 20 hours of game-play, then the entertainment cost is £2 per hour. Looking at the figures like this, game-playing actually seems to be a relatively cheap form of entertainment.

A console, though expensive, is usually supported by the manufacturers and games **developers** for about four years until new games are no longer produced for it. So, for example, a Wii bought for a RRP (recommended retail price) of £179 can be thought of as costing just over £44 a year, which is cheaper than the cost of a month's subscription to satellite television with all channels.

Key term

Developer – a company or an individual who develops computer game software.

As gaming becomes more popular, the costs are coming down and people can find pre-owned games and budget titles. There are also more games retailers competing on the high street, which results in lower prices for shoppers.

Separation from reality

Some people can get very confused after spending time playing computer games and new reports over the last 20 years tend to suggest that players who have psychological problems can lose their grip on reality and start to believe that the stories they are engaged with in a computer game can also be found in the real world. When games are immersive and engaging, people can start to believe that the characters are real and the situations they find themselves in could really happen.

However, this inability to separate games from reality is restricted to people who are mentally or emotionally unbalanced and it can be argued that they would be influenced by any kind of engaging story. In the news and media people often blame computer games for various tragic events that have occurred, but more tragedies have been associated with Hollywood films or novels than with games. Sadly these events tend to be violent or destructive and people often end up getting hurt as a result. It may be the case that the interactive element of computer games makes people believe they are really doing what the game is only simulating and this makes them want to do it in the real world, but this is hard to prove.

It cannot be stressed enough that these concerns are only applicable to a tiny minority of the game-playing population worldwide but as the results are often tragic, the incidents are reported far and wide. Parents will read these stories and, quite rightly, be concerned that their children's minds are being influenced by the computer games that they are playing. The PEGI website advises parents to play computer games with their children and keep an eye on them while they are playing. They also recommend that parents explain why certain games are not suitable to their children.

If someone has displayed psychological or emotional problems in the past, it is important that their access to highly violent games is restricted. Canis Canem Edit is an example of a game that was deemed to be excessively violent when in fact it wasn't, but there are a few games on the market that are very violent and some have even been banned from certain regions. Europe and Australia have strict regulations about what games can be sold and where.

Education

Concerns about the possible negative effects of computer games on children has diminished in recent years as games have become more prevalent in the classroom and are an acknowledged teaching tool. It used to be thought that playing too many computer games would make a child less intelligent, as all the child was doing was 'button bashing' for hours. As games have evolved and become much more detailed and complex, these concerns have gradually eroded – in fact, games have been proven to actually improve the intelligence and skills of players.

Computer games have been found to improve how nimble or dextrous a person's finger movements are. They can also improve tactical thinking skills, as a lot of games especially strategy games, demand that the player thinks about what they are going to do and the possible consequences, in a similar way to a chess player.

There are also a number of games on the market that are directly aimed at education. The best example of this is Dr Kawashima's Brain Training for the Nintendo DS®. This game has sold millions of copies and expanded the traditional games audience to include much older players. The Brain Training game is designed to give the player a number of daily tasks that will improve their maths skills, memory, reading skills and logic. There is also a claim that as you grow older, keeping your mind active and challenged will delay illnesses such as Alzheimer's disease, although this has not been proved and Nintendo® has not made such a claim.

Benefits

As mentioned above, the educational benefits of playing computer games are clear but there are other potential benefits, beyond the development of thinking and strategy skills.

Games in the classroom are now quite commonplace, as are games between family members, even between different generations of the same family. This means that game-playing can be seen to have a social benefit, rather than being an anti-social activity. This may have positive implications for the future.

Today, governments and businesses are using games as a method to advertise their goods or services. A website that would previously have just been information may now contain a fun game to play that helps people understand the policy or product that the company is trying to sell. This may lead to developments where TV programmes and films are interactive in the same way as games, using features such as the red button to engage viewers and draw them into their world. The technology may include use of the TV remote control to play simple games or could involve links to websites that contain more detailed games.

3D technology is another benefit that games will bring into the home. Whilst the games industry is expanding, more money will be spent on research into the different ways that games can be played. This technology will provide game players with increasingly immersive experience, as they will be able to see game elements in a similar way to seeing elements of the real world. There is also potential for 3D puzzle games or exploration games to achieve an extra level of difficulty, showing the player parts of the game world that they would otherwise be unable to see.

A further benefit of the growth of the games industry is the impact that games development has had on traditional application development. Programs such as Microsoft® Office® and Adobe® Photoshop® now show influences from developments made by games designers. The reason for this isn't immediately obvious. It concerns Human Computer Interaction (HCI), an academic study of how people interact with computer software. The study focuses on the different ways in which man meets machine and how the interface between the two is best designed. It is a very important area of design as it teaches people to learn from mistakes made in past interfaces and how to improve the experience for the user.

The most immersive games use HCI techniques to make the player forget that they are playing a game and become totally involved in what is going on. The key to this is making the different methods of communicating with the player as discreet as possible. For example, if you are playing a game where you are driving a car through a series of obstacles, if the condition of the car is represented by a 'health' bar at the top of the screen then the player has to redirect their attention from the car and its destination to the top of the screen to see how the car is doing. A more immersive approach would be to provide a series of visual cues that tell the player that the car is becoming damaged without drawing their attention away from what they are doing. The visual cues might indicate, for instance, that the paintwork has become distressed, a wing mirror has fallen off, the bonnet has started to flap open and ultimately smoke is coming out of the engine.

Good design using HCI uses colours and sounds before it uses text, as the designer understands that the focus of the player needs to be kept on the game. This is something that applications designers have started to learn. If you are working on a program in the Windows® 95 operating system and another program has an issue that needs your attention, the second program will pop up in front of the first and you may lose your place in what you were doing. Eleven years later, Windows® 7 uses a discreet glow on the icon of

the second program in the task bar so that you can decide when you want to shift your attention. This is an example of application designers looking at what games designers have done successfully and making use of these ideas.

1.2 Psychological factors

Computer games are popular because they affect us emotionally, in a similar way to films and music. Just as a horror movie makes you feel scared, a survival horror computer game can terrify you too. In some ways the game makes it feel more real because you are controlling the character, so what happens to the character can feel like it is happening to you. Games designers use the psychological factors to improve their games and make the experience of playing them more memorable. It can be done very simply and subtly, or it can be done in a very obvious way, depending on the needs of the game.

Use of sound

Sound can make you feel lots of different things – it can make you feel happy, sad, scared, brave. There isn't a single human emotion that hasn't been represented in music or sound effects at some point in our history. Games designers use this to their advantage and there will be an audio designer whose role is to pick the sound effects and musical scores that are used throughout a game.

High-pitched, fast-paced music or sound effects tend to make you feel more excited and as if you are in the middle of the action. Platform games and racing games use these features to add to the game's excitement and pace. Horror games use string instruments such as violins and the sound of creaking floor boards to make people feel tense in the same way that a horror movie does.

High score listings

In the early days of basic 2D arcade games, there was no option to play against anyone except the computer. Even multiplayer games were usually limited to two people. Single-player games today are often driven by the storyline and the player will continue playing to the end in order to find out what happens. In more basic games, however, this is not the case.

The high score table or list becomes the motivation to play again and again. If you feel compelled to improve your high score then you will keep on playing the game until you succeed and this means that you will get more game-play for your money. A high score list is an alternative to the storyline as a motivator for playing a game repeatedly. Some recent games, especially sports games and casual games, still include high score lists and you often have the option to publish your score online through the game so that you can compare yours to those of people across the world. In many **FPS** (first person shooter) games that have online multiplayer settings, you can have a world ranking which shows you how well you are doing in a similar way to a high score list.

Key term

FPS – stands for first person shooter. This is a game where the player sees through the eyes of the character.

Competitive games

Competition with others is a driving factor that makes people try to improve their skills and abilities. High score lists will encourage you to compete against yourself, but competitive games where you play against other people will make you even more motivated to improve.

Throughout our history there are examples of people competing against each other in order to prove that they are the best at something. The most well-known example is the Olympic Games, where people come together from every country in the world to compete, and the event generates a lot of international goodwill and excitement.

Inevitably there are occasions when people become over-competitive and the desire to win becomes a negative rather than positive motivation. On the whole, however, competition teaches people to be good losers, to push themselves and to analyse their skills and formulate plans to improve those skills. These are all positive attributes that make an individual successful in the world of work and are undeniably associated with being successful at computer games.

Since online multiplayer games have become mainstream, people have enjoyed playing a range of different games against friends or strangers. Some of the consoles that are aimed at younger children,

such as the Nintendo® Wii or DS, restrict online play to those who are known to the player in day-to-day life rather than introducing them to people through the game that they have never met face to face. The older consoles used to make use of LAN (local area network) gaming, where two consoles would be connected together with an ethernet cable, to double the amount of people playing the game. This would sometimes lead to LAN parties – larger groups of people meeting up with their equipment and playing games against each other. As the current batch of consoles and handheld devices include built-in wireless Internet access, playing competitive games online is very easy to do.

Did you know?

Some games make the experience seamless by allowing the user to go online without even interrupting the game play. Burnout Paradise is a really good example of this, as the player drives around a city picking different challenges and can, by pushing one button on the controller, get online instantly, without any kind of disruption.

Peer pressure

Another motivating factor that affects people psychologically is peer pressure. If friends, classmates or colleagues are pressurising someone to play the same games as them or to buy the same console, this can be a negative effect. Peer pressure is very powerful, especially with young people, because most people want to fit in with their peers. If everyone you hung out with was playing a certain game and you didn't have it, you would feel you were the odd one out, left out of discussions that they were having. Advertisers know that peer pressure is a powerful motivator for buying games and they use it to their advantage. Most young people will only be able to afford a new game from time to time, but as soon as one friend has bought an exciting new game everybody in the group will want it, and as soon as the majority have it, the person who doesn't will feel left out. Unfortunately the only way to combat peer pressure is to be sensible about the way that you make your games purchases and about who your friends are. If you know that you can only afford to buy one game a month, then make sure that you have read all the reviews of the games you might like and make an informed decision. If you are really enjoying the game that you have, then peer pressure won't make you want another game too badly. If you have friends who have bought a new game and are unwilling to share it with you or let you play, then this is a weakness of their character and not a reflection on your character.

Fun

Games are fun – that's why we play them. The games industry is part of a wider entertainment industry that aims to make us enjoy ourselves during our free time. At school or college, and then later on at work, we have a daily routine that finishes at a certain time and then, meals and chores notwithstanding, our free time is our own. People choose to have fun in lots of different ways, from playing a sport to watching a film. Games are a fun pastime because they challenge the player and often have gripping storylines. They have been getting better in quality every year for 30 years and can be played on one's own or with friends.

Games are fun because there are so many different types and, depending on what mood you are in, you can pick one that will satisfy you. Now that games are being embraced by whole families, game-playing doesn't have to be a solitary activity – it is something that can be fun whilst spending time with your family and also whilst learning or getting exercise.

Educational value

Games can be educationally beneficial, as mentioned above (see page 97), but games are also educational from a psychological point of view because they can teach us discreetly, whilst we think we are just having fun. Traditional toys and games, such as building

blocks and jigsaws for very young children, teach the child how to move their fingers, apply pressure and construct. Computer games can educate in the same way, teaching strategy or quick thinking. A game with a very strong storyline can also make the player think about how they would behave in a similar situation.

Expectations

People have certain expectations when sitting in front of a new game and one of the features that designers have to consider when planning their games is the element of surprise. When someone is surprised it is an enjoyable experience, even if it is associated with fear or shock, and this is a psychological factor that games designers use as often as they can. Some games have a storyline with a surprising twist whilst other games, such as action games, will have a surprising appearance of an enemy or special **power-up**. Regardless of what the surprise is, changing people's expectations is a great way of making them enjoy the game more. As there are so many titles available to each games player, they can sometimes be quite similar to each other, so the ones that change the expectations of the play are the ones that sell the most copies.

Key term

Power-up – a collectible item in a game that improves the abilities of the player.

Levelling

One of the satisfying factors involved in playing a lot of computer games is the principle of levelling. Many games involve a character that begins in a basic state and can be improved upon as the game progresses. This tends to involve the advancement of particular characteristics/skills such as strength, agility, magical powers, etc. The player will gain points in some way for progressing through levels or defeating enemies and achieving a certain amount of experience will allow the character to move up to the next skill level. This is known as levelling up. Role-playing games are dependent on levelling, as a higher level will allow the player to access new areas of the game or wield more powerful weapons. Psychologically, there is great satisfaction in moving up to the next skill level and this keeps the player interested in the game for longer.

Assessment activity 22.1 (P1) (D1) BTEC

Your class has been approached by a group of concerned parents who are worried about the negative effects of playing computer games and how games affect society.

1   In small groups discuss the influences that computer games have had on society as well as individuals. Record this discussion using either video, an online collaboration site such as Primary Pod, or just use a pen and paper. (P1)

2   Write up a report detailing the discussion and adding your own thoughts and opinions. (D1)

Grading tips

- The recording of your discussion will provide evidence for your assessment of (P1) and (D1).

- To achieve a (D1) grade, you must evaluate the influences of computer games across society and individuals. An evaluation has to be much deeper than a discussion and you need to get to grips with all of the information that people are talking about. You might want to do some extra research in order to make sure that you are aware of all of the issues that exist.

PLTS

You will demonstrate your skills as an **independent enquirer** by doing your own research.

You can practise your skills as a **reflective learner** by considering how games have affected your life.

An **effective participator** will follow the instructions of the assessment and work towards completion.

Functional skills

You will have the opportunity to improve your **English** discussion and report writing skills.

2 Know the different types of computer game

2.1 Types of game

In order to begin understanding how games are designed you will need to have a more in-depth knowledge of the computer games industry. Games have come a long way since the 1970s and, as with films, music and television, they can be categorised into different genres. These genres contain titles involving very different types of game design and complexity and tend to be available across different gaming platforms.

Genre of games

Categorising different games into particular genres can be subjective. These days, games can be a mix of more than one genre, for instance Fallout 3 by Bethesda is a role-playing game (RPG) because it involves a detailed storyline with side missions, levelling and character configuration. Fallout 3 is also a first person shooter (FPS) because it involves a first person view through the eyes of the main character and the player's gun is often in line of sight.

Genres can change and there are no perfect definitions: use Table 22.1 to familiarise yourself with different genres. The table also lists sub-genres which occur within the genres.

Gaming platforms/environments

The type of game that you can play depends on the different types of **gaming platform** available to you. One of the first-ever interactive games was made on an oscilloscope, a device used for displaying electrical current.

Key terms

Gaming platform – a physical or software device that allows the playing of games.

Blu-ray discs – a form of DVD that can store more data than other discs and allows for more detailed games.

Genre	Description/Sub-genres	Examples
Action games	Require the player to think quickly and reach goals Subgenres – fighting games, hack and slash games, platform games, maze games	Assassins Creed Prince of Persia Super Mario Bros
Role-playing games	The player develops characters' abilities whilst working through a story Subgenres – turn-based RPGs, massive multiplayer online RPGs	Final Fantasy 7 World of Warcraft
Adventure games	Tend to involve solving problems and puzzles Subgenres – point and click, interactive movies	The Legend of Zelda Professor Layton
Strategy games	Rely on tactical thinking and decision making Subgenres – real time strategy (RTS), tower defence game, turn-based strategy	Civilization Fat Princess
Simulations	Simulate real life activities in virtual worlds Subgenres – music and rhythm games, driving and racing games, life simulations, god games	Gran Turismo Nintendogs Guitar Hero
Sports games	Player takes control of sports teams or individual players	Pro Evolution Soccer Wii Sports
Combat games	Focus on combat and weapons Subgenres – first person shooter, third person shooter, light gun shooter	Metroid Prime Time Crisis
Educational games	Teach you how to do something or improve your skills	Dr Kawashima's Brain Training Mavis Beacon Teaches Typing

Table 22.1: Game genres

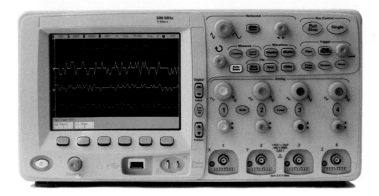

Figure 22.1: An oscilloscope

Today there is a wide variety of different electronic devices that allow games to be played. The most common platforms are games consoles or personal computers (PCs). Games consoles are devices that are designed primarily for playing games through a television. The consoles that are currently popular are the Sony PlayStation®3 (PS3), the Nintendo® Wii and the Xbox® 360. All of these devices play games that are bought separately on DVD discs (**Blu-ray discs** in the case of the PS3) and use their own controllers to move through menu options and control the characters or vehicles in the games. The consoles can also be connected to the Internet, which lets the players download extra content and new games and play multiplayer games against their friends.

Games consoles are the platform of choice for hardcore gamers because once they have been purchased they are dedicated to playing the games that are released for them. PC games, on the other hand, are reliant on a given technical specification which might be higher than that of the player's PC. However, PC games are popular because most homes have a PC in them so there is no need to buy a console. Many of the games that are available on consoles can be bought for the PC and there are some games which take advantage of the mouse and keyboard that are only available for the PC.

If the player wants to play games outside of the house they have the option of buying a handheld console. The Nintendo® Gameboy was the first of these to be released (1989) in black and white with very basic graphics. Now we can play richly detailed games on the Nintendo® DSi and the PlayStation® Portable (PSP™). These handhelds also have the ability to connect to the Internet and can come with extra software which allows them to be used as an e-book reader or even a sat nav.

While games consoles and handhelds were designed purely with games in mind, mobile phones are a device for which games have been developed despite gaming being far from their initial purpose. The early Nokia handsets all came with Snake, a basic maze game and now the iPhone® is considered to be a serious gaming platform in its own right.

Other gaming platforms are arcade machines (large single-game devices with a built-in screen that you might find in cinema lobbies) and TV set-top boxes such as Sky Digital, which come with games channels that allow the player to use the remote to control the game.

The environment that the game is played in also needs to be considered. Games can be:

- single player – where one player will play through a campaign, competition or story
- split-screen multiplayer – where two or more players play on the same screen
- network multiplayer – where players use a local network to connect devices together and play games against each other
- online multiplayer – where players in different homes, towns or even countries will connect their gaming platform to the Internet to play games against each other.

So the environment refers to virtual space in which the game player is playing – are they playing alone offline or as part of a large online universe? The environment affects the delivery of the game sometimes as well. Games can be purchased on a hard medium such as a DVD and bought from a shop. Alternatively, they can be bought on soft media, downloaded directly onto the player's console from retailers such as Xbox® Arcade or the PlayStation® Network.

Platform considerations

It is very important for games developers to understand the capabilities of the platform that they are developing for. PC games developers can state the particular technical specification that the PC needs to have but developers for the other gaming platforms need to work with the available hardware. A developer for a Nintendo® DS™ game can include touch screen controls in their game but this means that it can't be released for another platform, such as the PSP™. Similarly, a PS3™ game that has over 8.5 GB of data will not fit on a single DVD disc for the Xbox® 360. Multi-platform games tend not to take full advantage of the different systems they are released on and suffer in quality as a result.

When developing software applications, designers and **programmers** only really have to worry about the interfaces they are going to design and the code they need to write. The process for developing computer games, however, is different, as there are additional considerations, depending on the complexity of the game. You might hear a game being described as a 'triple A title' which tends to mean a game that has had a lot of money spent on it, but there are high expectations of sales revenue. An example of this is Too Human, a game on the Xbox® 360, which had a rumoured $60-million production budget. Although the game didn't get outstanding reviews, it did sell well and the money spent will easily have been made back in sales.

Key term

Programmer – the individual who writes the code that eventually becomes a game. A programmer may also be referred to as a developer.

Concept artist – the individual who will sketch or paint scenes from the game before it is made.

Object – a game element that has characteristics and abilities such as the main character, an enemy or an item.

NPCs – stands for non-player characters. Game characters which the player does not control, but does interact with.

Technology

There are certain development areas that a games producer must consider at the early stages of games design.

Graphics

Concept artists are traditional artists who draw sketches and paintings of the characters and environments that need to be created for the game. Their role is crucial at the early stages as it allows the rest of the development team to get a clear idea of the overall style and theme that the game should have.

A decision needs to be made early on as to the graphical style of the game. This may be influenced by the limitations of the platform or it might be a particular style that the developer is going for. Whatever the reason, the graphical style will dictate how detailed the game and therefore how extensive the development is going to be. If the game is a simple cartoon-style, 2D game it can be designed and programmed a lot more quickly than if it is to be a highly detailed 3D world. If the game is to have 3D graphics then a 3D modeller, animators and environmental programmers will need to be found. If it is a 2D game, then one programmer may be able to create all of the **objects** needed.

AI

AI (artificial intelligence) is very important in games development as it can dictate how challenging a game is. Games that rely on puzzles do not require any AI, but combat games such as Uncharted: Drakes Fortune are a lot more fun if the bad guys that you are shooting behave in a realistic way when you shoot at them.

Did you know?

How can companies spend millions of dollars on a game? Well, it depends on how detailed the game world they've created is.

Certain games fall into the Sandbox category and these are games that take place in a world that can be explored at the whim of the player. Sandbox games are massive and most of them take place in large cities that are copies of real-world cities. The player can go anywhere in the city and the majority of the buildings may be explored. This takes an enormous team of developers – some games are said to have up to 1000 developers working on them. There can be hundreds of NPCs (non-player characters) wandering around the city and each of these will have been modelled by a specialist known as a 3D modeller. Each building needs to be created, each type of car and boat and tree – the list goes on...

Basically, the bigger and more detailed a game, the more money has to be spent on it. Games are now being produced in a similar way to Hollywood films.

This is where AI programmers come in. Their role is to program rules that designate certain behaviours to computer game **NPCs**, so that the NPCs' actions and reactions can change and adapt to what the player does. The Elder Scrolls IV: Oblivion used AI to allow the NPCs to live their lives within the game, even when the player wasn't in the same area. AI isn't true intelligence though – it is only an illusion.

Audio

Computer games make a lot of noise and all of these need to be planned, recorded and then mixed. A lot of games use whole orchestras to create the same feeling as a classic Hollywood film. As well as music, games use a lot of sound effects that need to be recorded or created digitally. The final audio consideration is voice acting, as modern games use human voices instead of text. Actors need to be hired and their voices recorded in a studio. Their lines are then matched to the lip movements of the animated characters, in a similar way to a computer-animated film like *Toy Story*.

Game-play

The game-play needs to be carefully designed, as that is fundamentally what the player is interested in. Level designers meticulously plan the layout and exploration of levels and the puzzles or challenges that will be contained within them. The game designers will decide the kind of features that the game will contain and the abilities of the central characters.

Scripting

Any game with a storyline needs to be scripted in the same way that a television programme or a film does. The script is very important as it will be shared with the developers, the authors of the game's documentation and the voice actors, who will record any dialogue.

Did you know?

Rockstar studios invested in time-lapse cameras on the roof tops of New York to capture photos and footage of the city that were later used to create the virtual city in Grand Theft Auto IV.

Assessment activity 22.2 P2 BTEC

A software development company that currently makes office applications is thinking about branching out into games.

1 Put together a report for the company. Your report should contain sections that define and give examples of:

- different genres – what they mean and example games' titles
- types of platform and environment.

Grading tips

- Remember that you can't make assumptions about the reader's knowledge. Not everybody plays games, so you will need to explain the differences between the genres, and what common features of games qualify them for the genre. Make sure that you have given an example of each type of platform: console, PC, handheld, mobile, etc. Don't just list a few different products from one type of platform. **P2**

PLTS

Working on your report and researching genres will help improve your skills as an **independent enquirer**.

Functional skills

You will have the opportunity to develop your **English** functional skills and improve your report writing skills.

3 Be able to design and develop computer games

Computer games development is very different to normal software application development, as it is built using different elements and with a wider variety of staff bringing different skills. A software application is made by a programmer who may have help from a **tester** or a systems architect, depending on the scale of the project. Computer games are made up of graphics, menus, game-play rules, levels, sounds and control systems. This means that even a small casual game will have a large team working on it and it is extremely rare that one person will have all of the skills required to build a professional game on their own. This section will focus on the way that games are designed and how this design is then implemented by the developers.

3.1 Design

The design stage of a game's development is the most crucial time and decides how the game is going to look and play. The game's **producer** will have a clear idea at the beginning of the kind of genre that the game will fall under and some basic ideas regarding the game play, style and the platform that it will be released on. This information is then relayed to the designers who will start putting together the design documents that will be needed in order to start developing the game.

Storyboards

Games are very visual and even if they do not have a storyline, they still have a definite start, middle and finish, with the middle tending to be the bulk of the game. This means that rather than designing a software application that has certain features and abilities, a games designer focuses on the order in which the player is going to experience the game. Using a storyboard is one of the best ways to start this process. A storyboard is a series of simple drawings that show the different stages of the game and the order in which they will be played. The game can then be split up into different sections of development and allocated to different people. The storyboard itself is very simple and comprises basic impressions of what the different levels and menus will look like.

Key terms

Tester – the individual who usually works in a team to make sure that there are no defects or glitches in the game. (For more details, see the section 'Be able to test and document computer games', page 115.)

Producer – the individual responsible for overseeing the development cycle of the game.

Pseudo code

Writing programming code can be extremely complicated and the more detailed an application, the more difficult the code is to write. Programmers who work on games tend to have a good understanding of how their programming language is written but don't tend to be the people who design the game. The designer role is a full-time job and involves having an understanding of the games industry as well as having the relevant design skills. The designer needs to be someone who understands why certain games are popular and what features the game needs. This means that they probably won't have an understanding of the specifics of programming. Instead, designers use pseudo code as a meeting point between the two skill sets.

Pseudo code is an informal cross between programming code and normal English language and it is used to plan a program's structure before actually writing the code. This means that you don't have to

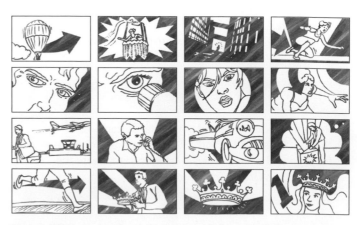

Figure 22.2: A storyboard is an excellent way of showing the game in the early stages of development.

have picked which programming language you are going to use before planning how the program will work.

Later in the unit (page 111) you will learn about programming structures and it will become clear how these can be planned using pseudo code, but here is an example for now.

```
If Sonic Collides with Enemy
        If Sonic has got any rings
                Then rings are dropped
        Else if sonic has no rings
                One life lost
        End if
End if
```

This sample of pseudo code is based on the game Sonic the Hedgehog™. In the game, the main character, Sonic, is vulnerable to enemies if he is harmed when he is not holding any rings. If he has rings and he is harmed, he drops them. The pseudo code above is not written in any particular programming language. It is written in normal English but by someone who has an understanding of how programs are put together and it would allow a programmer to quickly turn it into programming code.

Narratives

A narrative is a story and as a design tool it is a plan of the whole sequence of events in a story. When designing a game the narrative's author has to make the same considerations as someone writing a television series – some information must be kept back to keep the player guessing, there should be happy moments and sad moments, characters should be engaging and interesting. All of these considerations go into the narrative and it can be a very lengthy document, depending on how important the storyline is to the game.

If the game is very story driven then all of the developers will need access to the narrative document in order to make sure that the characters or environments that they create work together and don't contradict anything that happens in the story. For example, you might be developing a game where there is a major environmental incident such as an apocalypse. The developers will need to understand the storyline so that they can create the world before

and the world after the apocalypse. The character designers will need to know how the story dictates any technological or physical limitations of the people or creatures in the game. The environment artists will need to know if there are any plot mechanics such as lack of water or low temperatures that will affect their design of the game world.

The storyline can be crucial to the development process, as any inconsistencies in the game world will lead to a reduction of the feeling of immersion that a player seeks.

Action lists

Most games that are being developed will be overseen by a project manager or producer. The producer has a very important role because they decide exactly what needs to be done and who needs to do it. There are many different types of document that a producer may use, and for designing games, action lists are very useful documents.

An action list contains all of the tasks that need to be done to create the game, written in the order in which they need to be done and with details about how long they will take and who is needed to do them. The action list is distributed to the entire development team so that everyone knows who is doing what. This is important as some people's roles will be dependent on other's finishing the tasks they have been set, according to a deadline.

Graphical tools

All of these design documents can be created using different graphical tools. There are software packages available that will help you make storyboards but they are easily made using something like Adobe® Illustrator® or even Microsoft® PowerPoint®. Different development companies (often referred to as games studios) will have their own chosen tools, such as a graphics tablet, that they encourage everyone to use.

3.2 Program design

The design of the game is crucially important, as different teams may be involved in the process. The documentation of the design allows everyone involved to understand the purpose of the game and the different sections, or modules, that will need to be created in order for the game to work.

Algorithm	A series of coded steps that solves a particular problem
Data dictionary	A document that contains important details about the data that is used within a game and any rules that it must abide by
Instantiation algorithm design	In order to save time when developing the game and also to use less computer memory when running the game, the algorithms that are designed use different instances of the same object
Methods/procedures	Blocks of code that perform a specific function
Modularity	Designing the game's code so that it is made up of separate parts with common commands
Parameters passed	Data that is sent into a method to have an action performed on it; a parameter in a game could be the number of bullets available sent into a 'shoot gun' method
Return values	Data that is sent out from a method; based on the previous example the return value could be 'bullets left'
Scope	The size of the game and the amount of methods and objects that will need to be created
Systematic approach	Creating the code in a logical way and understanding which modules need to be created first as others may rely on them

Table 22.2: Terms used in program design

One important design document that is used throughout the development of a game is the data dictionary. It states the data types, any procedures that can be used on the data, any data that is passed in (called a parameter when it is moving between different code modules), any values that are sent out from the data, where it is used (referred to as its scope) and how it can be accessed (referred to as its visibility).

There are various types of visibility:

- private – the data can only be accessed within the same code block
- public – the data can be accessed by any other code block
- static – the data can be accessed but not changed
- friend – the data can be accessed by an allowed code block.

If you use an object-oriented programming language then your program design will include all of the different objects that the game uses. The advantage of using objects is that multiple instances can be created of the same object. This means that you can create copies. In the classic game Space Invaders, for example, all of those identical alien ships that slowly move down the screen are not coded separately, they are instances of one object.

Some important terms you might come across whilst looking at program design are listed in Table 22.2.

3.3 Develop

Programming a computer game can be very different to creating an office software application or a web application but in some ways there are still similarities. A game uses similar code to create menu structures and events that dictate the flow of the game from loading, and it accesses files in similar ways for game saves. When games programmers are deciding how to proceed from the design documents that they have been given, they usually have the first decision made for them: which programming language they should use. This decision tends to be taken out of their hands because the choice of platform will decide how the game is going to be built. There are still some choices available to the programmer but they are narrowed down a lot. Some computer games development companies will have a particular house language which they insist that everyone uses.

The implementation of the programming will also depend on the complexity of the game and the language that is being used.

Choice of language

The programming language that is used to make a game is a very important consideration but will often be decided by the platform for which the game is being developed. The more complex and detailed the game, the higher the level of programming language needed and therefore the more difficult it is to write.

IDEs

The software that a programmer uses to write and check the code is called the development environment. Certain development environments are extremely clever, finding problems in the code and fixing them. The use of a development environment is essential when working with graphical software, as it allows the developer to create the graphics and then write the code that runs behind it in order for the game to run. This could potentially be done by a number of different people, depending on how complex the game is. Some development environments have the programming language built into the software so that the programmer can write the code even faster – some of the code is even generated for them. These are known as integrated development environments or **IDEs**.

Once the language has been chosen, the developer can then look to see what different development facilities are available. Some languages such as Action Script or Visual Basic are written exclusively using a specific IDE, whilst others can be used in a variety of IDEs. More traditional programming can be done using a simple text editor, but this lacks many of the features that an IDE provides.

The programmer will use the available development facilities to write, save and edit their files. A normal software application will usually be made up of numerous files within a project folder. A game is made up of even more files, including code files as well as graphical and sound files. The IDE will manage all of these files and also take responsibility for building or compiling the code. This means that after the programmer has written the code using the correct programming language, the code is translated into machine code which is packed into fewer files and is much quicker to run. The IDE will identify any problems in the code which may stop it from compiling properly and some of the more sophisticated IDEs will even correct the problems for you using built-in help facilities.

Regardless of how sophisticated the IDE is, the code needs to be written in a way that the computer can understand. While small problems can be found and fixed properly, larger problems may take longer to find. It is common for multiple programmers to be working on one game at the same time and they will often turn to each other for help when they get stuck on an error in their code. Because of this, and because programmers will often pass their work on to another person to upgrade or complete, good programming practice is encouraged whenever writing code professionally (see Table 22.3).

Key terms

IDE – stands for integrated development environment, software which helps write programming code.

Container – a device for storing data that is used in the game.

Programming practice	Description/benefit
Using suitable comments	Developers can write comments in the code which is ignored by the compiler. This is a really useful way of explaining how a block of code works and what it should be doing.
Writing small unitary code blocks	By writing small blocks of code that produce a specific outcome, the developer can make the code easy to understand and easy to reuse.
Invocation	Developers can access existing code blocks from code that they have already written or code that has been written by others.
Using consistent indentation	Code can be very difficult to read and appears to be quite dense on a screen or when printed out. By using indents, programmers can show which lines of code are related to each other and also the order in which they should run.
Writing descriptive identifiers	All programs use **containers** called variables which store data. Variables have to be given identifiers – names, which separate them from one another. These names should be as descriptive as possible so that reading the name of a variable will let you understand what it is used for. An example of this could be Marios_Health which could store a numeric value that indicates how much health Mario has left.

Table 22.3: Good programming practice

Game Maker 8 is an IDE which is made by Yoyo Games. Using Game Maker it is possible to create 2D or 3D games very quickly by dragging actions and commands through a very easy-to-use interface. Game Maker 8 Lite is a complete IDE that is free and allows you to make 2D, single-player games. Upgrading to the Pro version enables you to make 3D games and multiplayer games.

Figure 22.3 shows the interface of Game Maker 8 and you can see the three distinct sections of the screen. The main window on the right-hand side is where the developer can view and edit the different elements of the game. The section on the left is a file structure of the game being developed, with the different elements split between folders. The top section contains menus and icons that allow for the creation and manipulation of the game elements. Using this IDE a programmer can make a game from scratch, including drawing animated **sprites** that can be used for graphics.

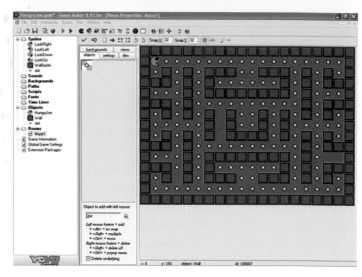

Figure 22.3: Interface of Game Maker 8, an IDE designed purely for creating games

Case study: Anatomy of a game – Hungry Joe

In Figure 22.3 you can see the development of a game called Hungry Joe. This is a simple maze game that is very similar to a 2D classic, Pacman. In Hungry Joe, Joe must move around the maze and eat as many yellow dots as he can find.

The game is made up of the following elements:

- six graphical sprites
- three game objects
- one room.

The room makes up the whole of the first level, and the only setting that has been changed from the IDE's default is the colour of the background, which is now grey. An animated GIF was created using Game Maker's image editing features – Hungry Joe facing right. This image was then duplicated three times and rotated to face up, down and left. Two more sprites were then created – one for the wall and one for the dot. The sprites are only the face of the object, though. They don't have any behaviour or actions yet, so this must be programmed into the object.

The objects consist of any parts of the game that need to have characteristics or functionality – so the

three that are in this game are Hungry Joe, the wall blocks and the dots. Hungry Joe has actions which respond to the player pressing the cursor keys on the keyboard. Depending on which direction is pressed, Joe will start moving in that direction and his sprite will change in the appropriate direction.

This behaviour is implemented in Game Maker 8 by dragging the icons into the event window on the Hungry Joe object. If you were using a more traditional programming language, you would need to type in the code line by line. This is where the advantages of an IDE really start to become obvious.

The wall object only has one action and that is to wait for a collision with Hungry Joe and to make his movement stop. In other words, when he hits the wall he comes to a standstill. The last object, the dot, also only has one action. It waits until it collides with the Hungry Joe object and it changes the player's score by an increase of one point. It then refreshes the score on the title bar and destroys itself so that, to the player, it disappears from view and looks like Hungry Joe has eaten it.

Key terms

Sprite – the graphical image that represents a game element.

Program structures – different ways in which the code runs. There are three main types: sequential structures run one line after another, selection lets code be run only under certain conditions, and iteration lets you repeat lines of code whenever necessary to save time and computer memory.

Input/output statement – a statement that either brings data into the current code block or sends it out. If, for example, a block of code deals with the amount of damage a sword attack will have on an opponent, the input statement may contain data about the power level of the sword and the output statement may contain the amount of damage that will be dealt.

Logical construct – terms which allow data and instructions to be linked together such as AND, OR and NOT.

If statement – a control structure in programming which decides the direction of code.

Iteration loops – a control structure in programming which repeats code for a set amount of time.

3.4 Coding

The practice of writing a program using a programming language is often described as coding and refers to writing any kind of programming language as long as there is some point where code is written by the developer.

Good use of program structures

The developer, or programmer, will need to make sure that the **program structures** that they are using are the most appropriate for the language they have chosen. Different programming languages are suited to particular program structures. For example, Visual Basic is well-suited to event driven programming – where the actions of the user direct the order in which things occur in the game.

An alternative to this would be a procedural language, where the code runs in a logical order, one command after another. Procedural structures are well-suited to embedded systems but are not well-suited to games development. A better approach is object oriented programming, which allows for game elements to be created once and then reused – a useful trick if you consider that most games involve encountering the same enemies multiple times.

The program is structured according to the type of language that is used, and the programmer is given the task of taking the design documents and deciding what approach to take. They will need to consider the experience of the player, the requirements of the game and the system on which it will be run.

Syntax rules for the language

All programming languages use a particular combination of words and symbols to achieve a particular outcome. The combinations of words and choice of symbols vary according to the language. We refer to these combinations and choices as the syntax of the programming language. When you learn how to use a particular language, what you are learning is how to write the code using the syntax rules for that language.

Syntax rules govern how values are assigned. They also determine how to use program structures, what operators can be used, how to input and output data (**input/output statements**) and which **logical constructs** can be used.

Selection methods

The code is constructed in a logical way and the programmer will consider how they are going to solve the problems that they face. They will choose appropriate selection methods such as **If statements** or user inputs, and will decide whether or not there is existing code in external procedures/methods that can be used to do a job that needs doing. For example, if a character's jumping ability needs to be added for an NPC, there might be a jump procedure already written for the main character.

Iteration loops

Iteration loops also provide the developer with some important decisions.

The loop may have a condition on it that starts it off. This is called a pre-conditioned loop and it is used when you know in advance how many times you want something to loop, such as a character who keeps on flying upwards depending on how many golden feathers they have before they start ascending.

A post-conditioned loop is where the loop will finish when it reaches a certain amount. So, using the previous example, one golden feather causes the character to fly upwards until the time limit runs out.

Worked example

```
// This code block allows racers in last
place to catch up
Var items, newItem, lives ;
if (Race_Position = Number_Of_Cars)
{
  If (items<MaximumItemsHeld)
  {
    newItem = findBestItem(Race_Position,
Current_Speed); //procedure to calculate
best item depending on position and speed
    Next_item = newItem;
  }
  Else
  {
    MaximumItemsHeld +=1
  }
}
```

This code snippet is written in GML the language that Game Maker uses. It is a short unitary code block that chooses the most appropriate power-up for a racer who is losing a race in a Mario Kart style game.

The first line is a comment to let the developers know what this code block is for. This is then followed by an If statement which is used for the program structure selection. The code says that if the current position is the same as the number of cars then start running the code below. So if there were eight cars racing and the current position of the player is eighth, that means that they are last and need a bit of help!

Inside the If statement there is another one. This checks to see if the player has got the maximum number of items using the < operator. If they haven't then it sets a new item which will be the best possible item, depending on the current position and speed. This line of code uses an external procedure that has been written separately. It will decide which is the most appropriate item given the circumstances. For instance, if the player is last but driving really fast then they might get a bomb to get rid of the competition. But if they are last and driving really slow then they might get a speed boost. If they already have the maximum number of items then the number of items allowed is increased by one using the += operator, which means the number will be incremented by one.

The last option that the programmer has when using iteration loops is a fixed loop which will always loop through the same code, the same amount of times and could be used in a racing game where the same amount of laps are used on every track.

3.5 Data representation

Computer games use data in lots of different ways, depending on the type of game that is being played. An action game such as Mirror's Edge has a countdown timer that sets the time limit for each level. This time limit data will be stored in a data container such as a variable or a **constant**.

Variables and constants

Variables were mentioned in the previous section (see page 109) and were described as containers for data. Constants are also data containers that games may use. The difference between a variable and a constant is that a variable can be changed but a constant will

Key terms

Constant – data that is stored that cannot be changed.

Path – a pre-determined route through the room that an object can take.

stay the same. If every level in Mirror's Edge had to be completed in a set time then the programmer would use a constant. If it changed from level to level, then they would use a variable.

These containers have to be set to a specific type of data, as this allows the programming language to treat it in an appropriate way. Data types vary depending on what kind of language is being used but will usually use a different type of number, such as integers (whole numbers) or real numbers (numbers with a decimal point), characters (a single number or letter) or strings (a string of characters, text). If the variable or constant

Case study: Anatomy of a game – Guitar Loser

In Figure 22.4 you can see an example of a game that is in development called Guitar Loser. It is a rhythm action game where you have to press the keyboard in time to the music. The coloured, musical notes fall down the guitar strings, and the player must press the space bar as they pass the yellow line at the bottom of the screen.

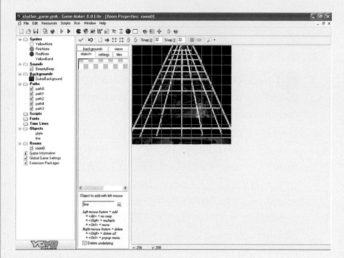

Figure 22.4: Game maker 8.0

Despite this being quite a simple game the programming behind the scenes is more complicated than you might think. The game has the following elements:

- four sprites
- one sound
- one background
- five **paths**
- two objects
- one room.

When the game loads, the background is visible in the room. There is an image of a guitar with the strings appearing closer together at the top of the screen and more spread out at the bottom, as if the base of the guitar is closer to the player. What the player can't

see is the plate object, which is sitting at the top of the screen without a sprite. This plate object will reflect a musical note.

The reason the player is not allowed to see the plate object immediately is to make the game seem more dynamic each time it is played. As soon as the game loads, a 'create' event begins within the plate object and it randomly chooses one of the three coloured note sprites.

The game has five different set paths. The five paths are invisible to the player and they have been drawn to follow each guitar string in the background image. The next event in the plate object randomly chooses between the five paths and then starts moving down the path to create the impression that it is a note moving down a string. The last action of the plate object is to start a timer which will set off an alarm event after a set amount of time. When the alarm goes off, it creates another instance (copy) of the plate at the top of the screen and the whole process starts again. When the plate moves off the screen it sets off an event that starts a second alarm and then destroys the instance of the plate that is out of sight. It is important that the instance is destroyed because otherwise it just uses up memory.

The game has to run within a set amount of time, as it is designed to be played for the duration of a recorded music track. When the line object is created at the beginning of the game, it sets a third alarm timer to limit how long the player can play. When this time is up, they are shown the message 'Time's Up' and the game ends.

The line object also has an event that occurs whenever the space bar is pressed. When this occurs the game checks to see if there are any coloured notes passing across the line at the bottom of the screen. If there are, the player gets a point, so whenever the player wants to score a point, they have to press the space bar as the musical note moves across it. A beep sound is heard whenever the player gets a point.

is set to a number data type then the programmer will be able to make calculations on it such as adding up scores to produce a high score. If the variable or constant is set to a string then the programmer will be able to change the case or add it to other text.

When the variable or constant is declared (created), it has the data type set to it. The values that are assigned will happen at the beginning of the code if it is a constant or at any other time if it is a variable.

Here is an example of declaring some variables as strings or integers and assigning values to them. This uses the Dark Basic programming language, which is a popular games programming language:

```
PlayerName$ = "Giles"
CatName$ = "Aslan"
```

```
PlayerHeight# = 5.6
CatAge = 2
```

When using Dark Basic the $ symbol represents the string data type, the # symbol represents the real number data type and if you don't use any symbol then it is assumed that the variable is an integer.

Assessment activity 22.3

1 You have been asked to design an original 2D maze game with a top-down view called Space Goblins Attack. The game needs to include:

- an opening menu which has simple instructions explaining the controls
- at least two levels with a different maze in each
- power-up items which increase the abilities of the main character in some way
- at least two different non-playable characters (such as enemies).

The rest of the game design is up to you, but make sure that you don't design anything that you wouldn't be able to make yourself.

Your evidence will include:

(a) data and interface requirements **P3**

(b) a storyboard **P3**

(c) some pseudo code **P3**

(d) an action list of what needs to be done **P3**

(e) a list of data types that will be used and an explanation of why they were chosen **M1**

(f) an explanation of how to declare any variables or constants. **M1**

After you have completed all of the documentation above, you can work towards a distinction:

(g) submit a short report that describes how the structure and design of your game would allow for easy maintenance should any problems be found, or expansion should the games studio decide that extra features are needed. **D2**

Grading tips

- **P3** requires you to provide evidence of planning the functional data and interface requirements of a game. You need to make sure that you plan the whole game and decide exactly how it should play. This means you need to make decisions about health, power-ups and scoring. These decisions will in turn allow you to plan the necessary variables and constants that will be needed. Your interface design will be shown in the storyboards but make sure that you include some annotations that help to explain exactly how the user controls the interface.

- To get the merit criterion **M1** your choices of data types have to be appropriate and justified. If you have a variable called CatsLives, then it should be a number and not a string, but you still need to pick the appropriate number format.

- The distinction criterion **D2** is looking for evidence that you understand why games are designed using modular code blocks and that you can show where the game could easily be fixed if there was a problem, or easily improved.

PLTS

As a **creative thinker**, you will need to come up with original ideas for a fun game.

Functional skills

You will have the opportunity to improve your report **writing** skills.

4   Be able to test and document computer games

Now that you have learnt all about the types of games that are produced, the effect that they have had and the way that they are designed and developed, it is time to test and document a game. Implementing a design is an exciting time but it still must be done professionally and the design documents should be in view at all times.

4.1 Testing methods

After the game has been created, it must be tested thoroughly. Games are often paid for by their players and they would not be happy if they have paid for something that doesn't work properly. Testing is taken very seriously and while a lot of people imagine it to be tremendous fun to play games for a living, the professional games tester needs to be able to understand both the design documentation and the programming code because this is what they will use as a reference when they are creating and executing their tests.

Test strategies

There are a few different strategies that can be used when planning the testing of the game and the producer or project manager will be responsible for

Did you know?

There are several types of games testing procedure:

- black box testing – testing based on how the game-play and features are described in the design documents
- white box testing – testing based on how the programming code has been written and the code paths are traced by the tester
- interface testing – testing of the game's interface elements
- iterative testing – testing the game at different stages of its development.

employing a test manager who will then choose the most appropriate test.

There are various different types of testing documentation that are created to plan the tests in advance and then record the results. Figure 22.5 is an example of a test plan where the first five columns are filled out in advance of the testing and the last two columns after the testing.

Game title: **Helen's Hamster**
Test type: **Black box**
Test focus: **Hamster navigation through Maze 1**

Test #	Date	Test description	Data	Expected result	Actual result	Corrective action
1		Move forward	'S' key press	Hamster moves forward	Passed	n/a
2		Move up	'W' key press	Hamster moves up	Failed	Check code
3		Move down	'X' key press	Hamster moves down	Passed	n/a
4		Move backward	'A' key press	Hamster moves back	Passed	n/a
...		...	...	...	...	...

Figure 22.5: Example test plan

The test plan covers the entire game's development and makes sure that there are no flaws in the game that is eventually released. This is a very large-scale task and if any problems are found along the way, the test plan will ensure that they are recorded and amended. Games that are released that have flaws or errors in them do not sell very well and receive poor reviews from games journalists.

Each test will have a test case, which is a particular scenario that the tester will undertake to try a feature or a command under certain conditions. These conditions might be the direction of movement or the amount of items in an inventory. It is important that the test cases cover as many different scenarios as possible so that there is nothing that the player could do when the game is sold that hasn't already been tried during a test.

The test plan is used as a test log, where all of the outcomes are recorded and an indication of what needs to be done to correct it is added. If a problem is found, the tester may take a screenshot to use as test evidence. This screenshot will then be passed on to the developer who will be able to get a clear idea of the problem and then start to fix it.

When all of the testing has been done a test report will be written to show where the problems were found and summarise any vulnerabilities in the software or issues that might resurface.

When a game has been tested to a satisfactory level it will then be released for sale.

4.2 Testing tools

One of the advantages of using an IDE instead of writing programming code directly into a text editor is that there are various testing tools that are available for the programmer to use to check their code. These testing tools are often referred to as debugging tools as their aim is to find any problems, or bugs, in the code and calculate the problems that they might cause when the game is running. Most problems that can be found in computer games involve the game crashing or the characters disappearing during game-play, which can be a cause of great frustration to the player.

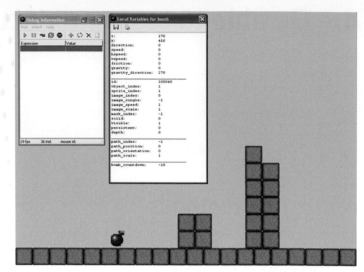

Figure 22.6: Errors found when the game is running can be tracked using debugging tools.

Debugging tools will check the syntax of the code as it is being written and will, in some cases, change the colour of the text, depending on what has been typed, so variables can be represented with one colour and procedures with another. This allows the programmer to instantly see when they have mistyped something, as it will not appear in the appropriate colour.

Another useful debugging tool is the trace facility, which allows you to watch the progress of a particular procedure or variable in a separate window. Figure 22.6 shows the debugging facilities in Game Maker which allow the programmer to slow the game down to almost a standstill and click through the game step by step which, when combined with a window showing the values attached to a particular object, lets the programmer understand exactly what is going on. In the screenshot the game is being 'stepped through' and the bomb object is being watched. If you look at the bottom of the local variables window you can see a variable called bomb_countdown which has reached -18. the programmer will see instantly that this is an error, as the countdown should stop at zero.

4.3 User documentation

Most computer games are still bought from a high-street retailer or large supermarket and will be sold in a display case that contains the game disk or cartridge and an instruction manual. This manual forms what the industry calls user documentation and includes any information that the user will need in order to play the game. It often includes:

- an introduction to the story of the game
- instructions on how to load the game
- screenshots of the opening menus
- a list of the control schemes and how to use them
- details regarding options that are available
- character details
- help and troubleshooting sections
- FAQs (frequently asked questions) section.

This will vary, depending on the type of game, and some will have very detailed user documentation whilst others will be very brief. Casual games do not tend to have detailed instructions while story-heavy RPGs may have quite a thick manual.

Some games are bought digitally, which means that they are distributed through a website or directly to the games console. When people buy games this way they download the games files, and the user documentation is often built into the download. In some cases the user documentation will only be available on a website, where it can be read, downloaded or printed.

Functional skills

Your **English** skills will help you write your user documentation effectively.

4.4 Technical documentation

The technical documentation that needs to be included with a games development will be crucial to anyone who needs to know how the game has been developed. The first recipients of the technical documentation will be the testing team, who will use it to trace back any problems with the code to the tests that they are running. After this the writers of the user documentation will receive a copy to use to help them understand how the game works and how to translate this into easier language for the users. If the game is going to have any expansion packs or sequels, then the technical documentation will be crucial for making sure that everyone working on the new code understands how it was put together originally.

The technical documentation will include the data dictionary, algorithm designs, user interface designs, and other design tools.

Data dictionary

As described earlier (see page 108), the data dictionary consists of a set of tables which lists all of the data (variables and constants) that is used within the game and tells the reader what it is named, where it is accessed, whether or not it has any validation and what kind of data type it is. This is a very important document, especially during the testing phase, as it provides an immediate overview of how the data is constructed.

Algorithm designs

This contains all of the game's algorithms – how each of the code blocks has been written in order to solve a different problem. You might have a car object in the game that needs to become more damaged each time it collides with the side of the race track. An algorithm will have to be written to deal with the way the damage is calculated and decide how it affects the game play.

User interface designs

The user interface is an important part of the game and needs to be documented thoroughly to ensure that it has been designed properly and then to show how it works. All of the menu and button functions of the user interface will be detailed here.

Other design tools

There is a wide variety of additional design tools that can be included as part of the technical documentation. These are mainly diagrams which are used by the programmers to design their code and understand how other areas of the code works. Action charts and action tables will demonstrate all of the actions and events that occur when the game is being played. There might also be input-process-output tables that show exactly where the data enters the game, how it is used and then how it is output. An example of this could be the route taken through the level converted into a percentage of how much of the level was navigated.

The programmer may also use class and instance diagrams. These represent all of the objects within the game, including details of the object's properties and the procedures that may be used. As well as data flow diagrams, which show the movement of data throughout a game, these diagrams are really useful to the programmer when planning the code and also to the tester.

Assessment activity 22.4

Using your design for the maze game Space Goblins Attack, you now need to create a working game.

You need to make sure that the game follows your design and that it contains:

- at least one user-controlled character
- health and score points for the main character
- collectable items – but no more than five on screen at any one time
- computer-generated and controlled enemies.

You need to create the game, write a test plan and user documentation for the game. **P4** **P5** **P6** **P7**

Make sure that you use control structures such as selection or iteration to improve your game-play. **M2** **M3** **M4**

You also need to produce thorough technical documentation for your game which must include a data dictionary **P7**

Grading tips

- Make sure that your game uses proper variable assignments which have some kind of process. The easiest way to do this is work out a scoring system where you get points based on items that you have collected and then increase the score using a multiplier based on how quickly the level is completed. **P4**

- When you are developing your game, keep taking screenshots whenever you find a problem, as this will provide evidence for your debugging. **P5**

- Your data dictionary needs to have as much detail in as possible and you should make sure that you use as many variables as necessary and that they have appropriate data types. **P7**

- For the merit criteria you need to make sure that you have used selection or iteration methods. A simple way to do this would be to have a specific number of enemies or items on the screen at all times, so if one has been defeated or collected, a selection method will create a new one. **M2**

- You will also need to gather some user feedback and reflect on this in order to suggest some improvements to the game. **M4**

PLTS

As a **creative thinker** you will use your creativity to think up an interesting and challenging game.

As a **reflective learner** you will think about the process you have been through and consider how your game could be improved.

Functional skills

You can use **ICT** to create your game design documents.

Gemma
Games journalist

Gemma is a games journalist working for a podcast magazine called *GameFrame* in South London. *GameFrame* is part of a larger publishing company and it publishes a fortnightly podcast that features games news and reviews.

Gemma's normal working day is spent researching the current games market and making sure that she is up-to-date with all of the news about future releases. She also has to test computer games and score them out of ten against different criteria such as game-play, storyline and graphics.

Gemma has to play all sorts of different games from different genres even though she's mainly interested in action/adventure. Since she has a good knowledge of games over the past 20 years, she is able to make comparisons between new and old games and predict which games might be a success. Gemma is considered an expert in games, as she has spent many years studying them and playing them.

Think about it!

1 Why is a games journalist an important job?
2 Do people rely on reviews?
3 What features of games are often popular with players?

Just checking

1. Why are people concerned about the amount of time spent playing games?
2. Can games be educational?
3. What sort of skills can be improved by playing games?
4. What is an FPS?
5. Name an educational game.
6. What is AI?
7. Name a home games console.
8. What is a storyboard used for?
9. What is iteration?
10. What is an instance?
11. What sort of game could you make with a scripting language?
12. Why is testing so important?
13. What is debugging?

Assignment tips

- When developing a computer game you need to work through the process of a software development cycle. The first stage is initiation:
  - What kind of game are you going to make?
  - Is there an audience for it?
  - What platform will it be on?
- Then you will need to start designing the game:
  - Which design tools will you use?
  - What is the best language to use?
  - What other areas of development must be provided? Sound/AI, etc?
- The next stage is development:
  - How much time will it take?
  - Are you following a systematic approach?
  - Are you using a data dictionary?
- Then finally, you will test your game:
  - Have you got a test plan?
  - Are you covering as many test cases as possible?
  - Have you recorded the problems that you have found?

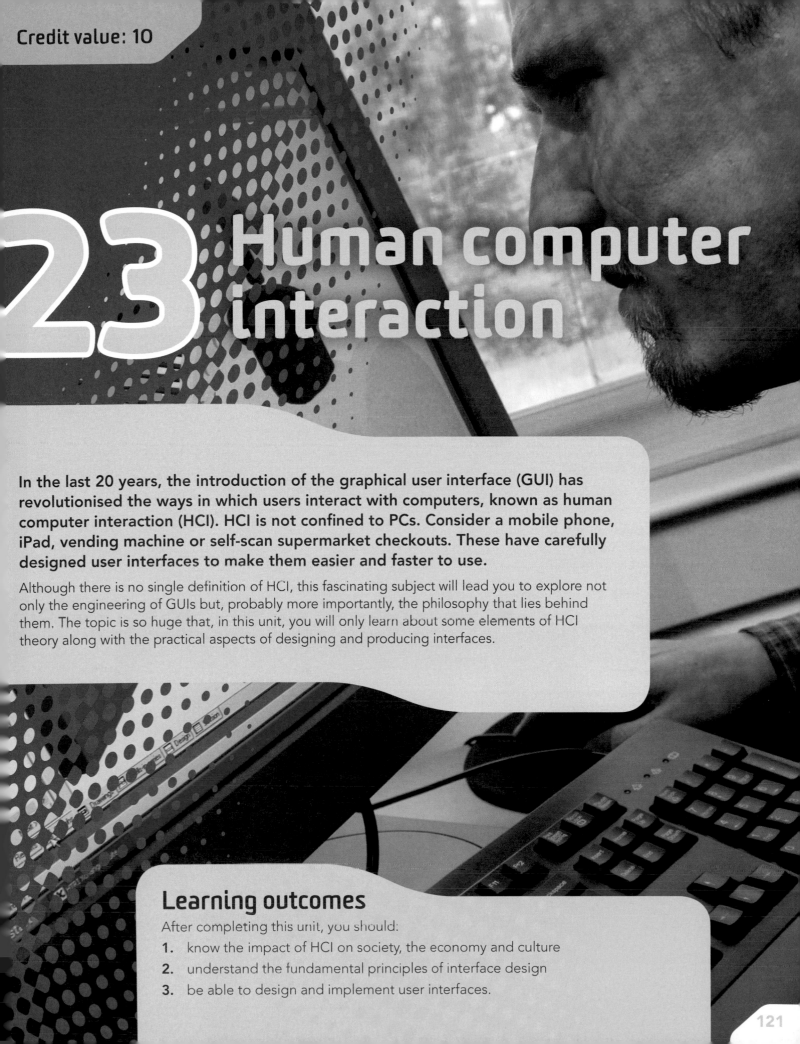

23 Human computer interaction

In the last 20 years, the introduction of the graphical user interface (GUI) has revolutionised the ways in which users interact with computers, known as human computer interaction (HCI). HCI is not confined to PCs. Consider a mobile phone, iPad, vending machine or self-scan supermarket checkouts. These have carefully designed user interfaces to make them easier and faster to use.

Although there is no single definition of HCI, this fascinating subject will lead you to explore not only the engineering of GUIs but, probably more importantly, the philosophy that lies behind them. The topic is so huge that, in this unit, you will only learn about some elements of HCI theory along with the practical aspects of designing and producing interfaces.

Learning outcomes

After completing this unit, you should:

1. know the impact of HCI on society, the economy and culture
2. understand the fundamental principles of interface design
3. be able to design and implement user interfaces.

Assessment and grading criteria

This table shows you what you must do in order to achieve a pass, merit or distinction grade, and where you can find activities in this book to help you.

To achieve a **pass** grade the evidence must show that you are able to:	To achieve a **merit** grade the evidence must show that, in addition to the pass criteria, you are able to:	To achieve a **distinction** grade the evidence must show that, in addition to the pass and merit criteria, you are able to:
P1 describe the impact of HCI on society, the economy and culture **See Assessment activity 23.1, page 137**		**D1** evaluate the impact of a potential future development in HCI **See Assessment activity 23.1, page 137**
P2 explain the fundamental principles of HCI design **See Assessment activity 23.2, page 145**	**M1** explain how an HCI could be adjusted for specialist needs **See Assessment activity 23.2, page 145**	
P3 design input and output HCIs to meet given specifications **See Assessment activity 23.2, page 145**	**M2** explain the fundamental principles which have been applied to the designs **See Assessment activity 23.2, page 145**	
P4 create input and output HCIs to meet given specifications **See Assessment activity 23.3, page 152**		
P5 test the HCIs created **See Assessment activity 23.3, page 152**	**M3** explain how the effectiveness of HCIs may be measured **See Assessment activity 23.3, page 152**	
P6 document the HCIs created **See Assessment activity 23.3, page 152**		**D2** evaluate the HCIs developed **See Assessment activity 23.3, page 152**

How you will be assessed

This unit will be assessed by assignments that will be designed and marked by the staff at your centre. The assignments are designed to allow you to show your understanding of the unit outcomes. Your assessment could be in the form of:

- presentations
- leaflets
- web pages
- storyboards
- flow charts
- diagrams
- notes
- annotated screen dumps
- reports.

Rob, BTEC National IT learner

I'm Rob and I'm mad on computers. I've discovered by working through this unit that what I am really interested in is the psychology behind the design.

What grabbed me was when I learnt about the creative ways that technology can help people who have disabilities or some kind of special need. This got me thinking about how I might be able to help my friend Cy. Cy was in a motorbike accident and is now a paraplegic. He can't fend for himself and has to have someone do practically everything for him. When I learnt about the different types of specialist equipment and software I got really fired up. I designed a system that could help Cy do things for himself and not feel a burden to other people. I mainly used haptic technology in my design and speech recognition software. The head-up display idea was really useful too and I found the case studies and activities helped me understand real-life situations.

I thought a lot about how Cy could help himself and how frustrated he could become if he couldn't get the design to work in a simple way. So I asked Cy to test my ideas and got other mates to test it too. It was really cool when my mates said it helped them appreciate how difficult life is for Cy. It was even more cool when I got a distinction for my work.

Over to you!

- **Do you have any friends or relatives who might benefit from what you learn in this unit? How?**
- **How are you going to tackle this unit?**
- **What will you do with what you learn in this unit?**

1 Know the impact of HCI on society, the economy and culture

With, what and how?

In small groups (perhaps four), using a piece of flipchart paper and marker pens, jot down examples of how you have interacted with technology. You might want to start with a definition of HCI in the middle of the paper, then each member of your group notes their examples in separate corners. You have no more than five minutes for this part.

Share your collective examples with another group. Are they similar or very different? You might want to take an image of the results using a mobile phone. You might want to do the same activity later in this chapter and compare results.

This section will help you to identify and understand the impact that HCI has on society, the economy and culture.

1.1 Development

This subsection investigates developments in HCI that have taken place over the last 20 years. Probably the most widely recognised GUI (pronounced 'gooey') is that used on PCs (personal computers). The most commonly used GUI is Microsoft® Windows®, which was based on the earlier Macintosh® model. Windows® version 1.0 (see Figure 23.1) was introduced in the mid-1980s, although this was by no means the first of its kind and did not go unchallenged. Almost all software introduced today uses GUIs, through which users (humans) interact with their computers: hence HCI.

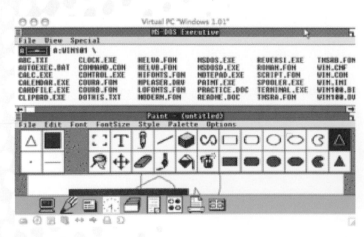

Figure 23.1: Windows 1.0

Activity: Microsoft® versus Macintosh®

1 Investigate the tension between Macintosh® and Microsoft® regarding the development of their GUIs. Produce a short account of why the tension arose, when and what happened as a result.

2 Prepare a presentation to give to your peers, which should take no less than five minutes and no more than ten minutes.

3 Include all your references.

Did you know?

You must always include references and a bibliography in any reports and presentations that you produce. By doing this, you ensure that the sources of information you present are credited and you also enable your readers to follow up any topics of interest.

Early designs

One early GUI design was developed in the early 1960s by a US graduate learner called Ivan Sutherland. He developed a computer graphics program called Sketchpad, which was inspired by research into how humans learn. This led to developments at Xerox during the 1970s which were based on the **WIMP** model – the concept became available in the early 1980s.

Meanwhile, Apple® computers continued to develop the WIMP concept and, in 1984, the Macintosh® computer appeared. These machines successfully made use of GUIs in the form of a computerised desktop with icons – small graphic images of paper, desktops, files and a rubbish bin. This concept, with the addition of a mouse, enabled the user to easily locate documents and click to open them, as well as pick up documents and put them in the bin. This early Apple® desktop design has truly influenced how users interact with computers today and has provided access to the world of computerised technology to millions of people.

Historically, early HCI designs were restricted by the hardware available. Users were required to type lengthy code into the computer just to log in. The highly popular Commodore 64 in the mid 1980s is one such example; at that time no GUI requesting

C:\ prompt on the Commodore 64

a username and password existed. Other examples included the BBC B Micro and Amstrad, all competing for the market share during the 1980s.

In these early designs, when switching on the computer, the user would be faced with an almost blank screen with just a C:\ prompt, as with operating systems such as MS DOS. Usernames were requested by some operating systems and, in some cases, followed by the need for a password. Developments such as Lotus spreadsheets still relied on user knowledge to interact with the program, as drop-down menus and GUIs had yet to be invented.

Activity: Alternative keyboard command

The forward slash (/), used to access a menu command in Lotus, is still operational today in MS Excel® – try it!

Probably the most widely recognised GUI today is the one used by Microsoft® Windows® – this was originally based on the Macintosh® model. The introduction of Windows® by Microsoft® promoted the use of a mouse as an alternative and, some might say, easier way to give and respond to commands. Other input devices and output tools which are now available are discussed on pages 146–148.

Activity: Crystal ball gazing

1 Carry out further research into the developments of the GUI from 20 years ago to the present day. Make notes.

2 Include the changes and developments in HCI for either PCs or Macintosh® and concentrate on one specialist system such as Sun or Unix.

3 Include the changes and developments that have taken place in one other device, such as mobile phones, cash registers or calculators.

4 Now list your prophesies – what do you envisage could develop in the future in each of the areas you have researched?

5 Present your findings in a short report of between 250 and 500 words. Include all your references.

6 Read ahead to the section on future development on page 129.

Extended command line editor (CLE)

Before the introduction of GUIs, the only way to interact with a computer was to enter a series of codes into the computer's operating system.

For example, the user would go into MS-DOS® (the

Key terms

CLE – stands for command line editor. It enables you to edit text files using the command line.

Dialog box – a window that responds to a command and allows you to make choices. In Office® applications, clicking on a menu item with three dots (…) after it will open a dialog box.

WUI – stands for web user interface. This is a series of processes and guidance for writing in a single language.

LCD – stands for liquid crystal display. This type of visual system is used, for example, in cash machines and mobile phones.

LED – stands for light emitting diode. This system is the same as LCD but with a different form of backlighting, usually resulting in a much slimmer model.

operating system) and the C:\ prompt would appear on the screen. By entering a series of codes, the user could create a structure such as copying, renaming and moving files – such structures are now built into modern-day computers and accessible through other means. The important thing about **CLE** was that it was a line of code, terminated by the Return key which handed control back to the computer. Typed text was ignored until the Return key was hit; then the computer interpreted the command and a response appeared on screen (or maybe not!).

Graphical user interface (GUI)

Microsoft® Windows® and associated application software, such as the Office® suite, rely on the extensive use of GUIs. These provide users with easy ways to access programs and carry out and give commands using **dialog boxes** (see Figure 23.2).

Web user interface (WUI)

A **WUI** generates a web page which the user can use to input or receive information via a web browser. Perhaps the most well-known programming language for this type of interface is JavaScript (a trademark of Sun Microsystems), although several others are used. A separate programme is created that enables users to interact in the here and now, without having to wait for a response.

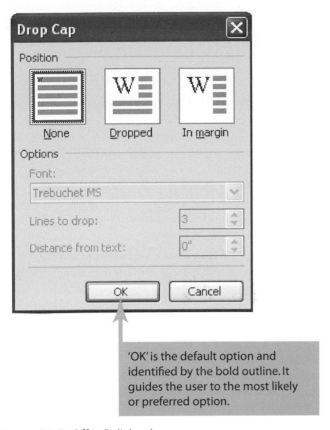

'OK' is the default option and identified by the bold outline. It guides the user to the most likely or preferred option.

Figure 23.2: Office® dialog box

Visual systems

Software developments have led to visual systems such as 3D pictures of the Earth's structure (See Figure 23.3) and reproductions of images, such as a scan of an unborn baby. 3D visual systems are now developing rapidly, with the availability of 3D televisions and systems that can be viewed without special 3D glasses. Many more films are being screened in 3D (such as *Avatar* in 2009) although a long time has passed since the screening of the first 3D film in the early 1920s.

Other types of visual systems include **LCD** screens, the more recently introduced **LED** and holograms such as those seen in *Star Trek*.

You are likely to be familiar with the display used to control a laser printer – this is very different from the primitive controls used on a dot matrix printer (see below).

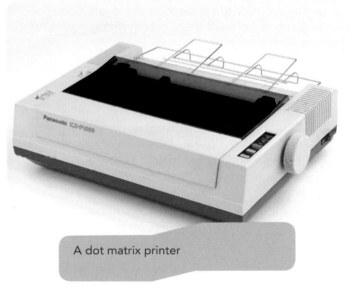

A dot matrix printer

Figure 23.3: A 3D picture of the Earth's structure

Activity: So what use is all this technology to my grandmother?

Put yourself in the shoes of someone you know who is in their twilight years. This could be your grandfather or grandmother, an elderly aunt or uncle or perhaps a neighbour.

1 Make a list of the technology you interact with on a regular basis. What do you use it for and how does it help you run your life?

2 Now consider it from the angle of your chosen elderly person.

• What technology do they interact with perhaps without realising it is a computer?

• What type of interface does this technology have – how does it work and how easy is it for them to understand and use?

• How often do they get frustrated with it when it seems to do something other than they wanted? Why is that? How can you help? Maybe they are expecting too much, too little, or perhaps there is something better for them out there?

3 Remember, it is not as easy to adapt as you get older, particularly when you haven't grown up with technology around you. You might want to take a look at how rapidly technology has developed by comparing what they use now and how they carried out the same actions and activities when they were your age.

4 You might also want to take a look at a BBC news article on the subject (go to http://news.bbc.uk/1/hi/technology/4540595.stm to learn more about claims that 'technology baffles old and the poor'.

Case study: Exciting ways in which technology can support users with disabilities or learning difficulties

There are many organisations involved in moving technology forward to provide a more independent way of life to those people who previously would have relied on someone else to carry out even the most basic of tasks. One such initiative is called MoLeNET (Mobile Learning Network) www.molenet.org.uk/projects.

The initiative has provided help and support for colleges and other training providers in maximising opportunities to learn, using advancements in technology. Tutors have developed new techniques for ways of interacting with technology that benefits learners across a variety of subjects in many ways.

Mobile technology (for example, **PDAs**, PSP®s, mobile phones and netbooks) has been used to benefit learners and tutors alike. On the MoLeTV www.moletv.org.uk website are numerous examples of learners with, in some cases, extreme learning difficulties and disabilities, accessing learning that had previously been too challenging.

Take a look through some of the examples. They could give you lots of ideas for your assignment.

Key terms

PDA – stands for personal digital assistant. It is a hand-held computer.

RSI – stands for repetitive strain injury. This common complaint can result from overuse of a computer mouse.

Specialised interfaces

Developments to HCI have led to specialised interfaces. It is only after mainstream development paid for itself that manufacturers started using their expertise to branch out into specialised markets and meeting specialist needs of users.

The development of specialist interfaces for individuals who have visual or hearing impairments has enabled such individuals to use computers in order to access and input information. For example, the National Library for the Blind has developed access to library services for users who are visually impaired, while the British Sign Language Society, in collaboration with tutors and hearing-impaired users, has recently developed a bank of sign language covering IT terms for use by tutors. A range of adaptive and assistive technology is now readily and cheaply available to support users with disabilities. For example, a tracker ball (see below) for a user with **RSI** or arthritis.

A tracker ball

In extreme cases, RSI can result in a permanent disability. Caused by overuse of muscles of the hands, wrists, arms and shoulders when using a computer, RSI can be worsened by awkward posture, excessive use of the computer and badly designed equipment.

Activity: Adaptive technology

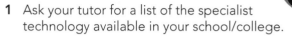

1 Ask your tutor for a list of the specialist technology available in your school/college.

2 Identify what each item is for and how it is used. Perhaps you could try it out.

Did you know?

When using the computer, avoid resting your wrists on the keyboard and typing intensively for long periods. Make sure you take regular breaks and have frequent changes in activity. By taking these precautions, you can avoid developing RSI.

Present and future development

The section above looked at specialist interfaces for users with disabilities. Other developments include robotic systems for the visually impaired and realistic computerised images, used in virtual reality computer games – 3D images that appear to leap off the screen. If you have ever watched a 3D movie or played a 3D game, you will have experienced the pop out effect

Case study: Star gaze or eye gaze?

Eye gaze technology is one approach to assisting people with multiple disabilities. *The New Scientist* has reported how a camera can be used to track eye movements and can assist independent living. More recently, its article 'Innovation: gaze trackers eye

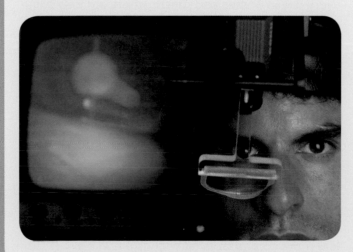

computer gamers' reports on improved interaction, using a variety of approaches, particularly to support people with disabilities. (To read the article, go to www.newscientist.com and search for 'Innovation: gaze trackers eye computer games'.

1 Using the Internet, research what the following universities' research and development teams are doing in the field of eye gaze technology:

• De Montfort University, Leicester, UK

• McGill University, Montreal, Canada

• You might also want to read about Tobii glasses (www.tobii.com/corporate/start.aspx).

2 How else might these technologies be useful?

3 What other innovations have you come across in your research?

with a fully 3D interface. This effect can be greatly enhanced by the use of **E-D** glasses.

Speech-activated software has improved greatly since its infancy in the 1990s, when the user had to speak slowly and with great clarity. Instructions were easily confused with narrative. For example, when the user spoke into a microphone, a lengthy pause was often needed to differentiate between words and punctuation. Developments have improved the speed at which the user can talk to the computer and speech recognition is now extremely accurate.

Thought input

There are different ideas about what thought input actually means. Some might say that since the introduction of computers, thought input from the individual has been minimised because computers often make decisions for us. An exaggerated example was portrayed in the TV comedy series *Little Britain* -– a customer asks for a bank loan, the bank employee types the details into the computer and responds with, 'The computer says no'. The computer had a set of criteria which it used to make a decision and the human interacting with it could not affect that decision.

Another example of the user's thought input being unnecessary is when the computer carries out a task such as generating a graph from a spreadsheet. The user only needs to enter the figures and the computer does all the work of creating the graph (see also Productivity per individual on page 132).

In the USA, research is being carried out into whether a user can 'think' commands to a computer. The study involves implanting micro chips into the user's skull. This technology could help users who are incapable of speech or movement to interact with computers and possibly carry out a number of tasks. In past research, similar devices have been used to enable a stroke victim to generate signals that move an on-screen cursor to select messages.

Realistic virtual reality

Virtual reality systems are used to train pilots, astronauts and racing drivers. They provide opportunities to gain experience and learn from potentially life-threatening activities without risking human life. These methods of training are also more cost-effective than real-life ones, as they avoid the need for aircraft or racing cars, racing tracks, fuel, etc.

1.2 Society

Developments in HCI have brought about a culture in which computers are used in everyday life. Much of the population now uses a computer of some form or another every single day. Lives depend on computers – consider, for example, their use in hospitals, transport and medical research. This section of the unit explores how technological developments both support and protect us. As well as the relatively simple GUIs used every day in homes and offices, there are also some extremely complex ones.

Improve usability

Users benefit from developments in HCI by being able to easily log into computers and load programs. Developers such as Microsoft® use a consistent approach to their tool bars, menus and GUIs. This consistency means that the user needs fewer technical skills and less specialised knowledge. For example, someone who has used Word® but not Excel® should already be familiar with some of the commands in Word®. So, when using Excel® for the first time, they feel more comfortable, as menus are in a similar format and location, the colours used in GUIs are usually the

Icons help to improve the usability of domestic appliances.

Activity: Location, location, location

Notice how GUIs generally appear in the same location on the desktop, that the colours are relaxing on the eye and that the terminology and format are usually consistent. (Colours are explored in more detail on page 138.)

1 Compare the page setup GUIs in Microsoft® Excel® and PowerPoint® with the GUI in Figure 23.2 on page 127, and make a list of all the similarities and differences between them.

2 Drag and drop one of the GUIs to another location on the desktop. Close it, then open it again. What happens? Try opening another GUI. Does this land in the same or a different location? Now try the original GUI again. Where does it land? Does the same happen when you use another Office package? If you have the chance, try other software and see what happens.

3 Keep a log of each activity, details of software and system, the response time by the user, the response time from the system and the date it was carried out.

4 Compare your list with that of one of your peers.

same, etc. This consistency simplifies input/output and is user-friendly because user confidence is increased.

Domestic appliance displays (see above) are often simple to understand and there is little need to read the instruction book first. In some cases, the instruction booklet is no longer supplied and if required, the user is directed to a website to download the manual. Another user-friendly aspect is the use of simple, almost cartoon-like images. This approach has the universal benefit of allowing people who speak different languages to use the same appliance.

The technological development that has impacted on most lives is the mobile telephone. This device is explored in detail in Unit 4: Impact of the use of IT on business systems, in Book 1. Its relationship with the way humans interface with computers is fascinating. Much research has been carried out, in particular into the multi-tap feature that enables one key to represent more than one entity. This is not the same as StickyKeys, which are referred to in the activity Office extras on page 146.

Specialised interfaces

Specialist software has been developed to enable those with sight or speech impairments to use computers.

• Voice recognition software converts spoken text into electronic text. The user speaks to the computer through a microphone (which may be built into the computer). The computer then interprets what is being said and the text appears on the screen as if it is being typed. In the very early days of voice recognition software, the user had to use very clear diction and identify clearly when saying 'stop' whether a full stop was required or the word 'stop' should be typed. The user had to talk very slowly and the reaction time before the text appeared on the screen was also slow. It took time to 'train' the computer to accept the user's voice and, in some cases, it only recognised one user. See also Present and future development on page 129.

- Software that converts text to speech, called speech synthesis, is also available. This works in a similar way to voice recognition, only in reverse. The user types in the text and the computer responds. An example is the software that enables the famous physicist Stephen Hawking to interact with other people. He uses a rod-like tool to tap out his text and the computer then speaks for him. The method used is a type of artificial intelligence and is also used in automated telephone services. It accounts for the occasional stuttering you may have noticed when using automated services on the phone when you are asked to press different keys on your telephone key pad. Try an automated service such as a telephone weather report or a satellite navigation system, and you will experience slight delays between responses (in the case of the weather report) and instructions (in the case of directions for travel).

- People who are visually impaired can now access library books through specialist interfaces, as identified in Specialised interfaces on page 128, while those with hearing impairments can turn on subtitles to television programmes, DVDs and many Internet sites.

- Language translators are also available. One such programme, *Talking Tutor*, enables interaction between different language speakers of more than 25 languages.

Interfaces for hostile environments

Robots with remote control devices are particularly useful and often life-saving in situations and activities in locations that are too dangerous for humans, such as locating landmines or landing a rocket on Mars to take samples. In these instances, remote control is necessary as it allows the user to be a considerable distance away and therefore danger free. A remote-controlled robot designed to gather information on Mars will include a data logger to record measurements such as temperature.

Complexity

As well as the relatively simple GUIs used every day in homes and offices, there are also some extremely complex ones. For example, fly-by-wire systems are used in aircraft to replace human actions. Additional

equipment such as a **head-up display** enhances the virtual reality experience – for example, simulated skiing down snowy slopes in the Alps.

Key terms

Heads-up display – a device worn on the head like glasses that can be used to watch DVDs or to experience a virtual activity.

Wizard – a program that enables a user to carry out a complex task by following a series of simple steps using dialog boxes.

Text reader – software that translates text into speech.

The latest developments in virtual activities require the user to make physical movements in order to interact with the gaming device in simulated sports such as golf and tennis.

1.3 Economy

The rapid developments in computers and the features offered have changed the way the economy operates. For example, automation by interacting with computers enables greater productivity, which equals reduced costs. The range and accessibility of interfaces, and the devices which they feature, support employees – for example, adjusting a robotic machine to cut sheet metal, operating a till in a supermarket or instructing a machine to bake another two dozen cakes.

Productivity per individual

In the world of business, time is money. Users being able to more easily and quickly give and respond to commands from devices through interfaces results in greater productivity. For example, it takes considerably less time and expertise to analyse data and produce a graph using a **wizard** than to produce one without a wizard or, indeed, without a computer. Another example is the speed and reliability with which a database can be constructed, also by using a wizard.

Alongside these obvious benefits, you should also consider the length of time it takes to develop HCI, the cost of production and how to make it user-friendly.

The cost of producing interfaces has become more competitive due to the increased number of experts with the knowledge and skill required worldwide.

Increased automation

When developing HCI, you will need to consider how to reduce user input by simplifying the amount of effort or knowledge required. A common saying by developers or users involved in the development of HCI is 'with every click the user loses interest'. One option might be to consider the use of **text readers**.

An example of a text reader is the BT voice message that relays a text message sent to a landline. Although the message is somewhat inhuman, it does enable the recipient to listen to a message while carrying out another task.

Automatic judgement of output

Another example of increased automation that impacts on the economy is automatic judgement of output. This system is commonly used in the grading of produce, such as apples, eggs or potatoes, by size and weight. The produce passes along a conveyor belt containing holes, and a predetermined grade of produce drops through the hole, thus batching items of equal size. In some wineries in Chile, for example, this method is used for separating the leaves and stalks from grapes before turning them into wine. In

Tasmania, however, they still grade apples by hand. Technology has impacted on organisations that are able to use computers to measure overall output. For example, in the nuclear industry, processes use online monitoring systems to test chemical make-up and ensure the quality of the end product. Technology now allows the decision maker to be the customer – for example, if a customer is able to provide an example of a desired colour some paint manufacturers have the technology to provide an exact match, thereby meeting the customer's requirements.

Voice input

Voice input has provided organisations with the opportunity to reduce the role of call centres. An example of this is telephone banking, which uses automated voice input to request, record and relay bank account details straight into a computer for fielding or dealing with enquiries. Utility suppliers also use this method for users to phone in with their meter readings. Some global satellite systems (GPS) respond to voice input and are an example of the consumer becoming part of the process – the GPS instructs the user to turn right, go straight on, etc.

Thought input

The subject of thought input was introduced above (see page 130). Software has been developed to

Activity: Just a click away...

How many times have you lost interest or become frustrated when you have tried out a new phone, electronic game or website? This is the impact that being more than 'one click away' can have on the user. If you are planning to go into software design of some kind, the number of clicks could potentially make or break the success of your product.

1   Choose a website, game or phone that requires the user to go through many steps to carry out a fairly simple, fundamental function. Ask your friends and family for their experiences.

2   Make a flow chart of the number of steps required to complete the task.

3   Now make an alternative flow chart of a more simplified action. Compare the two.

4   Get your friends and family (as guinea pigs) to try out the two versions. The existing version is easier, of course, because it exists. To be able to try out the non-existent version, you could produce a number of cards, each describing a different step, and get your 'guinea pig' to move the cards around to test out the scenarios.

5   What is the outcome? Did it work, what could be further improved? You could present the final version in a storyboard format, to share your ideas with those of your peers. (Storyboards are discussed in Unit 28: Website production, page 169.)

provide exercises for the brain and claims to boost cognition. You may be familiar with some of these games. For example, thought input type software claims to have enabled patients to communicate through the software, where speaking or gesturing has not been possible by other means.

Varied working environment

Employees are experiencing an ever-changing working environment because of advances in technology. The equipment used in the workplace has changed considerably over the last 20 years. In the 1980s, fax machines had only just been introduced, mobile phones were the size of bricks and very rare, and most administrative tasks were carried out manually, with little help from computers.

Today, not only is the equipment more varied, but also the environments within which we work. For example, there has been a considerable shift to home and remote working. Technological developments have made this possible. (Refer also to Unit 4 in Book 1.)

The range of mobile communications available, such as PDAs, mobile phones, wireless Internet connection and Bluetooth®, is a huge benefit to the world of work, allowing people to work in locations away from the traditional office.

1.4 Culture

The increased level of HCI has helped break down cultural barriers. For example, computerised translators enable users to type in words in their native tongue and vast dictionaries respond with translation in the chosen language. These translators are relatively cheap to buy and easily carried in a pocket or bag. Alternatively, translations are also provided on the Internet.

Activity: Je ne sais pas! Ich weiß es nicht!

1 Where else can you translate text, apart from using computerised translators and the Internet?
2 Find out which languages are available within operating systems (such as Windows®). How many languages are provided?
3 What other language features are available?

Activity: HCI influences

Investigate the influences of HCI on the following topics. Be prepared to discuss your findings in class.

1 Society: How does HCI feature in our lives? Keep a log over a week identifying every time you use a computer or computerised device. List the item, what you used it for, the day and date.
2 Economy: Investigate the impact of HCI on one of the following:
   (a) wealth: of a nation or an individual or the exploitation of workers
   (b) job changes: due to automation or the paperless office
   (b) market: growth in products, availability, desire to own the latest gadgets, etc.
3 Culture: Find examples of how HCI helps to break down barriers.

Activity: Technology in the working environment

1 Investigate the use of IT in BT (British Telecom).
2 Identify the way it is used and how it has impacted on jobs.
3 Put together a case for and against these developments – include the impact in the workplace and on the environment, society and culture.
4 Contribute to a debate in class. You will be asked to represent a team that is either for or against increased use of technology in the working environment.

The ways in which people use computers

Technological developments have supported employees and workers in carrying out everyday activities and have contributed to the growth in numbers of people working from home. For example, texting has grown rapidly and can be used as an alternative to speaking in order to confirm meetings with people in other organisations or to advise on delivery schedules. PDAs, mobile phones and other devices are used in addition to or as replacements for paper diaries and enable remote access to the Internet and file documents such as spreadsheets and databases. Emails have now mostly replaced internal **memos** and in many cases formal letters.

Key term

Memo – short for memorandum. It is a short note between colleagues.

As laptops become smaller, lighter and slimmer they are increasingly commonplace. They can be carried around inconspicuously and easily, and if you travel by train or plane you might see more people using laptops than not. Age does not discriminate in the use of computers and we are now in a culture of using our laptops for multiple activities, such as entertainment as well as computing. People use small laptops or netbooks for playing games and showing videos, particularly when they are travelling. The more recent introduction of the iPad® is taking human computer interaction even further.

Portable music has developed with the use of MP3 players and iPod®s. Increasingly sophisticated games are readily available through Xbox® and PlayStation®. However, there are some adverse effects of the increased use of computers, such as the reduction in verbal and face-to-face communication and the opportunity for employees to hide behind a computer rather than give verbal instructions or criticism. Some people might say that professionalism is being lost through the widespread use of email, as there is currently no universal protocol for email language and layout.

Domestic appliances

We might be hard pushed to find any domestic appliance that doesn't rely on technology. We are less likely to reach for a dustpan and brush as rush off and use a vacuum cleaner, available in hand-held versions for smaller tasks. The sales of worktop or slimline dishwashers are plentiful for those users either living in limited accommodation or on their own. We do very few non-automated tasks, even the most menial task can be done electronically.

Did you know?

Domestic appliances often rely on in-built computers.

Case study: Are robots taking over the world?

Robots are not new and are continually being improved through development. There are many examples of robots being used instead of humans, particularly for menial, repetitive tasks that require little skill or imagination, such as assembly-line work. As discussed in Unit 4 in Book 1, robots are also used to perform life-threatening tasks, where there is no room for human error.

A prominent feature in the news for many months in 2010 was the BP oil-leak disaster in the Gulf of Mexico. One article reported how, three months after the leak began, robots were used to attempt the blockage of oil flow at considerable depths in the ocean.

There are also examples of more realistic 'human' robots being developed and of scenarios where robots and humans interact together. In 2008, a robot was used in a Japanese school to reprimand children when they were noisy. It was reported that the children cried when told off by the robot. The same robot (Saya) was used as a receptionist in Israel. Interestingly, her movements in that scenario were deemed to be less than realistic.

Another example of developments in Japan (2008) was the creation of a robotic face replicating basic expressions in response to a limited range of words.

Previously, in 2005, Japanese scientists developed a female android that had flexible skin, fluttered her eyelashes and even appeared to breathe.

Work on robotic development is not exclusive to Asia. The Cogniron project, which is developing robots to communicate with humans, is being run by a consortium of European research institutes. Microsoft® unveiled a virtual human called Milo, as a means of interacting with humans referred to as a 'new revolution in storytelling'.

1 What is the value of this robotic development?

2 Is Milo a development of the virtual pet?

3 What do you envisage to be the next stage of development?

Psychological and sociological impact of IT

There is a psychological impact on workers and employees as a result of the development of HCI.

There is less variety of work in some environments, such as where robots are used in manufacturing, and the work is often less specialised. This is called deskilling.

The impact of deskilling work

Where automated systems reduce the complexity of the work required, this can lead to employees feeling less valued and motivated. Automated machinery has taken away the need for some specialist trades such as wood machining and milling or turning as automation reduces costs considerably.

Some trades are in danger of dying out or being so seldom available that costs have escalated. Examples include traditional furniture manufacture, stained glass making, dressmaking and tailoring. The division of labour and technological development have led to the reduction of the scope of an individual's work to one, or perhaps a few, specialised tasks. Work is fragmented and individuals lose the integrated skills and comprehensive knowledge of the craftsperson. (Read more about the impact of technology on businesses in Unit 4 in Book 1.)

Impact in the developing nations

One noticeable change over recent years is the increasing amount of overseas development and support that is provided to the UK. For example,

when you make a call to a service centre, it is more and more common for the call to be answered by someone in another country. Research carried out in 2009 identified that in India alone, there were then 555 million 'techno-savvy' 15–25 year olds using or working with computers. This has meant more jobs for those in poorer countries, but at what cost?

More products are sourced from overseas, possibly because of the lower cost as much as the available technology, but research shows too often that the conditions and pay are extremely poor. You might well ask the question: why, if the iPad® was designed in the USA, is it assembled in China?

Activity: In their shoes

1 Put yourself in the shoes of a worker affected by deskilling. Do the same for their family and then for the employer. What will be the psychological effects for each of these people? The employer may be content with the developments, as productivity is more reliable and costs reduced. However, the worker will not necessarily feel the same and this might also effect their family.

2 Research Samsung and LG products (from South Korea), Sony (Japan), Quanta (Taiwan) and China (more recently the microchip, iPod®s) and consider:

(a) if workers feel useful and motivated and whether they have job satisfaction

(b) the impact that changes in production methods have had in developing nations

(c) the impact on UK industry and jobs of production shifting to the Far East

(d) the way in which their 'new found wealth' impacts on nations such as China.

3 Be prepared to discuss your findings.

Assessment activity 23.1
P1 D1 :BTEC

The assessment tasks in this unit are based on the following scenario.

You are working in a temporary position for the local council as a software designer. You have been given an assignment in the education department to work on a project for the local nurseries, schools and colleges. You have been told that if this project is a success, you will be offered permanent employment and, depending on the quality of the outcome, promotion might also be possible.

The council is eager to provide pupils and learners in all their schools/colleges, at any age, a range of methods by which to learn and be assessed. However, you will need to enlighten managers in the council that your proposals and designs will benefit the end users, based on sound research and simple, easy-to-use products. This provides you with lots of scope for creativity and enables you to demonstrate your abilities in your quest to show how indispensable you are. You are reminded that, as you are the expert, you will need to indicate some of the principles applied and how the specialist needs are met.

Council managers have formed a review group with representative tutors from the local nursery, primary and secondary schools and colleges. Although very keen on your project, some of the tutors are unsure of how their learners will benefit from it.

Your starting point on this project is to identify the age range for your designs in order to choose the most appropriate devices for HCI development.

1 Describe one impact of HCI in recent years on each of society, the economy and culture. **P1**

2 Explain how modern advances in HCI design have contributed to the impact of computers on society, the economy and culture. (Be creative in the way in which you present your explanations.)

3 Evaluate the HCI developments over recent years, relating them to the impact on society, the economy and culture and offer a prediction for one potential future development and what impact it may have. **D1**

Grading tips

- Make sure that you describe an impact of HCI in your own words. Be creative in the way that you present your findings. Leaflets or media outputs (such as web pages) might be useful. **P1**

- Be really imaginative when thinking of a potential future development. It could be something that doesn't exist at all at the moment, rather than just developing something current. **D1**

PLTS

You could prove yourself to be a **creative thinker** in the ways that you present your findings and you will have many ways to solve your problem solving skills.

Functional skills

You may use both your **ICT** and **English** skills in this activity, researching HCI and presenting your findings.

2 Understand the fundamental principles of interface design

This section helps you to understand the essential values to apply when designing an interface.

2.1 Perception

Perceptions vary between the developer and the user. The user might not be aware of the fine detail in a GUI, such as the importance of colour or the positioning of the GUI on the desktop, and how these aspects may affect the ease with which it can be used. The developer may not be the same person as the designer or the one carrying out the interview with the client, so may not be fully aware of the client's needs. The client may not always be the user and most certainly won't be able to fully represent the desires or requirements of all the users.

Colour

When designing GUIs, you need to be very aware of the use of colour. Microsoft® Office® uses grey as the predominant colour, blue for the title bar and for enhancing drop-down lists and highlighting some text. Many users feel that grey is boring or dull. However, if bright red or black had been used, it would soon become uncomfortable on the eye.

Colours affect different people in different ways. For example, some individuals find yellow easier to read, while others find it difficult to deal with as it can appear fuzzy. Users with certain medical conditions such as dyslexia may be affected by colour in different ways.

If you decide to design a GUI with a 3D effect, you will discover the importance of the **trichromatic system**.

Luminance

The three colours of the trichromatic system are detected by three different types of cells on the retina of the eye, which are known as receptors. There has been a lot of work done on developing the theory of this system into a definition of the signals that these receptors generate and it is believed that these signals take the form of red-green, yellow-blue and black-white signals. These signals are called opponent colour channels because they relay information about opposite colours. The word luminance is used to describe these and the theory goes on to say that there is a hierarchy of luminance, (red-green – yellow-blue – black-white) and the early colour pairings cannot effectively display detail. This leads to a fundamental rule of design: to display the best detail we should always use luminance contrasts.

Activity: Colour me purple...

Create a screen background of graduated shades of one colour, from lightest at the top to darkest at the bottom. Now type a piece of text in a different colour from top to bottom of the screen. Where do you get most detail and the sharpest image. Why is that? Try this with different colour combinations.

Pop out effect

Where a display has a lot of symbols or imagery, how do you make one symbol or image stand out? It can be done by aligning them differently, colouring them differently or by adjusting to a different shape. This

Activity: What's in a colour?

1 Study three different types of GUI.

2 Identify the impact different colours have on you. Write down your experiences.

3 Identify any aspects of consistency and special features that you find useful. Make notes on what and why.

4 Compare your findings with some of your peers and note down any differences.

makes the symbol or piece of text or image, etc, stand out and is known as the pop out effect. More correctly it is called the preattentive processing theory. It is something with which you can experiment.

Our eyes observe colours using the trichromatic system, which comprises the three colours red, blue and green (not the primary colours red, blue and yellow). We can be tricked into believing that a wider range of colours has been used. Some devices rely on the luminance of colours. DayGlo colours might have value in some games, but unconsidered or excessive use can be irritating and might have adverse effects on individuals with certain health or sight conditions, as might the use of flashing images and lights. Nevertheless, if designing a GUI for use in poor light or at night, then luminance may be essential.

Most important is the market value of your GUI. In order to achieve credibility and status, it will need to look professional and stylish. Therefore, over-use and extremes of colour will reduce its professionalism. It needs to be fit for purpose.

Pattern

The user might think the word pattern refers to the picture on the GUI or its layout, whereas to the designer it might mean a template. For example, Microsoft® uses a template for its dialog boxes. The template provides consistency and evenness (symmetry). It aids the way the user relates to the interface, providing user-friendliness and **connectedness**.

Consistency helps the user to feel comfortable with what happens next (for example, clicking on Save As allows you to save with a new filename). Templates are likely to include colour, format, layout and common groupings (with menus, options). Early GUI designs (see page 124) laid the foundations and subsequent developments and changes have resulted in apparent simplicity (from the user's point of view), standardisation and consistency of interfaces (see page 130).

Pattern perception is one of the fundamental processes in our perception of displays and objects. A set of laws, originally the Gestalt laws, has been formulated to describe our pattern perception and form rules for our designs.

- **Proximity**: We view things which are close together as a group.
- **Continuity**: Smooth continuous lines are more easily interpreted than rapidly changing lines.
- **Symmetry**: We see symmetrical shapes more easily than unsymmetrical shapes.
- **Similarity**: We see similar objects as a group; dissimilar objects tend to be viewed as individuals (a manifestation of the pop out effect).

There are also laws that relate to common groupings.

- **Fate**: We see objects that move together as a group.
- **Region**: We see objects that are enclosed together, in some way, as a group.
- **Connected**: We see objects connected by continuous lines as related to each other.

Objects

All components of a GUI or any other form of image display are built using a number of separate objects. Each object appears in a hierarchical system; in other words, the images are layered. It is crucial to identify which image appears first and the subsequent images which overlay the first image. Otherwise, an interface might appear to the user as an incomplete object.

Activity: Connectedness

1 Pick up a GUI on your computer desktop and move it to another position. What happens the next time you instruct the same action, before closing and reopening the application?

2 What happens when you close and reopen the application, then reopen the same GUI?

3 Try the same exercise with other applications and note down what happens with each GUI.

4 Open three applications by the same software producer (eg Microsoft®) and make a list of the similarities and the differences between the applications.

5 Compare your findings with other members of your group.

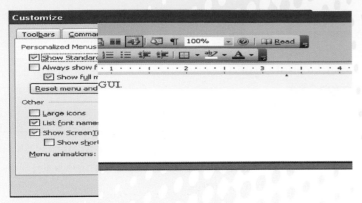

Figure 23.4: Desktop image on top of GUI

If images are sitting behind or in front of other images, then the entire interface will not be visible. An example is that the GUI should appear in front of any text on the desktop. If it is built incorrectly, it could appear behind the existing image on the desktop, which is visually confusing (see Figure 23.4).

To expand on the concept of positioning and layering further, if the positioning of the object has not been accurately arranged then the GUI, or parts of the GUI, may appear behind the main screen. The user will not be able to access the full range of commands, if any.

Another consideration is the positioning on the face of the interface. If the GUI appears too far across the screen, it may be difficult to see or it might obscure other features that need to be visible.

Geons and gross 3D shapes

Geons and gross 3D shapes are used to provide some consistency when reproducing images.

Geons are uncomplicated objects that are made of a range of essential properties that enable the viewer to identify the image from almost any angle. They are less complex to design and easier to recognise than 3D images. They are also relatively cheap to produce. In contrast, 3D images can more easily be misinterpreted due to the perception of the observer. You will need to consider how a user might view an object when designing your GUI.

Gross 3D shapes are used in video games and are also relatively cheap to produce. They do not require exact reproduction and are used to transmit images in **real time**, for example large screens at football matches and other sporting events or security X-ray machines.

Activity: All is not as it would seem

1 What springs to mind when you look at Figure 23.5?
2 Compare your results with those of your peers.

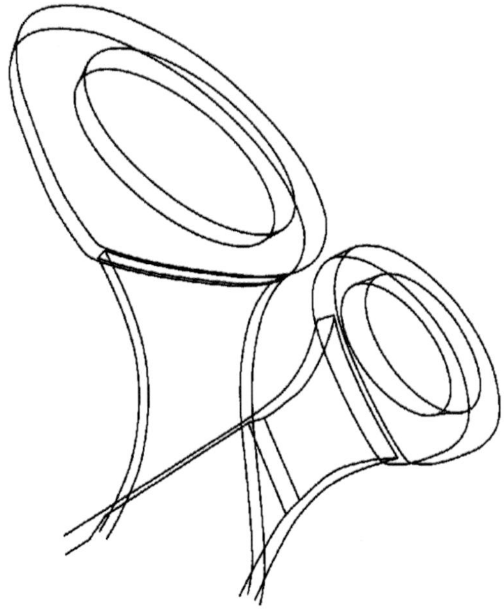

Figure 23.5: What is this 3D image?

Key terms

Geons – 2D images that are quickly recognisable by the user from almost any angle.

Real time – where audio and video signals are transmitted almost instantaneously.

Predictive model – an equation or calculation used to forecast an event.

As well as the cost involved, due to the time taken to design and produce an image, you also need to consider the cost and speed of running such an image. (For more on this subject, see Quantitative measures of effectiveness on page 150).

In some instances cost becomes less of an issue. For example, the use of a gross 3D image produced from a robot on a lunar landing might be essential to present a realistic picture and would be used almost regardless of cost.

As you know, 3D is now more widely accessible, not only on the big screen but also in games. The costs involved are dramatically less than five years ago or even last year.

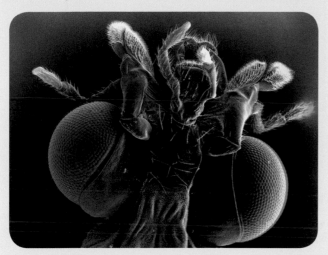

1 Using the Internet, research the topic of 3D to find answers to the following questions:
   - Where is 3D used and what for?
   - How is it designed and produced?
   - Who by?
   - What type of objects represent 2D, 3D, 4D?
2 Make a list of your findings and be prepared to share them with your peers and your group.

Activity: An icon

1 Design a very simple image that could feature on a dialog box/GUI as an icon to represent an action or instruction (eg a door representing exit, a pointing finger, etc).
2 Produce a storyboard identifying the stages for producing the image. (Storyboards are discussed in Unit 28: Website production, page 169.)
3 Produce your icon.
4 Note down exactly how long it takes to carry out stages 1–3 of this activity.
5 Ask one of your peers to review your icon and provide constructive feedback.

2.2 Behaviour models

There are a number of models that predict the way in which an interface or user will behave. Some of these are identified in this subsection.

Predictive models

There are a number of **predictive models** that provide guidance when designing interfaces and systems. This is a way of pre-empting what will happen without having to carry out lengthy research and delay the introduction of the interface while lots of people test it out.

The reaction time to respond to a command from a GUI will vary depending on the user. Consideration must be given to whether or not the interface will be responsive to time, eg shut down if a reaction or command takes too long.

The keystroke-level model (KLM)

KLM recognises very low-level actions. The model breaks down each sequence of operations into individual actions, such as hitting keys on the keyboard, clicking on the mouse, pointing the mouse, moving between using the mouse and the keyboard and back again. Each action is assigned a time in order to calculate how the system will respond.

Activity: I predict...

1 Write down how long you predict it will take to power up your computer, log in and access one application.
2 Carry out the activity while timing. Write down the results and compare with your peers.
3 Try the same activity using all mouse actions and then again, using all keyboard actions where possible.
4 Identify how long it takes for the system to respond.

The throughput (TP)

TP relates to the productivity of the computer. Throughput measures include the amount or speed of processing in response to a command. Other measures of productivity include performance in terms of speed of processing and any variation in relation to the number of tasks and complexity. This is called response time.

Fitts' Law

Fitts' Law is a method for calculating throughput in advance for any system design by predicting human movement and motion based on time and distance (called psychomotor behaviour). It was developed in 1954 to counteract the assumption that the time taken for something to travel from A to B is likely to be based on the distance between the two points. Fitts' Law identified that time depends upon the size of the object to be moved and the size of the object with which it is moved. User time will vary according to user, the location of an icon, menu or GUI, the click of the mouse button or hitting a key and even the pressure applied.

Descriptive models

This section considers three descriptive models:

- the key-action model (KAM)
- Buxton's three state model
- Guiard's model.

The key-action model (KAM)

KAM identifies the need to evaluate how the user will expect the computer to behave or react and how this may be different from how the computer actually reacts to commands. For example, when a user who is completely new to computers is logging onto a computer, they are likely to find it difficult to understand why they have to type in the username and password completely accurately, or cannot log on. Similarly, users will get confused and frustrated when they think they have selected Shift F (for a capital F) but the File menu drops down because they have accidentally hit Alt F.

Sometimes, there is a delay in the computer carrying out a command, perhaps because the system is carrying out a background save, but the user receives feedback with the egg timer, so knows there is something going on and that they need to wait for a while. How will you give your users feedback and how will you make sure that they know what it means and how long they have to wait before the operation is complete?

Other feedback examples include the depression and suppression of buttons on dialog boxes and invitations or steering to the next most likely command by highlighting a button (see Figure 23.6).

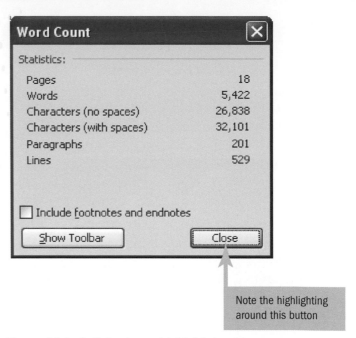

Note the highlighting around this button

Figure 23.6: A dialog box with highlighted button

Buxton's three state model

Buxton's three state model (see Figure 23.7) is concerned with the pressure and dexterity with which users make movements using mice and touchpads. When designing the interface, you should consider the amount of effort or pressure the user will need to make to give or respond to a command. For example, the interface will need to be responsive whether the command is via the mouse, a touchpad on a laptop or a roller button in the keyboard.

This model also identifies the relative ease of using a mouse as opposed to a touchpad. This may depend on the regularity of use. For example, someone who frequently uses a touchpad might argue that it is far easier and quicker to use than a mouse, which requires

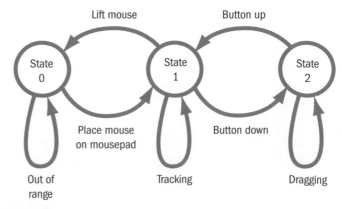

Figure 23.7: Buxton's three state model of graphical input with labels appropriate for mouse interaction

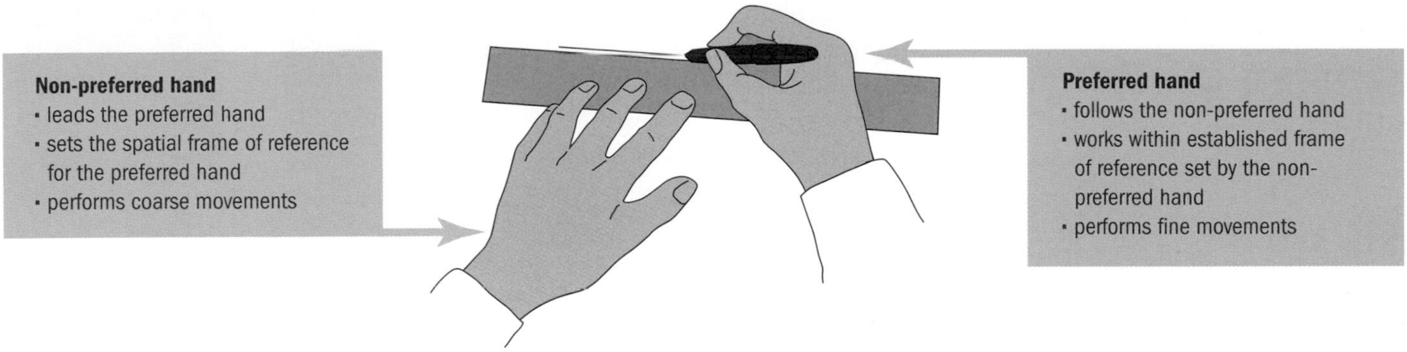

Non-preferred hand
- leads the preferred hand
- sets the spatial frame of reference for the preferred hand
- performs coarse movements

Preferred hand
- follows the non-preferred hand
- works within established frame of reference set by the non-preferred hand
- performs fine movements

Figure 23.8: The Guiard model of bimanual skill

taking a hand away from the keyboard. The same argument might apply to a keyboard user who prefers keystrokes to mouse use.

Guiard's model of bimanual skill

Guiard's model of bimanual skill (see Figure 23.8) relates to the preferred method of interacting with computers and input devices. For example, when designing your interface you must consider the ease of use and you must not rely on the user always inputting data or mouse actions using a preferred hand. The positioning on the interface must also be accessible and logically laid out for use by a left-handed person. Guiard's model identifies that users who use both hands are unlikely to be able to carry out equally effective actions with either hand.

2.3 Information processing

This section explores information processing – in other words, how information is processed (or to be processed) and how fast this is done.

Activity: This would be even better if...

The interface may require the user to make a decision and some decisions take longer than others to make.

1 Identify an interface, perhaps one you use regularly.

2 Make a list of the adaptations that you think would improve the way it currently processes information and/or the speed with which it does this.

3 Be prepared to discuss your results.

Humans as a component

One of the key variables in HCI design is the human end user! The human factor is not only difficult to manage but it can also be difficult to identify people's

Activity: Preferences

1 Select two different interfaces. One might be on the computer while another might be on a standalone game that uses a joystick. Alternatively, it might be the same interface using two different command methods, such as a game operated by a mouse or joystick and the same game using keystroke actions.

2 For each of the two interfaces, using your preferred hand, decide which interface is easier to use and why. Make a list of each action you carry out and its degree of ease. You can use a four-point scale to do this (eg 1 = very easy,

4 = very difficult) and the time (in seconds) it takes to carry out the action.

3 Identify response time and user time.

4 Now carry out the same actions but with your other hand and answer the same questions.

5 Compare the differences in your findings. Overall, which method was easier and with which hand? Why was this? Was the same method easier for both hands? Be prepared to discuss your findings.

needs and expectations. One way to prepare for all eventualities is to carry out a **risk assessment**. For example, if the user selects option X before option Y, what happens?

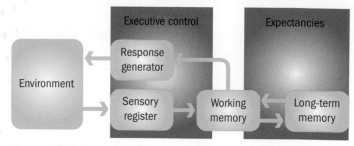

Figure 23.9: A model of human information processing

Key terms

Risk assessment – an analysis of a task against each of the steps that could be taken to achieve the task.

GOMS – short for goals, operators, methods and selection. It provides a model for how the user will behave when carrying out a series of tasks.

Human information processing (HIP)

Human information processing (HIP) means the way in which we absorb information, analyse it, use it and do something with it. Our brains (which can be compared to the hardware of a computer) take the information, then use the mind (the software) in order to process it. The output depends on our previous knowledge, our ability to interpret information and even our willingness to do something with it (as the decision maker).

Activity: How much of a risk?

1 Refer to Guiard's model (see Figure 23.8) and produce a risk assessment based on this question: What happens if the user gives an instruction to the interface with the mouse in the left hand and uses the right-hand mouse button instead of the left?

2 Repeat question 1 for this situation: If a key or the spacebar is selected instead of the mouse, what does the user have to do next if the Esc key is selected?

3 A flow-chart approach is effective in identifying possibilities such as 'If this route is taken what will happen?' In other words, 'What are the risks?' Be prepared to discuss in class.

4 Carry out some Internet research into human information processing and make notes on what you find out.

Improvements in HIP may be achieved by altering the information provided, by improving the ability of decision makers and by the construction of formal models of human decision making, such as the one shown in Figure 23.9.

Overview of goals, operators, methods and selection (GOMS)

The **GOMS** model can predict the time it will take for an action to be carried out or a command to be followed. The designer identifies a goal (outcome of intended action) when using a series of operators and lists the method and selection (ie mouse or keystroke) in order to carry out the action (or command). This enables the designer to calculate the time it will take to execute the action and identify any risks or loopholes – assuming the user carries out the instructions as anticipated. The designer can use the results to identify which method of user interface is more efficient, based on the user's requirements.

2.4 Specialist

To avoid producing an interface that is not accessible for specialist uses, such as for a user with a disability, you might consider designing an interface that uses speech-activated software for input or output for the visually impaired. However, you will need to consider how easy it will be to use if your user has a speech impediment such as a lisp. Would the interface work at all? Would it respond differently to such a user?

For users with visual impairments, refer back to the subsection on the pop out effect (page 138) and consider how it could enhance the appearance and usability of your interface

For those users who are both aurally (to do with hearing) and visually impaired, the most likely option is haptic technology (see page 147). Haptic technology might also be the only option for someone who is severely physically challenged and unable to use their limbs. A design that enables the user to use a pointer to select the desired options could enable independence. Remote control devices or head-up displays can also be used to input or receive output from the interface.

Activity: Accessibility for all

1 Do some further research on how technology can support those users with physical or other challenges.

2 Note down the key points and the sources of all information. Make sure you follow additional links to ensure your information is reliable, comprehensive and up to date.

3 Do you or a friend have a disability? How does the disability affect the ability to interact with

technology? Make a 'wish list' of improvements and research further to identify some potential solutions. Present as a case study or presentation (perhaps a podcast or short video).

4 Discuss with your peers. What else do you need to do in order to meet some or all of the items on the wish list? What is overall your aim and timeframe to achieve?

Assessment activity 23.2

As a result of the meeting where you presented your ideas, the group has asked you to design at least two input and two output interfaces to meet given specifications, using a variety of techniques. **P3** As all the schools and colleges in the area have a number of learners with specialist needs, you have been asked to explain how at least one of your designs could be adapted to meet a specialist need. **M1** At this meeting, they have asked to see an interactive computer input and output based on HCI principles. One member of the group has also asked you to design a DAB radio display or perhaps something for projection to an audience. At this stage, the request is only for the design as it might not be taken any further.

As the group only comprises representatives, they have asked if there is any way their colleagues might be able to experience your presentation. One of these ways might be to blog it.

To enlighten council managers, explain the fundamental principles of HCI design, particularly how it will benefit the tutors and learners. **P2** As you will want to give them the benefit of a range of options, the two input and two output designs need to be sufficiently different. Do not forget that the group are unlikely to have the level of understanding that you do and there are one or two techno-phobics. In order to help them overcome their limited understanding and experience, provide a variety of examples that illustrate or demonstrate these principles, including all

your planning material. **M2** You are hoping that they will be so impressed, you could secure that permanent contract as a result.

Grading tips

- The assignment could benefit from a presentation supported by design documentation (storyboards) and annotated diagrams/charts.

- Consider being creative in how you present your explanations, perhaps by adding audio to a presentation or providing a podcast. **P2**

- Although a glossary might seem like a good idea for those techno-phobics, a series of overlays showing and describing the input and output designs may be more visually illuminating. You could even represent them in model format. **P3**

- A blog has been suggested and this could encourage interaction from council managers. You could also include a FAQs section. To make it truly interactive, you could include a mini self assessment at the start of the presentation so managers could test their own perceptions and understanding and then an evaluation of their findings at the end! **M1 M2**

PLTS

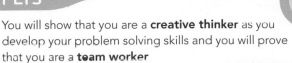

You will show that you are a **creative thinker** as you develop your problem solving skills and you will prove that you are a **team worker**

Functional skills

This task will use your **ICT** skills as well as your **English** speaking and listening skills.

3 Be able to design and implement user interfaces

When designing and producing your own simple interactive computer input and output, you will need to demonstrate that you have taken care to base all your decisions on the HCI principles covered in Section 2.

This section focuses on how these principles apply to input, output and specialist situations.

3.1 Input

This subsection relates to the tools that a user is likely to use to input information, such as the keyboard, mouse and monitor.

Keyboard/mouse/monitor

A simplified input might rely on mouse use only, with minimum use of keystrokes, which generally rely on memory. However, some users prefer to use keystrokes and some may not wish to use the mouse at all. Your system might rely on the mouse or keyboard for some commands or you could offer your users a choice, so that there is more than one way of carrying out the same action. If there is the chance of more than one user, then there is likely to be more than one preference.

Activity: More than one way

1 Compile a list of at least 20 different actions and list three (or more) alternative methods to carry out the same action.

2 Go back over the list and identify your preferred method for each action.

3 Compare your results with your peers or family members.

4 Continue to add to the list every time you discover another action and the alternative methods of carrying it out.

For any single Microsoft® command, there are very often at least four different ways to carry it out – for example, to save a file: File, Save; Ctrl S; Shift F12; or the Save icon on the toolbar. In some cases there is the shortcut menu option as well. The user may be particularly experienced (a power user) and equipped with a wealth of knowledge and techniques that they expect to use. Equally, the user may be a novice, new to interacting with computers. (This is discussed further in Unit 12: IT technical support, in Book 1).

Activity: How long?

1 Select one of the actions you identified in the previous activity and time how long it takes to carry out each of the methods. Write the times next to the method and then compare with your peers.

2 Once you have made these comparisons, consider whether they are fair comparisons. For example, if you click on the toolbar button to print a document, does the overall action take longer or less time than selecting from the menu, and is the result the same? Bring your results to class for further work.

Minimise keystrokes and mouse movements

Another consideration is the use of the mouse and how this will interact with the computer. For example, if the GUI interacts with the mouse, you will need to ensure that the user knows which mouse button and how many clicks are required in order to carry out a command. When designing your interface, you will also need to consider what is happening with the other mouse button, as it cannot just lie redundant.

To simplify your system and perhaps reduce the development time, you might decide to minimise the number of keystrokes and mouse movements. Pay attention to the layout of the interface so that users can locate commands and input areas without having to move around the interface in an illogical order – this would rely too heavily on the dexterity of the user.

Activity: Office extras

1 Try the Microsoft® option StickyKeys. What is its purpose?

2 Who would find it beneficial and why?

3 What is the narrator?

4 How can visually impaired users receive feedback from the keyboard?

5 Find out if there are any other adaptations included for users with disabilities.

6 What other extras does Microsoft® provide within Windows®?

Logical sequencing

You must consider whether a logical sequence to perform an action is necessary or whether it should be up to the user. For example, if your system expects the user to save after instructing a command or inputting data, this may not suit all users, some of whom may wish to save first or during the action to avoid losing the data. You will need to ensure the system responds in a consistent way, whether the user clicks softly or hits keys firmly.

Use of other input devices

This subsection explores other input devices that may be preferred by the user. For example, an end user might want to use a **concept keyboard**. Or you might be asked to design a system that responds to voice input or operates by using a **joystick**.

The benefit of using a joystick is that it is easy to use – no specialist knowledge or dexterity is needed to play a game. For example, in early versions of space invader games and flight simulators, specific keystrokes such as Ctrl + Shift + arrow keys were required.

Many devices used today have built-in **haptic technology**, enabling us to interact with the device using a touch screen. The user can drag and drop applications and files or carry out commands by touching the screen instead of the keyboard or mouse.

A concept keyboard

Research states that most, if not all, of us will experience a disability of some degree at some stage of our lives. The disability could be, for example, a broken wrist, RSI (see page 128), a bad back or even headaches. Each affects ways of working and may require specialist input devices.

Key terms

Concept keyboard – also called an overlay keyboard. This has keys that have been preset to specific functions. The keys often have images or symbols to guide the user. A concept keyboard can do anything a QWERTY keyboard and/or mouse can do. For example, it can be used to access the Internet, run programs, play movies and music.

Joystick – an input device that can be used for playing video games.

Haptic technology – technology that enables the user to interact with the device using their sense of touch. For example, ticket machines, cash points, computer games, mobile phones and other such devices, all use haptic (touch screen) technology.

DAB – stands for digital audio broadcasting. DAB radios require no tuning and provide a clearer, crisper sound than traditional radios.

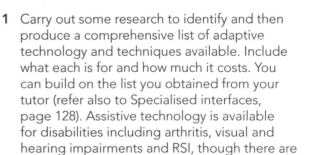

Activity: What does it do and how much is it?

1   Carry out some research to identify and then produce a comprehensive list of adaptive technology and techniques available. Include what each is for and how much it costs. You can build on the list you obtained from your tutor (refer also to Specialised interfaces, page 128). Assistive technology is available for disabilities including arthritis, visual and hearing impairments and RSI, though there are many more which you will discover during your research (eg StickyKeys).

2   You will need to bring this list to class for further work.

Designs for other input devices

Until now the focus has been mainly on designing a GUI for a computer, but GUIs are also needed for other devices, such as mobile phones and PDAs, as well as voice-activated systems for **DAB** radios.

3.2 Output

This section explores systems designed for the output of information.

Monitor or print

You will already be familiar with some output devices, such as the interface on a scanner or printer. Some printers do not require a computer to read the data or image in order to provide a print-out. These printers either take a memory card containing digital images from a camera or connect directly to the camera via a **USB** port. These types of printer can be used by someone who has little or no knowledge of how to use a computer, yet wants to print out photographs with ease.

Key terms

USB – stands for universal serial bus. It is a connection method that enables files to be transferred and stored.

Interactive whiteboard – a screen that has a touch-sensitive display and can connect to the Internet, file servers and computer applications. Information can be written on the screen with a special marker pen and changes can be made and stored in the same way as when working on a computer.

Activity: Finite steps

1 Identify the steps you would expect to take when printing directly from a digital camera to a printer. Include how to put a memory card into the printer and obtain print-outs.

2 Draw a flow diagram to set out these steps.

Use of other devices

There are other output tools which use on-screen GUIs such as data projectors for projecting images and presentations onto a screen. **Interactive whiteboard** menus are activated by using the mouse, touching the board with a special pen or using a finger.

These menus are used to access many of the features available on a computer, with additional features such as writing on the board, underlining text from the Internet and saving note pages for accessing later. Specialist software for interpreting text into speech for voice output is another output example.

3.3 Testing

A major part of design is testing. The testing of the design from a prototype stage is how the design can be perfected. It needs to be tested in many ways, under different circumstances, conditions and by different users. Each testing stage needs to be documented, along with the details of the when, where, who, how and what.

Testing will be carried out against the original specification to measure the impact and identify changes for improvement. The documented records will need to include anything appropriate and a description of how the result was achieved. The process of testing is usually captured in a test log.

Activity: The times when I'm the guinea pig

1 Make a list of any occasions you have tested a product or service and the nature of that product or service. Identify:
   (a) what was being tested
   (b) how it was tested
   (c) whether it was voluntary
   (d) how the designer or producer received feedback
   (e) whether changes were made as a result.

2 Now consider how you will test your design. Make a plan of how you will do this, when and with whom and most importantly, how you will gather the feedback. What types of questions will you need to ask? How much time will it take and how many times will you need to test it?

3 Design a test log and compare with those of your peers. Are they similar or different, could you combine several to result in a comprehensive test log?

Simple testing

The point of simple testing is to measure the fitness for purpose against the original specification at a fairly low level, to ensure it meets a set of predetermined quality standards. The testing will vary according to the product. When working within a closed system, the test will involve internal mechanics of some kind whereas a wider system will involve testing the behaviour and will therefore include sequencing. A wider system is likely to be more complex and the variables will be less controllable. For example, a closed system, such as a clock, is reliant upon its internal mechanics to keep it going, providing it is wound up or has a power supply. On the other hand, a computer or software working in a wider system may behave very differently, depending on the actions of the user.

Recording tests

There is software available that gathers information (intelligence) on user interaction. The actions performed on a computer are recorded and can be recalled. As the process is complex and variable, the recording gathers information such as the type of interaction, when it took place, how long it took and the sequence of events. This will enable a test engineer to evaluate the series of events and their impact and to consider what changes and further development may be needed.

3.4 Documentation

When creating a design, there is no hard and fast rule that says it must be done one way only or that it has to be done on paper. It is fine to use whatever method is accepted within the organisation. However, it is crucial to document work and therefore designs. Imagine if Louis Pasteur had not documented his medical findings in the 1800s that have saved billions of lives.

It is important to have a plan. In order to design something, you need to have an outline and key objective. At the same time, you may have experience of a design evolving through an iterative process (going over and over, refining and changing). This is also valid. Documenting the stages can be done through pictures or storyboards and flowcharts. (Storyboards are discussed in Unit 28: Website production, page 169.)

You could also use rich picture diagrams for the first stages in the design process. These are somewhat like mind maps, where the objective (main theme) is placed in the middle and link words are positioned around the outside. A good example can be found online, and can be accessed by going to www.technologystudent.com/PDF4/richyl.pdf.

Structured charts

These charts are hierarchical and used to display a breakdown of components to a reasonable level of detail (see Figure 23.10 below). They are used in structured programming to display the components of the program as a tree and provide a clear direction as to the relationships between the programme modules. You may be learning more about this type of structure in data engineering models.

When designing any form of system or product, the records should always be dated. As the design develops, progresses and changes are made, the records need to include written explanations and

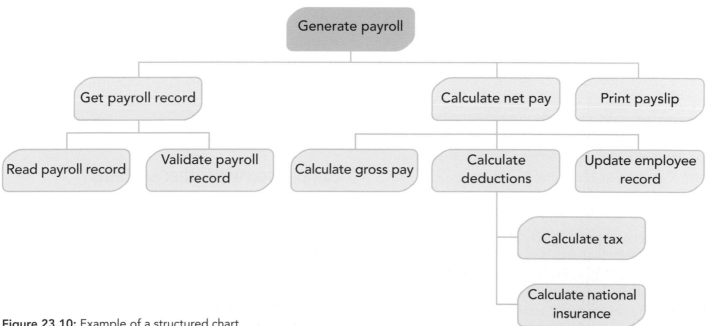

Figure 23.10: Example of a structured chart

annotations to ensure the process can be followed again. This will enable tracking of the evolution of the design to implementation and beyond.

3.5 Quantitative measures of effectiveness

It is clear that testing is a major feature of design and without it things will neither develop nor improve. The most effective and reliable way to identify differences and make comparisons is to carry out both **quantitative** and **qualitative research**. Research methods might include use of questionnaires or surveys, interviewing and reading. This section helps you to identify some areas you should include in this research.

Key terms

Quantitative research – involves collecting data that can be measured and counted. The data collected can usually be presented in the form of graphs, tables and charts. It is important to use a large enough sample to ensure that you have used sufficient 'quantity' for the results to be valid and not guesswork.

Qualitative research – involves collecting information about people's opinions, views and preferences about something. It allows you to make 'quality' judgements about your findings (based on fact, not on your own opinions).

Research can return different results, depending on the number (quantity) of responses to each question. This will determine the value of the research outcomes.

For example, if you ask three young people from a large city if they prefer ITV to Channel 4 and two out of three say yes, does this mean that the majority of the whole population of the UK also agree? You might have unknowingly asked predominantly ITV viewers, whereas if you asked another group of people (perhaps from a different place or of a different age or background), they might give you different answers.

You need to make sure that you ask a large enough sample of people, who are representative of all the people who will be using your interface.

When you carry out research you will need a checklist containing the questions you are going to ask, otherwise you may ask different questions to different people and the results of the research will not compare exactly. The saying often used is 'you can't compare apples with pears'.

Quantitative measures of research include speed, costs and comparisons with the original needs and with other systems. These all produce quantitative data that can be measured.

Input speeds

One of the features of an interface that is fundamental to its effectiveness is the speed at which it interacts with the user. Issues of speed include:

- keying – how quickly users can input a command
- throughput – the speed at which the user can (or has to) type in any data (does the GUI time out if reaction isn't fast enough?)
- the speed of throughput (such as the response back from the interface)
- speed of comprehension of output – the length of time it takes the user to comprehend the result.

Comparative costs

Another major factor to consider is the running costs of the interface in comparison to what was used before, which may have been a more traditional approach. If there are a large number of images on the interface or it relies on other programs to support it, then it is likely that the cost of power increases. In addition, you will need to consider whether the interface requires additional costs of staffing to use or maintain it.

Comparison with original needs

You will also need to make a comparison between the product you have provided and the original needs of the user. How closely does it match the original design or requirement of the originator? To find this out, you will need to ask questions such as:

- How many features are fully included?
- How many are partially included?
- How many features are not included?
- Does it meet the needs of the client/user?

Comparison with other systems

It is important for you to compare your system with other similar systems, as these will provide ideas for further improvements. However, bear in mind that 'you can't compare apples with pears' and be realistic with your evaluation. For example, if the system your interface is running on does not have the power or performance of the system you are comparing it with, it will not be a fair comparison.

3.6 Qualitative measures of effectiveness

Qualitative measures are more subjective and the value of the information you obtain will depend largely on the quality of the questions you ask. For example, if you ask a closed question such as 'Do you like food?' the answer is likely to be simply 'Yes'. This doesn't tell you what the person likes about food or what types of food they prefer. Therefore, any evaluation of the answers provided would not provide sufficient information to ensure the food was to the person's liking. However, if you asked an open question such as 'What type of food do you like best?' the answer would be far more informative. If you were then to ask 'Why?' you would be even better informed. The main difference between these questions is that the first question is a closed question (which returns a yes/no answer) and the subsequent questions are open and more meaningful.

Always try to avoid asking leading questions, as they encourage people to provide the answer wanted rather than one that reflects what they really think. This makes the answer unreliable. An example of a leading question is 'Do you like tomatoes best because they have a better flavour?'

Qualitative measures of effectiveness include user satisfaction. This will provide qualitative data because you will be collecting the users' opinions.

User satisfaction

An essential question is the level of satisfaction by the end user. The end user might not be the same person as the commissioner or originator. Therefore the questions you ask are likely to be different.

To establish the level of user satisfaction you can provide the user with a number of statements or questions and ask the user to grade each statement according to whether they agree/disagree or are satisfied/unsatisfied. Your grading system could use number 1 as the highest level and 4 as the lowest. It is a good idea not to use five grades, as many people tend to go for the middle number, as the easy option.

Using numbers makes the survey quick and easy to complete and is an easy way to make comparisons and identify trends. For example, you can identify whether the lowest level of satisfaction occurs among a particular type of user.

Don't forget to ask the people you are surveying to give details such as their job title and department, where they work and perhaps what they use the interface for (if there are different uses). Asking for their age and level of computer experience might also be useful. Questions you should include in order to determine user satisfaction should cover the following:

- knowledge required
- skills/expertise required
- time to use the interface
- ease of use
- limitations
- usefulness of results
- closeness to original requirement.

Comparison with other systems

When carrying out your research, include a question that asks the user to make a comparison with other similar systems they have used. This type of question can be graded 1–4 as discussed above. It might also be a good idea to include an open-ended question to get their opinion, for example 'In what ways is the new system better than the old one and in what ways is it worse?' This will help with your evaluation.

Evaluation of interfaces

Once you have carried out your surveys, using these guidelines and including some questions of your own, you need to aggregate your results. It is also a good idea to present the results in a graph, as this can be easier to evaluate.

Judgements of effectiveness

Every design must be tested during its build to ensure it meets the users' expectations and requirements. When you carry out these staged checks, use a checklist to remind you what you are going to test and how you are going to measure its effectiveness.

You will need to measure effectiveness and evaluate interfaces to demonstrate your understanding and analytical skills. You should refer to some of the experimentation, such as speed and ease of use. You will also need to identify how closely the system matches the original goal – that is, the degree to which it is fit for purpose.

Although you do not need to include exact costings, you should compare costs of different interfaces and to what degree the interface is value for money. You will need to identify the good points and bad points against which improvements can be made.

Improvements

Having carried out the evaluation, you will know what needs to be improved. You will need to identify a plan in order to achieve those improvements. It is also important to evaluate why each improvement is needed and how it enhances the design. For example, does the change make the design more effective or simply more colourful?

A major challenge is dealing with our feelings and emotions. Are we truly being objective or simply resisting change because we spent so long 'doing that bit' or felt 'that turned out really well, and is something to be proud of', yet it does not actually meet the need for which it was designed.

Activity: Gathering feedback

1 Explore the Internet for websites requesting feedback as a matter of course. How do they do it, what questions do they ask?

2 Consider how many times you have engaged in giving feedback and, if not, why not? Was it because you couldn't be bothered or you didn't understand the questions?

3 Now try to find a website or alternative place where you have been asked for feedback. In particular, try to locate an example where you receive feedback from your comments. Find any examples you particularly like and decide why you like them.

4 You are likely to be asked for your comments and suggestions at your place of work or study. What methods do they use? How do you find out what changed as a result of the feedback?

5 Decide how you will present your findings and share with your group.

Assessment activity 23.3

The group has met again to review your designs and is fairly confident that the concept of the project could revolutionise the way learners of all ages and abilities learn. The group has now requested that you create your designs, although they are prepared to accept that practically these might not be the same designs you presented at the meeting. **P4**

Discussions arose at the meeting where they discussed some changes. However, some of their suggestions might not be realistic, particularly in the timescale and with the resources you have to hand. So they agreed that where it is not possible to create all changes, existing designs could be used but have asked that you present your final designs with clearer and creative examples of how they will work. **P6**

You will need to clearly explain how to interact with your designs and also provide some context as to where they might be used. Explain how you tested the effectiveness of different designs and what further developments you carried out as a result of feedback. **P5**

Be prepared for their questions. You will no doubt be keen to give some indication as to how the effectiveness could be measured. You should also produce a report describing the good points and the areas for improvement about each and any potential improvements. To add context to what you present you will probably find it useful to make comparisons with those being developed commercially. **D2 M3**

Grading tips

- Have you thought about creating your design and making a short video of the different stages or key points you want to promote? **P4 P5**

- A blog, with images, would make interesting reading and bring to life your designs and proposals. You could also use screen dumps. **P6**

- To explain your designs in context, add some video to your presentation with your designs being tested or perhaps images of the stages with voiceovers. **M3**

- An interactive GUI with the option to record might enhance the feedback process. **D2**

PLTS

You will have many ways that you are a **creative thinker** by developing your problem solving skills and you will also need to be a **self manager.**

Functional skills

You will use your **ICT** skills as well as your **English** writing, speaking and listening skills.

Kelly works for her brother, who runs a small advertising company. They have lots of small clients. Kelly's job is to manage the administration and accounts, booking appointments and responding to any enquiries that come in via post or telephone. Their single-page website generates few enquiries. Her brother liaises with their clients and works hard at bringing in new clients.

Their mission is to be 'ahead of the game' but Kelly can see that her brother's mission might not be reflecting the company's practices. For a start, he seems to spend a lot of money on mass mail shots and expects her to trawl through trade magazines and other catalogues for new customers to bring on board.

It seems to Kelly that because her brother is so busy out on the road with customers, he doesn't have time to evaluate the cost in relation to the return of new leads.

Kelly thinks they should be practising what they preach and has some wild ideas, but doesn't know how to carry them out or even if they would or could be possible. She really needs a creative and knowledgeable 'IT person' to help them and is quite convinced that if she could find someone who understood their objective and could put together a 'whizzy' proposal with practical examples, her brother would be keen.

They are very eager to get advertising contracts with public and third (voluntary) sectors and would like to access the specialist market for those organisations working with disabilities and other special needs. They would like to be in a position of promoting charitable organisations, perhaps for free or not-for-profit, supported by larger contracts. If they could, they might be able to win some bigger contracts, perhaps with the local hospital, doctors' surgeries, clinics and such like. After all, they need to promote their services like any other business and their clients all have different abilities and needs.

Think about it!

1 How could you help Kelly and her brother to expand? Where would you start?

2 What suggestions could you make that would match their aspirational mission?

3 How would you present your suggestions so both Kelly and her brother can understand your proposals?

Just checking

1. What does predictive modelling mean?
2. What does a head-up display do?
3. What features does Microsoft® apply to GUIs to make the user feel comfortable?
4. What are the main features of the KAM model?
5. How could we improve the way in which we process information?
6. When would you apply the Guiard model?
7. Why are humans one of the key variables in HCI design?
8. What is the difference between descriptive and behaviour modelling?
9. Name at least five different methods for giving instructions to a computer.
10. Why might you decide to minimise the number of keystrokes and mouse movements used?
11. Give some examples of where output devices do not require a PC.
12. Explain the difference between open, closed and leading questions.
13. Give three examples of types of research that might be unreliable or of little value.
14. Describe how to carry out testing of a design.
15. What is the difference between quantitative and qualitative research?

Assignment tips

- Get in the habit of evaluating the effectiveness of the technology with which you interact. Make notes of what works well and what you would want to improve and why.

- Keep an ongoing record of all sources of information so you can refer back at any time.

- Keep screen dumps as you go along, you might find them particularly useful to annotate with your thoughts and ideas.

- Do question: why is it done that way, what influenced the designer, how user-friendly is it, how does it meet the need, what could be improved?

- Do involve other people as often as you can in helping you evaluate your work.

- Try to talk to someone who is involved in design, whatever the product.

28 Website production

The Internet is perhaps the most important IT development in the last few decades; it has provided new ways to communicate and share information and, in doing so, has revolutionised the way people and businesses use IT.

In this unit you will learn how to design and create interactive websites. You will also discover the factors that can improve website performance and security issues affecting websites.

Being able to build websites is an important skill and one which is in high demand in the modern working world. Some organisations choose to employ a dedicated web designer in their company who works solely on their site; alternatively some organisations will hire an external web design company to create and manage their site. However, not all businesses can afford this and some, especially smaller companies, will be looking for a member of their staff who can maintain their website. Therefore there is a strong career route and high levels of opportunity for those who wish to study web design further. Conversely for those who do not wish to take this further, it is still a very useful skill to have and one which may elevate you above the competition when looking for employment.

Learning outcomes

After completing this unit, you should:

1. understand web architecture and components
2. understand the factors that influence website performance
3. be able to design websites
4. be able to create websites.

Assessment and grading criteria

This table shows you what you must do in order to achieve a pass, merit or distinction grade, and where you can find activities in this book to help you.

To achieve a **pass** grade the evidence must show that you are able to:	To achieve a **merit** grade the evidence must show that, in addition to the pass criteria, you are able to:	To achieve a **distinction** grade the evidence must show that, in addition to the pass and merit criteria, you are able to:
P1 outline the web architecture and components which enable Internet and web functionality **See Assessment activity 28.1, page 161**	**M1** explain the role of web architecture in website communications **See Assessment activity 28.1, page 161**	**D1** explain the role of the TCP/IP protocol and how it links to application layer protocols **See Assessment activity 28.1, page 161**
P2 explain the user side and server side factors that influence the performance of a website **See Assessment activity 28.2, page 166**		
P3 explain the security risks and protection mechanisms involved in website performance **See Assessment activity 28.2, page 166**		
P4 using appropriate design tools, design an interactive website to meet a client need **See Assessment activity 28.3, page 174**	**M2** explain the tools and techniques used in the creation of an interactive website **See Assessment activity 28.3, page 174**	**D2** discuss the techniques that can be used on web pages to aid user access to information **See Assessment activity 28.3, page 174**
P5 create an interactive website to meet a client need **See Assessment activity 28.4, page 184**	**M3** improve the effectiveness of a website on the basis of a client review **See Assessment activity 28.4, page 184**	**D3** demonstrate that a created website meets the defined requirements and achieves the defined purpose **See Assessment activity 28.4, page 184**

How you will be assessed

For this unit you will complete four tasks:

- create a reference booklet explaining the hardware, software and other technology needed for a website

- write a short report on the user and server side features that affect website performance

- produce detailed designs for a website

- build and review the website you have designed.

William, BTEC National IT learner

I had always wondered exactly how websites worked and this unit gave me the answers. It was interesting in the first project to find out all the technology needed to create a website, then put it up on the Internet for people to see and use.

The second project looked at the performance on the website and all the different things that can affect it. I really enjoyed looking at the different file types and discovering that how you save your images will have an effect on your site. I was also interested in learning about the risks, such as hackers and viruses, and how you can protect your site against them.

The last two projects were really good, as I got to design and build my own website. When building it I had to be very careful to follow my design and make sure I met all of the user requirements, which helped me to achieve a distinction grade.

Throughout this unit I was fascinated by all the things we learned and was really happy with the website I made.

Over to you!

- **Which areas do you think you might find challenging about this unit?**
- **What might you do to prepare for this unit?**
- **Design and functionality of websites are important in this unit. Name five websites which you think are well designed and five websites which work well (eg are user-friendly, easy to navigate, etc).**

1 Understand web architecture and components

Perceptions of the Internet

The Internet has been around for only a relatively short time, coming into general use in the 1990s. There are differing opinions about it – some people think it is the best thing to have ever been invented, while others are still very wary of it.

- Create a set of questions to determine a user's perception of the World Wide Web.
- Ask these questions to as many people as possible, preferably from different age groups, and record their answers clearly.
- Analyse your findings and identify any patterns that emerge.

1.1 Web architecture

To allow a website to be seen across the Internet, it must be **uploaded** on to a **web server**.

The process of uploading involves a protocol called **FTP** (file transfer protocol). FTPing can be done straight through a browser or using a program such as CuteFTP.

It is not only the web pages that must be uploaded on to the web server, but all other associated files. This includes image, video and sound files. This is because these files are not embedded into web pages, but linked to them, remaining as separate entities.

Activity: Uploading to a web server

Research using the Internet to discover the difference between uploading through a browser and a program. Make notes for future use in your coursework.

A web server holds the live copy of the web page which can be seen by the public.

There are several web server software applications such as Internet Information Services (IIS), which comes bundled with modern versions of the Windows® operating system or Apache HTTP Server.

Key terms

Uploading – the process of putting a website on to a web server so it can be distributed across the Internet.

Web server – a server which distributes web pages on to the Internet.

FTP – stands for file transfer protocol. It is the protocol used to upload web pages on to a web server. Unusually, the term is used as both a noun and a verb.

IP address – a unique number which identifies a computer on a network, in the format of four numbers separated by full stops, eg 127.0.0.1

Hyperlinks – originally called hypertext, these are words that are interactive and, when clicked, open a web page or file.

Proxy server – a server that acts as a connector to other servers, either for security, speed or more dubious reasons, such as circumventing restrictions.

Router – a network device which can direct data traffic to the correct destination.

Internet service providers (ISPs)

An Internet Service Provider (ISP) supplies the connection with the rest of the world. They link a web server with the rest of the Internet. The ISP will usually determine what type of connection they have, for example if an ISP provides a maximum of only 1 Mb broadband, that is the fastest connection any user using that ISP can obtain. Most areas in the UK are serviced by several ISPs, each providing different competitive features such as different speeds of connection, levels of capping (maximum amount of download or upload per month), prices and additional features such as free email, web space on their servers or support. More remote places in the UK, however, have fewer ISPs and therefore fewer features and less competitive rates to choose from, but nationally the level of Internet connection is increasing all the time.

Web hosting services

To be available on the Internet all websites must be hosted on a web server. A website owner can host a site themselves but they must have the equipment and Internet connection to cope with the number of users accessing the site. It is usually easier and more cost effective to pay for web hosting services. This is where the website owner pays for space on an existing web server. These hosts not only provide space but website management facilities can also be included in the fee such as maintaining uptime, providing traffic monitoring and technical support. Fees are usually calculated based on estimated number of users accessing it, features on the site (eg a site hosting an eCommerce site will take more of the host's bandwidth than a simple static site) and additional features required.

Domains

Each website is identified by the **IP address** of its web server. However, they are difficult to remember, are meaningless in terms of what the website contains and are easy to mistype. Therefore a website on the Internet needs to purchase a domain name, which can be linked to the IP address. A domain name is the characters that appear between the prefix (eg www.) and the suffix (eg .com), for example 'google'.

A domain name should be easy for the user to remember, simple to type and meaningful, reflecting the site's content. Usually short names are best, but iwantoneofthose.com and webuyanycar.com are examples where whole phrases have been used successfully. A useful thing to remember is that the existence of a site will only spread by word of mouth if it is easy to say, as well as type.

Also consider purchasing similar domain names to the one you have chosen, in case a user mistypes it or

forgets a section. For example, www.edexcel.com also owns www.edexcel.co.uk, www.edexel.com and www.edecel.com.

World Wide Web

Although the terms Internet and World Wide Web are often used interchangeably, there is a subtle difference between them. Essentially the Internet is the collection of pages and the content of this huge network, whereas the World Wide Web is the technology that allows it to exist: the pages, the web servers, etc. Tim Berners-Lee was the inventor of hypertext, which we now call **hyperlinks**, the fundamental tool that underpins the World Wide Web and allows the content of the Internet to exist.

1.2   Components

There are many interrelated components on the Internet. They fall into the categories of hardware, software and networking.

The main hardware used for websites are servers such as web servers, email servers and **proxy servers**.

Routers are a key networking component in Internet networking and are usually used at the ISP level. They are the devices which can direct traffic to the right locations, whether going to a web server or back out to the user.

Did you know?

Data is transferred across the World Wide Web by bouncing data from node to node, to eventually reach the desired destination. A node may be a router or a web server or any piece of technology that can act as a conduit to pass the data package through. It is incredible to think that this transfer happens in less than a second!

The main programs used for the Internet are browser and email. A browser is used to view web pages. There are a variety available including Microsoft® Internet Explorer® (which comes standard with the Windows® operating system), Mozilla® Firefox® or Opera™ (free to download from the Internet) and Safari® (for the Apple® platform, including portable devices such as the iPhone®). Different browsers provide different toolbars and functionality, and arguably speed of loading pages, although this is more dependent on the user's Internet connection.

Email can either be accessed through a program, such as Microsoft® Outlook®, or on the Web. Some ISPs offer a free email address as part of their deal. There are a variety of email services on the Internet, some free such as Gmail, and some for which you pay a fee such as www.fastmail.fm.

Protocols

Protocols are the agreed way that different systems can talk to each other, sometimes called a 'handshake'. They work a little like a translator does when two people who speak different languages are trying to communicate.

TCP/IP (transmission control protocol/Internet protocol) is responsible for transporting data and making sure it reaches the right address. It consists of four layers – link layer, Internet layer, transport layer and application layer – and is included in every data package that is sent across the Internet. Each of these layers deals with a different issue. The link layer is the lowest and deals with hardware, navigating through the myriad of routers, servers and other machinery to reach its destination. The Internet layer focuses on targeting the IP address. The transport layer establishes communications between hosts and moves the package towards its destination.

The application layer, the highest layer, contains other protocols including HTTP, HTTPS and SMTP. The hypertext transfer protocol (HTTP – an acronym you may have noticed at the beginning of each web address) sends out a request to the client to establish permission to transfer data. The client may be the final destination or just a node on the journey. In HTTPS, the S stands for Secure and does the same job but ensures a secure connection. This is used in eCommerce, banking websites and where private data is being transferred. Simple mail transfer protocol (SMTP) is the main protocol for the transfer of email. Other protocols which you may have heard about include POP (post office protocol) and IMAP (Internet message access protocol) which operate at the client-level to access mail servers.

1.3 Web functionality

As technology improves new functionality is being created. Internet connections become faster and more reliable, and it becomes more affordable.

Web 2.0

Web 2.0 refers to a new range of uses for the web which are focused on interactivity, user content and information sharing. It does not refer to a new version of the Internet, but instead the new way it is being used. Rather than accessing information on the Internet in a passive way, Web 2.0 allows the user to interact, add their knowledge and opinions, contribute, share and challenge. It includes:

- Wikis – a place where all users can contribute to information, the biggest example of which is Wikipedia, an encyclopedia website where anyone can contribute to any article or even create new ones

- Blogs – online journals; any person can become a blogger and create a blog which is usually public (although there are some private ones); tools are provided for readers to comment and contribute

- Social networking – sites such as Facebook, LinkedIn and Twitter, which allow people to communicate by signing up and creating a profile; they are then given tools with which to correspond, for example through chatting or playing games and are encouraged to make 'friends'; there are also similar sites such as Flickr, which allow users to share photographs

- Online applications – rather than purchasing a program and installing it to a local computer, online applications allow the user to use programs on the Internet; this means they are accessible anywhere and are often free or have a small subscription fee; Google™ Documents is a good example of this.

One of the results of Web 2.0 is the possibility of cloud computing, an exciting prospect which is beginning to be realised, although there are still a number of issues surrounding it. Cloud computing is where programs, files and data are not stored on the user's computer or on a server, but instead in 'the cloud', where shared resources are joined together in one mass of on-demand technology. This is a huge shift in the concept of networking. The advantages include being able to access your programs and files from any computer which can connect to the Internet, and no longer having to worry about storage (hard drives, memory sticks, etc) as all files would be in the cloud. This would mean the nature of personal computers and laptops would change – true mobile working would be possible, from anywhere at any time. The disadvantages include a lack of trust that the cloud is reliable and that programs and data could be lost. Also, there may be concerns about the security of data, especially financial, personal or business data. As this is such a new and esoteric concept a large proportion of people are struggling to understand it and therefore mistrust it.

Did you know?

The term Web 3.0 is beginning to be used, although as it is so new there are disagreements as to its actual meaning and it will still be a little time until it is in common usage. Look up Web 3.0 and see for yourself what is being predicted for the future of the Internet.

Assessment activity 28.1

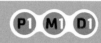

Fancy That! is a business selling fancy dress costumes. They want to create a website to advertise their business with a catalogue the customers can look through. They hope in the future to sell their products online.

1 Create a reference booklet for Fancy That! which will:

   (a) outline the web architecture and components that will enable Internet and web functionality for them **P1**

   (b) explain the role of web architecture in website communication **M1**

   (c) explain the role of the TCP/IP protocol and how it links to application layer protocols. **D1**

Grading tips

- The outline could take the form of a short report or flow diagram that shows the different stages and the information which passes through them. **P1**

- When discussing website communications, describe in detail how information is moved around and shared. Make sure to refer to Web 2.0. **M1**

- When describing the layer protocols, ensure it relates to TCP/IP. **D1**

PLTS

Use your skills as an **independent enquirer** to carry out further research, and as a **reflective learner** to use the research to compile your booklet.

Functional skills

Bringing information together for your booklet could provide evidence for **ICT** skills when finding and selecting information and developing, presenting and communicating information.

2 Understand the factors that influence website performance

2.1 User side factors

The capabilities of the user's system must be taken into consideration because, if not, people who may become potential users could be prohibited from using the site.

Download speed

The speed of the user's Internet connection will determine how quickly the web page is downloaded.

- **Dial-up**: This is the traditional method of connection. It uses the existing analogue telephone lines and it has remained popular for many years. The earliest type had an average speed of 56 Kbps.
- **ISDN** (integrated services digital network): To achieve faster speeds, digital lines needed to be connected. ISDN could reach speeds of 128 Kbps.
- **DSL** (digital subscriber line): Using these digital lines, DSL was introduced. It is the basis for broadband. The most common in the UK is ADSL (asynchronous digital subscriber line) and it can currently reach speeds from 1 Mbps to 8 Mbps, although Cable is also gaining popularity with a current maximum speed of 6 Mbps.
- **Broadband**: This technology is constantly being developed and faster speeds are already conceivable in the near future, with even 100 Mbps being proposed in Japan.

You should ensure that your website will work satisfactorily on a 56K modem as well as the latest broadband speeds. This way you will not exclude any potential users from your site.

PC performance factors

As the connection speed will determine the rate of download, so the computer's components will affect the speed with which it is displayed and with which users interact with it.

You must take into consideration that a user's PC may not have a fast processor or large memory capacity and so you must decide between a high level of user specification requirements and a high number of visitors.

2.2 Server side factors

If a website is slow to download, it is likely that it will struggle to retain visitors. There are various methods which can be used in conjunction with each other to reduce download time and make the site more efficient.

Web server capacity

As well as the capabilities of the user's computer, the capacity of the web server must be taken into account. This is true whether the web server has been bought or rented.

Bandwidth determines how much traffic can be handled by the web server, specifically how much material is able to be downloaded at any one time. Bandwidth can be thought of as a pipe from the web server to the users. The bigger the pipe, the more that can be sent down it. The larger the web page and its associated files, the less users can download at any one time.

Server side scripting on a website will also take up bandwidth. The more that is to be performed before page load, the slower it will be to download on a user's computer. Client side scripting does not have the same issue as it is executed on the user's computer rather than the web server. As a general rule, server side scripting should be carried out only where absolutely necessary and as efficiently as possible.

Key terms

Bandwidth – the capacity a network connection can conduct at one time.

Compression – where a mathematical calculation is performed on a file in order to 'squash' it and make it smaller.

Bitmap – a map of bits; each pixel is saved in its location.

Vector – an image which is saved as a mathematical algorithm. Each line is saved as co-ordinates of each point and details of colour, width, etc.

File types

By using smaller file types which use **compression** methods, the website will have a faster download time. When deciding on which file types to use, a developer must make a judgement in order to balance quality and file size because the higher the quality, the larger the file size.

Activity: User and server side factors

1 Investigate the Internet service providers (ISPs) who currently provide broadband over ADSL. Create a table comparing the speeds and prices.

2 Find out the Internet connection method and speed at your school or college.

3 Find out the specification of the computers at your school or college.

4 Discuss the choice of connection and specification, explaining whether you would make any changes to it. Take financial factors into account.

Image files

There are two image file types available: **bitmap** and **vector** (see Figure 28.1), which are compared in Table 28.1.

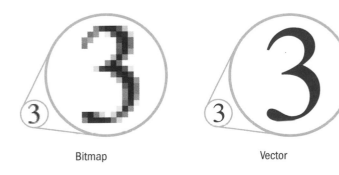

Bitmap   Vector

Figure 28.1: Bitmap and vector images

Bitmap file types include GIF and JPEG. A GIF has a maximum palette of 256 colours, therefore should be used for low colour images. A JPEG has a larger palette and is therefore better for higher colour images.

Bitmap	Vector
• Each pixel is saved individually with its location, colours and other details. • Generally has a large file size. • When resized, the image will become pixellated. • File formats include .bmp,.gif,.jpg. • Created by programs such as Microsoft® Paint and Adobe® Photoshop®. • Usually used in web pages as they are rendered by all graphical browsers.	• Co-ordinates of points and curves are saved as a mathematical equation. • Generally has a small file size. • When resized, image will retain clarity. • File formats include .pdf and .eps. • Created by programs such as Adobe® Illustrator® and CorelDRAW®. • Often used for graphics such as logos which need to be resized. • Shapes drawn in Adobe® Flash® are vectors.

Table 28.1: Comparison of bitmap and vector

Activity: Image file types

Look at an existing website, perhaps the one for your school or college. Open the code for that web page (in Internet Explorer® click View/Source). What image file types have been used and why?

Sound files

Sound travels in waves. These are continuous and called analogue. Digital sound waves are sampled at regular intervals with gaps so small the human ear cannot perceive them (see Figure 28.2).

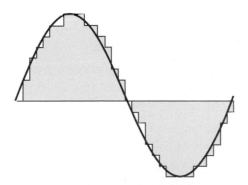

Figure 28.2: Close up of digital sound waves

Once these signals are combined the whole piece is a series of waves which denotes the characteristics of the sound (Figure 28.3). As a computer can only understand 0s and 1s, the value of each part of the wave is converted into a binary value, eg 0000, 0001, 0010, 0011, etc. These values are then translated by the computer into sound output.

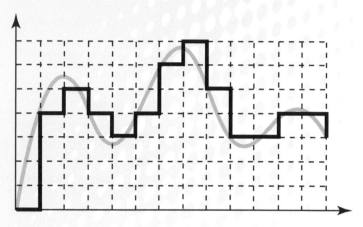

Figure 28.3: Full sound waves

There are several types of sound file type available, each with their own method of sampling and compression.

A .wav file has a high sample rate, which means the sound quality is closest to that produced by the actual instruments, but it is a relatively large file.

A .mp3 file has a low sample rate and therefore produces a smaller file size. This is how MP3 players manage to store such a high volume of music. However, there is a loss of quality, depending on the compression rate chosen. The higher the rate, the better quality but the larger the file size.

A consideration must also be made as to what types of music **plug-ins** a user is likely to have, as this may restrict the choice available.

Video and animation files

Video and animation can seriously affect the speed of a website and, in general, should be used sparingly. Both types can produce very large file sizes.

When uploaded onto a website, for a user to view video or animation files, usually they must click on them and download them. Due to the size of the files, this will often take a relatively long time and control a large proportion of bandwidth during the download, even with a high-quality Internet connection. A file such as

this will also take a large proportion of web server space. The more video and animation files used, the more web server space used and the slower the website will be.

A possible solution to this problem could be to **stream** the video file instead of the user downloading it in one go (see Figure 28.4).

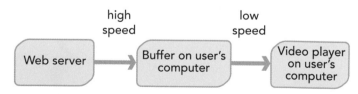

Figure 28.4: Video stream buffered to a user's computer

Conversion between formats

To convert a bitmap to a vector, the image has to be **traced**. This can be done in programs such as Adobe® Flash®, Adobe® Illustrator® and CorelDRAW®.

The conversion of a vector to a bitmap is a much simpler process, as it consists of opening the vector in a bitmap program and saving it. As the package's native file format is bitmap, anything saved in it will be saved as a bitmap. Programs such as Microsoft® Paint and Adobe® Photoshop® will perform this process, which is called rasterisation.

Conversion between sound files involves using the compression algorithm, either to make into a smaller MP3 or to convert back to a file type such as .wav. CD creation programs such as Nero have the facilities to perform this conversion. It is very important to check that the conversion of the file and inclusion on the website will not break copyright law.

Activity: Image file conversion

1   Design a new logo for your school or college.

2   Create this logo in a vector program such as Adobe® Flash® or CorelDRAW®.

3   Convert the logo into a bitmap using a program such as Microsoft® Paint® or Adobe® Photoshop®.

4   In both programs, try increasing their size by 200 per cent. Make notes on the effects you observe.

2.3   Security

There are several risks to the security of a website, which is especially important for eCommerce sites where hackers and viruses can steal customers' details and use them for fraud, such as identity theft (see below).

Developers must build protection mechanisms into their websites in order for users to feel comfortable using them. This is especially important for eCommerce sites. For more information see Unit 8: ECommerce, in Student Book 1.

Risks

Hacking is when someone attempts to access a computer system or data to which they are not permitted. They may do this to try to steal the data, change it, destroy it or cause a nuisance. Often they will look for 'back doors', ports on web servers which have been left unsecured, which they can utilise to gain entry. Alternatively, they may seek to obtain a username and password of someone who is allowed access to the data.

Viruses are programs which are malicious and cause an unwanted result when run. They can be aimed at causing disruption or stealing data.

Identity theft is where a person's private details are stolen and used by someone else. By pretending to be the victim the thief can do things like apply for credit cards and make purchases in the victim's name, knowing that the bank will target the victim rather than the thief to pay the debt.

2.4   Security protection mechanisms

There are several security protection mechanisms available, such as anti-virus software. However, those which relate specifically to websites are discussed below.

Firewalls

A **firewall** builds a protective barrier around a computer or a network of computers so that only authorised programs can access the data.

The firewall sets up a gateway and only allows authorised traffic through the gateway. Incoming data is inspected and only allowed through if it is legitimate. This is done by the opening and closing of ports. Ports connect protocols and IP addresses together. Each computer has several ports for data to pass through. They are virtual so they cannot be seen. Ports are like doors: each has a number to identify it and can be open or closed. There are some default ports – for example, port 25 is usually for email and port 80 is usually for the Internet, although these can be changed. For a web server, it is good practice to close all ports that are not being used. Otherwise, hackers can take advantage of open ports to get into the system.

Secure socket layers (SSL)

SSL is a cryptographic protocol which provides secure communication on the Internet. It provides endpoint authentication – this means that both the server and the client need to be identified and confirm they are who they say they are. This is done by **public key encryption** and **certificate-based authentication**.

Adherence to standards

It is vital for all computer users to use strong passwords. This is especially important for web servers and other eCommerce systems.

A strong password involves:

- both letters and numbers
- both capitals and lowercase
- symbols such as * or #
- being over eight characters long.

Hackers can take advantage of weak passwords, especially those which are easy to guess. If a password is related to the user, for example a pet's name, it will not take too much effort for a hacker to guess it. There are software programs which can run through many possible combinations of characters and test whether that is the chosen password. The stronger the password, the longer this software will take to work it out, and the more likely a hacker will go on to try a different website. They are not likely to spend time working their way into a well-protected site.

Activity: Security

1 Research the threats to websites including hackers and viruses. Make notes for future reference in your coursework.

2 Research the methods to protect websites including firewalls. Make notes for future reference in your coursework.

Assessment activity 28.2   **BTEC**

As we have seen, Fancy That! is a business selling fancy dress costumes.

1 Prepare a report for Fancy That! to describe:

   (a) the user side factors that influence the performance of a website **P2**

   (b) the server side factors that influence the performance of a website. **P2**

2 Create a leaflet to explain the security risks and protection mechanisms involved in website performance. **P3**

Grading tips

- Make sure the report covers both user and server side factors and deals with each one in enough depth. Also consider the limitations such as client or customer hardware and software. **P2**

- As well as discussing risks generally, include laws and guidelines that rule website production and to which developers must adhere. **P3**

PLTS

Self-managers can carefully organise this task to make sure both parts have enough time and are equally done to the best of your ability.

Functional skills

Your **English** speaking skills can be evidenced by you presenting information in two different formats.

3   Be able to design interactive websites

Before a website can be created, it must be designed. If this stage if skipped, it can cause major problems when building the website or errors might not be found until it 'goes live'.

3.1   Identification of need

By investigating the requirements of a project, a web designer can ensure they fully meet both the client's needs and those of the users.

Nature of interactivity

Most modern websites involve interactivity; **static websites** risk losing users.

It is important to decide how much interactivity will be in a **dynamic website**.

Too little interactivity and users may lose interest; too much and they may feel overwhelmed. It is important to get the balance right.

If a website is to be an eCommerce site, the designer also needs to decide how online transactions will be done. There are two parts to this issue:

1.   How will the user browse the catalogue?

2.   How will they make purchases?

Activity: Browsing and buying

1   Visit five websites which have e-commerce facilities. Note the URL and business name of each website you visit.

2   Make notes on the design decisions each have made.

3   Describe the interactivity possible on each website.

Client needs and user needs

Web designers must always have two sets of needs in mind: those of the client and those of the users. The client is the person who has commissioned the site to be made and usually they are also the person who holds the purse strings. If the client is not happy with the site, you may not get paid for your work.

The users are the visitors to the site. They need to be attracted to the site initially to make their first visit, and then encouraged to revisit. This may be for several reasons, for example, to make more purchases, to look at new content or take part in discussions on forums. One aim of websites is to persuade their users to bookmark the website, therefore increasing the probability of their returning on a regular basis.

Key terms

'Go live' – describes the first time a website has been uploaded to a web server and made available to the public.

Static website – one with no interactivity and is usually just a presentation of information. Changes have to be hard-coded into the site.

Dynamic website – can involve any level of activity from a simple feedback form to a database that personalises the website for each individual visitor. Changes can be made on the fly.

Activity: Bookmarks

1   Think about websites you have bookmarked in the past. Why did you choose them? What persuaded you to become a potentially regular visitor?

2   If you haven't bookmarked a website before, why do you think that is? Would you like to bookmark any you use frequently?

A website must convey the correct image, especially if it is for a business. It should be professional and demonstrate that the organisation can be trusted. Image can be conveyed through a clear layout, choice of colours and pictures and the content of the text.

A level of security must be decided upon as this will impact both the design of the website and its management. You will need to ask questions such as:

- Can anyone access the site, or will there be an account system with passwords, or a mixture of both?

- What protective methods will be used on the web server? (See Security, page 165.)

Development timescales must be agreed upon at the start of the project, preferably in a written form which both client and designer have signed. The schedule should be broken down into stages, with clear points of review where the client can check that the project is progressing to their satisfaction.

Support and maintenance contracts are important factors which need to be decided at the beginning of the project. The web developer might be contracted just for designing and building the website, or they might also be contracted to provide maintenance, updates and support when needed. The type of contract agreed on will naturally affect the cost of the project.

Pricing a website for a client is difficult. Items to consider when estimating costs include the size and content of the website, the timescale of the project and any aftercare requirements. Some developers charge by the hour for as long as the project takes. Others charge for each element in the website – the more that is in the website, the more expensive it will be. There might be very few overheads involved in website development (eg a freelance developer working from home), but on the other hand it is a very specialised area, so deciding on how much to charge can be difficult. A developer may select a price purely to undercut the competition.

Key terms

Search engine visibility – getting a website listed as highly as possible on a search engine. This will increase the number of visitors to a site.

Concept designing – outlining the overall design of the product. This gives the general feel of it and the effect it should have on the users.

Mood boards – a collage of images, textures and other items, aimed at providing an idea of the look and feel of a product. They are usually A3 size.

Storyboard – shows the sequence of a project. In web design, it shows how different pages will interrelate.

Other elements that a client may need include:

- logo design
- original images and photographs
- **search engine visibility**
- online advertising.

The user and client requirements are used as a benchmark of the success of a project. After testing, the website should be evaluated, including checking whether the requirements have been met. An explanation should be included for any requirements that have not been met (see Check against user requirements, page 184).

End user need

The other set of needs a web designer must consider are those of the users. This is difficult for sites intended for a large target market.

The website must be appropriate to the audience. The content must be suitable, which involves not using inappropriate language or technical jargon. The image should also be suitable for the wide range of people who may look at it. For example, the website for Disneyland Resort® Paris needs to be suitable for both children and adults and has to be careful to avoid excluding either of these target audiences. For children, there are colourful images and magical animations; for adults, there is information about the hotels, the parks and all the facilities available. The aim of the website is to encourage parents to book a holiday.

Considering the range of people who may use the site, the complexity of the site must be appropriate. This includes not just the content, but also the method of using it – for example, it must be possible to easily navigate round the site. Users with little Internet experience must also be taken into consideration.

One problematic area of web design is ensuring that client and user needs are compatible. For example, if the client wants to use a colour scheme of yellow and magenta but you know this would not be appropriate for the website's users, you will need to manage the situation and attempt to come to a compromise, such as using a header of yellow and magenta, but the rest of the website in more easily read colours.

3.2 Design tools

Several tools can be used to ensure that all areas are considered when designing websites. By producing a thorough design using the tools presented in this section and using this to communicate with your client, you can ensure that your client is happy with your plans before you build the site. This should reduce the problems you may encounter if there was a mismatch between client expectations and the actual outcomes.

Concept designing

To convey the concept of a site, you might use one or both of the following tools: **mood boards** and **storyboards**.

The aim of a moodboard (see Figure 28.5) is to produce something with the same feel as the website. They are useful way of focusing the design and demonstrating initial ideas to the client.

Storyboarding (see Figure 28.6) is key to structuring a website clearly and is a way of expressing a navigation design (see Navigation, page 175). It is not just used in web design; it is often used in the design of moving images such as animation or film.

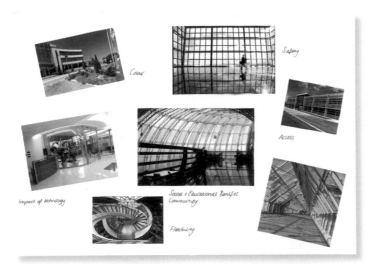

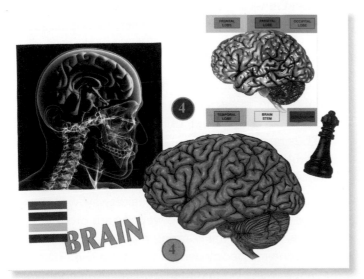

Figure 28.5: Examples of mood boards

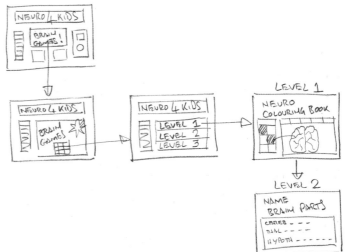

Figure 28.6: Example of a storyboard

Activity: Storyboarding

Think of a scene from your favourite cartoon or film. Create a storyboard to show what happens. Use a minimum of 10 boxes and a maximum of 20. Add any notes underneath each box to explain what is happening.

Layout techniques

As well as the structure of the overall site, the layout of the individual pages must be designed. There are several methods which can be used to arrange items on a web page, including **frames**, **tables**, **DIVs** and **SPANs**.

Key terms

Frame – a section of a web page which, when used with other frames, can make up a page of independently functioning sections.

Table – a collection of cells placed on a page, and data (text, images, etc) can each be placed in separate cells, which is a very good way of controlling layout.

DIV – a method of defining a style for a block of HTML (hypertext markup language). It includes an automatic paragraph break.

SPAN – a method of defining a style for a block of HTML (hypertext markup language).

The simplest method of layout is to use frames (see Figure 28.7) but this is considered 'old-fashioned' in the industry. Each part of the page is contained in its own file and there is a master page which pulls each part in like a jigsaw.

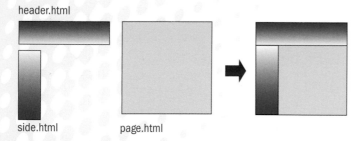

header.html
side.html
page.html

Figure 28.7: Example of frames

A table (see Figure 28.8) holds all the content on each page, with each cell having an individual part. It is a good method to ensure the layout is retained on the different browsers on which users may view the page. However, the more complicated the table, the longer it will take to load for the user. If a page takes too long, a visitor may lose patience and leave the site, perhaps never to return.

DIVs and SPANs are used to define styles within blocks of HTML; for example, `<span class="red small">some text</span>`.

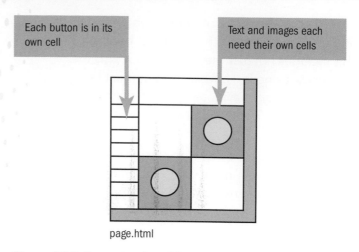

Each button is in its own cell

Text and images each need their own cells

page.html

Figure 28.8: Example of a table

However, a more useful method is to combine them with CSS (cascading style sheets) formatting style. For example, in the code `<span class="warning">some text</span>` the "warning" style would be defined earlier in the CSS (see Cascading style sheets, page 182).

The main difference between DIVs and SPANs is that a DIV includes a paragraph return, whereas a SPAN does not. They are efficient methods of laying out and formatting a page, especially when used in conjunction with effective CSS.

Templates

Templates are used to make the process of adding content simpler, and are often used to provide an easy maintenance system for users with minimal web knowledge. A template keeps the design and content separate. Generally, a template will provide full design, connection to any other systems such as a database, and all interactive coding. The only thing that usually needs to be added is the actual content.

Templates can be quite expensive, depending on the level of design, especially if a company has asked for a unique creation. However, using templates can mean that a business that does not have someone with web skills within the organisation does not need to employ someone to create the website.

A recent development has been 'takeaway' websites. This is where all the parts of a website are provided and a user can add the content, mainly targeted at non-technical people who want to put their own personal website on the Internet. The result could be a high number of websites that look very similar and have low-quality content.

Colour schemes

The colours selected for a website can encourage or deter users, so the selection must be made with care. Several questions must be asked when deciding on a colour scheme.

- Do the colours combine well? Are they aesthetically pleasing?
- Are the colours appropriate for the target audience? For example, primary colours might be used for a children's website.
- Is the text readable? Black text on a purple background may give an atmospheric effect, but it is not easy to read.
- Does it fit with the business's house style?

Activity: House styles

1 Find three websites with distinctively different artistic styles. Describe the artistic style used on each website.

2 For each of your chosen websites, describe how a house style has or has not been carried through the website.

3 Explain why a house style has or has not been used for each website. In your opinion, is this effective for that website?

Screen designs

To visualise what the pages will look like before building them, designers create screen designs (see Figure 28.9). These are mock-ups of the actual page, concentrating on layout rather than content.

Activity: Screen designs

Choose an existing website and produce a screen design to show how the designer has created the layout (following the example shown in Figure 28.9). Label the colours, fonts and other specifications. Estimate sizes and give the images suitable labels.

Outline of content

As screen designs deal with the layout of the page, the content must also be considered. Generally, at this point, only headings will be defined.

Activity: Content design

1 Select two different websites about the same topic (eg computer). Compare the design of their content. Write a list of pros and cons of the quality of their content

2 Explain whether you think each website has fulfilled the users' needs in terms of content.

3.3 Software

It is only possible to choose the correct web development software once you know exactly what will be in your website. Otherwise, part of the way through a build, you may find you need another piece of software which will cost money and may take time to learn.

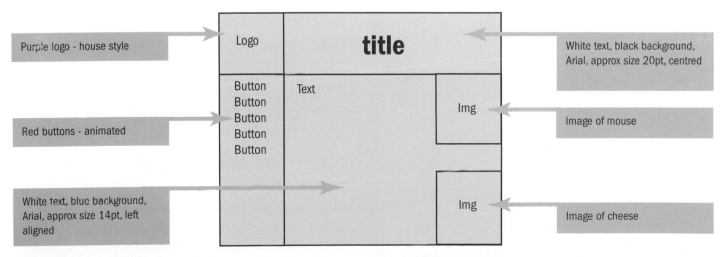

Purple logo - house style

Logo

title

White text, black background, Arial, approx size 20pt, centred

Red buttons - animated

Button
Button
Button
Button
Button

Text

Img

Image of mouse

White text, blue background, Arial, approx size 14pt, left aligned

Img

Image of cheese

Figure 28.9: An example screen design

Markup languages

HTML (hypertext markup language) is the most commonly used markup language – so much so that all others are just about extinct. It forms the basis of all World Wide Web pages, even if other languages are used.

HTML uses a system of tags (indicated by angle brackets, `<` and `>`) which contain the instructions. Almost all tags come in a pair of open and close tags enclosing the content to be affected, eg `<font color="red">Some text</font>` would produce Some text. Note that American spelling is used in HTML.

HTML pages should start with `<html>` and end with `</html>` tags to declare the language being used. If other languages are used, they will need to be declared (see Client side scripting languages below).

Every web page is divided into a head and body section, each of which is defined by its tags. The head section is unseen by the user and can be thought of as the brains of the page. It contains all the information for the page to function correctly. The body is the part seen by the user and contains all the content of the page. A well-designed page should have reusable code in the head and minimal code in the body.

How to... Create a simple HTML web page

1 Open Notepad (or a similar text editor).
2 Enter this code:
```
<html>
<head>
<title>My First Web page</title>
<bgcolour="white">
</head>
<body>
<font color="blue"><b>Hello World!</b></font>
<font color=#000000><i>This is my first ever web page</i></font>
</body>
</html>
```
3 Click File / Save As.
4 Delete the Filename and type mywebpage.html, then click Save.
5 Navigate to where the file is saved using My Computer. Notice how the file icon is your Internet browser icon.
6 Double click your file. It should open in your browser.

Activity: Using HTML

Even though there are several web design environments available, it is still important to understand HTML. The best way to do this is to use Notepad (or a similar text editor) to create a web page using purely your own code.

1 In a browser, open a website with which you are familiar, such as your school or college website. View the HTML (eg in Internet Explorer® click View / Source or Tools / View Source). Examine the code and compare with the visual version in the browser.

2 Write down all the tags you recognise and what effect they have on the display of items on the web page. Try to find examples of all the tags listed in Table 28.2.

Client side scripting languages

Even though HTML is the basis of all web pages, as a language it is quite limited and so other languages need to be brought in to create more advanced features. A **client side scripting** language is code which is embedded into the HTML. When the web page is downloaded onto the user's browser, the script is run on the user's computer.

Key term

Client side scripting – when the script is executed on the user's computer. This is the opposite of server side scripting, which is executed on the web server. Server side scripting is used for more advanced interactive features such as connecting to a database and is not covered by this unit.

Features and advantages of software languages

There are several languages available for a web designer to use. At a basic level, all websites must have at least a foundation in HTML, even if that is just used to support the other languages.

Open tag	Close tag	Purpose	Example
`<font>`	`</font>`	Changes text. Open tag can have parameters such as colour, size, face.	`<font face="Arial" size="16">Text</font>`
`<b>` or `<strong>`	`</b>` or `</strong>`	Makes text bold	`<b>Text</b>`
`<i>` or `<em>`	`</i>` or `</em>`	Makes text italic	`<i>Text</i>`
` `	No close tag	Starts a new line. One of the rare tags that is not in a pair.	`Text` ` ` `Text`
`<li>`	`</li>`	Creates a list with bullet points	`<li>first item</li>` `<li>second item</li>`

`<table>`	`</table>`	Creates a table (`<tr>` creates rows and `<td>` creates columns)	`<table border=1>`
			`<tr>`
			`<td>top left</td>`
			`<td>top right</td>`
			`</tr>`
			`<td>bottom left</td>`
			`<td>bottom right</td>`
			`</tr>`
			`</table>`

`<img>`	No close tag	Inserts an image. One of the rare tags that is not in a pair.	`<img src="Images\logo.gif">`
`<a href>`	`</a>`	Creates a hyperlink. Can be used around text or an image.	`<a href="index.html">Go to home page</a>` `<a href="index.html"><img src="Images\logo.gif"></a>`

Table 28.2: Common HTML tags

CSS (cascading style sheets) is used to ensure standardised formatting across a website – this also makes the site easier to maintain. In order to make a formatting change to a website that is formatted in HTML, the designer would have to search through the whole code, finding every instance of the format that needed to be changed. There could be hundreds of entries so this is a very time-consuming method and it is likely to produce errors in consistency. By using CSS, on the other hand, only one formatting entry need be changed and it will be immediately applied throughout the whole site for every instance of the formatting style.

ASP (active server pages) and PHP (hypertext preprocessor) are server side web languages. This means that the code is executed using the web server's processing power. The result is that the code and the data are very secure and can be executed efficiently. Both these languages can create interaction on a website, particularly involving connecting to databases.

VBScript® and JavaScript® are client side web languages. This means that the code is executed using the user's computer and not the web server. This frees up the processing power which would otherwise have been used. Both languages can create interaction on a website, such as forms, searching and even games.

Software development environments

There are several software development environments available. Microsoft® FrontPage is the most popular web authoring application for beginners, as it uses a similar layout to the other Office® programs and is very user friendly. However, the functionality can be limited.

Adobe® Dreamweaver® is the current industry standard. Although more difficult to learn, it provides a wide range of tools to create a website and supports several client and server side scripting languages.

Using a development environment such as FrontPage or Dreamweaver® is not absolutely necessary – as you have seen from the previous examples, it is possible to write the code using a text editor. However, using a development environment can make coding quicker and formatting easier.

Activity: Web design software

1 Explain the advantages and disadvantages of using a text editor (eg Notepad) for creating a web page.

2 Explain the advantages and disadvantages of using web authoring software (eg FrontPage or Dreamweaver®) for creating a web page.

Assessment activity 28.3

 **BTEC**

Fancy That! want to create a website to advertise their fancy-dress business that includes a catalogue the customers can look through. They hope in the future to sell their products online. They want the website to have at least five pages and at least one interactive feature.

1 Using the appropriate design tools, design an interactive website to meet the requirements of Fancy That! **P4**

2 For each design tool used, add an explanation of the technique to describe it in general, how you have used it and how it will help you create the website. **M2**

3 Add a discussion of the techniques which can be used to aid user access to information in your design. **D2**

Grading tips

- The website that is designed must be a multi-page, two-way interactive site. **P4**

- Link the descriptions of tools to the site you are designing. **M2**

- Consider all elements of design and functionality that could improve accessibility. **D2**

PLTS

Creative thinkers can make inventive designs and **independent enquirers** might want to look at other existing websites for ideas.

Functional skills

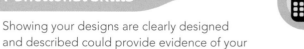

Showing your designs are clearly designed and described could provide evidence of your **English** skills.

4   Be able to create websites

Once the design is entirely completed and the client is happy with it, the website can be built. Prototyping is often used in the first instance. This is where a test version of the website is built to ensure that the functionality is correct and the specifications are to the client's liking. By using a prototype the designer can save time and money.

The first element of the creation of a website is the structure. This will provide a solid basis for the content, which can then be easily inserted. Extra features, such as interactivity and audio-visual elements, can be added. At this point the website should be complete. All parts must then be tested to ensure they are functioning correctly. Once the developer is happy that there are no bugs in the site, it can be uploaded to a web server and go live on the Internet.

4.1   Structure

Before adding any content, the fundamental structure of the page should be put in place. Otherwise, you may have formatting problems later in the implementation.

Layout of pages

In your design, you will have decided whether you are going to use frames, tables or DIVs and SPANs. You should also have your layout exactly planned in your screen designs.

Navigation

The location of your buttons and hyperlinks should be in your screen designs. Your storyboard will show how the pages will link together. For example, in a matrix-style website all the pages will have buttons to all the other pages.

How to... Create tables in Adobe® Dreamweaver®

1 Open a web page in Dreamweaver®.

2 Select Insert / Table or click on the Table icon in the top toolbar (see Figure 28.10).

3 Enter the number of rows and columns required.

4 Select border thickness (0 is invisible, 1 and over are increasingly thick).

5 Test your page in the browser by pressing F12 or selecting File/ Preview in Browser.

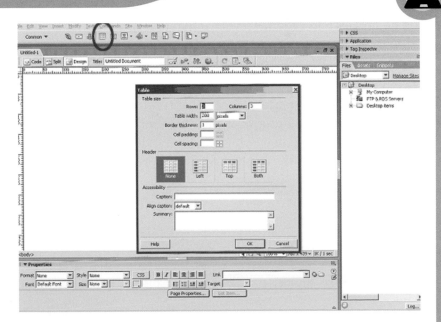

Figure 28.10: Dreamweaver® Table icon and Table Properties box

How to... Create Flash buttons in Adobe® Dreamweaver®

1 Open a web page in Dreamweaver®.

2 Select Insert / Media / Flash Button (see Figure 28.11).

3 Choose your settings: the style of the button, the text written on the button, font and font size, where the button should link to, and the 'save as' name – note that each Flash® button should be saved as a separate image.

4 Once you have selected the settings, click OK.

5 Test your page in the browser.

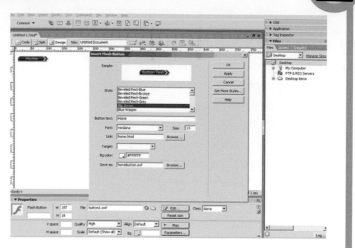

Figure 28.11: Dreamweaver® Flash® Buttons Properties box

Format of content and cascading style sheets (CSS)

There are several ways of formatting text on a web page, including font, size, emphasis (bold), italics, underline and lists. In Dreamweaver®, when text is selected the Properties Inspector (see Figure 28.12) will change to offer all the font formatting options.

Formatting can also be done using CSS (see Cascading style sheets, page 183) which ensures it is efficient and consistent throughout the website.

Interactive features

Interactivity involves two-way communication between the user and the computer. In other words, it requires input from the user which provokes a response from the computer. This could include giving feedback, searching a catalogue of products or purchasing a product from a website. To have a full catalogue of products would require a database and server side scripting, which are not covered in this unit. However, the functionality can be simulated using client side scripting.

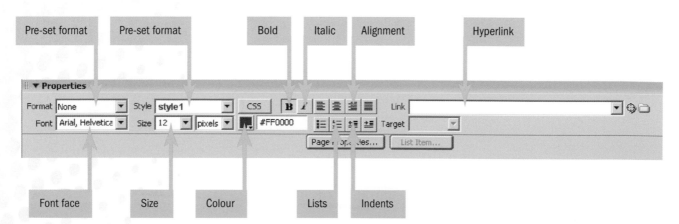

Figure 28.12: Font Properties Inspector

How to... Create a feedback form in Dreamweaver®

1 Open a web page in Dreamweaver® (either a blank one or one you have prepared for the form).

2 Change the toolbar drop-down to show the Forms toolbar (see Figure 28.13).

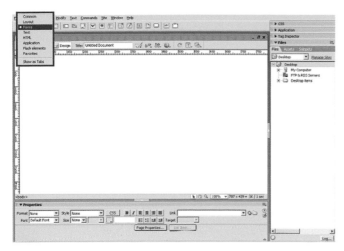

Figure 28.13: Dreamweaver® Forms toolbar

3 Place your cursor where you want the form to go and select the red dotted square (see Figure 28.14).

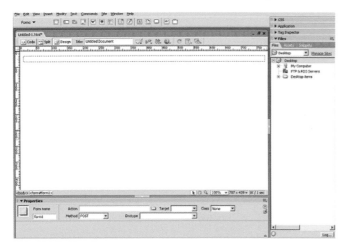

Figure 28.14: Dreamweaver® form outline

One will be automatically drawn on your web page. Everything within that red square will be part of the form.

4 Using the Forms toolbar, insert the fields you want, eg a textbox with the label Name.

5 When you have all your fields, insert two buttons at the bottom, still inside the red square, with no labels. They will automatically both be called Submit. Leave one as Submit and change the other to Reset using the Properties Inspector at the bottom of the screen.

6 Using the tag selector at the bottom left of the page (see Figure 28.15), select the Form tag. The Properties Inspector will show an action box. Into it, type mailto: followed by the email address to which you want to submit the form.

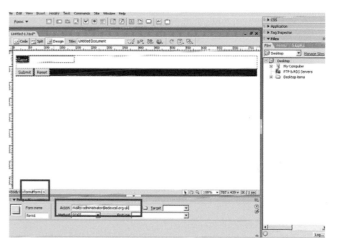

Figure 28.15: Dreamweaver® tag selector and completed action box

7 Test your page in the browser.

How to... Create a simple catalogue search using JavaScript

1 Create your catalogue web page with three products.
2 Above the `</body>` tag, enter this code:

```
<script>
necklace = 1
chocolates = 2
toy = 3
product=prompt("Please enter search
product", "")
if (product=="necklace")
     {document.write("Item found.
Catalogue number " + necklace)}
     else
```

```
if (product=="chocolates")
          {document.write("Item found.
Catalogue number " + chocolates)}
          else
          {document.write("Item found.
Catalogue number " + toy)}
</script>
```

3 Amend your code to match your three products (by changing the words in red).
4 Run the page in a browser to test if it works for all three products.

How to... Create a shopping cart system

1 Open a web page in Dreamweaver® (a blank or one you have prepared for the form).
2 Above the `</body>` tag, enter this code:

```
<script>
necklace = 25.99
chocolates = 5.95
toy = 4.51
product=prompt("Please enter product to
be purchased", "")
document.write("You have purchased ")
if (product=="necklace")
     {document.write("a fabulous
necklace: £" + necklace)
     total = necklace}
     else
     if (product=="chocolates")
          {document.write("a luxury box
of chocolates: £" + chocolates)
          total = chocolates}
     else
     if (product=="toy")
          {document.write("a cuddly toy:
£" + toy)
          total = toy}
          else
          {document.write("nothing")
```

```
          total = 0}
document.write("<br>Total to pay is £"
+ total)
if (total != 0)
{alert("Are you ready to enter your
details?")
name=prompt("Please enter your
name:","")
dob=prompt("Please enter your date of
birth:","")
ccnum=prompt("Please enter your credit
card number:","")
document.write("<br><br>Customer
details: <br>Name: " + name + "<br>Date
of birth: " + dob + "<br>Card number: "
+ ccnum)
alert("Thank you for making your
purchase")
}
</script>
```

3 Amend your code to match your three products.
4 Run the page in a browser to test if it works for all three products.

Note: *This unit will not show you how to process customer purchases, only how to collect their order and payment details.*

Activity: Using JavaScript®

1   Using your knowledge of JavaScript®, and referring to books and the Internet as necessary, amend the shopping cart code so it allows the user to purchase more than one item at a time.

2   Change one of the prices in the shopping cart exercise to £4.50. Notice how the zero is missed off when it is written to the web page. Research why that happens and how it might be fixed.

Images and animation

A web page should not be littered with images because they increase the download time of a site (see Image files, page 163) and can make the page look amateurish. Choose images and animations wisely so that they enhance the content on the website.

Similarly, animation can have a serious effect on the performance of a website and should, therefore, be limited to only where it is essential. There are several animation programs available, the most popular being Adobe® Flash®. When creating a Flash® animation, the working file is saved in the .fla format, but it is then converted to a movie file (.swf) so it can be added to a website. The user will need the plug-in Flash® Player® to be able to view the Flash® animation. However, most modern browsers already have the player built in. Animated GIFs can also be used as animations on a website. These provide a smaller file type but a lower image quality in playback and are therefore more suitable for small, simple animations. Animated GIFs can be made by several programs, including Adobe® Photoshop® and CorelDRAW®, and can be rendered on most browsers without the need for a plug-in.

4.2 Content

After the web page has been structured and all the coding features are finished, the content can be inserted. This includes text, more images and other features which are not part of the structure which give information to the user. It is pointless to have a website which looks stunning but which does not hold well-written, accurate, informative content.

The content of each page should be planned, remembering that generally users will not want to read an essay, but they must be able to obtain all the information they need. The use of language should be concise and precise.

Proofed, correct and appropriate

All text in a website should be proofed for both spelling and grammar mistakes. The website you are creating will be your client's presence on the web and as such it is an extension of them and their business. If it is an eCommerce site and there are mistakes in it, customers may not have confidence in the site and decide to shop somewhere else.

The content should be correct, accurate and up to date. If descriptions of products are incorrect then the client could be prosecuted under the Trades Description Act (1968). Prices must also be correct; if they are lower than they should be, your client may lose money.

Check also that there is no inappropriate content on the site. Not only could inappropriate content deter potential users, it might also contravene the Obscene Publications Act (1959), which can be applied to UK websites. In legal terms, the act says that 'an article shall be deemed to be obscene if its effect ... [is] such as to tend to deprave and corrupt persons who are likely, having regard to all relevant circumstances, to read, see or hear the matter contained or embodied in it.'

Reliability of information source

It is essential that the information given on a website is correct; otherwise, users may lose trust in the site and stop visiting. This is most important for an eCommerce site. When creating the content of the website, if a designer is taking information from other places, they must ensure that it is reliable. If the designer puts out incorrect information, even though it is from another source, they could be held responsible.

A legal disclaimer is usually included on the bottom of a website home page to ensure that the owners are not held responsible for incorrect or changing information. It can also include other legal information about viruses, data protection, copyright and trademarks.

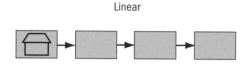

Case study: Edexcel

Edexcel is the largest awarding body in the UK and offers a wide range of opportuntities to help people achieve their full potential.

Their website provides information for tutors, learners and others involved in education.

1 Visit the Edexcel website www.edexcel.com and read the disclaimer.

2 Find two more websites with disclaimers

3 Compare the three disclaimers:

   (a) What elements do they have in common?

   (b) What dissimilar elements do they have?

4 Write a disclaimer for the website you are designing.

Structured for purpose

The content of a website should be structured so it is easy for the user to read. Lists should be put into bullet-point form and complex data should be put into tables. Prose should be ordered in a logical sequence.

Case Study: Nestlé

Nestlé is a multinational organisation with products including Nescafé® coffee, Kit Kat® chocolate bars and Ski® yoghurts. Their UK website is well-designed and rich with content.

The website uses several techniques to present the high volume of textual information effectively.

1 Go to www.nestle.co.uk and find examples of these formatting features:

   (a) bold text

   (b) uppercase

   (c) bulleted list

   (d) highlighting with colour.

2 How has the web designer ensured that the text is clear and readable? List a minimum of five methods.

4.3 Tools and techniques

There are several tools and techniques which can be used to create a website. It is only by combining these that an effective site can be produced.

Navigation diagram

There are three main methods of connecting web pages together in a **navigation diagram**: linear, hierarchy and matrix (see Figure 28.16).

Key term

Navigation diagram – a diagram that shows how the different parts of a project will combine. In web design, it shows how different pages will interrelate.

Linear

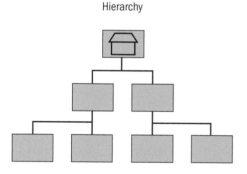

Hierarchy

Matrix

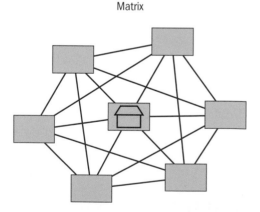

Figure 28.16: Website structures

Activity: Navigation structures

Analyse each type of structure. Name two positive points and two negative points about each one. Consider the needs of the designer, client and user.

Building interactivity tools

Client side scripting languages include JavaScript® and VBScript®. These can be used to create simple feedback forms which are emailed to an address when submitted or something as complex as arcade-style computer games. The essential purpose of the languages is to create two-way communication between the user and the website.

How to... Create a simple JavaScript® web page

1   Open Notepad (or a similar text editor).
2   Save the file as myjavascript.html.
3   Enter this code:

```
<html>
<head>
<title>My First JavaScript</title>
</head>
<body>
<script>
age=18;
document.write("My age is: ");
document.write(age);
</script>
</body>
</html>
```

4   Save the file.
5   Navigate to where the file is saved using My Computer.
6   Double click your file to open it in your browser.

Activity: Using JavaScript®

1   To receive input from the user, the following JavaScript® can be used:
```
age=prompt("Please enter your age: ","").
```
Use this new code to alter myjavascript.html so the user can input their own age.
2   Add the ability for the user to input their name so it will be displayed on the web page.

Pseudo code is a method of designing code, forming an intermediary step between an explanation in English and the coding language – See Table 28.3.

Pseudocode	JavaScript
age = input from user	`age=prompt("Enter age","");`
if age >= 18 then	`if (age>=18)`
print onscreen "i am an adult"	`{document.write("I am an adult");}`
else	`else`
print onscreen "i am x years old"	`{document.write("I am " + age + " years old");}`

Table 28.3: Example of pseudo code used to plan JavaScript

By using pseudo code, a designer can plan what the code will do, without having to worry about ensuring the correct words and syntax are used. It is also easier to convert into the full programming language by using this transitional step.

Adding animation and audio/visual elements

It is good practice to save your images and animations in a folder called 'Images' and to store this folder in the same folder as your web pages. Keeping all your website files in one place means that when you come to upload them there is less chance you will miss any out. Also, it reduces the amount of code needed to link to an image or create a hyperlink.

How to... Insert an image in Adobe® Dreamweaver®

1   Open a web page in Dreamweaver®.
2   Select Insert / Image.
3   Browse to the image you want to insert and click OK.
4   Test your page in the browser.

How to... Insert a Flash® animation into Dreamweaver®

To use a Flash® animation in Dreamweaver®, it needs to be saved as a .swf file. This compiles it into a movie file that can then be linked to a web page.

1 Open a web page in Dreamweaver®.
2 Select Insert / Media / Flash.
3 Browse to the animation you want to insert and click OK.
4 Test your page in the browser.

How to... Insert sound into Adobe® Dreamweaver®

To insert sound as a link:

1 Open a web page in Dreamweaver®.
2 Highlight the text or image you want to link for the sound.
3 In the Link box in the Properties Inspector, type in or browse to the music file.
4 Test your page in the browser.

To embed as a background sound:

1 Open a web page in Dreamweaver®.
2 View the code by selecting View / Code or by clicking the Code button in the top left.
3 Between the <head> tag and the </head> tag, insert <bgsound src="mysound.wav" loop=50>. But instead of mysound.wav enter the file name of your sound and instead of 50 set the loop number to the amount of times it should play. (Note: loop can be set to infinite.)
4 Test your page in the browser.

Ensuring compliance with W3C

The W3C (World Wide Web Consortium) is a body which promotes the standardisation of web design, especially of HTML. This is to ensure universal **accessibility**, including the ability of websites to be displayed on a variety of browsers and resolutions and be used by users with special needs.

Key terms

Acessibility – the ease with which websites can be accessed by users, especially referring to those with particular technologies or special needs.

Spider – a type of bot (short for robot – a computer program that runs automatically) used by search engines to find websites for search engines.

Meta-tagging

Search engines do not literally search the whole Internet every time a search word is entered into a search engine. Instead, they use enormous databases to store information about all the websites of which they are already aware and it is these databases which are searched. Search engines use **spiders** to trawl the Internet for websites to include in their databases.

The spiders examine each web page encountered and send information back to be stored in the database. To ensure that the spiders list the web page correctly, the web developer can include meta-tags in the coding for the web page.

How to... Create meta-tags in HTML

1 Open your homepage.
2 Below the <head> tag, enter this code:

```
<meta name="description"
content="Cheeseworld - all you need
to know about cheese">

<meta name="keywords"
content="cheese, fromage, brie,
cheddar, dairy">
```

Notice there are no spaces between the keyword and commas.

3 Change the description and keywords so they are relevant for your site.

This code cannot be tested, but can be read by spiders to be listed in search engines.

Cascading style sheets

CSS (cascading style sheets) can be used to control the formatting of a website efficiently. They can appear in the head of a particular web page to which they are to be applied or in a separate file so that they can serve

How to... Create a simple CSS page

1 Open Notepad (or a similar text editor).

2 Save the file as myCSSweb page.html.

3 Enter this code:

```
<html>
<head>
<title>My First CSS</title>
<link rel="stylesheet" type="text/css"
href="myCSS.css">
</head>
<body>
Here is some normal text.
<br>
<h1>Here is the text with CSS tags.</h1>
</body>
</html>
```

4 Save the file.

5 Create another new file and save it as myCSS.css.

6 Enter the following code:

```
h1 {
font-family: Arial;
color: red;
font-size: 20pt;
}
```

7 Save the file.

8 Navigate to where the.html file is saved using My Computer.

9 Double click your html file to open in your browser.

Note: Make sure the.html and .css files are saved in the same folder.

---

the whole site. CSS makes formatting easier. All the formatting is done in one place, meaning it is easier to preserve a house style. If alterations are required later on, only one change in the CSS needs to be made, rather than several in the HTML which may be hard to find.

Activity: Using CSS

1 In myCSS.css, change the font to Wingdings. Save the .css file and refresh the .html file in the browser.

2 In myCSS.css, change the colour to blue and the size to 100pt. Save the .css file and refresh the .html file in the browser.

4.4 Review

After the website is built, it is essential to test it to make sure all parts work correctly. This allows an opportunity for bugs to be removed and for the website to be perfected before it goes live.

Functionality testing

All the elements of the website should be tested. For example, when the page loads, the correct images should load in the right places. Also, each hyperlink should be tested to ensure it goes to the right page.

The user environment needs to be tested as well, to make sure it is in fact easy to use. This is often done using a usability group. This is a group of people who fit into the target market who will use the system. They provide feeback on the website when there is still time to make changes.

A test plan such as the one shown in Table 28.4 can be used.

Content

The content of the website must be proofread to check that there are no spelling and grammar errors and that the information is accurate and appropriate for the target audience.

Test number	Test element	On page	Test data	Expected result	Actual result	Success or failure	Screenshot reference
1	Home button	About.html	Left click	Load index.html	Load index.html	Success	S1
2	Logo.gif	Index.html	Load page	Appear in top left corner	Appear in centre of page	Failure	S2

Table 28.4: Example test plan

Check against user requirements

The final website should be compared with the user requirements which were defined in the design. The requirements that have been met should be assessed according to how well they have been met. If any requirements have not been met, this must be justified, giving valid reasons.

Activity: Meeting user requirements

1. Choose a website with which you are familiar. Identify the target audience and write a list of ten user requirements this site would need to meet.

2. For each user requirement, state how the web designers have or have not met it.

3. If any requirements have not been met, explain how the designers could improve the website to ensure that all requirements are met.

User acceptance

Once the website has been tested for functionality and been corrected, it is necessary to test if it is suitable for the designated audience. A focus group of people from the potential target market are selected to test the website and provide feedback. One very useful aspect of this will be to test whether the website is user friendly, as this is difficult to measure.

Audit trail of changes

An audit trail will track all the changes made to a web page. This can be used to trace all the developments made, especially useful when making changes due to testing.

In addition, tracking the changes made allows the possibility of reverting to a previous version if an amendment has caused a problem. For example, testing the JavaScript® might produce an incorrect result but when the code is changed it could stop asking the user for data to be inputted. If the developer has tracked the changes, instead of trying to repair this new error, they can easily change back to the original version and redo the repair of the script.

Assessment activity 28.4  (P5) (M3) (D3) BTEC

1. Using your design from Assessment activity 28.3, build the website for Fancy That! This includes the HTML, CSS and server side scripting. A web authoring package should be used. **P5**

2. Improve your website based on a client review. **M3**

3. Demonstrate that your website meets the defined requirements of the client and achieves its desired purpose. **D3**

Grading tips

- Any method or software can be used to create the website, but it must be multi-page with two-way interaction as designed. **P5**

- The improvements should be measurable. Explain how they will make the website better in terms of design or functionality – for your client or the user. **M3**

- Meeting the requirements can be demonstrated with annotated screenshots. Make sure each original requirement is addressed. **D3**

PLTS

Self-managers should use their time management skills to make sure their project does not overrun and **creative thinkers** can use their originality to translate their designs into a real website. **Reflective learners** will test and find improvements.

Functional skills

This task allows you to use **ICT** to carry out complex and non-routine tasks.

Jared
Web designer

There are two main areas of website production: designing and developing. Working as a web designer means that I concentrate on the artistic elements of the sites.

A large part of what I do is making sure the website's brand is used throughout the site and this is done by having a house style which defines the fonts, colours and other styles. These must be used consistently in all the site's pages.

Designing pages can involve working on large graphics for the whole layout, for example where the navigation will be on each page, or it could be small elements such as logos or individual buttons. Sometimes it can be more challenging working on the smaller parts, as you need to convey a company's logo and colour scheme in a very small space.

All the time I am working on a site, I have to remember two things:

- the client's needs – if the final product does not suit their requirements or does not fit the brief they have given me, then they might reject it

- the user's needs – the client needs a website which people will want to visit and be able to use easily.

Balancing these two sets of needs can be difficult, but when the final website is completed it is very rewarding.

Think about it!

Select three websites which you think are well designed and carry out the following tasks:

1 Write down five requirements that the client may have stated when requesting their website.

2 Write down five user needs for the website which will encourage them to keep visiting and using the site.

3 Compare these lists. Are any the same for client and user? Do any contradict each other?

4 You have identified these websites as being well designed. What specifically do you consider to be well designed on each site? What can you learn from them?

Just checking

1. Sketch a simple diagram to give an overview of how Internet technologies work together.
2. What are the four layers of TCP/IP and briefly what do they each do?
3. How does a firewall use ports to protect a web server?
4. What is the difference between static and dynamic websites?
5. How does bandwidth affect website performance?
6. What is compression and how does it aid website performance?
7. What is interactivity?
8. What are the advantages of using CSS?
9. How can meta-tags help a website move up the listings in a search engine?
10. What is house style and why is it used?

edexcel

Assignment tips

- Getting your head around Internet technologies can be a bit tricky because you need to imagine activities that are happening all over the world, numerous times every second. Try focusing on just one data package or one website and then expand it to consider what is happening across the whole of the Internet.

- When thinking about website performance, nanoseconds can make a big difference. Remember that it is important for websites to perform their actions as quickly as possible in as few clicks as possible.

- When designing your website, consider the time limit you are working to. Ambitious sites are impressive, but sites that are unfinished are not and could result in your achieving a lower grade. Strive for the best website you can make but be realistic about your deadline.

29 Installing and upgrading software

The performance and reliability of a computer system is extremely dependent on the correct selection, installation and configuration of its software. Without proper consideration of these factors, people often find that their computer systems are inefficient and in some cases unusable. This unit will give you the opportunity to install and upgrade software following agreed procedures, to ensure an effective installation is performed. It is important for you to understand how to recognise the need for an upgrade or new installation – for example, how to fix an identified bug, to allow a device to run more efficiently or to allow the device to operate with other components or software. You need to understand the role of software in controlling devices and systems as well as where the software is stored and the processes involved in upgrading software.

Within an organisation it is extremely important that all installations and upgrades are thoroughly planned to make sure that the work will complement the existing systems and that all resources are available. It is also important that structured procedures exist for the installation and upgrading of software so that there are clear and coherent records for all installations and to ensure that each job is completed properly. You will investigate these procedures and follow them when completing your own installations and upgrades.

Learning outcomes

After completing this unit, you should:

1. understand why software needs installing or upgrading
2. know how to prepare for a software installation or upgrade
3. be able to install or upgrade software
4. understand the completion and handover process.

Assessment and grading criteria

This table shows you what you must do in order to achieve a pass, merit or distinction grade, and where you can find activities in this book to help you.

To achieve a **pass** grade the evidence must show that you are able to:	To achieve a **merit** grade the evidence must show that, in addition to the pass criteria, you are able to:	To achieve a **distinction** grade the evidence must show that, in addition to the pass and merit criteria, you are able to:
P1 describe the potential prompts that initiate the installation of new or upgraded software **See Assessment activity 29.1, page 193**	**M1** explain the advantages and potential disadvantages of installation or upgrade of new software **See Assessment activity 29.1, page 193**	**D1** justify a particular installation or upgrade **See Assessment activity 29.1, page 193**
P2 describe the potential risks of installing or upgrading software **See Assessment activity 29.1, page 193**	**M2** explain the requirements in preparing for a software installation and upgrade **See Assessment activity 29.2, page 199**	**D2** evaluate the risks involved in the installation or upgrade of software and explain how the risks could be minimised **See Assessment activity 29.1, page 193**
P3 plan an installation and an upgrade **See Assessment activity 29.2, page 199**	**M3** design and implement a procedure to preserve data integrity during an upgrade **See Assessment activity 29.2, page 199**	
P4 record and complete a software installation **See Assessment activity 29.3, page 206**	**M4** design a procedure to back out of software upgrades **See Assessment activity 29.2, page 199**	
P5 record and complete a software upgrade **See Assessment activity 29.3, page 206**		
P6 explain the importance of the user acceptance process **See Assessment activity 29.4, page 210**		

How you will be assessed

By completing a number of assessments you will develop the required knowledge and skills to plan, implement and record a software installation and upgrade.

These assessments might include:

- verbal presentations
- case studies
- practical tasks
- written assignments
- PowerPoint® presentations.

Märit, BTEC National IT learner

I really enjoyed this unit as it allowed me to learn how to effectively install and configure different software and upgrades.

In my assignment I designed and planned procedures for the safe installation and upgrade of software in an organisation and then got to actually implement my procedures to effectively perform the installation and upgrade.

I found it really interesting to see the amount of planning and detail that has to go into a software installation or upgrade within an organisation. It is much more complicated than a home installation, as you have to consider the effects on the running of the business and how you can reduce these effects.

I also had to look at the prompts and justifications that lead to organisations actually installing and upgrading software. I discovered that just because a new piece of software or an upgrade is available this doesn't mean an organisation will actually install them. I also had to write about the risks and requirements involved in a software installation and upgrade. I found this tied in closely with the justification for upgrades, as one of the reasons a business may not upgrade is because of the potential risks involved, such as loss of data and computer system down-time. It was interesting to look at these risks and justifications and I really enjoyed having to justify an installation to an organisation to help me gain my distinction.

Over to you!

- **What was the last software application you installed?**
- **What did you consider before you installed the software?**
- **What sort of risks do you think might prevent an organisation from upgrading their software?**

1 Understand why software needs installing or upgrading

Prompts in your system

Have a look at the software currently installed on your computer system.

- What do you think would make you upgrade or install new software to replace what is currently on your system?
- Does any of the software have an automatic update feature?
- What upgrades or alternatives are there available for you to install?

This section will help you to identify and understand the reasons why we install and upgrade software as well as the factors we must take into consideration when deciding on whether to go ahead with an installation or upgrade.

1.1 Prompts for change

There can be a huge variety of reasons that would prompt you to install or upgrade your software. It could be in response to a bug that has been identified or it could be to allow for a hardware device to run more efficiently or with greater functionality. You must be aware of these prompts so that you can act on them in a timely manner, as in some situations they are important for ensuring the security of your computer system.

Problems with existing systems

There may often be problems with your existing computer system that a new software installation or upgrade can fix. It could be that the software currently on the system is unstable and has a tendency to cause the system to crash, or that it is no longer supported by the manufacturer and so you no longer receive user support or updates for it. There could be security issues with software you are currently running – in other words, it is at risk from malicious attacks. You could even find that your current software is incompatible with a newly installed operating system. In these situations it is very important to upgrade your software or install new software so that you can continue to make full use of your computer system.

Additional functionality required

Sometimes a person or organisation will want additional functionality from their software. For example, someone using Windows® XP may require some strong parental control facilities and so purchasing Windows Vista® or 7, which have these, would be a good solution. Another example could be that you have anti-virus software but you would like to have anti-spyware and firewall software as well to ensure the security of your computer system. You could install a fully integrated Internet security suite that offers these tools and many more to better protect your computer system. When additional functionality is required there will usually be an upgrade available that offers the new facilities. However, there will be some situations where a completely new installation will be necessary.

New hardware requiring new or upgraded software

When you install new hardware into your computer system you are often required to install a program called a **device driver** in order for it to be fully compatible. These drivers inform the operating system about how to communicate with the new piece of hardware, so without them it will not work. Sometimes when you have installed the hardware it will detect an existing device driver. However, it is always important to make sure that you are using the latest device driver to ensure greater systems stability and compatibility. Alternatively, hardware providers will also include software programs that allow you to use, configure and manage the hardware device more effectively, so it is a good idea to install this software.

External prompts for software bug fixes

Although software will be extensively tested before it is released, it is very rarely released without a single bug or error. These errors may cause the software to **hang** or **crash**. When bugs are identified by the software developer they will work on a 'patch' which can fix the problems and then make the patch freely available to download. Often the software will automatically check for these bug fixes and if any are identified it will ask you if you wish to install the update. Microsoft® Windows® operating systems have an update program that can be set to automatically detect and update the software. This can be for relatively minor fixes, which are flagged as optional updates, or major security-related fixes, which are flagged as important. Without these regular bug fixes your software can be extremely unreliable and insecure, so paying attention to these external prompts is very important.

Key terms

Device driver – a program that tells a computer system how to communicate with a hardware device.

Hang – when a computer program or an entire system stops responding to input.

Crash – when a computer program stops working and communicating with other parts of the computer system altogether.

Other

There are a variety of other reasons why a software installation or upgrade would be necessary. One of the most important of these is to do with company policy. Many organisations have a policy defining a specific piece of software the company will use. This is done to ensure greater compatibility of document types, so information can be shared between employees more easily. It also means that training and maintenance is far easier as, for example, training for only one word processing application would be required for all employees. It is also likely that there will be a policy on when new installations and upgrades will be carried out. This means that companies will upgrade

their software at specific intervals, such as on a daily, weekly or monthly basis, allowing them to easily track when software has been updated and ensure that the software is up to date.

Activity: Windows® update

Go to http://windowsupdate.microsoft.com and check for updates.

- Does it find any software updates? How many?
- How can you tell which of these updates are urgent and which are not?
- Explain why it is important to pay attention to these update prompts and to install them as soon as possible.

1.2 Justification for change

Just because there is a prompt for change, it doesn't mean that an organisation will agree to the change going ahead. Installing new software is often expensive, as is upgrading in many situations. This isn't just the cost of the software – there will be additional costs such as training and the down-time needed to install the software. Therefore, it is important that there is a good business case made for the change to go ahead. This means that the perceived benefits must be shown to outweigh the costs of the new software or upgrade. The benefits could be many things, such as greater efficiency or improved systems security. Whatever they are they must clearly outweigh the costs for the organisation before installation can go ahead.

Activity: Justifying a change

1. In small groups discuss what the new features and benefits are in using Microsoft® Office 2007 over Microsoft® Office 2003.

2. In the same groups discuss the potential costs of upgrading from Office 2003 to Office 2007.

3. Together, create a presentation that identifies these advantages and costs and then justify whether you think the upgrade should be completed.

1.3 Risks

When installing and upgrading software you must always be aware of the variety of risks involved, such as the down-time on the system required as well as the danger of incompatibility issues. It is extremely important that you plan how to mitigate the effect of these risks before starting with the installation so that you are prepared in case the worst should happen.

Potential loss of service

When installing software there may be a certain amount of time when your system will be inactive while the installation takes place. Although this may not be a significant amount of time, in some situations it can take over an hour, especially if the installation needs to be completed on multiple computer systems. This period of system inactivity may cause major disruption to a business's trading. For example, if you were upgrading the operating system on your server it would probably mean that any network resources and the Internet connection would be unavailable for the period of time it takes to install and configure the new operating system. There is a real risk that this down-time will reach unacceptable levels and so plans should always be made to minimise any disruption.

Incompatibility issues

Another major risk when installing new software is that it may cause incompatibility issues with existing software, hardware and data files. For example, if you were using an operating system such as Windows® and switched to Linux there is a good chance that some of your software would not work on Linux as it may only be compatible with Windows®. Additionally you would need to find alternative drivers for your hardware devices, as the Windows® drivers would not be compatible with the Linux operating system. This doesn't just apply to something as drastic as switching from one operating system to another. When upgrading from Windows® XP to Windows Vista® you will find that older software on your system may not be compatible with Vista and is unusable.

So, before you perform an installation, it is very important that you make sure your new software is compatible with your existing system. Otherwise you will find yourself unable to use the system and normal business trading could grind to a halt.

Risk reduction measures

It is important to identify the risks involved with any installation or upgrade and to have risk reduction measures in place. There are three main methods for reducing the risks involved:

- **Backups**: Before making any installation attempt you should back up all data and software. This way if your installation damages the existing data and software you will easily be able to replace it from your backup.

- **Installing at low risk times**: If you install your software during your busiest business hours it can be very costly as you will be unable to use your computer system for a fairly significant amount of time (especially if something goes wrong). By performing installations at quiet times, such as overnight, the negative effects of any down-time will be greatly reduced and it will allow you plenty of time to rectify any problems that arise.

- **Incremental installation**: If you're going to be installing new software on a large number of computer systems you can reduce the risk by installing the software on only a few systems initially, to ensure that no problems arise, and then gradually install it on further systems. This means that you will be able to continue running your business while the installations are happening and identify and resolve any issues on a smaller number of computer systems.

Activity: Reducing risks

1   If you were a high-street shop that was installing new till system software, how would you reduce the effect of losing the use of your tills while the installation is being completed?

2   During the installation an error occurrs that causes your sales data to be lost. What could you have done to reduce the effect of this risk?

Assessment activity 29.1

P1 P2 M1 D1 D2   **BTEC**

You have recently been hired as an IT consultant by a small charity that wishes to advertise itself with a website and take donations. They have asked you to look at their current computer systems and advise on any new software installations or upgrades that may be necessary.

You have noticed that their anti-virus software is out of date and they do not have anti-spyware or firewall software. You have decided to advise them that upgrading their anti-virus software to an up-to-date fully integrated Internet security suite would be advisable.

Write a report to the managers of the charity to explain your decision and advise them on what they should be doing to prepare for the software upgrade.

1   Describe the prompts that might lead you to consider a software installation or upgrade. **P1**

2   Explain the advantages and disadvantages of installing and upgrading software. **M1**

3   Justify to the managers why upgrading their anti-virus software would be advisable. **D1**

4   Describe the potential risks of installing or upgrading software. **P2**

5   Evaluate the potential risks of installing and upgrading software and explain how the risks could be minimised. **D2**

Grading tips

- A paragraph or two describing the different prompts that have been looked at in this section will meet this criterion. **P1**

- A quick Internet search will identify many of the range of benefits of different software packages. A table comparing the advantages and disadvantages of installations and upgrades would help achieve this criterion. **M1**

- You have already identified the prompts, advantages and disadvantages of software installations and upgrades. You must now use these to create a report that makes a good business case for upgrading the charity's anti-virus software. **D1**

- You can use the Internet to research the risks of upgrading software. You need only write a paragraph identifying and describing these risks to achieve this pass grade. **P2**

- You have already described the potential risks. A report that evaluates the risks and explains how to minimise their effects will help you meet this criterion. **D2**

PLTS

Researching into different software packages will provide evidence that you are an **independent enquirer**.

Functional skills

The research you will undertake in this task will use your **ICT** skills and the writing of the report will use your **English** writing skills.

2 Know how to prepare for a software installation or upgrade

This section will help you to understand the important processes and preparations that you must carry out before performing an installation or upgrade in order to ensure it is completed efficiently and effectively.

2.1 Installations and upgrades

When an issue has been identified with the software in your existing computer system you will need to decide on whether a new installation is required or if upgrading the existing software is a satisfactory solution. This decision can have a major effect on the costs and preparations involved with the task.

Installations

A software installation that requires the addition of completely new software to a computer system is usually a much more expensive process than upgrading existing software. Additionally, a new installation will often take more time than upgrading the software and there will also be a greater chance of problems arising, as you will have had no experience with the software to date. This also means that more training will be needed so that employees are able to use the software effectively. The advantage of a new installation is that you will be able to choose software that has all of the features you require, which an upgrade may not offer.

Installations do not always involve new software. If for some reason a current installation is no longer functioning properly it may be advisable to uninstall the software and then reinstall it.

Upgrades

A software upgrade involves replacing the software that is currently on the computer system with a newer version, which usually offers greater tools and facilities. This is generally cheaper than purchasing entirely new software so it is usually the best option when you require new features from your current software package. It also has the advantage of requiring less training, due to its similarities with the earlier versions of the product, and the relative ease and reliability associated with carrying out an upgrade. As a rule, you are better off upgrading software rather than

completing a new installation unless an upgrade fails to offer the features you are looking for.

Activity: To upgrade or install?

1 In small groups list three advantages of upgrading Windows® XP to Windows Vista®.

2 In the same groups list three advantages of installing a Linux operating system instead.

3 Discuss which would be the better choice of the two and the reasons why you come to the decision, eg cost of installation, cost of training, compatibility with existing systems.

2.2 Planning

Before you start any software installation or upgrade it is extremely important to have thorough plans so that the process can be completed as smoothly as possible.

Sequence of activities

You must first have a clearly defined sequence of activities to follow in order to ensure the installation is completed successfully. These activities are as follows.

- Check to ensure that the system(s) used for the installation meet or exceed the software's minimum requirements.

- Decide on whether a fresh installation is required or if installing over existing software is appropriate.

- Ensure that the installation method is suitable and capable. For example, if the installation files are stored on a DVD your system requires a DVD drive that supports the specific DVD format (eg DVD-R).

- Select the most appropriate location for the application to be installed. This could be the main hard drive, an external hard drive or a remote network drive.

- Define a suitable procedure for the installation or upgrade. This will usually involve steps such as checking contents, reading manuals, performing virus scans, backing up data, configuring the software and problem solving.

Materials

When planning for an installation or upgrade you need to make sure that you have all of the materials you will need available to you and that they are fit for purpose. The materials include:

- the computer system
- the software installation media
- installation guides
- license keys.

For more information on this subject, see page 197.

Activity: Planning for your materials

1 Use the Internet to research the procedure for installing Adobe® Dreamweaver® CS4.

2 What materials will you need to gather when installing this application? Remember to consider the software's minimum requirements.

3 What formats can Adobe® Dreamweaver® CS4 be installed from (eg CD, DVD, downloaded file, zip file)?

Timing

Installations and upgrades are not usually performed during the hours when a business is operating so that the amount of disruption and loss of businesses efficiency is kept to a minimum. The most common time for carrying out upgrading or installation work is late evenings. Some businesses run 24 hours a day, so for these it is best to carry out the work during their non-peak hours.

Communications

It is important that you have well-defined communication procedures planned for every installation. This means you must consider who needs to be communicated with during the various installation stages as well as how you will communicate with them. It is usual to keep the following people informed during an installation.

- **End users**: These are the people who will be using the system. They need to be kept informed about when the installation is going to happen and how long they will be without a system as well as any problems that arise during the installation. This information is very important to the end user, as all of the factors can have a major effect on their productivity.

- **Management**: The management within an organisation will be very interested in being kept informed during the installation process so that they are aware of when their employees will be able to start making use of the new software. They will also need to be aware of problems that have arisen, as this may have serious effects on the running of the business.

- **Software vendors**: If problems arise with a software installation or upgrade you will often need to contact the software vendor to find a solution. It is important therefore that you have your lines of communication to the software vendor defined before you start the installation.

The most common form of communication within a business is email. It is popular because it is fast and allows for storage and filing, for referencing at a later date. Contacting the software vendor can usually be completed through a variety of methods. The most common methods are phoning, instant messaging or using a web contact form.

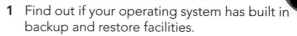

Activity: Contacting software vendors

1 Use the Internet to find the different ways you can contact Microsoft® for software support.

2 Choose another software vendor and find out the different ways to contact them for support.

3 Compare these different methods with another learner and list the most common methods offered to contact the software vendors.

Back-out procedures

Sometimes you will find that an installation or upgrade will cause problems with your current system that you had not foreseen and you will need to reverse the changes you have made. For example, you may have upgraded your operating system only to discover that many of your software applications and hardware devices are incompatible with the new operating system. To help recover from these situations you will need to have a clearly defined **back-out procedure**.

Key terms

Back-out procedure – restoring the system to the state it was in before the installation took place.

Administrator account – a user account that has total access rights and permissions. This allows total unrestricted access to all hardware and software resources.

There are a variety of procedures that you can put in place. The first of these is to ensure that you have your software and data backed up before you complete the installation. This will allow you to restore the system to its previous state easily. Another would be to uninstall the new software or upgrade. This combined with having your software and data backed up should allow you to return to the stable state you had before the

installation. Your final procedure would be to have system recovery points set. This is a series of points that you can roll back to should a problem arise, and it is a common feature in modern operating systems.

Activity: Backup software

1 Find out if your operating system has built in backup and restore facilities.

2 List the different types of data that the facility can backup.

3 Follow the steps given by the facility to create a backup of your document files.

Gaining permissions and access

Due to the importance of security within an organisation it is usual for workstations to be kept secure by requiring staff to use usernames and passwords and by limiting access rights to software and data that they do not need to use. This means that to install new software you will need to have access to an **administrator account**. You may also need to be aware of user login details to ensure that the correct users will have access to the software once it has been installed on the system.

Activity: Classroom access rights

1 Find out who has administrator privileges on the computers in your classroom.

2 What access limitations are there on your account? Can you install software or change settings?

3 What access limitations do your tutors have? Can they install software or do they need to contact an IT services department to get this done?

Other

Most installations will be subject to a SIP (software installation plan). This SIP is a document that contains contractual agreements about things like installation details, timescales for completion of the work and details on after-sales support and customer training. This document will obviously have a major effect on your planning, as you must make sure that you meet all of the defined criteria – otherwise your customer will be able to use the document to refuse to pay you for the work.

2.3 Guidance

As part of your preparation for any installation you will need to ensure that there is suitable guidance available for the end users. The procedures and availability of support should be clearly agreed upon before installation takes place.

Providing guidance on procedures

Whenever software is installed or upgraded within an organisation there will be a period of time during which users will be unfamiliar with the software and will need guidance on how to use the software's various features. This will vary greatly from very simple problems that can be easily and quickly resolved to much more complex problems that may need to be escalated to a higher level technical assistant. The amount of requests for help can be reduced greatly by giving the users training on the software before the installation is completed. Without giving the training you will likely find that the amount of requests for help will be unmanageably large.

Activity: Providing guidance

1   Perform an Internet search for people requesting help in using Microsoft® Office. How many results did you find?

2   List five of the help requests that you found.

3   Try to resolve the problems yourself or, if you can't, see if you can find the answer using the support features built into Microsoft® Office.

4   Did you find that most problems people need help on were fairly simple? Share your findings with other learners in your class and discuss.

Selecting software loading facilities to be used

It is important to consider the software loading facilities that are going to be used because you will need to ensure that they that are compatible with the media on which the software installation files are stored. In the preparation stage you must check that you have the correct software loading facilities available so that the installation can actually proceed. For more information please see Loading facilities, page 205.

Escalation procedures

Many requests for guidance will be simple problems that can be dealt with by low level IT support assistants. However, there may be more complex issues that arise that cannot be solved by these assistants and so need to be referred to higher level IT support assistants so that the issue can be resolved. This process of referring these difficult to resolve problems to more highly trained technical staff is known as escalation. It is important that the procedure for escalation is well defined so that it is clear in which situations to escalate the problem and who is the correct person to escalate the issue to. Without having these procedures well defined you can often find that the request for help will be passed between people and so the problem may take far longer to be resolved that it should do.

2.4 Materials

When preparing for an installation it is very important to ensure that you have a clear understanding of the materials and resources that you will require and you have them all available to you in a usable format.

Obtaining and allocating required materials

Naturally, the first thing you should make sure you have available to you is the computer systems that require the installation or upgrade. You will need to check that these meet the minimum requirements of the software application, otherwise the installation will not be possible. You should also ensure that the computer system has a software loading facility that can use the installation method. For example, if the software is stored on a DVD and the computer system only has a CD drive then you will not be able to perform the installation.

As mentioned above, the method of installation, such as CD or DVD, is also something that needs to be planned for and obtained before the installation can take place. It may be accessed from a server via an internal network or it could be a downloaded installation file from the Internet. Whichever method, you must ensure that your computer system can make use of these resources. For more information on software loading facilities, see Loading facilities, page 205.

Resource allocation

As well as allocating the correct materials it is also important to allocate the correct resources, including manuals, installation guides and **license keys**. The manuals and guides are a very helpful resource when you perform an installation or upgrade for the first time as you will be unfamiliar with the procedures. They would be a first line of support before having to contact the software vendors.

Correctly allocating the license keys is important, as you will need a valid license key for each installation. If you install more copies of the software than you have license keys then you will be running the software illegally. It is possible to purchase a site license, which allows you to have as many installations of the software as you need within the organisation. This is significantly more expensive than individual license keys but easier to manage and allocate where needed.

Key term

License key – a software key certifies that the copy of a program is original and not been illegally copied.

Case study: Allocating resources

Microbyte Systems is a small computing retailer run by Paul Clews. He has recently hired you to manage the installation of the Windows® 7 operating system on his computer systems. He has five computers, all of which are currently running Windows® XP. The specification for the computer systems is as follows:

- 3 GHz Pentium 4 processor
- 1 Gb DDR2 RAM
- 250 Gb hard disk
- 512 MB DirectX compatible graphics card
- CD-RW optical drive.

1 What issues may arise when collecting the materials to install Windows® 7 32 bit using the current hardware system?

2 What additional issues may arise if you were installing the Windows® 7 64 bit operating system?

3 What resources will you need to collect before installing Windows® 7?

Assessment activity 29.2

The small charity has accepted your proposal of upgrading their anti-virus to a fully integrated Internet security suite. They currently have five computers, all of which require the software upgrade. They have asked you to create a comprehensive plan showing the procedures you will be following when upgrading the software. They have also requested that you plan for the installation of Open Office.

1   Explain the requirements involved when preparing for a software installation or upgrade. **M2**

2   Plan an installation and an upgrade. **P3** Design and implement a procedure to preserve data integrity during an upgrade. **M3**

3   Design a procedure to back out of software upgrades. **M4**

Grading tips

- A report explaining the various processes that you should follow before installing or upgrading software would meet this criterion. **M2**

- To meet this criterion you should explain the process you will follow when carrying out the software installation and upgrade requested by the charity. **P3**

- Choose a method of ensuring the integrity of data that is suitable for the upgrade and document this process. A witness statement by your tutor would demonstrate your ability to implement the procedure. Alternatively, you could use screen recording software to document your implementation. **M3**

- This time, select a procedure for backing out of a software upgrade that is suitable and document this process. **M4**

PLTS

Deciding on the best process for the installation and upgrade will show that you are an **independent enquirer**.

Functional skills

Your report will give evidence of your **English** writing skills.

3   Be able to install or upgrade software

In this section you will learn what processes are involved in a software installation or upgrade. You will also be given the opportunity to practise the practical skills needed to install or upgrade software.

3.1 Installation/upgrade processes

There are a number of processes involved in the implementation of an installation that must be completed to ensure that the installation is successful

and that it is possible to recover if there is a problem with it.

Backing up the current system

The first process you must complete when installing or upgrading software is to back up the current system. The main purpose of this is to make sure that you are able to go back to a working system should any major problem arise after the installation. When backing up the current system you have two main options:

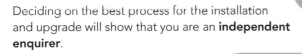

- **Image-based backup**: This is a backup of your entire hard drive. If your main disk is damaged this allows you to quickly recover, as every piece of data will be stored in the backup, even software applications and registry data. The down side of image-based backups is that they can take a very long time to complete.

- **File-based backup**: This is a simple process of copying files from the computer system to another source for the purpose of data recovery. You can use backup software to choose what types of file to back up and then automate the procedure or you can do this manually, although this would be quite time consuming. The advantage of a file-based backup is that the resulting backup is much smaller and so takes less time to complete. The disadvantages are that it is always possible to forget to back up files, and when your main disk fails you will need to reinstall all of your software before you can use your backup to restore the files.

Activity: Backups

1 If you were upgrading your operating system, which type of backup would you use first?

2 In pairs, discuss what you thought was the best kind of backup to use and explain why you came to that decision.

Disaster recovery plan

Another important process that must be completed before performing the installation or upgrade is to ensure that you have a disaster recovery plan in place and that all pre-installation tasks have been completed. The purpose of the disaster recovery plan is to give you a defined process for recovering from damage to your computer system so that you can continue running your business. It will usually be in the form of a detailed written plan that defines how you will recover from the loss of network services, application software and data files, as well as explain who will be responsible for the repairs and what the priorities for recovery are (what must be restored immediately and what is less important to restore in order for business to recommence). It will also usually include a checklist and test plan for ensuring that the computer system has returned to a fully functioning state.

Case study: Recovering from disaster

Banoop is a website development company run by Simon Cross. They recently moved to a new operating system but this caused some major problems, with many of their software applications not working and other compatibility issues. The result is that individual workstations cannot communicate with the company's server, and therefore cannot access either their files or the Internet.

1 What should Banoop have done before installing the new operating system to ensure that they could recover from this problem?

2 If they had performed the actions you advised after the problem had occurred what would their recovery process have been?

3 Create a report where you explain your answers to the above questions. Also create a checklist for Simon to follow to ensure that everything is restored to its original working state.

The installation process

After you have completed all of your pre-installation tasks you will finally reach the installation process. Some software is simply designed to be copied to its destination and so there is no formal installation process to be followed. However, with most installations you will find that a range of tasks is involved, including:

- reading and agreeing to a software license
- selecting a location for the installation
- unpacking compressed files
- creating a folder structure and copying files to the new location
- creating Windows® registry entries
- creating the software configuration files
- creating links and shortcuts.

These tasks are usually simplified into an installer program that will allow you to choose exactly what you wish to be installed and then will automatically complete all of the required tasks to fully install the software. You may then wish to manually perform actions such as creating further shortcuts, manually configure the software and update the software.

Activity: Installing software

1 Download CCleaner 2.30 (you should find a link easily if you use a search engine to search for it).

2 Run the executable that you downloaded, select English from the language selection dialog box and select OK.

3 Select Next and then read through the license agreement before choosing 'I Agree'.

4 Select the destination for the software to be installed to (you can just use the default location) and then click Next.

5 Read through the different installation options and choose the options you wish to be completed and then click Install.

6 Once the installation is completed click Finish.

The upgrade process

The updating software process usually consists of many of the same tasks that are in the installation process. The major difference is of course that the folder structures, files, registries, links and shortcuts are already created. The upgrade process itself involves replacing many of the files and potentially creating additional files and folders as well as adding and modifying registry entries and software configuration files. The process is simplified through the use of a

Activity: Upgrading software

1 Run the CCleaner program that you just installed in the previous activity.

2 On the bottom right-hand side of the user interface you should see a link that says 'Check for updates…'. Click this link.

3 A webpage will load that identifies whether you have the latest version of the software.

4 Download the installation file and once it is downloaded run the installer.

5 To complete the installation follow the same steps that you followed in the installing software task.

6 Try running CCleaner and clicking the 'Check for updates…' link again. Does it find any more updates?

software upgrade program. Once you run the program you need to identify the location of the original installation and then it performs all of the creating, moving and editing of files to complete the installation process.

Many software applications will have an upgrade facility built in so that it is easy to keep up to date with the latest version. This facility either automatically downloads the software upgrade installation file and starts the upgrade process or it takes you to a site where you can download the upgrade.

Selecting installation/upgrade procedures

When selecting an installation or upgrade procedure you need to take a variety of factors into consideration. The first of these concerns the agreements you have made with the company about your payment for completing the software installation. These could include agreements such as when the installation will be completed and how long it will take.

The type of software installation or upgrade that you are completing will also affect the procedure followed. The simple upgrading of word processing software will be unlikely to cause major damage to the system and so your preparation for disaster will be quite a simple task. However, if you are going to install an entirely new operating system then you will need to spend a large amount of time performing extensive backup, configuration and testing procedures. The procedures you follow will vary, depending on the individual circumstances of each installation and upgrade.

Following agreed processes

You should always follow the agreed installation or upgrade processes closely. The agreed upon processes are designed to ensure that the installation or upgrade can be completed as smoothly as possible, causing little or no negative effect on the running of the business. If you deviate from the agreed process, for example by starting the installation later than agreed, then you may find that your installation will not be completed as smoothly as planned and problems could arise. As this process is one that has been agreed with your employer, it is likely to be part of the contractual requirements for the installation. Therefore, if problems do arise you may find that it will affect your payment for the work that you have completed.

Contractual requirements as potential constraints to processes

The contractual requirements are part of the agreement with the organisation that is employing you to perform the installation and as such they will be used to assess the success of the installation. If you fail to meet all of the requirements that are defined within the contract the employing organisation may judge that the work has not been completed acceptably and this may affect the payment for the work you have completed. These contractual requirements are likely to be to do with what you are installing, where you are installing it, when you are installing it and how long it will take to install. They allow little margin for error when performing the installation, which is why thoroughly planning your installation and upgrade procedures is so important.

Case study: Constrained by requirements

Matthew Charman is the owner and manager of a small coffee shop called Matt's Mocha. The shop has recently purchased new software for their EPOS system and have hired you to manage the installation process. They're open from 9am to 5pm, seven days a week, although they're far busier on the weekend. Matt is very concerned that the installation will require the store to be closed and therefore have a very damaging effect on sales.

What time and day should the installation take place to help minimise disruption to the business?

What other requirements might need to be agreed that will constrain the installation process (eg data that must be protected)?

3.2 Installation/upgrade procedures

While the installation and upgrade procedures are quite easy to carry out now due to installation programs, as a whole they involve a variety of extra tasks that must be followed to ensure that the installation is successful.

Installation

The installation process involves completing a series of tasks to fully deploy a software application on a computer system. The tasks include agreeing to software licenses, copying files, creating files and registry data and creating links and shortcuts. For more information, see 3.1 Installation/upgrade processes, page 199.

Configuration

Once an installation is complete you will need to configure your new software to ensure that it fully meets the needs of the organisation and integrates with the business's other systems. Some common configuration tasks that you might complete on newly installed anti-virus software include:

- how often and when the automatic scan will run
- how often and when the virus definitions will be updated
- whether incoming and outgoing emails should be scanned
- whether to ignore certain warnings and errors that arise
- what size the quarantine zone should be and whether to automatically delete infected files.

In individual software applications most of the configuration can be completed in an options section within the application itself. However, in software such as a newly installed operating system there is likely to be a range of areas for completing the configuration. For example, in Windows® operating systems you would use the user accounts section to configure new user accounts and access rights, whereas you would use the network and sharing centre to configure your network connections. To make finding these various areas easier, Windows® and other operating systems have a control panel that contains the various tools for configuring your operating system.

Activity: Configuring software

1 Run the CCleaner application that you installed previously.

2 Go to the options menu by clicking on the Options button.

3 Configure the application from this menu so that it will run CCleaner when the computer starts, automatically check for updates and close the program after cleaning.

4 Investigate the other configuration options available for CCleaner.

Testing

Once the new installation or upgrade is configured you will have to perform thorough tests to ensure that the system works fully and meets the requirements that were agreed upon with the company employing you. It is now that the test plan you created during the planning stage of the software installation or upgrade should be completed. The specific tests will vary greatly depending on the software you are installing or upgrading, but some of the more common ones are:

- Does the application run?
- Have all the settings you configured been applied correctly?
- Can you save files?
- Do all other applications and hardware still work?
- Have you deleted temporary files?

You will also need to perform actions such as running a disk checking application and running the software's automatic update tool. Your test plan should be detailed and specific so that you can ensure that the work you have carried out will be accepted as completed.

Activity: Testing software

1   In pairs create a list of features that you would need to test to ensure you have installed and configured CCleaner correctly.

2   Discuss the tests you have chosen with the rest of the group and see if there are any tests you hadn't thought of.

3   Use this test plan on CCleaner and record what happens for each test. Did they all work correctly?

4   If any tests didn't work as you expected, record what did happen and how you fixed the problem.

Delivery

The software installation process will not be completed until the computer system is delivered to your employer with its software fully working and meeting all requirements that have been defined. This means that you must ensure that the computer system is safely delivered to the client, whether this is by the client collecting the system from you, you personally delivering it or you having it sent to the client via a courier service. If something were to happen to the system in the process of delivery you would be responsible for the damage, so it is vital that all deliveries are checked and signed for on receipt.

Shipping

If you are using a courier service to deliver the completed computer system then you must be aware of the method of shipping used and pack the computer system appropriately. If it is being shipped internationally then this obviously could mean that the delivery will need to go through a variety of different stages such as airmail, lorries and vans. Making sure that the system is well packaged to protect it from damage, using a company that is reliable and ensuring that the contents are checked and signed for on receipt are all very important stages that should be completed when shipping.

Storage

When storing a computer system that you are performing a software installation or upgrade on you must ensure that it does not get damaged and is returned to your client unharmed. The basic rules for storing a computer system are that the storage location is dry and at a temperature of between 5 and 25 degrees. It should also be well ventilated and the computer positioned so that all its ventilation holes, including those of the monitor, are exposed. It goes without saying that the computer should be on a secure surface where it cannot be easily knocked over by someone passing by.

Software storage locations to be used

When installing the software it may not be a simple case of choosing the default location for storing your installed application. By default the software will usually be installed on your main hard drive. If the hard drive has been partitioned then you will need to make sure you are installing the software on the correct partition. Other location options include a separate hard drive or a file server. The choice of location is important, as if you make the wrong choice you will need to uninstall the software and reinstall it in the correct location, which will waste a lot of valuable time.

Specifications of the software

All software will have specification requirements that must be met for the software to be successfully installed. These specifications will usually require you to have an appropriate:

- operating system
- processor
- system memory
- hard disk
- graphics card
- display monitor
- optical drive.

There may be other requirements defined such as having an appropriate sound card.

To be able to successfully install a software application you must meet the minimum requirements for that specific application. While meeting the minimum requirements will allow you to install and use the software, there will also be recommended requirements that are necessary for the software to work efficiently and allow you to make full use of all the features.

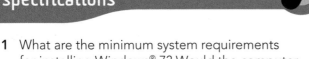

Activity: Discovering software specifications

1 What are the minimum system requirements for installing Windows® 7? Would the computer you are currently working on be able to support these requirements?

2 What are the recommended system requirements for installing Windows® 7? Would the computer you are currently working on be able to support these requirements?

Communicating the progress and outcome of the installation/upgrade

During the planning stage you should have clearly defined who you will need to communicate with during the installation/upgrade and how you will communicate with them. This is not just a practice exercise – you must communicate regularly with all of the relevant people to make them aware of how the installation is progressing and when it has been completed. This allows all of the parties involved

to react to any complications that happen during the installation or as a result of it. If you have not communicated with the appropriate people then these complications will get worse and resolving them will take longer. This is turn causes problems for your client and for you, as you may fail to meet the agreed deadline requirements.

Information recording

During the installation procedure you will need to record a variety of details. The sort of information that should be recorded includes:

- software license keys
- software versions installed
- date and time of the installation
- how many and which specific computers were installed with the software.

This data will later be passed on to the customer, allowing them to keep track of the installation after the handover has been completed. It will be extremely useful should the software ever need to be uninstalled, upgraded or replaced.

Obtaining access

To protect a business's computer systems and data most employees will only receive limited access rights, to prevent them from making unauthorised changes. You will therefore need to obtain access rights that are of a high enough level to perform the installation or upgrade – usually administrator access rights. When using this level of access you must obviously be extremely careful as it allows you to perform any changes to a computer system, which is potentially very damaging.

Security

In addition to having administrator access rights, you will also have access to all the company data stored on the computer system. For this reason you will need to ensure that your login details and the company's data is kept secure. Appropriate security policies must be put in place to ensure that only the people that need to have access to the computer system will have access to it. If administrator login details or private business data were to be accessed by unauthorised personnel, major damage could be caused which would damage the reputation and finances of both your client and yourself.

Confidentiality

As well as ensuring that the computer system is kept secure, the data stored on it must also be kept confidential. As you will have total access to the computer system it is reasonable to assume you will have access to private business data. It will be your responsibility to make sure that this data is not viewed by people unauthorised to do so and is only viewed where it is necessary for the installation process. Any information that is viewed should not be repeated to third parties. The confidentiality of the data will be considered a paramount requirement of the business and **non-disclosure** agreements may need to be signed before access to the data is given.

> ### Key term
>
> **Non disclosure** – an agreement used to protect the confidentiality of information when it is shared with a third party.

3.3 Loading facilities

There are a variety of loading facilities available to complete a software installation or upgrade and choosing the best option available is important to ensure that the installation runs as smoothly and efficiently as possible. Some of these options include CD, DVD, floppy disk and downloaded installation file. However, there are further considerations such as whether the CD is CD-ROM, CD-RW or one of the many other forms of CD.

> ### Activity: Choosing loading facilities
>
> 1 If you were asked to install a software application that takes 1 GB of storage space, what loading facilities would be available for you to use?
>
> 2 List each of these loading facilities and name an advantage and disadvantage of using each one for this application.

The capabilities of available software loading facilities

Loading facility	Positive capabilities	Negative capabilities
CD	• Almost all computer systems have a CD drive or a compatible DVD or Blu-ray drive • Storage capacity and read/write speeds are fairly good • Fast data transfer speeds	• Not all types of CD are compatible with all CD drives, eg a CD-R will not work with a CD-ROM drive • Storage size is often too small for modern software applications • Read/write speed is not the fastest
DVD	• Large storage capacity • Fast read/write speeds • Almost all modern computer systems will have a DVD drive or a compatible Blu-ray drive • Fast data transfer speeds	• Not all types of DVD are compatible with all DVD drives
Hard disk	• Very large storage capacity • Very fast read/write speed • Fast data transfer speeds	• Internal hard disks are not portable and external hard disks are less portable than an optical disk
Internet download	• The software will often be cheaper due to savings in resources, eg no disks or packaging	• Downloading the file will usually take a long time, even using a broadband connection
USB drive	• Very large storage capacity • Compatible with almost all modern computer systems • Good read/write speed	• Data transfer speeds are currently not as fast as modern hard disks and optical disk drives

Media

The media format of the installation files will naturally have a major influence on the loading facilities that you use. If the installation is stored on a DVD and your computer system only has a CD drive then there is obviously going to be a problem. Modern software is rarely stored on CDs due to their low storage capacity and the high availability of DVD drives. This consideration doesn't just apply to optical drives but also for formats such as ZIP files, which require special software to decompress the files.

Speed

The speed with which the loading facilities can read the installation files will significantly affect the overall completion time for the installation. The read speed of CD-ROMs can vary greatly from 150 **KB/s** (1×) to 10,800 KB/s (72×). DVD read speeds are significantly faster. A 16× DVD drive can read 21.13 **MB/s**. This would be equivalent to a 144× CD drive. So, as you can see, if you install software from a DVD it will take significantly less time than if you use a CD.

Key terms

KB/s – stands for kilobytes per second. It is a data transfer rate measured in 1000 bytes per second.

MB/s – stands for megabytes per second. It is a data transfer rate measured in 1,000,000 bytes per second.

GB/s – stands for gigabytes per second. It is a data transfer rate measured in 1,000,000,000 bytes per second.

Connection

The connection used by the loading facility will also potentially slow down the time it takes to install an application, as the data will need to be transferred from the loading facility to the computer's hard disk. Modern optical disk drives will transfer data using a SATA 2 connection. This offers transfer rates of 3 **GB/s**, which is obviously very fast and will enable you to transfer the data quickly. However, if your software installation files are stored on a network resource or on the Internet itself, you will be limited by your network speed. Broadband Internet runs at a variety of connection speeds but 10 MB/s is fairly common. This is obviously far slower than transferring from an optical disk drive.

Assessment activity 29.3

Now that you have agreed the installation and upgrade for the small charity and have designed the procedures to be followed, they would like you to complete the installation and upgrade.

1 Install Open Office on your PC, following the procedure that you planned in the previous assignment. Record the installation process and any important information that the client might require. **P4**

2 Upgrade your current anti-virus software package, following the procedure that you planned in the previous assignment. Record the upgrade process and any important information that the client might require. **P5**

Grading tips

- You can download the Open Office installer online. Print-screening each stage of the installation process would be a good way of recording it. **P4**

- If you haven't got an anti-virus software package or there isn't an available upgrade, then download and install a free anti-virus package eg AVG. Make sure you don't download the latest version, so you can then upgrade it for the activity. Print-screening each stage of the upgrade process would be a good way of recording it. **P5**

PLTS

Looking at improvements for the charity will show that you are an **effective participator**.

Functional skills

This assessment activity will require that you use your **ICT** skills.

4 Understand the completion and handover process

The final stage of installing and upgrading software is the completion and handover process. At this stage you will perform the final tasks to be completed after installation (eg registering the product) and then hand over the product to the customer.

4.1 Handover

The handover process occurs when the fully functioning computer system is returned to the customer. If the client does not accept that the work which has been completed meets the requirements for the installation satisfactorily then they will not accept the handover until any outstanding issues have been resolved. It is therefore important that the installation is fully completed to the agreed requirements before attempting the handover process.

Configuration to meet customer/user needs

As the customer has the right to refuse to pay you if the installation doesn't meet the agreed requirements it is important that you have configured the software to meet their needs completely. The task of configuring the software is not complicated but it must be completed and the software tested to ensure it works as expected and required. For more information on configuring software see page 202.

Handover to the customer/user

Formal handover to the customer involves not only handing over control of the computer system with new software installed. It also requires handing over installation details, technical manuals, user guidance documentation, contact details for technical and user support as well as any other materials that were used in the installation that belong to the customer. All of this information is extremely important to the customer so that they can make effective use of the software installation.

Customer/user acceptance

Once you have completed the formal handover the customer will need to formally accept the installation or upgrade as having been completed satisfactorily. Before they do this they may subject it to **user acceptance testing**. At this point the customer will normally sign a release form that confirms the installation has been accepted as complete.

If the customer does not accept the installation has been completed satisfactorily you may need to spend more time working on it. This is why clearly defined requirements with the customer are so important. If there is a dispute over whether the job has been completed you will have a document that proves you have completed the installation to meet the requirements that were agreed.

> ### Key terms
>
> **User acceptance testing** – a process carried out by the user that involves completing a series of tests on the newly installed software. Each feature of the software is individually tested to ensure that it is in fact a working application. This helps the user to confirm that the installation has been completed effectively.
>
> **Full image backup** – a single file that stores all contents from a storage device such as a hard drive.

Backing out

If the installation has not been successful then it is likely that you will be expected to back out of the installation. As described earlier (see page 196), this involves uninstalling the new software, reinstalling the previously installed software, recovering any lost data files and reconfiguring your system settings. This process will be greatly simplified if you took a backup of the system before you started the installation process, especially a **full image backup**. This would enable you to restore all software applications and systems settings from that one backup. (For more on hard drive images, see page 210.)

1 Create a list of materials you would need available to you if you were backing out of an installation.

2 With a partner, design a procedure for preparing and implementing the backing out of an installation.

3 Implement this plan by installing a software application and then backing out afterwards. Make sure you check that the back out was completed successfully.

4.2 Product registration

Once an installation is completed you should register the new software with the software vendor. Although this step is not mandatory there are a range of benefits to registration with no drawbacks, so you should do this for every installation that you complete.

Purpose of registration

When you install a new software application you will almost always be asked to register your software with the vendor via a simple electronic form. This data will then be sent to the vendor over the Internet. Registering your software is very important to the vendor. It supplies them with a variety of information on the people using their software such as:

- what kinds of people or business are using the software
- what the software is being used for
- your contact details
- how you discovered the software.

Activity: Registering software

1 Run a software application that you have recently installed but have not registered (eg AVG anti-virus software is free to install if you don't already have an application that you can register).

2 Find the register option and select it. You will usually find this under the Help menu option.

3 Fill in the registration form and submit it. What information did they wish to collect? Why do you think they want that information?

Registration will also prove to the vendor that your installation is using a legal license and it can include you in a bug reporting scheme to help them improve the reliability of the software.

Benefits of registration

Because of the advantages that registering software offers the vendors it is important that the vendors offer real benefits to the user to encourage them to register. Many vendors will require you to register your software to receive user support and software updates. If you are not able to access the software updates then you may find that problems will arise, as software is often released with many bugs still present that the updates will fix. Registering may also offer you such benefits as being kept informed of future releases and upgrades, giving you a replacement license key if you lose yours and discounts on future purchases.

Activity: Benefits of registering

1 Use the Internet to research the benefits of registering your Microsoft® Office product. Does it offer additional features or special offers?

2 Choose another application and research the benefits of registering this application.

3 Share your findings with another person in your group and create a complete list of the benefits of registering your software.

Licensing

When you install a new piece of software you will need to agree to a EULA (end user license agreement). This is a legal agreement between you and the vendor that defines how you can use the software. If you purchase an off-the-shelf software application you will usually have a standard single user proprietary license. However, there are other kinds of licenses such as:

- OEM (original equipment manufacturer) license – for software that is purchased by a hardware supplier and comes with your computer system
- site license – an unrestricted license that allows you to install the software as many times within your organisation as you need to

- open source license – a license that not only gives you access to the software but also lets you view, modify and share changes to the actual source code.
- freeware license – for software that is completely free to use, although sometimes there will be an optional payment.

Activity: Choosing a license

1 Research the price difference between an OEM license and a standard license for Microsoft® Office 2007 Professional.

2 What reason is there for the price difference? Why couldn't a standard user buy and install an OEM licensed software package?

3 Share the answers to these questions with the rest of your group.

Contractual implications

When you agree to an EULA (end user license agreement) you agree to a number of contractual implications. These implications can vary significantly, depending on the type of license that the software uses, but whatever the implications are you must ensure that you are not in breach of any of the terms or you will be breaking the law. A major part of most license agreements is the limited liability of the software vendor if the software causes damage to the end user's computer system. This has important implications, as you will not be able to claim for damages if your system is affected by the installation. There may also be agreements to prohibit users from reverse engineering the software as well as limiting the number of times the software may be installed. People rarely read the entire EULA when installing software but within an organisation it is important to understand exactly what you are agreeing to.

Dongles

Dongles are used by software vendors to protect their software from unlicensed use. The dongle itself is a small piece of hardware that must be connected to the computer system every time you run the software. If the dongle is not attached then the software will only run in a restricted mode or not at all. Dongles are used because they are difficult to replicate and this adds another layer of security. The vendors of AutoCAD® software commonly use dongles.

4.3 Data integrity

Whenever you are performing a software installation there is always a chance of causing damage to the data that is stored on the computer system. This is why measures must be put in place to ensure the integrity of data is retained.

System recovery point

A system recovery point is also known as a snapshot and it is a backup of your system at a specific point in time to which you can roll back should a problem arise in your computer system. System recovery points can be created manually or automatically and will usually be made before major changes to your system are carried out, such as the installation of a new piece of software. By creating these recovery points it is very easy to recover from any damage to data integrity.

Activity: System recovery points

1 Run the System Restore application that your Windows® operating system will have installed.

2 Look through the list of restore points that have been created. Is there one from before your last installation?

3 Roll back to before the most recent restore point. What aspects of your system have changed?

Copy of registry data

The registry data stores configuration settings and options that you have set on your operating system, software applications and hardware. Damage to registry data can cause applications, hardware and the entire computer system to become completely inoperable. Due to the serious effects caused by damage to the registry data you must always have a backup copy of this data.

All operating systems will have an application that will allow you to browse the registry data and take a copy of it – for example, Windows® operating systems have an application called regedit. However, there is also a variety of third-party software applications that will perform these actions.

Activity: Copying registry data

1 Run the regedit application that is installed on all Windows® operating systems.

2 Use the File menu to export the registry data to your documents folder.

3 Once this process has completed try importing the copied data back using regedit.

Copy of user data

User data refers to the files created by the user while using the software applications. This could be word processor documents, spreadsheets, presentations, web pages or game save files. It is important to keep this data secure, as it could include important information such as customer details, employee payroll data or financial information. There are huge amounts of user data stored by businesses that are absolutely vital to the running of the business. It is therefore extremely important to keep a copy of this data, which can be used in the event of damage to the data that is currently stored on the system.

It is quite easy to manually copy the user data on your hard disk to another location using the document explorer. However, this can also be time consuming as well as risky, as you could easily miss some files. There are a huge number of applications designed to automate this process such as the backup and restore program of the Windows® operating system.

Activity: Copying user data

1 Identify, with a partner, all of the types of user data they have stored on their computer (including emails and game saves).

2 List these different types of data and where the files will be stored on your computer.

3 Copy all of this data onto an external hard disk, USB stick or optical disk.

4 Did finding the data add a significant amount of time to the process? Would using a program to automate the process be advisable?

Prior image of hard drive

Creating a full image of the hard drive is the best way to ensure you will be able to recover all data on your computer system should there be damage to the data. Restoring from the image is a time-consuming task and as such it is usually used as a last choice, should your system recovery points and other backups not resolve the problems that arise. There are a variety of software applications available for creating a hard disk image, eg Norton Ghost™ or Acronis® True Image.

Assessment activity 29.4

You have completed the installation and upgrade for the small charity and have reached the handover and acceptance stage of the procedure.

Explain to the small charity why the user acceptance process that is followed during the handover stage is so important. **P6**

Grading tips

- A short report that clearly explains the different reasons for the user acceptance process would be acceptable for this criterion. **P6**

PLTS

Looking at improvements for the charity will show that you are an **effective participator**.

Functional skills

Your report will give evidence of your **English** writing skills.

Steve
IT technician

Steve Denham is an IT technician for a large university in the southeast of England. In his role he is responsible for:

- planning, implementing, configuring and testing new software installations and upgrades
- resolving issues that are discovered during testing and arise while in use
- setting up, adjusting and installing new computer hardware
- arranging for the repair of equipment where the need arises
- organising and performing routine maintenance tasks on the computer systems.

Due to the nature of Steve's job he very rarely sits still in his office. He is constantly moving around the university, performing his duties in the classrooms and offices of other employees, ensuring that they can perform their own duties.

He keeps in contact with his fellow IT technicians through the use of a PDA (personal digital assitant), which allows him to view new job requests and record how and when he completes any work. As he has to work closely with staff across the entire university he needs to have strong communication skills. In fact, it is communicating with so many different people that he enjoys most about his job.

Think about it!

1 What areas have you covered in this unit that will help you perform the role of an IT technician?

2 What skills would you need to develop? For example, do your hardware maintenance skills need to be developed?

3 What would you most enjoy about a job like this? Would all of the roles and responsibilities appeal to you?

Just checking

1. What are the prompts for installing or upgrading software?
2. Describe the risks involved with performing an installation or upgrade.
3. What is the difference between a clean installation and an upgrade?
4. What are the key stages involved in any installation or upgrade procedure?
5. Identify the resources and materials required to successfully complete an installation.
6. What processes can be performed to ensure that disaster recovery is possible, should a problem arise?
7. Give three examples of software loading facilities and identify their relevant advantages and disadvantages.
8. Identify and explain the different types of license agreements.
9. List the purpose and benefits of product registration.
10. Describe the different methods available to ensure data integrity is kept during an installation or upgrade.

edexcel

Assignment tips

- Download free software available on the Internet such as Open Office, CCleaner, Mozilla Firefox, Ubuntu and AVG. Try installing these and think about the similarities and differences between each installation process.

- Look through all of your installed software and see if any upgrades are freely available. What are the advantages of these upgrades and what steps must be followed to complete the upgrade?

- Research the different backup tools that come with your operating system. Does it regularly create system restore points? Create a new system restore point, install some software and then roll back to the restore point. Have any problems arisen? Is the software still there?

- Find out what type of license agreement is used with each piece of software you have on your computer system. Were you already aware about the type of license? Can you install the software on another computer without any further payments?

30 Digital graphics

Digital graphics are found in many places, including promotional materials, documents and websites. This unit will give you an awareness of the software currently available to create and manipulate images. It will show you techniques that you can practise to enhance your graphical skills, as well as the hardware required to capture, edit and print digital images.

When you have completed this unit you will have improved your technical skills in using both vector and bitmap software packages. You will learn the importance of choosing an appropriate file format for saved graphics, with an appreciation of the issues around resizing images and pixellation distortion. You will need to understand how to use formal checking to ensure that a final product meets the requirements and that artwork keeps within the laws of copyright.

Learning outcomes

After completing this unit, you should:

1. know the hardware and software required to work with graphic images
2. understand types of graphic images and graphical file formats
3. be able to use editing tools to edit and manipulate images
4. be able to create and modify graphic images to meet user requirements.

Assessment and grading criteria

This table shows you what you must do in order to achieve a pass, merit or distinction grade, and where you can find activities in this book to help you.

To achieve a **pass** grade the evidence must show that you are able to:	To achieve a **merit** grade the evidence must show that, in addition to the pass criteria, you are able to:	To achieve a **distinction** grade the evidence must show that, in addition to the pass and merit criteria, you are able to:
P1 describe the hardware and software used to create and edit graphic images **See Assessment activity 30.1, page 232**	**M1** compare the limitations of different hardware and software packages used in graphics work **See Assessment activity 30.1, page 232**	**D1** evaluate the impact of evolving output mediums on the design and creation of graphic images **See Assessment activity 30.1, page 232**
P2 explain how different types of graphic images relate to file formats **See Assessment activity 30.1, page 232**		
P3 demonstrate the use of editing tools to edit and manipulate images **See Assessment activity 30.2, page 237**	**M2** justify the software, tools, file format, image resolution and colour depth used for creating graphic images. **See Assessment activity 30.2, page 237**	**D2** discuss the impact that file format, compression techniques, image resolution and colour depth have on file size and image quality. **See Assessment activity 30.2, page 237**
P4 create original graphic images to meet a defined user need **See Assessment activity 30.2, page 237**		
P5 modify images as a result of user feedback **See Assessment activity 30.2, page 237**		
P6 explain the potential legal implications of using and editing graphical images **See Assessment activity 30.3, page 238**		

How you will be assessed

This unit will be assessed by internal assignments that will be designed and marked by the staff at your centre. It may be subject to sampling by your centre's Lead Internal Verifier or an Edexcel Standards Verifier as part of Edexcel's on-going quality assurance procedures. Assignments are designed to allow you to show your understanding of the unit outcomes. These relate to what you should be able to do after completing this unit.

Your assessment could be in the form of:

* presentations
* case studies
* practical tasks
* written assignments.

Dan, BTEC National IT learner

When I first started my National Diploma course, I already had a massive love for graphics. When I discovered I could carry on with graphics on the course, I was over the moon.

Our graphics course was built over three assignments that were fun, but at the same time took a while to get our heads around. We have been able to use all types of new software packages, and I have improved my skills so much by learning how to use them and being able to access them any time I needed.

In the final assignment, we had to pick an unknown company and design a brochure for them to use. I really enjoyed the assignment, picking a local band called Tom + Olly from Brighton. I got to try out new ways of making logos and editing pictures to make them look the way I wanted them to look. We were allowed so much time and freedom in this assignment that it was possible to really put my own mark on the brochure and be happy with the final outcome.

To sum up my graphics course at college, it has been fantastic and I have learnt so much over the year of studying the subject. I have improved my skills by a huge margin, and now feel confident in new areas and even more confident in the areas I knew something about before.

Over to you!

* What planning do you think Dan needed to do before he could produce his brochure?
* Can you find any graphics software applications that include templates to help produce brochures?
* Identify and explain at least three ways that a template could help to produce a brochure?

1 Know the hardware and software required to work with graphic images

Start up

Can we believe our eyes?

Many modern images are faked or enhanced to help them become more effective, especially when used in adverts.

- Go to www.life.com/game/realfake to look at some images on the Life website. Find out how well you can pick out the fake photographs on this website from real ones.

- Search the Web for photographs that interest you. Identify photographs that you think:
  - o are enhanced to help sell a product
  - o are faked to give a wrong impression
  - o have been edited into a humorous image.

1.1 Hardware

Working with graphic images requires suitable **hardware** and **software** to produce the best results. The hardware used can have a dramatic impact on the ease of working with graphical images. Large amounts of data need to be moved between components such as the hard disk and RAM and video display, which can result in a frustratingly slow system if the components are not ideal.

Slow systems are not only more difficult to use, but they can also stifle the creative side of anyone using the system. If a wrong click of the mouse makes the system unusable for a minute or so while the hardware struggles to catch up, then there is less incentive for the user to try new things.

Graphics should be fun and any computer system that is used to work with graphics should be fast enough to make it a pleasure.

Suitable hardware for a graphics system should include these components at appropriate performance levels:

- graphics card – needed to produce a display at a **resolution** and **colour depth** that meet the needs of the user within the capabilities of the monitor

- internal memory (RAM) – to hold the running software and graphic images

- processor – to run the software and work out the calculations needed to manipulate digital graphics

- digital card reader – to quickly and easily accept graphic images from a digital camera

- file storage – to save the graphic images

- USB devices – to plug in pen drives to input or move graphic images to other devices or other USB devices, such as digital cameras

- input devices – to capture graphical images and transfer them to the computer system. Graphical input devices include digital cameras, scanners and graphics tablets.

For a computer system that is used for graphics, the higher the spec the better. A high-resolution display with good colour depth is essential for most graphic designers.

Key terms

Hardware – the physical part of a computer system, including components inside the system unit, peripherals such as monitor and printer, as well as specialised devices such as a digital camera.

Software – the collection of programs installed on the computer.

Resolution – short for display resolution. This is the number of pixels (see below) or lines to the inch on the screen or other output device. It is usually written as two numbers: the number of pixels across then the number down. So a 1024 × 768 display resolution has 1024 pixels across and 786 down, giving 786,432 dots on the screen.

Colour depth – the number of bits used by the graphics system to hold the colour of each pixel on the screen. A 24-bit colour depth means the number of colours available on a computer system will be 16.7 million.

Pixel – short for picture element. It is a dot of colour on a screen or other output device..

RAM – stands for random access memory. It is the name given to the electronic memory plugged into the main motherboard inside the system unit. RAM is often 1 GB or more in a modern computer system. This component is often replaced when a PC has a memory upgrade.

Cache memory – very fast electronic memory between RAM and another device, used to make the system run faster.

Digital graphics are an art form, so you need to have some artistic ability as well as a suitable computer system before you can create outstanding images.

Graphics cards

The graphics card takes digital information from the operating system specifying what is to be shown on the screen and makes this into a signal that the display understands. The signal usually travels along a video cable to the monitor, which uses it to create the picture.

Most modern graphics cards are very capable of producing an image that meets the highest needs of any monitor without noticeably slowing the system down.

Professional graphic designers value a DVI (digital visual interface) connection between graphics card and monitor in preference to the older VGA (visual graphics array) cable connection, as it gives a better picture.

Professional graphic designers often work with 32-bit colour depth, which gives 'truecolor' – this is a system where 32 bits are used for each **pixel**: 24 bits for the colour and the other 8 bits giving transparency information of 256 values, from fully opaque to fully transparent.

Internal memory

The internal memory of a computer system is called **RAM**. It is primarily used to hold programs when they are running and any documents or graphic files that the user has opened.

There is a constant flow of data between the hard disk, the RAM and the processor (see Figure 30.1). When a software application is run, the program is first copied from the hard disk to RAM. Once in RAM, the program can travel at very high speed to the processor where the program code can be run. RAM works at the speed of electricity, much faster than a hard disk, which works at the speed the disk spins.

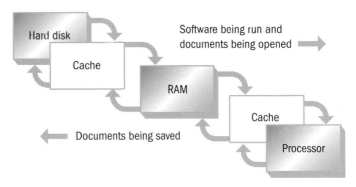

Figure 30.1: Data flows in a computer system

Similarly, when a document or data file is opened, it is first copied from the hard disk to RAM. Once it is in RAM, the file can be worked on by the user.

Most modern hard disk drives have **cache memory** built into the control electronics to help the drive work faster.

The cache is used so that:

- the **FAT** is copied from the disk to cache to make finding disk addresses faster, as fast electronic cache is used rather than slow disk to access FAT

- if data is needed from a drive, the required data is brought to cache, as well as the next data on the disk, so if the computer needs this as well, it is already in the cache, ready to go

- when data is written to disk, it is very quickly sent to cache so the drive electronics can then write the data to disk at slow disk speed without reducing performance in the rest of the system.

Usually there is some cache memory between processor and RAM. This cache may be on the motherboard or part of the processor. The processor works a lot faster than RAM, so needs a good supply of data and software to keep running without slowing the system down. Processor cache is a type of very fast RAM, keeping the processor from slowing down in a similar way to how disk cache helps the hard drive work faster.

Graphic files can be huge, so everything that the hardware can do to make rapid transfers of data helps.

Processors

The processor (or **CPU**) is the heart of a computer system, allowing the operating system and other programs to run. Every program consists of instructions for the processor that are decoded and actioned inside the processor to make them work.

When running a program, the processor has to make every instruction work, usually one after another, but some modern processors can run processes side by side. The quicker the instructions are run, the quicker a program responds to the user.

The processor is very important in maintaining performance with complex digital images, so it's important to choose a system with a powerful CPU.

The power of a CPU depends upon:

- processor speed – the faster the circuits are driven, the faster the computer runs

- processor design – the way the circuits have been designed has a massive effect on performance. Modern CPUs may have single, duo or quad cores with a lot of variation within these designs.

The core of a processor is a collection of circuits that run programs. For early CPUs, there could only be one core, as the technology of that time needed all the circuits on the chip just to make the processor work. Technology has advanced so much that now manufacturers can include two or more cores in the same chip, equivalent to having two or more CPUs in the same component.

There is a lot of choice of processor designs and it takes research to find out which performs better.

Some graphics manipulations are easy for the processor, eg loading a graphic from disk to RAM, which is delegated to the **DMA** controller(s).

Many graphics operations involve a lot of processor work, such as:

- rescaling an image, so the picture is a different size

- saving or exporting the image into another format, eg converting a bitmap file into a JPEG file (see page 227)

- applying a complex effect to a graphic, such as adjusting the tone or colour balance (see page 234).

All of these operations needs good, fast processor(s) to operate effectively.

Other hardware

Digital cameras and card readers

IT professionals who work with digital graphics often need to bring pictures from a digital camera into the computer system. There are four methods for doing this: cable, card, wireless and cradle.

Cable: Most digital cameras have a cable to connect the camera to the computer so pictures can be transferred, usually from camera to hard disk. The cable will probably be USB, but other standards, such as the faster FireWire®, are also available.

Card: Virtually every digital camera on the market uses a flash card to store the pictures taken with it. There are several types of card currently available, each with different sizes and different connections:

- SD (Secure Digital) – a secure stamp-sized digital camera memory card

- SDHC (Secure Digital High Capacity) – offers high storage capacity, currently to 256 GB

- CF (Compact Flash) – the world's most popular type of digital camera memory

- Memory Stick – from Sony, used in a wide range of Sony products

- MMC (MultiMedia Card) – a very small card which can also operate in SD devices

- XD – from Fujifilm and Olympus, with a very small footprint of only 20 × 25 × 1.7 mm

- SM (Smart Media) – from Toshiba, now becoming less popular.

Usually only one type of card will fit the camera, but many computers used for digital graphics have a card reader which can accept many types of card, often in the same slot.

The card can easily be removed from the camera and then inserted into a card reader to allow a very quick and effective data transfer of the pictures from camera to computer.

Wireless: Cameras offering **WiFi** radio connection to a network or PCs are now on the market. This allows a fast data transfer of the pictures without the need to use cables or remove the memory card. Bluetooth® is a slower wireless technology that can be used to transfer images between a mobile phone and a computer.

Digital camera cards

Cradle: Some digital cameras use a cradle to attach them to the computer system. This is a quick and easy method for transferring pictures to the computer as the camera simply pushes into the cradle that is already cabled to a computer.

Many cradles recharge the camera and can create a slide show of pictures.

Digital camera cradle

A cradle is similar to most hardware, in that it will need a driver to make it work properly, probably on an installation CD that is bundled with the cradle.

File storage

Graphic files need to be stored so they can be used again, modified, **backed up** or sent to a third party, such as a client.

Key terms

Back up – to copy computer work to another place so that it is kept safe in case of emergency such as file corruption, fire, flood or theft. Many users back up to CD-ROM, then store these somewhere secure, such as a fireproof safe or off-site in another location.

Solid state device – a device that has no moving parts. USB pen drives are solid state because they store data onto electronic circuits which hold their values even when unplugged. USB hard drives are not solid state because the hard disk spins (moves) when used.

File storage is needed to store files such as:

- hard drive
- CD-ROM and optical drives
- flash cards
- USB storage devices.

Hard drive

The hard drive is the obvious place to store graphical files as it is quick and the graphical software will

look there first to open or save work because of the computer system default settings.

- Modern hard disks are very quick and spacious, with lots of room for work. Hard disk drives also have cache memory (see page 217) to improve the disk performance.

Did you know?

Even the best computer systems fail sometimes, so you should regularly back up your work.

CD-ROM and optical drives

Most computer systems have CD-ROM and/or DVD drives – these are optical disks used to install software, play DVDs and to store files.

For an optical drive to store files, it must be of the right type. Table 30.1 shows the bewildering choice of standards available for optical drives. Fortunately for most IT professionals, the choice is a simple one: usually a DVD +/- RW drive for reading and writing DVDs that also handles the CD-RW standard for writing and reading CD-ROMs.

Flash cards

Digital cameras and other devices often use a flash card to store pictures or other data.

There are several types of flash card, each with a different size, shape and connectors (see Digital cameras and card readers, page 219).

USB storage devices

There are many USB storage devices currently available to plug into the USB port of a computer system.

External USB hard drives are quite popular as a means of backing up data and to take a substantial amount of work between computers.

USB pen drives are **solid state devices** that have become increasingly popular as they are cheap, robust, quick and offer reasonable capacity for storing files, especially to move from office to home or client. A lot of organisations now find them cheap enough to send through the post or even to give to a client with their completed graphic images.

CD-R	Compact Disc-Recordable: also referred to as Compact Disc-Write Once (CD-WO). A type of disk drive that can create CD-ROMs and audio CDs, allowing users to 'master' discs for subsequent publishing.
CD-ROM	Compact Disc-Read Only Memory: a standard for compact disc to be used as a digital memory medium for personal computers. The 4.75-inch laser-encoded optical memory storage medium can hold about 650 MB of data, sound and limited stills and motion video. A CD-ROM player will typically play CD-DA discs but a CD-DA player will not play CD-ROMs. The standard used for most CD-ROM formats is known as Yellow Book, based on the standard published by Philips.
CD-ROM XA	CD-ROM Extended Architecture: a hybrid format, promoted by Sony® and Microsoft®, that combines CD-ROM and CD-i capabilities. The extension adds ADPCM audio to permit the interleaving of sound and video data to animation and with sound synchronisation. It is an essential component of Microsoft's plan for multimedia computers and also the physical format for Kodak's Photo CD format.
CD-RW	Compact Disc-Rewritable: once known as CD-Erasable, or CD-E.
DVD	Digital Versatile Disc: the replacement for the ubiquitous compact disc. Like the CD, it is available in a number of different formats. Unlike the CD, it is available with a number of capacities ranging from 4.7 GB to 17 GB.
DVD Multi	A logo program that promotes compatibility with DVD-RAM and DVD-RW. Putting the emphasis for compatibility on the reader, not the writer, it defines a testing methodology to ensure drives are able to read both DVD-RAM and DVD-RW media.
DVD+R	A write-once optical media format designed for use by devices using DVD+RW technology.
DVD+RW	A competing (with DVD-RAM and DVD-RW) rewritable DVD standard being promoted by Hewlett-Packard, Philips and Sony®. Unlike the DVD-RAM standard, DVD+RW allows the use of bare discs. All three standards are incompatible. At one time the DVD-Forum – which does not support the standard – was insisting on the name being changed to '+RW' – but this appears to have had little effect.
DVD+RW Alliance	A voluntary association of industry-leading personal computing manufacturers, optical storage and consumer electronics manufacturers.
DVD-R	DVD Recordable: the write-once DVD format. DVD-R discs are the DVD counterpart to CD-R discs.
DVD-RAM	A rewritable compact disc format that provides much greater data storage than today's CD-RW systems. The caddy-mounted discs will initially provide 2.6 GB per side on single or double-sided discs.
DVD-ROM	The read-only format supports discs with capacities of from 4.7 GB (enough for an MPEG-2 compressed full-length movie) to 17 GB and access rates of 600 KBps to 1.3 MBps. Backward-compatible with CD-ROMs.
DVD-RW	Pioneer's rewritable DVD format, incompatible with the rival DVD-RAM and DVD+RW formats but generally compatible with DVD-ROM drives and consumer DVD players.
DVD-Video	A consumer DVD format for displaying full-length digital movies. DVD-Video players attach to a television like a video cassette player. Unlike DVD-ROMs, the Digital-Video format includes a Content Scrambling System (CSS) to prevent users from copying discs. This means that today's DVD-ROM players cannot play DVD-Video discs without a software or hardware upgrade to decode the encrypted discs.

Table 30.1: Optical drive formats

Input devices

An input device is anything that can be used to feed data into a computer system or to control the system.

The mouse is an almost essential input device for computer systems, but some IT professionals who specialise in digital graphics prefer a graphics tablet.

Graphics tablet

A graphics tablet often has a special pen to operate it in a similar way to how a mouse is used. The great advantage of the graphics tablet is that it is much more precise than a mouse and positioning is absolute, because when the pen is touched to a point on the tablet it will always represent the same spot on the screen. In contrast, if a mouse is lifted and then put down on a different part of the surface, the mouse pointer will continue from where it was on the screen.

The pen of a graphics tablet usually has a pressure-sensitive tip, so if the user presses harder the line thickens. This gives the pen a very natural feel.

Graphics tablet

Graphics tablet with LCD screen

Key terms

Megapixel – a million pixels. It is a unit of image-sensing capacity in a digital camera.

CCD – stands for charge-coupled device. It is an image sensor used in digital cameras and other devices that converts the image to digital signals.

CRT – stands for cathode ray tube. CRT is an old screen technology that uses a phosphor-coated glass tube to display images. The tube makes the unit quite deep, especially for large screens, as electron rays need to be fired at the display from the back of the tube, with room to spread out to the size of the display. This technology uses a lot of electricity and older models can produce some radiation, which concerns many users.

Colorimeter – a light-sensitive instrument that can be used to calibrate a computer screen to match the colours produced by a printer.

Some top of the range graphics tablets also have LCD screens built into them so the graphic designer can use the pen directly on the image (see below left).

Digital camera

Digital cameras have become better and better and are now very impressive devices with good optical lenses, high resolution and low costs.

Choosing a digital camera involves finding the best mix of price, lens and how many **megapixels** it has.

The lens is more important than you might think, as this is the component that provides the image to the camera's **CCD** for converting into a digital image. If the CCD does not receive a good image it cannot produce a good picture.

The lens should provide an optical zoom to give control over how much is in the picture. Digital zoom can be carried out later using a computer with photo-editing software.

The number of megapixels in a digital camera is how many pixels the CCD can capture. A 12 megapixel camera will be able to take pictures in a variety of sizes, up to 12 million pixels, which is big enough for a 4000 × 3000 picture to be taken. A lot of pixels are useful if you want to be able to use small parts of the picture later, when editing or if the picture is needed for a very large print out such as a road-side poster.

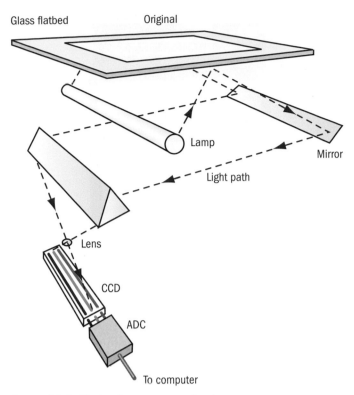

Figure 30.2: Flatbed scanner mechanism

Scanner

Scanners are still the best way to input paper images into a computer. They have a similar mechanism to a photocopier, with a scanning bar moving across the length of the scanner under glass.

The document is placed face down onto a glass window and a scanning mechanism moves back and forth underneath the glass. Light from the lamp bounces off the original and is reflected by the mirror into the lens. This focuses the image into the CCD, which digitises the results via an analogue-to-digital converter (ADC), to send the resulting information to the scanner's own hardware and then to the host PC.

1.2 Output medium

Output media for digital graphics include: printers, computer monitors, mobile phones, PDAs, plotters and vinyl cutters.

Printer

A printer is a device that produces hard copy by printing onto paper or another medium such as an overhead projector transparency or T-shirt.

There are different printer technologies available, each with their own characteristics, strengths and weaknesses. The choice of printer technology should match the user needs.

Below are the printer technologies that are of most interest to IT professionals working with digital graphics:

- **Inkjet printers**: have small nozzles that squirt tiny droplets of ink onto the paper. They are cheap to buy and run but can be slow for complex printing. Inkjets can produce near-photographic prints onto a wide variety of paper and other materials with a good choice of sizes.
- **Colour laser printers**: have cyan, magenta, yellow and black toners. They are usually more expensive than inkjets, with similar running costs and can be a lot faster, especially when printing the same page many times.
- **Dye-sublimation printers**: use dyes that vaporise and seep into the paper surface. They are usually more expensive than colour laser printers to buy and run but are quite slow. The great strength of these printers is that they produce real photo-quality prints.
- **Solid ink printers**: make use of sticks of a wax-like substance, which are melted and then applied to the page. They produce quick, quality prints. They are usually more expensive to buy but have low running costs, which can make them a cheaper option over time if they are well used.

Inkjet technology is the most well accepted of these technologies, with laser printer technology next.

Computer monitor

A computer system needs a monitor or display so the user can see what is happening. Traditionally, monitors have used **CRT** technology, which has many disadvantages, especially the space the monitor occupies and the heat produced. CRT screens have now been mostly superseded by flat screen displays.

Some professional displays feature hardware calibration to adjust and match the screen display colours to printers, image setters and other digital devices. A **colorimeter** is used to help with this.

Flat screen monitors have become much larger and cheaper in recent years and are now the natural choice for any new computer system.

Other media

There are other media that can display digital graphics.

Mobile phones can use images that are captured using the phone camera or are downloaded from another source. Many **PDAs** also have a built-in camera and can display pictures on the device screen.

Plotters are used for large prints onto paper, material or other materials.

Vinyl cutters are used to cut signs from vinyl in the shape of the graphic image; the sign can then be peeled from its backing fabric and stuck onto a surface, such as the side of a van.

Vinyl cutter

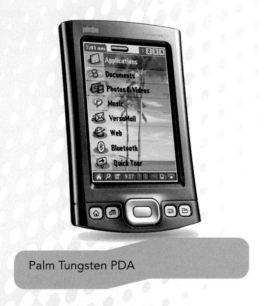
Palm Tungsten PDA

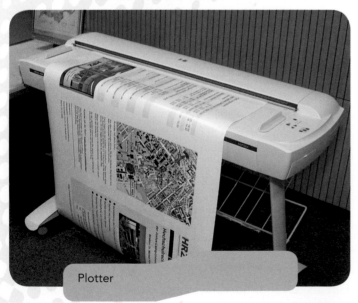
Plotter

1.3 Software

Software is the term used to describe the programs that run on a computer. Application software is used to help people produce work. There are many types of application (often called 'apps') that can be used to create, manipulate and view digital graphics.

Vector-based graphics software

Vector graphics are different from **bitmap graphics**. The main features of vector graphics are:

- small file size when saved to disk
- no loss of print quality when enlarged or reduced in size
- vector pictures are made from objects such as circles and rectangles
- each object has an outline and/or fill
- objects may be grouped together.

Vector graphics are very good for diagrams.

Key terms

PDA – stands for personal digital assistant. This small hand-held device offers a calendar, contact list and other useful programs.

Vector graphics – define objects as coordinate points and use mathematics inside the software to calculate how to display the image onto the screen or printer.

Bitmap graphics – also called raster graphics, they are made from lots of pixels, each with a colour.

Examples of vector drawing packages include CorelDRAW® (see Figure 30.3), Autodesk AutoCAD (see Figure 30.4) and Microsoft® Visio® (see Figure 30.5).

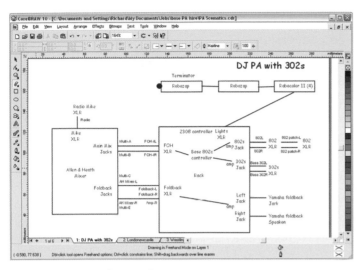

Figure 30.3: CorelDRAW®

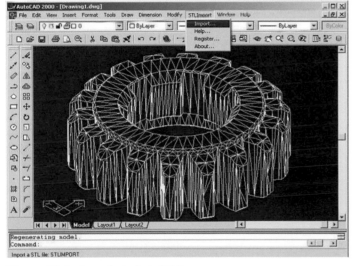

Figure 30.4: Autodesk AutoCAD

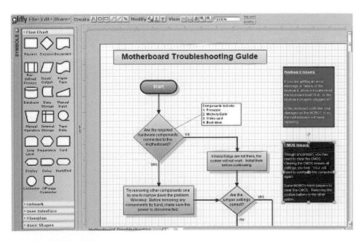

Figure 30.5: Microsoft® Visio®

Bitmap software

Bitmap graphics are different from vector graphics. They have a large file size when saved to disk and print quality can become 'blocky' when enlarged or reduced in size. Bitmap graphics can be created when a picture is scanned into a computer system using a scanner or from a digital camera.

Bitmap graphics are very good for screenshots and web page illustrations. Examples of bitmap drawing packages include Corel Paint Shop Pro® (see Figure 30.6) and Microsoft® Paint® (see Figure 30.7).

Figure 30.6: Corel Paint Shop Pro®

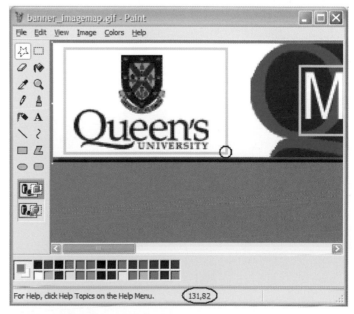

Figure 30.7: Microsoft® Paint

Photo manipulation software

Photo manipulation software applications are specialist bitmap programs with tools that are specialised for manipulating photographs.

Examples of photo manipulation software applications include Corel Photo-Paint® (see Figure 30.8) and Adobe® Photoshop® (see Figure 30.9).

Other graphics-related software

There are many utility programs available to help graphics professionals work more effectively.

Image viewers

Image viewers are programs that give a view of a folder with previews of the files there. Microsoft® Windows Explorer® can be used as an image viewer if the user chooses to set the view to medium icons, large icons or extra large icons.

Photo galleries

A photo gallery is a program that displays a collection of images for people to look at and enjoy. A photo gallery is often a collection of web pages showing photos that people post up there.

File conversion

File conversions can often be done by using the File Save As menu in a graphics app then choosing the type of file that the image is to be saved to. Microsoft® Paint is bundled in with Windows® and can do this to save an image as a BMP, JPG, GIF, TIF or PNG file.

Other file conversion apps have a wider range of file types available and may be able to batch convert a number of files automatically into another graphics file type. More information on converting files can be found on the next page.

Figure 30.8: Corel Photo-Paint®

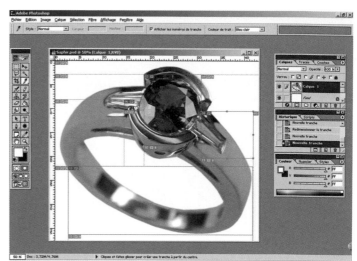

Figure 30.9: Adobe® Photoshop®

2 Understand types of graphic images and graphical file formats

As discussed earlier, there are two main types of graphic images and many graphical file formats. The bitmap (also called raster) type stores an image as lots of pixels, each with a colour. The vector type stores the image as a collection of objects, each with coordinate points to define size and position, as well as mathematical formulae defining line curvatures, thickness, fills and other properties. Each of these two types can be saved in many different formats to the disk.

2.1 File handling

Converting files

Files can usually be converted from one format to another. Many IT professionals simply use the File menu of their favourite graphical application to export or save as a new file type. There are also utility programs available that convert between formats and may offer batch options in order to automatically convert a collection of files from one format to another.

File sizes

The size of a bitmap graphic file saved to disk depends upon the format of the file and the options taken when saving it. Vector files are usually a lot smaller and do not have save options for controlling file size.

The same graphic would have different sizes in different formats (see Table 30.2).

BMP	GIF	JPG	PNG	TIF
2305 KB	209 KB	440 KB	348 KB	2305 KB

Table 30.2: Graphic sizes in different formats

Controlling the file size is achieved by setting the compression or quality level when saving the graphic. The same graphic file might have the sizes shown in Table 30.3 using JPEG quality settings.

100%	90%	60%	40%	10%
440 KB	216 KB	116 KB	92 KB	41 KB

Table 30.3: Graphic sizes with different JPEG quality settings

File formats

The file format is the way the graphic is internally structured. Each file format uses a different structure – a program using that format must be able to understand the structure so it knows how to show the graphic on the screen, print, edit and so on. Table 30.4 below shows some of the more common file formats.

File extension	Graphics type	Proper name	Description
.ai	vector	Adobe® Illustrator® Artwork	Vector format for Adobe® Ilustrator® (originally a subset of PostScript®, if an appropriate header was present).
.bmp	raster	Windows® Bitmap	Commonly used by Microsoft® Windows® program and the Windows® operating system itself. **Lossless compression** can be specified but some programs use only uncompressed files.
.cdr	vector	CorelDRAW® Document	Default proprietary format for CorelDRAW ®2D documents. Features include multiple import/export filters, 3D special effects and object/image layering.
.cgm	vector	Computer Graphics Metafile	Defined by ISO Standard 8632. Often used for complex engineering drawings, eg in the aviation industry.
.cpi	raster	Cartesian Perceptual Compression	Hyper-compressed format for black-and-white raster images. Typically compresses images 5–20 times smaller than corresponding TIFF or PDF version, leading to dramatic reductions in download times and server network traffic.

File extension	Graphics type	Proper name	Description
.cpt	raster	Corel Photo-Paint® Image	Default proprietary format for Corel Photo-Paint® documents. Has many extra features such as image layering. Supported by very few image editing programs other than Corel Photo-Paint®. Photo-Paint® images are usually smaller than Photoshop® documents.
.dxf	vector	ASCII Drawing Interchange	Standard ASCII text files used to store vector data for CAD programs.
.eps	raster/vector	Encapsulated PostScript®	A PostScript® file that describes a small vector graphic, as opposed to a whole page or set of pages.
.emf	vector	Windows® Enhanced Metafile	An enhanced version of Windows® Metafile. Supported in Windows® NT and later.
.exr	raster	Extended Dynamic Range Image File Format	OpenEXR is the Open Source high dynamic-range (HDR) file format developed by Industrial Light & Magic for advanced imaging in movie production. The main advantages of that format are up to 32-bit floating-point pixels and multiple lossless image compression algorithms up to 2:1 lossless compression on film grained images.
.fh	vector	Macromedia Freehand Document	Vector format for Macromedia Freehand.
.fla	vector	Flash® Source File	Shockwave® Flash® source file, only usable by Adobe® (previously Macromedia) Flash® authoring software
.gif	raster	Graphics Interchange Format	GIF is used extensively on the web. Supports animated images. Supports only 255 colours per frame, so requires **lossy compression** for full-colour photos (dithering); using multiple frames can improve colour precision. Uses lossless LZW compression, which used to sometimes make GIF undesirable due to LZW patent (now expired) issues.
.igs	vector	Initial Graphics Exchange Specification	IGES is an ASCII text neutral data format used extensively for CAD/CAM data exchange. It supports 2D and 3D curves and surfaces, as well as solid models and annotation.
.jpeg/.jpg	raster	Joint Photographic Experts Group	JPEG is used extensively for photos and other continuous tone images on the web. Uses lossy compression by trying to equalise eight by eight pixel blocks; the quality can vary greatly depending on the compression settings.
.jpg2/.jp2	raster	Joint Photographic Experts Group 2000	JPEG 2000 is the successor of popular JPEG. A new wavelet-based file format that includes both lossy and lossless compression options. It is commonly considered the actual state-of-the-art lossy format for photographic imaging, but its support in modern systems is still weak due to heavy requirements for hardware and many patents for software.
.mng	raster	Multiple-image Network Graphics	Animation format using data streams similar to those of PNG and JPEG, originally designed to replace the use of animated GIF on the Web. Free of the patent (which expired in 2003) associated with animated GIF.

File extension	Graphics type	Proper name	Description
.pcx	raster	PCX	Developed by ZSoft Corporation. Uses a simple form of run-length encoding. Supports palette-based and 24-bit RGB images.
.pdf	raster/vector	Portable Document Format	A page description language (loosely based on PostScript, but not a programming language), which allows for files containing multiple pages and links. Works with Adobe® Acrobat® Reader or Adobe® eBook Reader, or third-party compatible software. It is the native metafile format for Mac® OS X.
.pict/.pct/ .pic	raster/vector	Picture	Default for Macintosh® operating systems before version OS X.
.png	raster	Portable Network Graphics	PNG is an image format with lossless compression, offering bit depths from 1 to 48. It was mainly designed to replace the use of GIF on the Web. Free of the patent (which expired in 2003) associated with GIF.
.ps	vector	PostScript®	Generic vector-based page description language, created and owned by Adobe®. PostScript® is a powerful stack-based programming language. Supported by many laser printers.
.psd	raster	Photoshop® Document	Default proprietary format for Adobe® Photoshop® documents. Has many extra features, such as image layering. Also supported by some other image editing programs than Adobe® Photoshop®.
.sgi/.rgb/ .rgba/.int/ .inta/.bw	raster	Silicon Graphics Image	Native image format for Silicon Graphics workstations.
.svg/.svgz	vector	Scalable Vector Graphics	An XML-based vector graphics format, as defined by the World Wide Web Consortium for use in web browsers.
.swf	vector	Small Web Format (referred to as Shockwave® Flash®)	Flash® is a web page plug-in that displays vector-based animations contained in SWF files. Several applications can create SWF files; these include the Flash® authoring tool from Adobe® (previously Macromedia).
.tiff/.tif	raster	Tagged Image File Format	TIFF is used extensively for traditional print graphics. Lossy and lossless compression are available, but many programs only support a subset of available options.
.wmf	vector	Windows® Metafile	Stores vector graphics and raster graphics as a sequence of commands to be issued to the graphics layer of the Microsoft® Windows® operating system.
.xaml	Vector	XAML	The XML-based file format for representing a document built using a Windows® Presentation Foundation application (pre-installed on Vista). Can declare 2D vector graphics (and include references to external bitmaps for imaging), textual documents (with or without page fidelity), 2D user interfaces and renderings of 3D models (with a fair amount of baseline support for lighting, materials, etc).

Table 30.4: Graphic file formats

File management

File management involves the methods used to look after work saved to disk or USB drive, including the following.

- File naming simply means giving names to your files. Learners often give files joke names, making them very difficult to identify later. IT learners and professionals recognise that naming a file is important because the name must represent what the file is. Look at Table 30.5. Which type of file name would you rather see if you were looking for the second assignment for Unit 30 about vector software?

Joke file name	Professional file name
Itchy	Unit 30 assignment 1 Bitmap software
Scratchy	Unit 30 assignment 2 Vector software
Bart	Unit 30 assignment 3 Utility software

Table 30.5: Showing filenames

- Folder structure is one of the most powerful tools that IT professionals can use to help organise their work. Folders give a structure to the disk that can be used to help locate files easily and quickly. There are many ways to organise folder structures. The correct one is usually the one that is most obvious to the user.

- Moving a file involves cutting it from a folder then pasting it to another folder or drive. You may need to move files when tidying up your folder structures, so that the files are in their correct locations.

- Deleting a file removes it from the drive so it cannot be used again.

Compression techniques

Compression techniques are used to reduce the disk size of a file. File size is important if the file is to be transmitted to another location (a small file arrives faster) or if there is a small amount of storage space and the file needs to be reduced in size to fit.

2.2 Graphic images

Vector graphics

Vector graphics follow mathematical rules. Shapes are understood by vector graphic software as coordinate points joined by lines with a defined fill (see Figure 30.10).

A line joining points may be straight or curved and has properties such as thickness, colour, solid or dashed and so on.

There could be no fill, making the shape transparent, or it could have a colour, more than one colour, texture, etc.

Figure 30.10: A vector image

Bitmaps

Bitmap (or raster) graphics are pixel-orientated, meaning that a bitmap image is made from lots of pixels. Each pixel is a tiny dot in the image with a colour.

Bitmap software can usually zoom the graphic large enough to edit individual pixels (see Figure 30.11).

Figure 30.11: Bitmap pixels

Comparison between types of image

There are big differences between vector and bitmap images (see Table 30.6).

	Vector	Bitmap
File size	Small	Large files sizes, especially big pictures with large colour depth
Scaling	Very scalable to any size	Pixellation occurs
How created	User created with mouse or graphics tablet	Scanner or digital
Typical uses	Diagrams	Photographs

Table 30.6: Relative features of vector and bitmap images

The mathematical way in which vector images are stored and manipulated by software makes them easy to edit and resize and results in small file sizes.

Bitmap images allow editing that is much more complex than that possible with vector images, which means that skilled IT professionals can manipulate photographs into anything they can imagine.

Resizing a bitmap needs software to analyse the pixels in the image, then recreate a new set of pixels to make the image the new size. Modern software can be amazingly good at this complex task, but there will still be a loss of quality. There will always be a limit to how large a bitmap image can be acceptably enlarged.

As the colour information of every pixel needs to be stored in a bitmap image, the file size can be enormous.

File format features and typical uses

Vector file formats are usually **proprietary**, with few open or common standards to share between vector software applications.

There are many file formats commonly used for bitmap files – bitmap applications can usually open, edit and save many of them. Bitmap file formats are less likely to be proprietary than vector files.

BMP bitmap files are often used for scanned images that need to be saved at best quality. For this reason, BMP files are often quite large.

JPEG bitmap files are often used when a smaller file size is needed, for example so that Internet graphics take less time to download and to show in the browser.

Assessment activity 30.1

You have always enjoyed creating computer graphics, ever since the first computer was brought into your home. Friends and family are very impressed and encouraging towards the images you've created, so you have decided to set up as a freelance graphics designer.

To do this, you will need some financial investment to purchase the hardware, consumables and software needed for your business, as well as some other spending on marketing, such as business cards and advertising.

The owner of a small chain of convenience stores, where you have a part-time job, is interested in sponsoring your start-up but needs to be convinced that you know what you are doing and are not going to incur debt by spending on anything that is not essential.

You are to produce a report with the following sections:

- Hardware
- Software
- File formats
- Comparisons
- Output media.

1 Create the Hardware and Software sections of your report.
- The Hardware section needs to focus on components such as the graphics card and how their features impact upon graphical work.
- The Software section needs to identify the vector and raster software applications you would wish to use as well as other software. **P1**

2 Create the File formats section of your report, explaining how different types of graphic images relate to file formats. This should include sections explaining differences between vector and raster images, with some examples of the file formats that can be used to save them to storage media. **P2**

3 Create two sub-sections in the Comparisons section of your report, one for hardware and the other for software packages used in graphics work.

Add to the hardware sub-section, identifying the limitations of the following devices compared to others in the bullet point:

- file storage media: CD-ROM, hard drive, flash cards, USB storage devices
- input devices: graphics tablet, mouse, digital camera, scanner.

Add to the software sub-section, comparing the limitations of vector and raster software applications. **M1**

4 Create the Output media section of your report, evaluating the impacts of evolving output mediums on the design and creation of graphic images.

Research the marketplace to find current developments in both hard and soft copy for graphical work. **D1**

Grading tips

- Make sure all the hardware and software you describe relate to creating graphics. **P1**
- You must relate the graphic images you use to their file formats. **P2**
- For the merit criterion, limitations need to be compared, both of the hardware and software packages used for graphics. **M1**
- You may find it useful to find actual products used as output media. **D1**

PLTS

You can show you are an **independent enquirer** when you analyse and evaluate information, judging its relevance and value by creating the Hardware and Software sections of your report.

Functional skills

Choosing graphical software will utilise your **ICT** functional skills when you select and use software applications to meet needs and solve complex problems.

3   Be able to use editing tools to edit and manipulate images

Editing tools are designed to help the user change a graphic and can be very powerful. This section explains the uses of some of these tools.

3.1 Graphic creation

Graphic images can either be obtained from another source, or created using specialist software.

Obtaining images

Many digital graphic artists use editing tools to enhance an image that is obtained from somewhere else, usually photographs or other sophisticated graphics. Images may be obtained by:

- scanning – using a scanner to capture an image from paper or other hard copy
- importing – using the File Import menu option to bring in a graphic file from another place
- digital camera – transferring photographs taken by yourself or another person using the camera to your computer system.

Image creation

Many tools exist to help the user create an image, including freehand drawing techniques, which allow the user to draw with a mouse or graphics tablet directly into the application.

It is more common to create images from scratch with vector software rather than bitmap software, as vector graphics are often logos, diagrams or similar that do not already exist and so need to be created.

Using vector software to create images often involves assembling shapes such as rectangles, circles, curves or similar into the graphic. These shapes can be grouped together so they can be used as a single object.

Pre-existing material can often be found in clipart or other sources. It is always important that any copyrights are honoured.

3.2 Tools and techniques

The computer can be a very powerful asset in creating or editing graphics, enabling the user to do things that would be very difficult otherwise.

Standard software tools

Most graphics software applications offer several standard tools, including freehand draw, rotate, flip, crop, group/ungroup and resize.

Freehand draw

This tool is best used with a graphic tablet, rather than a mouse. Freehand draw allows the artist to draw directly into the artwork with an on-screen pencil. Most software offers a choice of colours and line width.

Rotate

Rotate is a common tool for both vector and bitmap applications. As you might expect, this tool turns the selected image round by a specified amount. The rotation might be done using the mouse to drag it round or by selecting an angle to rotate.

Flip

Flip is a common tool for both vector and bitmap applications. It is used to create a mirror image of part of an image. Often there is an option to create a new flipped image while keeping the existing selection, or to change the selection so that it is mirrored. Mirroring an object horizontally flips it from left to right; mirroring an object vertically flips it from top to bottom.

Crop

Crop is usually a bitmap tool used to cut off the edges of an image so that the parts of the image that are not wanted are removed. The overall size of the image becomes smaller, but the contents of the image remain the same size. For example, a photograph of a person may be cropped to remove some of the background but the size of the face stays the same.

Group/Ungroup

Group/Ungroup is usually a vector tool. As vector images are created using many objects, it is often sensible to group some or all of them together to make it easier to work with them. For example, if a logo is created using several objects, then grouping them creates a single object that is much easier to select and work with. Grouped objects can be ungrouped to split them up into the original collection of objects – this is useful if one or two of the objects in the group need changing. They can then be grouped again once the changes have been made.

Resize

Resize is a common tool for both vector and bitmap applications. Using this tool makes the selection bigger or smaller. Vector images resize without losing quality because the image is kept inside memory as coordinates, with the computer recalculating the image to whatever resolution is needed for the screen, printer or any other device. When a bitmap is resized the software needs to examine the existing pixels, then determine the colours of the new pixels to reproduce the image – this is a complex operation that inevitably reduces image quality. Resizing bitmaps well is one of the benefits of using expensive, professional software applications.

Special effects

Special effects give you a lot of control and power over the image. The skilled IT professional can use these bitmap tools to make a bad picture spectacular – unfortunately, an unskilled user can use the same tools to make a spectacular picture bad!

Soften

The soften tool is used to smooth and tone down the harsh edges in an image without losing much of the important image detail.

Sharpen

Sharpening an image can increase the contrast, enhance image edges or reduce shading.

Watermark

A watermark in a word processor such as Word® places an image behind the page giving the appearance of printing using watermarked paper.

Similarly, specialist graphic software may also have this tool, which can be used, for example, for adding a translucent copyright watermark over the image to identify it as your own work.

Invert

The invert tool reverses the colours of an image. Inverting an image creates the appearance of a photographic negative.

Colour

Specialist IT professionals can use colour tools to enhance and edit images.

Colour balance

The colour balance tool or filter lets you adjust an image by shifting colours between complimentary pairs of primary RGB (red, green and blue) colour values and secondary CMY (cyan, magenta and yellow) colour values. For example, to tone down red in a photo, you can shift the colour values from red to cyan.

Colour depth

Colour depth is also important as it controls the file size and overall quality of the image. **8-bit** (256 colours) is still popular for web images as they load up a lot quicker than 16-bit (64,000 colours) or 24-bit (16.7 million colours), while still maintaining an acceptable picture quality.

Layering

Layering is a very useful technique for creating and editing images. An image can be divided into layers, and then a single layer can be selected for editing with all the other layers locked. This makes it impossible to accidentally change part of the image that has been completed.

Layers can also be set as not visible, allowing the user to see only the part of the image they want to work on.

Printing is another operation where layering can help the user. Unwanted layers can be marked as non-printable, so the hard copy will only show the parts needed by the user.

Advanced techniques: 3D images

There are many ways of representing 3D images using digital graphics, including:

- 3D drawing tools in a vector drawing package
- rendering a wire-frame model in a CAD application
- defining a digital landscape using games generation software.

3D drawing tools

Using 3D drawing tools in a vector drawing package can produce some excellent effects. For example, CorelDRAW® offers the Extrude dialogue box. This gives control over how the 3D effects are applied, including from which direction the object is lit and the position of the vanishing point – shown in Figure 30.12 as x under the shape.

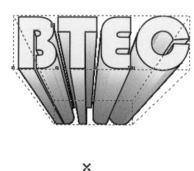

x

Figure 30.12: CorelDRAW® 3D Extrude tool

Rendering a wire-frame model

CAD applications such as AutoCAD® allow the user to define complex and precise objects using **wire-framing** (see Figure 30.4 on page 225 for an example).

Figure 30.13: A 3D graphic created using AutoCAD®

The object might be a component designed for manufacture, an architectural drawing or other 3D design. Many CAD applications can add texture to the wire-frames to produce a realistic impression of what the design will look like when it is produced (see Figure 30.13).

Masking

A regular **mask** is a selection tool, such as a simple rectangle, circle, freehand shape or lasso, to isolate the area that you want to protect from changes.

The image can be cropped to a mask, so only the part inside the mask remains.

A colour mask is used to protect colours in an image – the mask will apply only to the pixels within the colour range that you specify in the mask, using the magic wand, lasso or colour mask tool. This technique can be used to separate part of an image such as a car or person from the background.

3.3 Editing graphics

Editing a graphic is when an existing image is changed in some way using some of these tools and techniques to improve the image or to correct identified problems.

4 Be able to create and modify graphic images to meet user requirements

In professional graphical work, you need to meet the user requirements, which will be specified at the beginning of a project.

4.1 User need

Client needs

Clients and users may have different needs from digital graphics.

The client is the person or organisation that has commissioned and will pay for the job, so their needs are the most important. Their needs might include such aspects as:

- keeping to a corporate style
- using file formats that are compatible with their software
- keeping within their guidelines for file sizes that are appropriate for website download times and any other bandwidth or storage considerations.

The user is anyone who sees the digital graphics. Their needs include:

- images having enough resolution to make the picture quality acceptable
- images that clearly convey intended information.

Target audience

Identifying the target audience is important because it will help you to be clear about who will be seeing the completed images and why. Understanding this makes a big difference to the effectiveness of images, as knowing the reasons for creating them will help you to target them better.

When the images are near to completion, you can show them to people selected from the target audience for feedback on how well they meet the user needs.

User requirements

You will need to set out the user needs in a document or part of a document stating what is wanted by the people who will be viewing the end result of the production.

Constraints

Most graphic productions have constraints to help make the production practical and useful. Constraints may include:

- house style – so the graphic fits in with the rest of the document and other publications from the client organisation
- image size – to ensure that the graphic meets requirements such as acceptable load times for web pages or acceptable resolution for printing
- intended use – to make sure the graphics are appropriate for their target audience
- file size – particularly important for web page load times, but may also be an issue if the graphics are to be delivered on CD-ROM or other media where there is a limited amount of space
- production costs – to keep within budget and to not make work unprofitable
- timescale – as an image completed after the rest of a job is published is of little use.

Output media

The output medium is whatever is used to convey the image to the end user. Output media include:

- paper
- vinyl
- textiles
- display screens
- plates (for printing).

User feedback

User feedback is useful at every stage of producing professional computer graphics to confirm that the work is progressing towards a satisfactory end-product and to guage how effective the work is in meeting the user needs.

4.2 Reviewing

Reviewing is a vital part of the design and creation of graphical work to ensure the work meets acceptable standards and meets the client needs.

Checking work

When a job is close to completion, it should be checked against the client and user needs to ensure it is fit for purpose and suitable for release. The client will be meeting the cost of the job, so it is particularly important to check that the work meets their need. This will involve looking again at the client needs document and carefully considering each of the requirements to ensure the work matches them.

The user need is what the work should actually achieve. This check will be to make sure the end-product has the desired effect on people who see or use the graphic.

Proofing

Proofing is when the image is output to see (roughly) what it will actually look like when completed. An image may be proofed to an inkjet printer by the designer to check that the parts of the image look right before sending the image to a **bureau** for the final print.

Key term

Bureau – an organisation that carries out services, such as printing, for other businesses or clients. A design studio may not have expensive specialist printing facilities, so sends work to a bureau to make use of their printing equipment.

Image resolution

Part of the review process is to confirm that the image resolution is appropriate for the purpose of the digital graphic.

Graphics for web pages need to have an acceptable balance between the resolution and picture quality. Lower resolution means poorer picture quality but faster web page loading and downloads.

Graphics for publication need to match the resolution to the printer. Either a lower or higher resolution will result in poorer picture quality when printed.

File formats

The review process should involve checking that the file format meets the needs of both client and users. The file format should not cause any compatibility issues that would result in problems loading or using the graphic.

Other needs

Any other identified needs from the image specification, such as the speed of loading, should also be reviewed to confirm that all the image design needs have been met.

Assessment Activity 30.2

You have set up as a freelance graphics designer and received financial investment from the owner of a small chain of convenience stores.

The owner has commissioned you to produce a flyer advertising the stores that can be used for pushing through letterboxes in the area.

The flyer must contain:

- at least three photographs of products on special offer
- maps showing where the stores are located
- an overall colour scheme using the shop colours of purple and white
- telephone, email and website contact information for the stores.

1 Create a flyer using original graphic images to meet the user need. **P4**

2 You need to show your flyer to your tutor for their opinion, then modify the images as a result of this user feedback. **P5**

3 The owner's children are interested in computer graphics so you are to produce a collection of some annotated screenshots demonstrating the use of editing tools to edit and manipulate images. **P3**

4 Add a section to your document with annotated screenshots to justify the software, tools, file format, image resolution and colour depth used for creating your graphic images. **M2**

5 Add another section to your document discussing the impact that file format, compression techniques, image resolution and colour depth have on file size and image quality. **D2**

Grading tips

- There must be evidence that you've used some tools to edit and manipulate images. **P3**
- Your graphics must meet the defined user need. **P4**
- You need to respond to actual user feedback. **P5**
- This merit criterion needs you to justify the choices you made to create your graphic images. **M2**
- You need to relate how choices around file size impact on image quality. **D2**

4.3 Legislation and guidelines

Identifying ownership

Identifying ownership is an important first step towards finding out whether a graphic can be reused. Many images have the owner name or copyright printed on or close to the image, which makes this task easy.

If there is no name printed near the graphic, then the ownership will probably be with the publisher of the web page or book where you found the image.

Copyright

A piece of work such as an image is copyright when it has an owner with control over how the work is used or copied.

It must always be assumed that an image already has copyright and that permission must be sought from the copyright owner before the image can be reused.

Copyright free

Copyright-free images can be freely used by anyone. Such images may be found on web pages that are clearly identified as copyright free, included with graphics software or from other sources.

Gaining permissions

Any image that is not clearly identified as copyright free needs the permission of the owner if it is to be used. Permission should be requested from the owner and this will often involve paying a fee before the image can be reused.

If you take your own photographs of people, you need them to sign a model release form, giving you permission to use the photographs as you wish.

Jane
Graphic designer

I have always had a good eye for colour and composition, a love of technology, and enjoyed communicating ideas – so it was brilliant to get a job as a graphic designer in a well-known design studio not far from where I live.

I am responsible for a great variety of tasks, ranging from when a job is first discussed with the client through to creating the artwork and working with third parties such as printers to produce the end-product.

When we first receive a user requirement we meet to brainstorm how we approach the job and mock up some design ideas. I often meet with the client to present our ideas. We need to sell our ideas to the client and work with them to achieve the end-product they want, so may need to adjust our designs to fit in with their needs or taste.

Sometimes I am asked to produce the budget and schedule, but this is usually done by my team leader.

For me the best part is using computer software such as Photoshop® to actually execute the design. I really need to be organised here in order to meet our deadlines and stay within budget.

Even though computer software and technology have revolutionised the graphic design industry, there is no substitute for the artistic sensibility of people like me! Knowledge about design elements, such as colour and composition, is important for graphic designers but artistic ability and creativity are essential.

Graphic design is an exciting brainteaser. Choosing the exact right fonts, colours and lines, while also conveying the meaning, is complicated. If you want to succeed in a graphic design job, you must have strong problem-solving skills and love a good challenge.

Think about it!

1 Jane and her team like to brainstorm how they approach each job and mock up some design ideas. What methods do you think would be used to create the design mock ups?

2 Jane is sometimes asked to produce the budget and schedule for a new job. Can you produce a schedule for a job where the design studio is asked to create animated adverts for London Underground subway escalators?

3 Jane talks of how computer software and technology have revolutionised the graphic design industry. Can you find out what techniques were used before computers?

Just checking

1. How can photographs be captured and transferred to a computer system?
2. How can digital graphic files be stored?
3. What input and output devices are suitable for a computer used for editing graphics?
4. Identify some software applications suitable for creating and editing images.
5. What are the differences between vector and bitmap images?
6. Identify four graphic formats, with examples of where their use would be appropriate.
7. Give three examples of how a digital image may be sourced.
8. Identify and explain how four software tools may be used to edit digital images.
9. Identify and explain how four special effects may be used with digital images.
10. What is the client need?
11. What are user requirements?
12. What is meant by constraints?
13. What are the purposes of reviewing a completed job?
14. Explain the issues around copyright and digital images.

edexcel

Assignment tips

- You will need to obtain some real user feedback on your work before modifying it to respond to their comments.
- Remember, you need to compare the limitations of some different hardware and software packages used in graphics work.
- You will need to research evolving output mediums which are new on the market so you can evaluate their impact on the design and creation of graphic images.

31 Computer animation

Computer animation is the art of creating moving images using computers. It brings together computer graphics and animation techniques. Animation does not require computers, but the increasing power of computers to create and manipulate sets of images has allowed animation to reach new levels of sophistication and realism.

Animation is increasingly created by means of 3D computer graphics, although 2D computer graphics are still widely used for low bandwidth and faster real-time needs. In this unit only 2D graphics are required.

Learning outcomes

After completing this unit, you should:

1. understand the types and uses of animation
2. know the software techniques used in animation
3. be able to design and implement digital animations.

Assessment and grading criteria

This table shows you what you must do in order to achieve a pass, merit or distinction grade, and where you can find activities in this book to help you.

To achieve a **pass** grade the evidence must show that you are able to:	To achieve a **merit** grade the evidence must show that, in addition to the pass criteria, you are able to:	To achieve a **distinction** grade the evidence must show that, in addition to the pass and merit criteria, you are able to:
P1 explain the different types of animation **See Assessment activity 31.1, page 258**	**M1** explain persistence of vision **See Assessment activity 31.1, page 258**	
P2 explain different uses of animation **See Assessment activity 31.1, page 258**		
P3 discuss the advantages and limitations of animated GIFs **See Assessment activity 31.1, page 258**	**M2** compare different animation formats **See Assessment activity 31.1, page 258**	
P4 describe the software tools available for animation **See Assessment activity 31.2, page 267**		
P5 describe factors that need to be taken into account when creating animations for the web **See Assessment activity 31.2, page 267**	**M3** explain particular techniques that are used to minimise the file size of animations **See Assessment activity 31.2, page 267**	**D1** compare different specialist computer animation software packages **See Assessment activity 31.2, page 267**
P6 design computer animations using different animation techniques **See Assessment activity 31.3, page 272**		
P7 implement animations using different animation techniques **See Assessment activity 31.3, page 272**		**D2** evaluate the tools and techniques used to create animations **See Assessment activity 31.3, page 272**

How you will be assessed

In this unit you will carry out three projects. The first involves creating a series of detailed, illustrated posters to explain a variety of topics, including different types of animation and the ways in which animations are used. In the second project you will make a presentation on the tools for animation, two leaflets on good practice and a short report comparing different animation software. Thirdly, you will design and make your own animation, evaluating it at the end.

Peter, BTEC National IT learner

This unit was brilliant. I was able to be really creative and I could draw on my own knowledge of computer games and animated films.

The posters we made for the first project were useful because we were learning the theory of animation but presenting this in an imaginative way. I had to find a balance between all of the information I knew and what I could fit on the poster – I had to be succinct and make sure I included all the important points.

During the second project we began to focus on how animations were actually made and to make decisions on the tools and software we might want to use.

The third project was the best as I got to put all my learning into practice and create my own animation. I was really glad I was shown how to design it first as I realise now how important it is to have solid ideas before trying to create it.

Being able to compare the software was quite straightforward for D1 but the evaluation for D2 was tricky. I had to make sure I focused on the tools and techniques I used and not get distracted by the visual elements. Overall I feel I have really benefited from this unit and plan to look into animation more – hopefully to study it further in the future.

Over to you!

- What skills do you think you will need for this unit?
- Which of these skills may you need to develop? How do you think you might do this?
- Why do you think Peter said designing the animation before making it was really important?

243

1 Understand the types and uses of animation

Animation is a way of creating the illusion of movement. It can be used to create a fantasy world or to recreate reality, and is a medium that is both exciting and popular.

The development of animation technology began as a quest to capture the real world on a fixed medium. Before the invention of the camera, it was impossible to acquire a picture of reality. Before inventions such as the zoetrope and cinematograph, it was difficult to show natural movement. Nowadays we are quite used to seeing the real world captured in a photograph or a strange new world animated in a movie. But try to imagine that you have never seen such things and think about the dedication and creativity it must have taken to create these exciting visual experiences that we take for granted today.

1.1 Origins

At the core of animation is how the human eyes and brain allow us to see movement, particularly the theory of the persistence of vision. This theory explains how we can see and make sense of animations. Thanks to the pioneers and inventors of animation and film making, it has become possible to create masterpieces – the scale of modern animations and films would have been unimaginable to the early pioneers. Traditional techniques have paved the way for more modern techniques, although most are still used today in some form.

Persistence of vision

Movement in animation can seem very smooth, but in fact what is being seen is a series of individual images joined together and shown at speed. The animation appears continuous due to **persistence of vision** (see Figure 31.1).

Figure 31.1: Separate images which are seen as continuous

Key terms

Persistence of vision – refers to the ability of the human eye to preserve the image it has just seen for a brief instant. Therefore, when the eye sees a series of images that follow each other, it retains each image and the brain processes it as a continuous image.

Fps – stands for frames per second (fps), or the number of individual images that are shown every second.

Zoetrope – originally known as the daedalum, a machine invented by William Horner in 1834. It spun a strip of images at high speed in order to show movement.

Flipbook – a very simple type of animation where drawings are put on separate pages and then flicked through to animate.

An animation appears smoother and less jerky when there are more **fps** (frames per second) and more intermediary steps in the images that build up the illusion of movement.

The more frames which are shown during one second, the fewer gaps the eye and brain have to fill in and so the more continuous the motion appears.

An early example of this principle was the **zoetrope** (see Techniques, following). The faster the zoetrope was spun, the smoother the animation appeared.

Computer animation is generally created at 12 fps, as this is a sufficient speed to prevent jerkiness in the series of images, although the number of frames per second can be raised if necessary. The higher the rate of frames per second, the more images are needed in the animation. Cartoons that are made on a tight budget sometimes have a reduced rate of frames per second, such as 8 fps, so they need fewer images and can be finished more quickly and cheaply.

Pioneers

If it were not for the pioneers of animation who pushed the boundaries of technology, progress would not have been made so quickly. There were numerous people involved in the development of the capture of the still image (the camera) and then the motion picture – each one has contributed to modern animation and film making. Described here are three people in the history of this technology – without them, modern movies may never have become a reality.

Techniques

William Horner

In 1834, William Horner invented the daedalum (which means 'wheel of the Devil'). The name was later changed to zoetrope ('wheel of Life') (see below). It became a popular item, especially as the animations could be changed.

Activity: Persistence of vision

Figure 31.2: Layout of flipbook

1 Create a **flipbook** of at least 20 images to demonstrate persistence of vision in action:

(a) Use either a small book or pieces of rectangular paper cut to the same size and stapled (see Figure 31.2).

(b) Starting with the back page, draw a picture at the right-hand side of the page.

(c) Draw a picture on each page, moving forward, making slight changes on each new page.

(d) Test your flipbook by flipping through the pages quickly. Instead of seeing a set of different images, persistence of vision should mean that you see movement.

2 The average speed of an animation is 12 fps. Research the speed for movies, computer screens (refresh rate) and computer games. Why do you think they are different?

A zoetrope

The zoetrope was a cylindrical device, about 30 centimetres in diameter, with slits cut into it at equally spaced intervals. Animation strips were placed inside with images that had slight differences between them. Then the cylinder was spun and, by looking through the slits which were spinning past, the images appeared to be animated. The zoetrope achieved about 14 fps and the images appeared to be moving naturally.

The zoetrope is considered to be the forerunner of cinema film.

Thomas Edison

Thomas Alva Edison was a prolific and successful inventor – he developed three ideas which have become crucial to modern animation and cinematography.

Edison was working to improve the efficiency and quality of the telegraph message, when he noticed that the transmitter would emit a noise that resembled the spoken word. By developing this further, he discovered he could record and play back voices, using two needles and a wax-coated cylinder. When someone spoke into the mouthpiece, one of the needles would indent the cylinder according to the sound vibrations in the voice. The other needle would then 'read' these indentations and play it back. He completed his first **phonograph** (see below) in 1877. It became hugely popular, as it could be used for numerous purposes, such as dictation, books for the blind, children's toys and recording messages.

Key term

Edison is most popularly known as the inventor of the electric lightbulb. However, he didn't actually invent it but improved an idea that had been conceived 50 years earlier. His major achievement was that he made electric lighting safe, practical and economical. As a replacement for gas lighting, the electric light bulb was a huge hit and made Edison famous and rich. His company, Edison General Electric, merged with its competitor and became the US company General Electric.

In 1888, Edison was visited by Eadweard Muybridge who was the inventor of the **zoopraxiscope** (see page 247). This was an early form of projector – images on glass were lit by a lantern and projected onto a screen, producing a continuous moving image.

Muybridge was interested in Edison's phonograph and proposed a collaboration of moving images and recorded sound. Edison, possibly considering the

A phonograph

Key terms

Phonograph – invented by Thomas Edison in 1877 to record the spoken word.

Zoopraxiscope – invented by Eadweard Muybridge, it was a development of the zoetrope. It used light which was shone through images on glass.

Kinetoscope – invented by Thomas Edison, it was an early projector using perforated film.

Cinematograph – invented by the Lumière brothers in 1895, it used 35mm celluloid film.

A zoopraxiscope

A kinetoscope

zoopraxiscope to be an inefficient way of producing moving images, declined. However, he was very much interested in the idea. He invented his own version – the **kinetoscope** (see below) – which became the forerunner of modern projection. It involved a sheet of perforated film being moved over a light to give the illusion of movement.

Further experiments to combine a moving image machine with a pre-recorded sound machine were partly successful, but quality was an issue and it was difficult for the technicians operating the machines to keep the images and sound in time with each other.

Lumière brothers

There had been several attempts at making motion picture cameras before 1895, but the Lumière brothers created a camera that was portable and could film, process and project all in one unit. The **cinematograph** (see below) is considered the invention that began the era of motion pictures. It used 35mm perforated celluloid film. Although Edison (and others such as the Skladanowsky brothers) had preceded them in projecting film to an audience, the first screening made by the Lumière brothers is considered by film historians to be the birth of cinema.

One of their first films, *The Arrival of a Train at the Station*, showed a train entering a station diagonally across the screen and reportedly had audiences screaming and ducking out of the way. This was a new

A cinematograph

and exciting medium and it was now practical to bring it to a mass audience.

Now the technology had sufficiently developed, filmmakers became interested in the entertainment value of film and began to make historical, fantasy and horror movies. As demand increased, music halls, theatres and opera houses were converted to allow the showing of moving pictures and audiences flocked to see the new exciting shows.

Traditional techniques

There are many techniques available to animators. Some have been developed into more modern methods using technology and some are still used in their original form today.

Drawn animation is where each **frame** is hand drawn or painted onto a frame of film (see Figure 31.3).

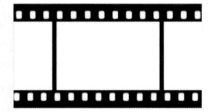

Figure 31.3: Frame of a film

This method works in a similar way to a flipbook, as each frame is drawn slightly differently from the previous one. When played at speed, the frames create movement. The advantage is that every single frame can be drawn in immense detail. The disadvantage is that this is incredibly time-consuming. Saturday morning children's cartoons have always been in high demand and studios have felt pressured to produce new material every week with very limited budgets. To combat these challenging circumstances they drew fewer frames per second, which meant that less work and fewer resources were required; however, the animation appeared shakier.

Another method of saving time and money using traditional techniques is to use **limited animation**.

Images are drawn onto **cels** and then overlaid to create a composite image.

One cel would contain the background and others would contain the moving parts. The background could remain the same throughout the scene and only the moving cels would need to be redrawn. This can be seen in cartoons such as Hanna-Barbera's *The Flintstones*. For example, Fred Flintstone could be running along a street, so he would be the moving part that needed to be redrawn. However, the same background would be used throughout the scene, so he would pass the same house and the same lamppost over and over again, but giving the illusion of distance.

Claymation is a type of stop-motion animation where a scene is set up, a picture is taken on a camera, then the scene is moved, another picture is taken and so on.

Although called claymation, models can be puppets or made out of clay, plasticine, wire or any other material that is malleable but will stay still during the taking of the shot. Claymation provides a 3D effect that is often lacking in other traditional techniques. The models can be reused over and over again throughout the filming and this can aid continuity. However, making a claymation film is a very time-consuming process. For example, the makers of the film *James and the Giant Peach* could only film about ten seconds of the movie

Key terms

Drawn animation – where animators draw each frame of the film.

Frame – a single section of film that contains one image of the animation.

Limited animation – where the same cels are used over and over again.

Cel – a piece of transparent film that can be drawn on then overlaid with other cels to create a composite image.

Claymation – where models or puppets are moved frame by frame to create an animation.

Cut-out animation – where shapes are laid against a background and moved for each shot of the camera.

Tweening – short for 'in betweening'. This is where the animator states where point A and B are and the computer fills in the intermediary movement.

Mask – used to cover part or all of an image and can be moved to reveal the image beneath.

each day because of the number of joints belonging to each character – the centipede alone had 72 moving parts.

Cut-out amimation uses a similar method to claymation – parts are moved, then a shot is taken, then moved again and so on.

A background is created, then the cut-outs (the moving parts) are placed on top. This can be a very quick method of creating animation – much quicker than the other traditional methods discussed – but it can result in quite jerky movements. The cut-out method is rarely used in modern animation; however, Matt Stone and Trey Parker have had worldwide success with their creation, *South Park*. It originally used traditional cut-out methods but moved on to use computer animations to simulate the effect of cut-out.

1.2 Types of animation

Animation involves three mains types of progression: movement, masking and morphing.

Movement

Movement is the development of an object from position A to position B. Movement can be achieved frame by frame or by using **tweening**.

Activity: Moving in Adobe® Flash®

1   Create the ball described in the How to feature. Make it bounce by adding another key frame at frame 20 and tweening it from the bottom middle of the stage to the top right.

2   Create two more tweens to make the ball bounce back again (at frames 30 and 40).

How to... Create a simple motion tween in Adobe® Flash®

1   Open a new Adobe® Flash® document.

2   Select the Circle tool.

3   Choose any fill colour and no outline:

4   Draw a circle (hold down the Shift key to make it a perfect circle).

5   Place your circle in the top left of the stage.

6   Right click on the circle and select Convert To Symbol.

7   Call it 'ball' and select the type: graphic. Click OK.

8   On the timeline (at the top of the screen), right click on frame 10 and select Insert Key Frame.

9   Make sure the key frame at 10 is highlighted and move your ball to the bottom middle of the stage.

10 On the timeline, on the grey section between the two key frames, right click and select Insert Motion Tween.

11 The grey part should turn blue and an arrow should point from the first key frame to the second one.

12 Test your movie by pressing Control and Enter together.

13 The ball should move from one position to the other.

Masking

Masking involves an image being shown or hidden by a **mask**.

Some of the effects that can be produced can resemble a camera lens or spotlight.

How to... Create a simple mask effect in Adobe® Flash®

1 Open a new Adobe® Flash® document.

2 Create a text box and type in your first name.

3 Create another text box and type in your last name.

4 Create a new layer – right click on Layer 1 beside the timeline, Insert Layer. (For more on Layers, see page 259.)

5 Make sure your cursor is on the first key frame in this new layer.

6 Draw a circle and fill it entirely in a solid colour (eg black).

7 Animate the circle using motion tweens so it moves around the two text boxes.

8 Right click on the layer name (Layer 2) and select Mask.

9 Test your movie by pressing Ctrl and Enter together. The circle should now act as a 'spotlight' and only the area underneath it should be visible.

How to... Create a simple shape tween in Adobe® Flash®

1 Open a new Adobe® Flash® document.

2 Select the Text tool, draw a textbox onto the stage and enter the text '1'.

3 Format the 1 so the font is Arial and the size is 48pt.

4 Use the Align palette (Control + K to open) and centre the 1 to the exact centre of the stage.

5 Highlight the 1 and use Control + B to break it apart until the shape is dotty (not highlighted with a blue box).

6 Create a key frame at frame 20 (right click, Insert Key Frame).

7 Replace the 1 with a 2 and ensure it has the same formatting, is in the centre of the stage and is broken apart.

8 On the timeline, on the grey section between the two key frames, left click so the highlight appears on it.

9 In the Properties Inspector at the bottom of the screen, choose Tween: Shape.

10 The grey part should turn green and an arrow should point from the first key frame to the second one. Note: If the arrow is dotted, the shapes probably need to be broken apart again.

11 Test your movie by pressing Ctrl and Enter together.

12 The 1 should morph into a 2.

Morphing

This is the changing of an object from shape A into shape B. Morphing can be done frame by frame or by using tweening.

Activity: Morphing in Adobe® Flash®

1 In a new document, morph a green square into a red circle.

2 In a new document, morph your first name into your last name.

3 Use the Help files to learn how Shape Hints work. (Hint: They are under Modify). Add Shape Hints to your name morph and see how the transition improves.

1.3 Uses

When someone thinks about animation, often the first thing that comes to mind is entertainment: animated films and cartoons. However, animation has so many other uses and is so widespread in our lives that sometimes you may not even realise when it is being used.

Advertising

Television advertising makes good use of animation to provide imagery that would not be possible in the real world.

Kellogg's use characters over long periods in their advertising

Animation can be used to make the products fun and can be especially effective with adverts for children. For example, Kellogg's has used animated characters throughout a long-running series of adverts for Coco Pops. The characters are now well-known to the television-viewing population, even though they are only on-screen for a few minutes at a time.

Other uses of animation can involve suspending reality in order to entertain television audiences during the advert or wow them by the product. For example, in a series of Citroën adverts, a car morphed into a robot figure and took part in activities such as dancing and ice skating. This conveyed an exciting message to the audience about the product that was being sold.

Activity: Animation in advertising

The next time you watch television, pay close attention to the adverts. Choose five adverts and, for each one, write down:

• the product being sold

• whether animation is used

• the purpose of the animation

• whether, in your opinion, it is an effective advert.

With the rise in popularity of the Internet and the speed at which people can access it in their own homes, there has been an increase in opportunities for advertisers on the Web. There are three main types of advertising on the Internet that use animation:

• banner adverts that appear either across the top of a web page or down the side

• pop-up adverts that open in a new window when a web page is opened

• centre-screen Flash adverts.

Generally the aim of the animation in these adverts is to attract the attention of the visitor to the web page and to encourage them to buy the product, visit the advertised site or do whatever else the advert wants them to do.

Billboard advertisements now also use animation, due to the increased availability and affordability of the technology. In Piccadilly Circus in London, the famous illuminated adverts span the whole height of the buildings (see below). Traditionally these were made

Piccadilly Circus then and now

Case study: The Uncanny Valley

Animated films such as *The Polar Express* and *Monster House*, were hailed by critics as being revolutionary for their use of **performance capture** for human characters. However, this acclamation did not translate into as much box office profit as might have been expected. The reason given was a theory called the **Uncanny Valley** (see Figure 31.4).

The theory states that humans or humanlike figures (such as androids), which are not real but look very real, make us feel very uncomfortable as our brain has difficulty recognising what it is seeing.

As technology develops, it is thought that the Uncanny Valley will become an increasing problem.

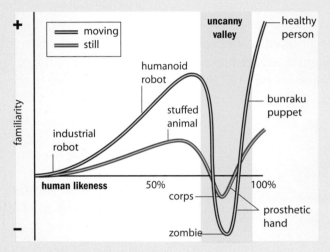

Figure 31.4: Diagram of the location of the Uncanny Valley

For example, as computer games characters become more realistic, players might feel uncomfortable being represented on-screen by a person who is no longer a fantasy figure but a character who looks and moves completely realistically.

For example, in the game Gears Of War (released on Xbox® 360 by Epic Games), the main character Marcus Fenix is very realistic in the way that he moves and there is great detail in his face. However, he has been drawn out of proportion, so there can be no doubt that he is a fantasy figure. This means that the animation does not fall within the Uncanny Valley.

1 Research three animated films: one from before 1990, one from between 1990 and 2005 and a very recent one. List the key animation features of each, focusing on how animation techniques have changed over time and the effects on the visual experience for the audience.

2 With reference to the Uncanny Valley, explain why an animated film and a computer game might have different consequences. How does the audience/player experience differ?

3 Discuss and debate with your friends whether you think the Uncanny Valley actually exists. Although there is research and anecdotal evidence, it is just a theory at present. Argue for and against the theory. What do you think will happen as animation technology continues to improve?

Key terms

Performance capture – where human acting is 'captured' by a computer and then used by animators to create the images.

Uncanny Valley – the theory that if animation looks too real, audiences will feel uncomfortable.

CGI – stands for computer generated imagery and is where computers are used to create animation to be integrated into the live action in a movie.

up of fluorescent and neon lighting, but they are now being replaced by full-screen animations. This means that advertisers are no longer limited to one advert but can change it easily whenever necessary.

Entertainment

Animation used for entertainment can take several forms, from a cartoon 'short' lasting only a few minutes between programmes to feature-length films. The first full-length animated film to be widely successful in the Western world was *Snow White and the Seven Dwarfs*, produced by Walt Disney Productions in 1937. It used traditional animation techniques, took three years to make and was a risky enterprise for Walt Disney – he reportedly had to mortgage his house to finance the project. However, the international success it acquired has justified Disney's decision and it changed animation history. In making this film, techniques (such as realistic human movements and weather effects) were developed that would be used in future films.

Modern animation films generally use computer techniques throughout and examples of this can be seen in films such as *The Incredibles, Ice Age* and *Toy Story*.

Bob Hoskins starring alongside Roger, the animated rabbit, in *Who Framed Roger Rabbit?*, 1988

Activity: CGI in movies

Research and make notes on how the following films used computer animation:

- *Tron*
- *Flight of the Navigator*
- *Labyrinth*
- *The Abyss*
- *The Mask*
- *The Matrix*
- *Lord of the Rings*
- *Star Wars.*

However, the 1993 film *Jurassic Park* revolutionised CGI techniques and proved that convincing digital animation was achievable and desired by audiences.

Education

Animation is becoming more frequently used in education: from demonstrating a scientific idea that would be difficult to carry out in the classroom, to grabbing and maintaining learners' interest in a topic by using a computer game with strong educational content.

A study carried out for the Department of Education and Skills in 2002 by Teem investigated whether computer games could be used as an educational tool and found that when learners were stimulated by the content they were more likely to learn successfully and develop knowledge. They also found that various skills developed during gameplay.

There are many educational games available and most rely on animation to ensure users find them entertaining while they learn. They cover a wide variety of topics including school subjects, such as science, life skills and healthy eating, and they can even be used in training for adults, such as in driving simulators.

Animation can also be used in conjunction with human acting. An early example of this is in the 1964 Walt Disney Productions film *Mary Poppins*, starring Julie Andrews and Dick Van Dyke. Although most of the film is acted by humans, there is a sequence in which they are acting alongside animated characters. There are some clever interactions where the humans talk to the animated characters and objects are passed between them.

The penguins from the animation in *Mary Poppins* reappeared as waiters and bartenders in the 1988 film *Who Framed Roger Rabbit?*, which was a landmark film involving animated characters and humans in a real environment. Bob Hoskins stars alongside a cartoon rabbit called Roger in a world where humans and 'Toons' exist together. The animated characters were all created using traditional techniques after the shooting of the live action, which meant the actors were acting against thin air. This film led to other human/animation interaction movies such as *Space Jam* (1996), *The Pagemaster* (1994) and *Casper* (1995).

CGI (computer generated imagery) is used widely in modern films and can create fantastical scenes such as flying through space. It can also be used to replicate objects and show, for example, a fleet of ships filling the ocean to the horizon. At first CGI used stop-motion techniques, which created a slightly unrealistic effect.

Activity: Animation in education

1. Think about your education to date. Has animation been used in any area to develop your learning?

2. List all the subjects you are currently studying. For each one, name at least one way animation could be used to assist your education.

Other uses of animation

Animation can be used for simulations of places or situations that would be too difficult or dangerous to deal with in the real world. In architecture, animated simulation can predict what would happen to buildings in certain weather conditions, such as hurricanes or floods. Architects can test the buildings for every possible eventuality before the actual building work is done. This means they can refine and perfect the structures to make them as safe as possible.

The military also uses simulations as part of its training. Military personnel are able to take part in realistic, interactive and repetitive military scenarios to develop their reaction times and strategies for similar circumstances in the real world. Animations are also used to model what would happen in situations such as a bomb hitting a certain target, demonstrating the impact on the surrounding areas.

Driving simulators work in a similar way, allowing drivers to gain confidence in driving and a feel for the car before driving in the real world. They can also be used to teach hazard perception, ie awareness of potentially dangerous situations and knowing how to avoid them.

Television weather forecasting exposes a huge amount of people to high-quality graphics every day. Early weather forecasts were illustrated with hand-drawn symbols, some held in place on a map with magnets. Now animations are used to show more detailed and accurate forecasts (see below).

Activity: Animation in weather forecasting

Watch the weather forecasts on BBC 1, ITV and Channel 4 and compare the different styles of animation and artwork used.

1.4 Digital animation formats

When creating an animation, you must consider the format in which you will create it. The choice will depend on the level of complexity of the animation and where it is intended to be used. It may be important to have a relatively small file size, perhaps to be used on a web page, or the animation needs to run equally well on different platforms such as Windows® and Macintosh®.

Animated GIF

GIF (pronounced either 'gif' or 'jif') is a **bitmap format**, which means that each pixel is saved in its location like a map. This is opposed to **vector format**, in which the graphical information is saved as a mathematical algorithm that is recalculated on each opening of the file. (For more information on bitmap and vector formats, see page 262.)

A GIF uses a maximum palette of 256 colours, which means it can hold less colour detail than a **JPEG**.

Weather forecasts then and now

Figure 31.6: Dithering

Key terms

GIF – stands for graphics interchange format. It is a bitmap image format that can support animations.

Bitmap format – saves the image as a map of pixels.

Vector format – saves the image as a mathematical algorithm.

JPEG – stands for joint photographics expert group. It is a bitmap image format that can hold more than 16 million colours in an image.

Dithering – uses in-between colours to reduce the harsh contrast of two colours.

JPEGs are more suited to images, such as photographs that need more detail to be stored, whereas GIFs are more appropriate for images with fewer colours, such as logos or graphics. One useful feature of GIF is that it supports transparent backgrounds.

GIF is an unusual file format in that it also supports animation. In the file of an animated GIF, a set of images are stored together with the instructions of how they should be played, including the order of the images (see Figure 31.5).

Figure 31.5: Frames in an animated GIF

GIF images are smaller than pure bitmap (.bmp) files, due to compression. They use a type of lossless compression called LZW, which attempts to make the file size smaller without significantly degrading the image quality. The more times a file is saved in a compressed format, the more quality is lost – for example, if a file is saved as a GIF, then saved again as a GIF, the compression algorithm will have been performed on the image twice. It is better to work in a full bitmap (for example, a .psd file in Adobe®

Photoshop®) then compress only once when the image is finished.

To try to include more colours in a GIF image, a technique called **dithering** can be employed, although this will decrease the amount by which the file size can be decreased and can cause some loss of definition in the image. The aim of dithering is to reduce the 'blockiness' that GIF images can have and give the impression of a more photographic quality to the image (see Figure 31.6).

The advantages of animated GIFs include:

- lossless compression
- relatively small file sizes
- supports transparent backgrounds
- suitable for inclusion in online content.

The disadvantages of animated GIFs include:

- maximum palette of 256 colours
- colours can appear 'blocky' in photographic-quality images
- dithering reduces the amount the file size can be compressed.

Alternative animation formats include DHTML web pages, Flash® animations and multimedia products created for specific players such as QuickTime® or Shockwave®.

Other animation formats

Dynamic HTML

Dynamic HTML (DHTML) is a form of **HTML** combined with client side scripting languages (such as JavaScript), **CSS** and a **DOM** (document object model).

DHTML can be used to create animation on a web page, such as a rollover button or drop-down menu, as well as being used to make browser-based games. However, due to the different ways browsers interpret web languages, there were platform problems with DHTML, for example between users using Internet Explorer® and Netscape Navigator. DHTML has become less popular in recent times and the features of DHTML are now usually created in CSS or client side scripting languages by themselves. The features of DHTML can also be made in Flash®, and Flash® websites are becoming more popular.

Flash®

Adobe® Flash® (previously Macromedia® Flash®) is a multimedia authoring application, although the term can also be used to refer to Flash® Player, the virtual machine used to run animations made in Flash®.

The program allows users to create animations frame by frame using vectors or imported bitmaps and including scripting in **ActionScript.** Sound and video can also be included.

A working Flash® file is a .fla, which means that it is opened and edited in Flash®, whereas a compiled, uneditable file is a .swf.

Flash® can be used to create animations for entertainment, examples of which can be found across the Internet. Elements of a web page, such as rollover buttons, can be made in Flash®. The whole website can even be a Flash® animation – this can create an impressive effect but causes problems for users with slow connections or who block Flash® content. Flash® has also been used more recently in online advertising, either in banner or centre-screen adverts. In addition, Flash® games and content for mobile phones are becoming popular.

Flash®is becoming the industry standard for lower-end animation and as a teaching tool in education. Due to the thorough help tutorials and its similarity to other Macromedia® and Adobe® products, Flash® is relatively easy to learn, as opposed to many other animation programs.

Shockwave®

Adobe® Shockwave® (previously Macromedia® Shockwave®) was introduced prior to Flash® and was Macromedia®'s first successful multimedia player. Whereas Flash® focuses more on 2D animation, Shockwave® specialises in 3D graphics, streaming videos and has a faster **rendering** engine.

Shockwave® was designed to work with the Director application, which can compile several types of **asset** into one multimedia product, on a larger scale than Flash®.

Key terms

HTML – stands for hypertext markup language. It is the language used as a basis for all web pages.

CSS – stands for cascading style sheets. It is a form of web language which standardises the layout through a website.

DOM – stands for document object model. It is used to integrate styles, content and formatting for web pages.

ActionScript – a language used in Flash® animations, for example to create buttons.

Rendering – the process combining audio and visual elements with any applied effects to produce a file that can be played in real time.

Asset – any type of object within a multimedia product, such as an image, movie clip or sound file.

QuickTime®

QuickTime® is made by Apple® but can be used on both Macintosh® and Windows® platforms. It is a multimedia player that supports animation, sound, video and other types of media clips. To accompany it, products such as QuickTime Broadcaster® (for producing live events) and QuickTime Pro® (for creating movies) can be purchased.

QuickTime® comes bundled with modern Macintosh® operating systems (Mac OS) and rivals Windows® Media Player, which is embedded in Windows® platform products. Although the number of Windows® users is higher than those of Apple® (see Table 31.1), Apple® is more commonly used in the design industry – therefore, the competition is still raging fiercely.

Windows®	Apple®
"More than a billion people around the world use Windows® every day."	"Apple® has seen the user base grow from 25 million to near 75 million users today, in 2009."
(From the official Microsoft® website, 2010)	(From the official Mac News Network www.macnn.com, 2009)

Table 31.1: Comparison of operating systems sales figures

RealPlayer®

RealPlayer is a cross-platform multimedia player that can support both QuickTime® and Window® Media formats. Although this player might seem to be a solution to the issue of different formats needed for QuickTime® and Windows® Media Player, RealPlayer® has received a lot of criticism for displaying adverts and pop-up messages during use. RealPlayer® has an advertising-free version for businesses. However, this does not give the user access to all the features available in the full program.

A version of RealPlayer® is used by the BBC website for playing the audio files of radio shows in its Listen Again service.

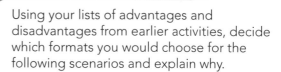

Activity: Multimedia players

1 Create a list of advantages and disadvantages of creating animations for each of these:
   - Shockwave®
   - QuickTime®
   - RealPlayer®.
2 Compare your three lists of advantages and disadvantages. Name situations where you would choose to create an animation for each individual multimedia player.

Activity: Which format?

Using your lists of advantages and disadvantages from earlier activities, decide which formats you would choose for the following scenarios and explain why.

- An animated logo for a website
- Rollover buttons for an Internet website
- Rollover buttons for an intranet website
- Short animated movie to instruct workers in a company how to lift boxes safely
- Animated introduction to a CD being delivered to design companies.

Note: You can choose a combination if required.

Assessment activity 31.1

Digital Myths is a small business that creates animations for schools. You are the newest member of the team and as a first assignment they have asked you to produce some materials for the schools with which they work. These will be displayed in classrooms for Year 10 and Year 11 learners to help them begin learning animation.

1 Create a series of detailed, illustrated posters to explain the following topics:

(a) different types of animation **P1**

(b) persistence of vision **M1**

(c) the ways animations are used in advertising, entertainment and education **P2**

(d) the advantages and limitations of animated GIFs **P3**

(e) the advantages and limitations of other animation formats **M2**.

Grading tips

- It is useful for you to have a wide range of experiences of different types of animation. Try to watch as much as possible, choosing different styles and viewing each of them with an analytical eye. **P1**

- On the subject of persistence of vision, include both old and new ideas, as opinions are changing as new research is done. **M1**

- When discussing how animations are used, give examples. **P2**

- With regard to animated GIFs and other formats, make sure you discuss both the positives and negatives of each. You may wish to use a table format to compare the formats. **P3** **M2**

PLTS

You can demonstrate your skills as a **creative thinker** by making your posters attractive and eye-catching while making sure the information is clear for the audience.

Functional skills

You can show your **English** skills by presenting your information appropriately for your audience and communicating information, ideas and opinions effectively and persuasively.

2   Know the software techniques used in animation

There are several tools and techniques that are used throughout all digital animation development. Although some of the topics discussed in this section will also be applicable to other types of animation, this unit focuses on digital animation which constitutes the majority of the modern industry.

2.1 Tools

Tools such as layers and frames are the basic building blocks of creating animations and are found in all animation applications. Other methods, such as scripting, can be used to add interactivity for products such as games.

A frame (see Figure 31.7) is a single image within an animation. It is the equivalent of a single frame in a strip of celluloid. Frames are played in sequence at a specified rate (fps) to create the illusion of animation.

Key frames (see Figure 31.7) are special frames where an animation begins or ends (see Key frames, page 269).

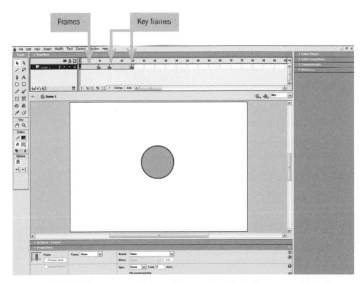

Figure 31.7: Frames and key frames in Flash®

When using tweening, each tween must begin and end with a key frame.

How to... Use frames and key frames in Adobe® Flash®

1   Open a new Adobe® Flash® document.

2   Draw a picture of a bee.

3   Highlight the whole bee, right click on it and select Convert To Symbol.

4   Right click on the circle and select Convert To Symbol.

5   Call it 'bee' and select the type: graphic. Click OK.

6   Create a key frame at frame 10.

7   Motion tween your bee to move from frame 1 to frame 10.

8   Continue animating until your bee flies all over the stage.

9   Test your movie by pressing Ctrl and Enter together.

Layers

A layer (see Figure 31.8) is a separate element of an image. When layers are viewed together, they become an amalgamation of the separate images. Layers are similar to the cels used in hand-drawn animations, where transparent films are placed over each other to create a composite image.

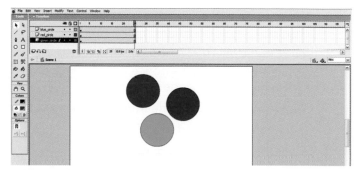

Figure 31.8: Layers in Flash®

When animating several assets, each asset must be on a separate layer.

How to... Use layers in Adobe® Flash®

1 Open a new Adobe® Flash® document.
2 Name the layer 'branch'.
3 Draw a picture of a tree branch, similar to this:
4 Convert the branch to a graphic symbol.
5 Create a new layer and call it 'sun'.
6 Draw a sun in the top right corner.
7 Convert the sun to a graphic symbol.
8 Create a new layer and call it 'caterpillar'.
9 Draw a caterpillar.
10 Convert the caterpillar to a graphic symbol.
11 Animate the caterpillar so it crawls up the tree (from off screen) and along the branch.
12 Test your animation.

Activity: Layers in Adobe® Flash®

1 Create the animation described in the How to… feature on layers. Continue the animation so the caterpillar turns into a chrysalis.

   Hint: You might need to use both types of tweens.

2 Continue the animation so the chrysalis turns into a butterfly and flies off screen.

Controls

Controls are the tools available in the animation application. They are usually contained in the Toolbox palette (see Figure 31.9).

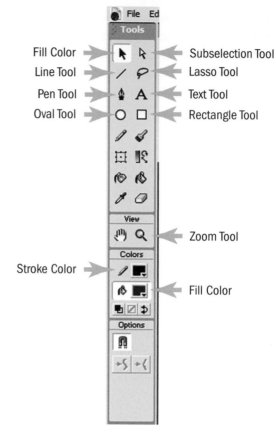

Figure 31.9: Controls in Flash®

How to... Use some controls in Adobe® Flash®

1 Open a new Adobe® Flash® document.
2 Select the Line Tool and draw a line on the stage.
3 Select the Text Tool and click on the stage to start a text box – type your name in the text box.
4 Select the Arrow Tool (black arrow) and click on your line and your text – notice how the Properties Inspector options change for each asset.
5 Change the style of the line from solid to dotted.
6 Change the colour and size of the text.
7 Select the Oval Tool and draw a circle.
8 Draw another circle but hold down Shift while drawing it – notice how this produces a perfect circle.
9 Select the Rectangle Tool and draw a rectangle, then a perfect square.
10 Select the Arrow Tool (black arrow), right click on your oval and select Free Transform. Notice

how black **handles** appear. These can be used to adjust the shape. Try pulling and pushing the handles and rotating the shape.

11 Hold down the Alt key and drag the oval shape to another part of the stage. Notice how, instead of moving the shape, it creates a second copy.
12 Select the Subselection Tool (white arrow) and click on the edge of your square. Notice how white handles appear. These can be used to adjust the individual points in a shape. Try turning your square into a diamond.
13 There are two colour tools in the Toolbox: Stroke Color and Fill Color. Change the Fill Color to a colour you have not yet used in this activity and use the Paint Bucket Tool to change the colour of one of your shapes.

Key terms

Handles – markers on a shape that show where a shape can be adjusted.

Ease – (also known as the fairing) the speed at which a tween is performed.

Activity: Adobe® Flash® Controls

1 Use the controls described in the How to… feature on controls.

2 Use three more tools not yet tried to change your shapes in some way.

Tweening

Tweening can create movement (such as a motion tween) or morphing (such as a shape tween). The tween itself also has properties that can be altered, for example the **ease**.

Others

Other tools at the animator's disposal include:

- **Buttons**: These can be used to control the play of an animation or alter the sequence. For example,

Activity: Using easing in Adobe® Flash®

Create the movie described in the How to… feature on easing. Describe what easing is. Explain why easing makes the movie look more realistic.

at the beginning there could be a 'Start' button to begin the playing of the animation; at the end there could be a 'Play again' button to restart the animation; there could even be 'Scene selection' buttons like the ones on a DVD which would take the viewer to a particular part of the animation.

- **Libraries**: Symbols, tweens and other assets are stored in libraries within animation software so they can be reused. Reusing assets means that the animator does not have to create the same thing over and over and also it means that there will not be any differences in assets that are meant to be the same. For example, if an animator wants to have three butterflies flying up the screen, instead of drawing three butterflies they can draw one and reuse it three times. This would mean they were identical and would save time.

How to... Use easing in Adobe® Flash®

Create a bouncing ball in Adobe® Flash®:

1 Open a new Adobe® Flash® document.

2 Draw a line across the lower part of the stage (this will be the 'ground').

3 Create a new layer.

4 On that new layer, draw a circle, convert it to a symbol and call it 'ball'.

5 At frame10, motion tween the ball to the ground.

6 At frame 20, motion tween the ball back into the air vertically, but not as high as it started.

7 Create three more bounces down and up, with the ball moving less high into the air each time.

8 Test the movie and think about how realistic it looks.

For each tween, change the ease:

9 To change the ease, click on the tween itself in the timeline and change the Ease option in the Properties Inspector.

10 Each time the ball moves towards the ground, set the Ease to 100 In.

11 Each time the ball moves away from the ground, set the Ease to 100 Out.

12 Test the movie. Why does this look more realistic than before?

To make the animation even more realistic, squash the ball slightly as it lands on the ground:

13 Create another symbol called 'squashedball' – the same ball but slightly flattened.

14 For a few frames on each bounce, when the ball touches the ground, change the ball symbol to the squashedball symbol.

- **Integrated media**: Other types of media can be integrated into an animation, such as video and sound. These can add a powerful effect to the animation but can sometimes be awkward to include and can raise the file size dramatically.

- **Preloaders**: These can be displayed to the user to indicate that a file is being loaded. They are generally used for larger files which take time to load or files uploaded to the web as the animator does not know what equipment the user has and so cannot predict how long the file will take to open. Preloaders generally display a progress bar and can also have additional information such as the title, the animator's name, a short description and even a mini-animation.

- **Scripts**: To make animations more versatile, scripting languages can be used, such as ActionScript in Flash®. These can change a simple linear animation into one with more potential and can also allow user interactivity.

2.2 Animation software

There is a multitude of software available to animators, from simple 2D beginner packages to complex 3D applications. Which software to use depends on the animation to be created and its purpose – for example, if it is to be used on a web page or whether the file size is important.

Vector graphics

A vector file consists of a mathematical algorithm that is recalculated every time the file is opened. This means that the file size is generally smaller, as it only holds data about the picture rather than an actual image. Because the file is a set of calculations, the image can be resized as much as necessary without any loss of quality (see Figure 31.10).

Adobe® Flash® is a vector-based program – although bitmaps can be imported to be used, any images created in Flash® are vectors. Other vector-based programs include Adobe® Illustrator® (.ai files) and CorelDRAW® (.cdr).

How to... Create buttons using ActionScript to control playing an animation

1. Open a new Adobe® Flash® document.

2. At frames 1, 2 and 3, create a green, yellow and red circle respectively. These will serve as markers to show the buttons are working.

3. Click on key frame 1 and open the Action palette (just above the Properties Inspector).

4. Make sure you are in Expert Mode (use the Help if you are unsure).

5. Enter the following ActionScript: `Stop();`

6. Enter the Stop command in key frames 2 and 3 in the same way.

7. Create a new layer and add key frames at 1, 2 and 3.

8. Click on key frame 1 and draw a green square.

9. Convert it to the symbol type: button.

10. Do the same for key frames 2 and 3, adding a yellow and a red square respectively.

11. Click on key frame 1 and highlight the green square.

12. Open the Action palette and enter the following ActionScript:

```
on (release) {
gotoAndPlay(2);
}
```

13. Do the same for the button on key frame 2, changing the middle line to gotoAndPlay(3);

14. Do the same for the button on key frame 3, changing the middle line to gotoAndPlay(1);

15. Test your movie and try clicking the buttons.

7× Magnification

Vector

Bitmap

Ice Cream

Figure 31.10: Comparison of enlarged vector and bitmap images

Bitmap graphics

A bitmap file is made up of individual pixels, essentially a map of where each one is and what colour it is. This results in a larger file size than vectors. The files can be compressed to make them smaller using formats such as GIF or JPEG but this results in a loss of quality. The

more times a file is saved in a compressed format, the more quality is lost.

Due to the image being stored with the pixels in place, when it is resized larger they become stretched and this causes a pixellation effect (see Figure 31.11).

Applications such as Adobe® Photoshop® and Microsoft® Paint® are bitmap-based and file types include .gif, .jpeg and .bmp.

Specialist software packages

There is a multitude of specialist animation packages available. Some used in the design, film and games industries include:

- Dream Studio
- Bryce
- Maya
- Blender
- trueSpace
- Lightwave
- 3D Studio Max
- Softimage XSI
- Flash®.

Some specialise in particular areas – Bryce focuses on building environments. Others tackle characters and objects as well. Some are good as learning application, such as Flash®, while others can be quite complex. Most are relatively expensive, but Blender is an open-source program and is free.

Figure 31.11: A bitmap image – small and enlarged (pixellated)

Activity: Animation applications

1 Select three specialist software packages and research each one. Make notes on:

- who produced it and what other products are available from them

- how much it costs and how it can be obtained (eg general release in stores, download from Internet, etc)

- what it is used for in the design industry

- its key features and in what situations it may be used.

2 Select two of your three packages and compare them using the points from question 1.

3 Select one of your two packages and evaluate it, using your own opinions.

2.3 Animating for the web

When animating for the web, file size is not the only constraint. In this medium, the animation is generally not the focal point but is used to enhance the content of the site – for example, buttons or logos. A house style may have to be followed so that the animations blend with the site as a whole.

Special techniques

Animated rollovers are buttons which perform an action when an event triggers them, for example when a mouse hovers over them. They usually have three states: up (where the button is unaffected), over (where the mouse hovers over the button) and down (when the mouse clicks the button).

How to...Create a rollover button in Adobe® Flash®

1 Open a new Adobe® Flash® document.
2 Draw a blue square on the stage.
3 Convert it to a symbol called button and type Button.
4 Double click button – you are now inside the button. Notice how the timeline is split into four actions: Up, Over, Down, Hit.
5 Add a key frame to the Over action and change the square to green.
6 Add a key frame to the Down action and change the square to red.
7 Add a key frame to the Hit action. This will be invisible when the movie is played but will define the clickable area of the button. Draw a large square over the top of button.
8 Just below the timeline, click Scene 1 to take you back to the main stage.
9 Test your movie and notice how the different actions affect the button.

How to... Create a moving rollover button in Adobe® Flash®

1 Open a new Adobe® Flash® document.
2 Draw a red square on the stage.
3 Convert it to a symbol called button and type Button.
4 Double click button.
5 Add a key frame to the Over action and the Down action.
6 Click on the Over action and convert the red square to a MovieClip.
7 Double click the square – you are now inside the MovieClip.
8 Using a shape tween, animate it so it grows longer.
9 Just below the timeline, click Button to take you back to the button.
10 Click on the Down action and change the red square into a yellow square.
11 Just below the timeline, click Scene 1 to take you back to the main stage.
12 Test your movie and notice how the different actions affect the button.

Email attachments and e-cards

A popular use for animation is to attach them to emails. They can include humorous jokes, inspirational messages and other entertaining distractions. Once they have been sent to one group of people, they are generally passed on and can spread all round the world. In a busy modern life, where people sometimes don't have time to write a full email message, they can send them an animated email message to let the person know they are thinking about them.

Viral advertisers have taken advantage of this new phenomenon and use it as another way of spreading news of their product, using digital word-of-mouth.

E-cards are digital cards that are sent via email in place of traditional paper-based cards. E-cards are generally animated and often have sound as well. E-card sites will often offer a few cards for free, but charge for the cards with higher-quality animation or messages. Parts of the e-card are usually customisable, including the heading, the greeting, the message and the goodbye message. For example, a sender could personalise a birthday card by writing 'Happy Birthday, Simon' instead of the generic 'Happy Birthday'.

Output devices

When creating animations, attention should be given to the devices on which it will be viewed.

Monitors can be set at a variety of resolutions so the animator cannot know which will be used. Common practice is design animations for the most popular resolution at the time – this will influence the animator's decisions on size of stage and other factors.

Some animations are designed for portable devices such as mobile phones and PDAs. Although a large percentage now have full-colour screens, some are still monochrome which should be borne in mind when creating animations for these devices.

If an animation is to be projected on to a screen, some quality may be lost as it is enlarged, and the animator must take this into account.

Activity: Animating for the web

Research and make notes for future use on factors which need to be considered when creating animations for the Internet.

2.4 Files

Before starting to animate, it is useful to know what file type will be used as this may influence the software or the method of saving used.

File types and features of each

Each file type is associated with a set of characteristics and the file type will often denote how the files are saved or how they can be played. Table 31.2 describes some of the most commonly used file types.

It should be noted that .mp4 and .mp3 (an audio-only file type with which you will be familiar) formats are related but not as closely as you might think: .mp4 is the MPEG-4 standard, whereas .mp3 is MPEG-1 Layer 3.

Converting files

Once files are in a compressed format, it is difficult to convert between them. However, during the editing stages it is possible to save files as many different types.

File types	Full name	Features
.gif (animated)	Graphics Interchange Format	• Maximum 256 colour palette • Supports transparency • Compresses file using lossless compression • Generally used for web animations and therefore playable on most platforms
.swf	Small Web Format Shockwave® Flash®	• Created by Adobe® Flash® • Locked and uneditable (as opposed to .fla files) • Files are compressed • Often used for online content
.mov		• Designed for QuickTime media player • Able to contain graphics, video and audio
.mp4	MPEG-4 Part 14 Moving Picture Experts Group	• Based on the .mov format • Can contain graphics, video and audio • Mainly playable on Apple® software or specialist hardware, including iTunes®, QuickTime®, PlayStation®3, Xbox® 360, iPod®
.wmv	Windows® Media Video	• Created by Microsoft® and popular on Windows® platform (Windows® Media Player is built into Windows® operating systems) • Can contain graphics, video and audio • Recently developed to store high definition files as WMV HD

Table 31.2: Comparison of some popular animation file types

Importing and exporting files

An animation will quite often include images and animations from other sources, rather than all assets being created for that project. The animation software being used will determine what can be imported and how but in general terms, both bitmap and vector static images will be accepted, as well as other animations made in the same program.

Exporting files involves publishing them in a viewable format that makes it possible to distribute. For example, when an Adobe® Flash® animation is published, it is then viewable using Flash® Player and can be watched on a computer that doesn't have the full Flash® application installed.

Activity: Converting files in Adobe® Flash®

1 Create a simple animation to save in Adobe® Flash®.

2 Save the animation in different formats:

- Save your animation in the normal way (File / Save) – this saves it as a .fla file, a working Flash file.

- Select File / Publish Settings. A new window should open with all the file type options: .swf, .html, .gif, .jpeg, .png, .exe, .hqx, .mov

Save your animation in each file type then try opening it. Make notes on what happens and try to explain why.

File management

Keeping files organised is a skill that you need to develop. One method is to keep all working files in one folder and all finished files in another. This should prevent working on a compressed file such as a GIF and compressing it further each time it is saved.

In addition, backing up is crucial, especially when working on large files, which is common for animations. Saving regularly can also prevent data loss.

2.5 Managing file size

The file size of an animation is crucial, especially if it is to be used on the Internet. If the file is too large, it will take too long to download and the user may lose patience and navigate away from the site.

Balance against quality of image

Images that are of a very high quality generally have the largest file sizes. In a bitmap, if the **resolution** is high, more pixels need to be stored in that image.

The more detail that needs to be recorded about an image, the larger the file size. In addition, if the image is detailed, the more likely it is that compression will have a detrimental effect on the image. When an image is compressed, some loss of quality will always occur and with detailed, photographic-type images, this degradation is usually more noticeable. An animator must choose whether it is more important to have high-quality images and a large file size, lower-quality images and a small file size or to find a happy medium balancing the two.

Use of special techniques

Optimisation of animation files is quite a complex process and can involve a detailed understanding of the file type and any compression methods that are used. Two common techniques are frame disposal and autocrop.

Frame disposal is used to prevent **artifacts** appearing. This is where a previous frame remains on-screen and is shown through the transparent areas of subsequent frames. To avoid this happening, frames should be disposed of and the background restored.

Autocrop is used to ensure that only the area that contains images is shown; areas with no images (which are transparent or a solid colour) can be trimmed (see Figure 31.12).

Activity: Managing file size

1 Create a simple animation without any optimisation techniques applied.

2 Using your animation, demonstrate how frame disposal optimises animations.

3 Using your animation, demonstrate how autocrop optimises animations.

Figure 31.12: Example of autocrop

Key terms

Resolution – the number of pixels per inch in an image.

Frame disposal – determines whether the frame continues to be displayed throughout subsequent frames or is discarded.

Artifacts – unwanted visible elements in a picture or animation.

Autocrop – a function that trims unwanted edges from an image or animation.

Assessment activity 31.2

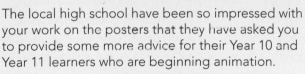 **BTEC**

The local high school have been so impressed with your work on the posters that they have asked you to provide some more advice for their Year 10 and Year 11 learners who are beginning animation.

1 Create a presentation describing the tools available for animation. **P4**

2 Produce a leaflet describing the factors that need to be taken into account when creating animations for the web. **P5**

3 Produce a leaflet explaining the techniques that are used to minimise the file size of an animation. **M3**

4 Create a short report comparing different specialist computer animation software packages. **D1**

Grading tips

- Make sure you include all the tools listed in the book and feel free to include others that you may have used. **P4**

- As you are creating leaflets, which have limited space, you need to make sure that you cover all the information you want to – choose your words carefully! **P5 M3**

- When comparing different software packages you could look at what the software can do, the price, which platforms it works on and the quality of the results. **D1**

PLTS

You can show you are a **reflective learner** by using your new knowledge to create these different documents and a **creative thinker** by making them visually appealing.

Functional skills

Finding relevant information and combining it in this range of documents could use your **ICT** skills.

3 Be able to design and implement digital animations

When creating animation there are generally three stages that must be performed: planning, creating and reviewing. The planning stage includes all the designing of the animation. The creating stage is the implementation of the design. The review involves testing the functionality of all elements of the animation and evaluating the animation to see whether it fulfils the client brief and is satisfactory for the viewers.

3.1 Design

Before beginning to animate, it is crucial to design it first. Although design can take a lot of time, it will save so much more during the actual implementation. Designing animation can involve storyboarding, calculating times and naming scenes.

Figure 31.13: Example of an animation storyboard

Storyboarding

Storyboarding (see Figure 31.13) is key to structuring an animation and deciding on the sequence of frames. In animation, a storyboard shows how different frames and scenes will interrelate.

The storyboard can simply be an overview of key scenes or it can be done in extensive detail, almost down to each frame being modelled, depending on how the animation will be made.

In a storyboard, boxes represent the screen and the designer draws the images to appear on screen, within the boxes. (If items are drawn outside the boxes, it means that they are off-screen and invisible to the viewer.) Drawings (or even photographs, if appropriate) are put inside each box to show what will appear in a particular frame or scene.

The designer includes notes under each box about what is happening. For example, 'Boy moves to centre'. These annotations can include film or theatre notations if these are understood by the animators involved. For example, 'Boy enters stage SR to CS, camera pans L à R' (which means: 'Boy enters stage right to centre stage, camera pans left to right').

Storyboarding can be a rough noting of ideas done in draft form or formally drawn for a team of animators to follow throughout the project.

Timings

Timing in an animation is quite an art and can be the element that draws the viewer into the action or leaves them feeling cold. For example, have you ever seen a film in which the speaking is out of sync with the picture? What effect did that have on you as a viewer?

The frames and their times can be planned using a log sheet or a bar sheet. The complexity of the animation will determine the intricacy of the sheets. Figures 31.14 and 31.15 on the following page show templates for bar and log sheets that may be suitable for your animations during this unit.

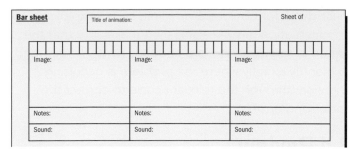

Figure 31.14: Bar sheet

Log sheet

Frame	Real time	Layer	Assets	Actions	Sounds
1	00:00				
2					
3					
4					
5					
6					
7					
8					
9					
10					
11					
12					

Figure 31.15: Log sheet

Key frames

When designing an animation, you need to identify where key frames occur, as these are the beginnings and ends of actions. These can be noted on the log sheet or bar sheet.

It is useful to know the frame numbers of each particular action (for example, when the key frames take place). In addition, it is good practice to name sections so they are easier to refer to, especially when working with a team of animators. If an animation has 2000 frames it is cumbersome to keep referring to the frame numbers of a particular scene. You could number the scenes, but again this doesn't give a clear indication of where the scene comes in the animation. It is, therefore, useful to name scenes in the animation, with meaningful names that reflect the content or action.

3.2 Implement

Create

When creating an animation it is important to follow the design you have produced. You may find that small adjustments need to be made and this is fine, as long as they are noted on the design as amendments.

Animating can be a very time-consuming, absorbing task so it is important to make sure that you have agreed to a realistic deadline. You need to pace the work sensibly, as leaving it all until the last minute is bound to result in a very poor animation.

Test

Testing is crucial to ensure the animation works as it is meant to. For more on this subject, see the Test section on the following page.

Review

After the specific, focused checking of the test stage the review stage provides an overall opinion of the animation. A review by the client or a member of

Activity: Creating animation

Sweet As is a business based in County Durham that produces honey from its own bees. The company has a website but the owners want to improve it by adding animation. They also want to use an animated advert on the Internet.

They have asked you to produce:

- a logo to be displayed large in the centre of the home page and smaller on each subsequent page
- a rollover button that can be used several times on every page for all of the navigation
- an advertisement for their special offer: 25% off for first-time buyers – to be shown on other websites with a link back to the Sweet As website.

Their website has a black background with yellow and white text. The logo must be completely in vectors so it can be resized. The rollover must have an action for up, over and down. The advertisement must involve some bitmap graphics.

1 Produce three draft designs for each animation using a pencil and paper. Choose the best design for each animation to produce for the business.

2 Create a detailed storyboard for each animation.

3 Create a log sheet or bar sheet for each animation.

the animation's potential audience is ideal. However, simply having feedback from someone with a different pair of eyes can be helpful.

Document

Documentation may seem boring in comparison to animating but it is very important to maintain it as you produce your animation. If there are changes to be made or the animation needs to be updated in the future, you – the original animator – may not be the person who does the work. So it is very important that good documentation exists alongside the animation.

3.3 Test

To confirm the functionality of an animation, it must be tested in several ways.

Test functionality

The movie needs to be tested in great detail to see if it plays correctly. It should be viewed scene by scene and all the way through at a much slower frame rate, in order to find small faults. Then it should be viewed at normal speed, to see what the viewer would see, again scene by scene and all the way through.

If there are any elements of interactivity, they should also be tested to make sure they work in the correct way.

It is advisable for not only the original animator(s) to test the movie but also other members of the team and an external tester or focus group. A focus group could consist of members of the potential target market. For example, the creators of an animated Walt Disney film will invite a focus group of children and their parents to watch the new movie before its release and will even adapt the film according to their feedback if necessary.

Debug

A bug is an error in a piece of code that causes a problem when the animation is run. It may be a typo or incomplete pair of brackets but it can bring the whole animation to a stop. Debugging can be done in many ways, although a manual check may be the best option because the code is spread out and attached to different key frames, symbols and objects. A manual check involves logically checking each bit of code that has been written and making sure that the relevant animation runs correctly. If it doesn't, you must check for obvious errors first, such as spelling or punctuation mistakes and then make sure that the symbols, variables, etc, are correctly named. You need to identify exactly where the problem is occurring and work through the relevant code to correct the underlying error.

3.4 Review

It is vital to review an animation project once it is complete to ensure that it successfully fulfils the client brief and is functionally sound. In other words, it must do what it is supposed to do.

Compare with original design

Using the documentation, it should be possible to review the project to see if it matches the original client brief. Does the animation fulfill its purpose? Does the description of the project reflect what has been created?

In addition to this, there should be an analysis of the user requirements to see if they have been satisfied by the animation. If there are any requirements that have not been achieved, you must be able to give a suitable reason as to why not – for example, a requirement may have been technically impossible.

Suggest improvements

Once testing has been completed, amendments can be made based on the results of testing. If errors or problems with the functionality have been found, they should be rectified and retested.

Activity: Designing animation

Sweet As is a business based in County Durham that produces honey from its own bees. They have asked you to produce:

- a logo
- a rollover button
- an advertisement.

Using your animations from the Creating animation activity on page 269:

1 review the functionality of each animation

2 make any amendments necessary

3 evaluate each animation, assessing it against the original client brief in the Creating animation activity.

Once the animation has been fully tested and corrected, the animators should be ready to present the completed project to the client for their approval.

3.5 Document

Although at the moment you will be creating animations on your own, in the design industry it is common for animators to work in teams. Therefore, documentation is needed so that everyone in the team understands the process and the progress being made. In addition, if an animator is absent for a period of time, the documentation will allow others in the team to carry on with the work or bring in another animator. In a situation where there is no documentation, a team member's absence might disrupt creation of the product, resulting in the deadline not being met and the client not paying the fee.

Purpose and description

The documentation must clearly state the objective of the project and contain a detailed description of how this will be achieved. This should be based on the client brief.

The purpose should include a clear explanation of the core objective and other details such as where it might be displayed. For example, the purpose of an animation might be to provide an introduction to a DVD. More detail could be added as to the subject of the DVD, how many buttons are required, what language it needs to be in, etc.

The description should then add considerably more detail including:

- any ideas the client has had for the project – this will assist in ensuring that the client is satisfied with the resulting product
- design elements such as storyboards – these should be amended as the project progresses, so that at any time they are an up-to-date representation of the animation
- clear user requirements, which can be used to review and evaluate the project on its completion.

Format, target file size and other documentation

The format of the animation will need to be decided before beginning the implementation of the design.

The decision will include:

- the platform on which to create it (Apple®, Windows®, etc)
- the software to be used and the format of the files
- the choice of bitmaps, vectors or both, as well as the file types and compression methods
- the media players for which they will be designed.

The target file size will help determine the complexity of the animation and also the amount of compression needed in order to make it suitable. For example, if the animation is to be used on the web, the file size will be crucial to its success; whereas if it is to be included on a CD, the file size may not be quite so important.

Storage of the animation during production needs to be decided and known by all animators involved. For projects such as games development, the competition is fierce and robust security is needed to ensure that projects remain secret until the publishers are ready to release them. A breach in security can destroy months of careful and expensive advertising that has built anticipation among consumers. In addition, backing up files is essential. For larger projects, several backups need to be made, at least one of which should be held off-site in a fireproof, waterproof container.

Source of images

Animation projects sometimes use images from other sources. These might be stock images that the company already has or images from services such as Getty Images or Stock.Xchng which provide (mostly photographic) images to subscribers. The documentation should include a record of all images that are not original, so that the legality of using the images can be checked at any time.

In the creative industry, copyright is a prevalent issue and animators must be careful not to breach it. Otherwise, they may find themselves involved in legal disputes. In UK law, copyright exists on any piece of work once it has become tangible (in a fixed form) and is protected by the Copyright, Designs and Patents Act 1988. This means that using other people's work without their permission is a breach of copyright. It also means that your own work is protected by copyright law.

Assessment activity 31.3

Digital Myths create animated stories for primary school children, ages 5 to 11. Some are based on classic fairy tales or nursery rhymes, others are new – written especially for the purposes of the animation. The aim is to encourage reading, educate about creative writing and, most importantly, entertain.

All the stories are subtitled, approximately five to ten minutes in length and appropriate for the specific age group. They are usually published on CDs, which are purchased by schools, but the company has recently begun to set up a website to distribute their animations.

Digital Myths have been so impressed with you that the boss has asked you to join their main animation team. Your first assignment is to create a short demonstration piece to advertise the type of work the company does. This should be an animated story with subtitles but does not need to be a complete story, being just one to two minutes in length. The narrative can be a classic fairy tale or nursery rhyme, or a new original story.

1 Create a storyboard for the whole of the story. **P6**

2 Create the animation, using different animation techniques. **P7**

3 Evaluate your animation, describing the good and bad points and how you would improve it in the future. Focus on the tools and techniques used. **D2**

Grading tips

- This activity is quite involved so you will need to know when your deadlines are and make sure you manage your time carefully. You should divide your time between design, creation and evaluation and, if you can, split each of these phases into separate tasks. The better you plan your time before you start, the better chance you have of meeting your deadline.

- Do not be tempted to start creating your animation before you have designed it. It will actually be counter-productive, causing more problems and time delays than if you took the time to create the design first. **P6** **P7**

- Make sure you leave time for your evaluation. It is an important part of the process. **D2**

PLTS

Being a **creative thinker** is a strong element of this task, however **reflective learners** will also be able to use what they have learnt and **independent enquirers** can look at other animations for ideas. **Self-managers** will make sure all parts of the task are done well and before the deadline.

Functional skills

Evidence for using **ICT** could be created when designing, creating and evaluating your animation as you use ICT in complex and non-routine tasks.

Jonathan
Animator

I work at a games design studio in the north of England and I'm part of the animation team.

How did you get this job?

I have always been into computer games and have played a wide range of different types, enjoying the different graphic styles. At college I was lucky enough to study a couple of multimedia units as part of my ICT qualification and found I had a real passion for it. I went on to university and started on a general Multimedia degree but then transferred to a specific Games Design course when it became obvious that that was where my talents lay. My tutors on the course encouraged me to put together a digital portfolio on CD of the pieces I was making and when I was in my final year and looking for jobs, I sent my portfolio with my CV and a covering letter to different games studios. Luckily the studio I work at now liked my work, thought I had potential and took me on. I began in a probationary position on a temporary contract and after sixth months, when I had proved myself, they employed me permanently.

Describe your work

Our team has to work very closely because we don't want to end up duplicating any animation work. Equally we don't want to miss anything out. At the beginning of the project, we are part of the design process and we will say what we think is possible and what is not, and whether we think the timescales are reasonable. Then the tasks are divided up between us. The more experienced animators take the main tasks, such as working on characters, whereas those new to the team, like myself, usually animate smaller elements such as the environment. Also, some animators will be dedicated to impressive sections such as cut scenes or advertising trailers.

We have to maintain a good relationship with both the graphics team, who draw the images, and the programming team. Communication is very important!

Think about it!

1 Jonathan says that communication is important. In what ways do you think the animators and the different teams communicate with each other?

2 Other than communication, what other skills do you think might be important in this job?

3 Use the UCAS website www.ucas.com and find out approximately how many games design courses are available at UK universities. Select one and look in detail at what topics are studied on this course.

Just checking

1. How does the theory of persistence of vision relate to animation?
2. Name three pioneers of animation and their key inventions.
3. What is CGI and where is it used?
4. Name three adverts which have involved animation that you have seen within the last week.
5. What is tweening?
6. What is a frame and what is a key frame?
7. Name five tools you might find in the toolbox of an animation program.
8. What are the key differences between a bitmap and a vector?
9. What is storyboarding and why is it important?
10. Why are log sheets and bar sheets used?

edexcel

Assignment tips

- When you are designing and making your animations, you need to achieve a balance between creating something that looks interesting and retelling a well-told story. Think of computer games you may have played where the graphics were really good but the storyline was poor, or vice versa. A good animator considers both visuals and story.

- Always remember the audience when creating your animations. If you put text on the screen, make sure it is on long enough for the user to read it. Remember that you know what is happening but your audience will be seeing it for the first time. Do not rush your animation. Perhaps ask a friend to watch it and see if it runs at an appropriate speed.

- Be careful with your timescales and make sure your designs are achievable within the deadline you have been set.

42 Spreadsheet modelling

Spreadsheet modelling is essential for many businesses and organisations, as spreadsheets are used for many of their activities, such as credit control, sales forecasting and stock analysis.

Spreadsheet software can support organisations, helping them to keep track of numerical information and analyse it quickly and more easily than paper records. The inbuilt functionality helps users to understand the data without the need for specialist mathematical skills.

Utilities such as ordering, sorting and filtering will show the same data in different ways. Charts and graphs help to display information more visually. Complex calculations can be carried out using library functions or users can choose to create their own formulae.

Spreadsheets can be set up as reusable templates that produce immediate results when data is input, such as payroll or invoice templates. Spreadsheet software can be customised with buttons and macros. For example, features are available, that restrict user access to whole workbooks, spreadsheets or parts of spreadsheets.

As an IT practitioner, you need to be able both to use spreadsheet software competently and to support users as part of a technical or help desk role.

Learning outcomes

After completing this unit, you should:

1. understand how spreadsheets can be used to solve complex problems
2. be able to develop complex spreadsheet models
3. be able to automate and customise spreadsheet models
4. be able to test and document spreadsheet models.

Assessment and grading criteria

This table shows you what you must do in order to achieve a pass, merit or distinction grade, and where you can find activities in this book to help you.

To achieve a **pass** grade the evidence must show that you are able to:	To achieve a **merit** grade the evidence must show that, in addition to the pass criteria, you are able to:	To achieve a **distinction** grade the evidence must show that, in addition to the pass and merit criteria, you are able to:
P1 explain how spreadsheets can be used to solve complex problems **See Assessment activity 42.1, page 283**		**D1** discuss how organisations can use interpretation methods to analyse data **See Assessment activity 42.1, page 283**
P2 develop a complex spreadsheet model to meet particular needs **See Assessment activity 42.2, page 299**	**M1** refine a complex spreadsheet model by changing rules and values **See Assessment activity 42.2, page 299**	
P3 use formulae, features and functions to process information **See Assessment activity 42.2, page 299**		
P4 use appropriate tools to present data **See Assessment activity 42.2, page 299**	**M2** analyse and interpret data from a spreadsheet model **See Assessment activity 42.2, page 299**	
P5 customise the spreadsheet model to meet a given requirement **See Assessment activity 42.3, page 306**		
P6 use automated features in the spreadsheet model to meet a given requirement **See Assessment activity 42.3, page 306**	**M3** compare different automation methods **See Assessment activity 42.3, page 306**	
P7 test a spreadsheet model to ensure that it is fit for purpose **See Assessment activity 42.4, page 310**		**D2** evaluate a spreadsheet model incorporating feedback from others and make recommendations for improvements **See Assessment activity 42.4 page 310**
P8 export the contents of the spreadsheet model to an alternative format **See Assessment activity 42.4, page 310**		
P9 produce user documentation for a spreadsheet model **See Assessment activity 42.4, page 310**	**M4** produce technical documentation for a spreadsheet model **See Assessment activity 42.4, page 310**	

How you will be assessed

This unit will be assessed by a number of internal assignments that will be designed and marked by the staff at your centre. It may be subject to sampling by your centre's External Verifier as part of Edexcel's ongoing quality assurance procedures. The assignments will be designed to allow you to show your understanding of the unit outcomes. These relate to what you should be able to do after completing this unit.

Your tutor will tell you precisely what form your assessment will take, but it could be in the form of:

*   output from practical exercises such as printouts of worksheets, charts and graphs

*   test plans providing evidence of the testing you have carried out to check accuracy of calculations

*   observation and witness statements, eg of your converting files from one format to another

*   user documentation and technical documentation.

Kevin, BTEC National IT learner

I know how to use spreadsheets for simple tasks – like recording a measurement over a period of 30 days – and feel confident about getting the software to add up a column of numbers or produce a graph from the data.

I'm also happy with structuring a spreadsheet, including formatting certain cells, rows or columns to make the data more accessible, but I want to progress further.

In the past, the scenarios have been scaled down – Mickey Mouse situations – and not overly realistic. I'm looking forward to solving some real problems using real data and developing real spreadsheet models.

Also, up until now, I've never felt motivated to explore some of the complex facilities that spreadsheet software offers the user – like pivot tables – and this challenge excites me. I have dabbled with what-if scenarios but not really got the hang of them. I'm hoping I'll be able to crack this, this time around.

In particular, I'm looking forward to automating a spreadsheet – lots of buttons for the user to press – and getting to grips with macros and Visual Basic so I can show how good I am at using this type of software.

Over to you

*   **How confident are you in using spreadsheet software?**
*   **Have you ever tackled some of the more complicated aspects – like pivot tables or automating a spreadsheet?**
*   **What is it that you are most looking forward to in this unit?**

1 Understand how spreadsheets can be used to solve complex problems

1.1 Uses of spreadsheets

Any problem involving a lot of calculations and analysis of numerical data is ideally suited to being modelled using spreadsheet software. So, it is commonplace for the accounting and finance departments of an organisation to use a series of worksheets within a spreadsheet file to record the transactions made by that organisation. In the past, you needed special training to understand the accounts. Nowadays, users can benefit from the inbuilt functionality of spreadsheet software – it helps them to understand the data without needing specialist mathematical skills. Data can also be presented in graphical form at the press of a button.

For most organisations, worksheets have replaced manual pages in ledgers, where income and expenditure were organised into rows and columns. The basic design of a worksheet echoes the two-dimensional table of rows and columns.

- The rows of a worksheet are numbered 1, 2, 3, ...
- The columns of a worksheet are lettered A, B, C, ...

Each cell has a cell reference based on its row number and column letter: A7, B2, etc. In its simplest form, each cell can then contain one of four types of data:

- text – including titles, headings and labels, as well as names, addresses and telephone numbers

- numeric data – any type of number – can be formatted as currency, percentage or date, for example

- **formulae** – involving single operators, relative cell references and simple **functions**

- left blank – useful for creating white space on a worksheet, which makes the rest of the data easier to read and understand.

Key terms

Formula – (plural 'formulae') an expression written in terms of cell references and operators, which specifies a calculation that is to be done. The result of the calculation appears in the cell in which the formula is stored.

Function – a command that results in a value being returned.

Range – defines a rectangular shape within a worksheet, for example the range A3:B7 includes columns A and B, and rows 3 to 7.

Having thought through how you want to design your spreadsheet model, so that you know what data you plan to put in and where, you can physically create the spreadsheet model using spreadsheet software. For each worksheet, this involves entering a title, column headings and row labels. You then enter text, numeric data and formulae, and format all these cells appropriately.

If the spreadsheet model does not quite fit the purpose intended, you may need to refine it.

- You can change the 'shape' – or design – of the spreadsheet by inserting or deleting rows and columns, or adding additional worksheets.
- You can change the values held within particular cells or the rules – the formulae that act on the data in those cells.

Did you know?

To change the contents of a cell, the cell has to be selected first to make it the active cell (as specified in the Name Box) before you can overwrite its contents. If you only want to make a minor change, you can do so in the Formula Bar.

Manipulating complex data

While spreadsheet software is perfect for simple calculations, taking the tedium of some tasks away, it is also an excellent tool for manipulating complex data.

- Additional worksheets may be created and links formed between them (see page 284).

Complex formulae (see page 285) can be set up to perform more sophisticated calculations that might be needed for a statistical analysis.

Presentation to requirements

The spreadsheet data will be visible on-screen, but may also be needed in hard copy form. With a worksheet, controlling the pagination is not as straightforward as in some other applications. If there are too many columns to fit across a single page, even in landscape orientation, your printout will present only a **range** of cells on each page, and it might prove difficult to see how it all fits together (see Figure 42.1).

Activity: Setting a print area

1. Use the Help feature to discover how to set the print area on a particular worksheet. Select a range of cells that you want to print and set the print area for these cells.

2. Use View / Page Break Review to see what the worksheet will look like, printed out with your current settings for page size, orientation and margins.

3. Experiment with changing column widths, orientation and margins to fit more (or less) onto any page.

Supporting decision making

Spreadsheet software offers functions that can be used to support decision making, providing timely and accurate information in a variety of situations.

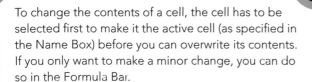

You can choose to turn on/off the page break review option.

The dotted lines show where the pages will start and end.

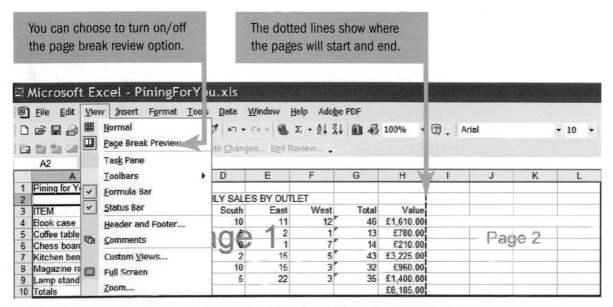

Figure 42.1: How a large spreadsheet is split into separate pages for printing

- **Analysis of data**: This is more easily achieved when data is summarised in some way or is presented graphically. This is especially true for large amounts of data when it is necessary to rely on **representative values** (like averages) and there is too much data to spot a trend among thousands of individual data results.
- **Goal seeking**: If you know the result that you want from a formula, but are not sure what input value the formula needs to get that result, using the Goal Seek feature does the job for you.
- **Scenarios**: If you create and save different groups of values as scenarios on a worksheet, you will then be able to switch between these scenarios to view the different results.
- **Regression**: This is a form of statistical analysis used for forecasting. It is time consuming to perform manually but easier if you use a spreadsheet to do all the calculations for you.
- **Data mining tools**: These help the user to derive patterns and trends that exist in complex data. For example, all credit card transactions are stored by the various credit card agencies and the data is analysed to spot possible fraudulent activity.

1.2 Complex problems

Essentially, spreadsheets are models that simulate a real-life situation. Spreadsheet models can be used to solve a number of problems, such as cash flow forecasting, budget control, sales forecasting, payroll projections, statistical analysis and trend analysis.

For example, in one spreadsheet model, the rows could be used to list the variables that relate to a situation, and the columns could reflect the passing of time (see Figure 42.2). The cells will be allocated to contain relevant data and to show the results of any calculations. Some values are fixed, whereas others will change. Some values will depend on other values within the spreadsheet.

The formulae that are used reflect current thinking on the 'rules' that apply in real life. For some formulae, there is no debate. For example, the cost of a product including VAT can be calculated with a degree of certainty. However, the effect on future sales of a price increase might be based on past experience but is, at best, an educated guess.

Having set up a model, it can then be used to simulate a situation and to forecast what might happen, given certain circumstances.

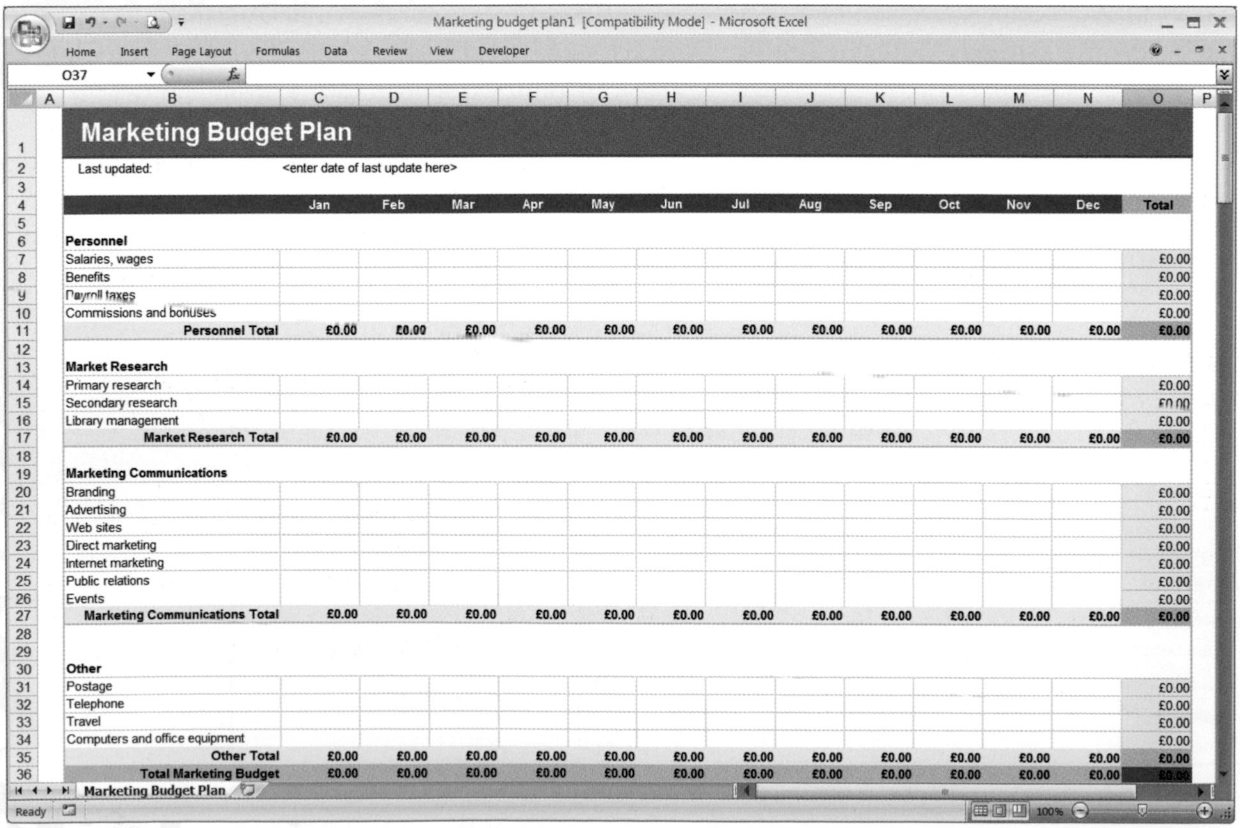

	Jan	Feb	Mar	Apr	May	Jun	Jul	Aug	Sep	Oct	Nov	Dec	Total
Personnel													
Salaries, wages													£0.00
Benefits													£0.00
Payroll taxes													£0.00
Commissions and bonuses													£0.00
Personnel Total	£0.00	£0.00	£0.00	£0.00	£0.00	£0.00	£0.00	£0.00	£0.00	£0.00	£0.00	£0.00	£0.00
Market Research													
Primary research													£0.00
Secondary research													£0.00
Library management													£0.00
Market Research Total	£0.00	£0.00	£0.00	£0.00	£0.00	£0.00	£0.00	£0.00	£0.00	£0.00	£0.00	£0.00	£0.00
Marketing Communications													
Branding													£0.00
Advertising													£0.00
Web sites													£0.00
Direct marketing													£0.00
Internet marketing													£0.00
Public relations													£0.00
Events													£0.00
Marketing Communications Total	£0.00	£0.00	£0.00	£0.00	£0.00	£0.00	£0.00	£0.00	£0.00	£0.00	£0.00	£0.00	£0.00
Other													
Postage													£0.00
Telephone													£0.00
Travel													£0.00
Computers and office equipment													£0.00
Other Total	£0.00	£0.00	£0.00	£0.00	£0.00	£0.00	£0.00	£0.00	£0.00	£0.00	£0.00	£0.00	£0.00
Total Marketing Budget	£0.00	£0.00	£0.00	£0.00	£0.00	£0.00	£0.00	£0.00	£0.00	£0.00	£0.00	£0.00	£0.00

Figure 42.2: Marketing budget plan

Cash flow forecasting

Forecasting is inherently difficult. How can you possibly tell what is going to happen in the future? The answer is: you can't. But you can make an educated guess if you have sufficient information about how things have worked out in the past, and you have the tools to process this data. You can take measurements today and, if you have a formula that you think will work, you can calculate the values for tomorrow, the day after and so on. Then, as time passes, you can check the accuracy of your forecasts and amend your model – the formulae that you used – until they more accurately forecast the future.

A spreadsheet is particularly useful for forecasting because it will do all the calculations for you. Each new row (or column) can be used to represent the next day (or whatever time interval you choose for your model).

For cash flow forecasting, data that relates to past events will show what today's situation is: today's bank balance. This can be reconciled with bank statements and you can be sure it is accurate at a given date. Having sent out invoices, it would be reasonable to record these amounts as coming in against some future date. If known outgoings are also recorded – such as cheques already written but not yet showing on a bank statement, or regular payments that will happen at known times such as payroll payments or amounts due to the Inland Revenue or the VAT man – the net effect on today's balance can be projected forward. The cash flow forecast will then show on what date, for example, there won't be enough to meet an expense unless monies are received in good time from customers.

Accounts departments need cash flow forecasting data so that they can chase payments to avoid problems, and they may use this data to forestall outgoing payments if they know there is not enough money to honour a payment.

Budget control

Spending can't just happen; there ought to be plans made so that the expected revenue for a company can be used to fund all outgoings and still leave an amount – profit – with which to reward shareholders. Agreeing a budget together with targets for the sales force will provide a framework – a business plan – which can be checked before costs are incurred which might lead to bankruptcy.

If the budget is put into a spreadsheet, actual income and expenditure can be entered too, with any discrepancies being identified as soon as they happen. This knowledge of what is actually happening – against budget – provides budget control.

When a new year starts, the data from last year can also be used to inform the decision makers as to what can be achieved and where they perhaps ought to make changes.

What-if scenarios

A simple what-if might involve only changing one variable and seeing what happens to one other value in the spreadsheet. However, the more complex a scenario is the more realistic the model and the more useful the answer. Goal-seeking tools and scenario tools (page 280) make the more complex **what-if questions** easier to answer.

The underlying power of spreadsheet software lies in the facility to recalculate the contents of cells that hold formulae and to display the revised contents almost instantly. This means that you can answer what-if questions using a spreadsheet model.

Key terms

Representative values – single values that represent many items of data. They include mean, mode and median, as well as other statistical values.

Goal seeking – working from a known numerical goal back to whatever data entries are needed to achieve that goal.

Scenario – a set of values that you can substitute automatically on your worksheet.

Regression – type of analysis that estimates the relationship between variables so that a given variable can be predicted from one or more other variables.

Data mining tools – tools that involve the automatic collection of large amounts of data and then analysing the data for trends and patterns.

What-if questions – situations where the result depends on a number of input variables and you want to know the effect on the result if you were to change one or more of the input variables.

How to... Answer a what-if question

1. Set up the data in a spreadsheet to create a model of some real-life situation.

2. Identify the result cells, ie the cells that hold the data you are trying to maximise or minimise or that indicate you have met some criteria.

3. Identify the input data, ie the cells that hold data you might change.

4. Change the input data in some way and note any changes in the displayed output of the result cells.

5. If the new value made the situation better, can you make it better still? If it made it worse, undo the change and consider changing the data in the other direction.

6. Repeat steps 3-5 until you are as close to a solution as you want to be.

Sales forecasting

Sales forecasting goes hand in glove with budget control and cash flow forecasting and is an essential tool for all commercial organisations.

Sales forces need to be motivated and the management need to know what they can afford to give by way of salary and commission to reflect the revenue a salesperson brings to the organisation.

Sales projections also impact on production. If the sales force plans to sell one million new mobile phones, can production turn them out fast enough to meet this demand?

Payroll projections

The cost of a workforce is often the largest bill an organisation has to face. This cost will drop if employees resign, and rise if new staff are recruited. As employees progress they expect salary increases, either just by moving up a scale or through some promotion. As well as the salary paid to the employee, there are amounts to be paid to the Inland Revenue for National Insurance contributions and amounts to be set aside for pension provision.

Since these costs play a major role in the overall budget, projecting what the payroll bill will be in three months or six months or next year is important. Spreadsheets can be used to good effect for this forecasting task.

Statistical analysis

To make sense of a lot of numeric data, statistical analysis can provide insights into trends and arrive at representative values of the data.

To design spreadsheet models for statistical analysis requires considerable knowledge of statistics, and the formulae can be complex. However, using them, once the model has been set up, should be easy if the user interface has been well designed.

Trend analysis

If measuring some variable on a daily basis, such as your weight, there are bound to be variations, and it may be difficult to spot whether the overall trend is up or down. The same goes for numerical data such as the value of stocks and shares, and the various indices that the government uses to measure the economy.

What does help is to step back to look for a trend in the data. Spreadsheet software, as will be seen in Section 1.3 (page 283) is perfect for trend analysis.

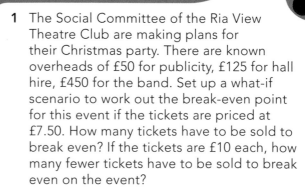

Activity: What if?

1. The Social Committee of the Ria View Theatre Club are making plans for their Christmas party. There are known overheads of £50 for publicity, £125 for hall hire, £450 for the band. Set up a what-if scenario to work out the break-even point for this event if the tickets are priced at £7.50. How many tickets have to be sold to break even? If the tickets are £10 each, how many fewer tickets have to be sold to break even on the event?

2. The Committee want to know what is the lowest break-even price they should charge If they expect to sell 75 tickets. Use goal-seeking tools to find the answer to their question. And find out what profit they'd make if 100 tickets were sold.

3. The Committee are also thinking ahead to next year's event and may want to change the venue (resulting in the price being something between £100 and £200) and the band (costing between £250 and £500). If they fix the ticket price at £10, what effect does this have on potential profits?

1.3 Interpretation

Once all the data is in your spreadsheet, how can you interpret it? Two interpretation methods are discussed here – comparison of totals and trend analysis – but what other ways might you use?

Comparisons of totals

To compare totals, you must first calculate them.

- The SUM function will add the values in consecutive cells of a row or column.
- The SUMIF function could be used to include in the total only those values that meet some criteria.

You can then see which is the highest total and which is the lowest total.

- The MAX function returns the maximum value in a range of cells.
- The MIN function returns the minimum function.

You could work out the difference between the highest and lowest values, which might give a measure of range.

- The formula =MAX(A1:A10)-MIN(A1:A10) will return the range (difference between the lowest and highest values).

Activity: LARGE and SMALL

1 Find out what the LARGE and SMALL functions do.

2 Investigate some other functions. Choose ones that you have never used before.

Trend analysis

Some variables change over time and it helps to see what the trend is. It's not important whether the values go up and down on a day-to-day basis. What's the trend (say) over a week, over a month or over the years?

The easiest way of illustrating a trend is to turn the data into a chart or graph (see page 303) and the most appropriate is a line graph, with the variable on the vertical axis and time on the horizontal axis.

Activity: Reading a trend graph

Using a set of data supplied by your tutor, generate a trend graph and make statements about what you read from the graph.

Assessment activity 42.1

The Ria View Theatre Club organises 30-40 theatre trips per year for their 200+ members.

Subscriptions are paid annually and this income is expected to cover the cost of all expenses such as production of the programme which is mailed out every 2-3 months and postage.

For each event, the costs to the club are the ticket price to be paid to the theatre plus the coach hire. The theatre charges a set amount times the number of seats booked less maybe some discount if more than 20 seats are booked. Coaches are available with 20, 29 or 49 seats and are priced according to the size of the coach and the destination. Before each programme of forthcoming events can be published, the club has to set a price for the trip, low enough so as to encourage as many members as possible to book for an event and yet not so low as to make a huge loss. There is no need to make a profit on each event but the club cannot afford to make a loss over any three-month period.

The Treasurer of the Ria View Theatre Club has asked you:

1 to provide information as to how a spreadsheet could be used to solve complex problems such as setting the trip price **P1**

2 how tools to analyse data might be employed to provide summary information to members at the Annual General Meeting of members of the Ria View Theatre Club. **D1**

Grading tips

- Assume that the Treasurer is competent in using spreadsheets for normal calculations and purposes but has never set up a spreadsheet with more than one worksheet and has no experience of using more complex functions. **P1**

- Include examples of how the Treasurer might model the finances of the Ria View Theatre Club, how the data might be interpreted and how the summary information might be presented to members. **D1**

2 Be able to develop complex spreadsheet models

A complex problem tends to need a complex model to hold all the necessary data and provide the analysis that the problem requires before a solution can be found.

2.1 Complexity

Complexity in a spreadsheet model can arise from a combination of factors: multiple pages, complex formulae, large data sets and cell linkage between worksheets.

Making life simple for the user also requires a more complex spreadsheet model design: data entry forms, data validation and error trapping, using lookup tables and nested IF functions, designing templates and setting up cell protection.

Multiple worksheets (with links)

Rather than having a single worksheet, you may design a spreadsheet model to have several separate worksheets and there are a number of benefits of linked worksheets.

- You can streamline the development of large, complex models by breaking them down into a series of interdependent workbooks. You can then work on the model without opening all of the related sheets. Smaller workbooks are easier to change, they don't require as much memory and they are faster to open, save and calculate.

- You can link workbooks from several users or departments and then integrate relevant data into a summary workbook. When any of the data in the source workbooks is changed, the summary workbook changes automatically.

- You can enter all the data into one or more source workbooks and then create different views of this data by setting up a report workbook that contains links to only the relevant data. For security purposes, you may restrict access to the source data but provide open access to the reports for those who need to see this information.

So, depending on the purpose of your model, you may have one worksheet per month, one per employee or one per event. The first worksheet may summarise the data held in subsequent worksheets and that's where the answer to the problem may be displayed.

Case study: Knits4U (1)

Knits4U use different worksheets, within the same spreadsheet file, to hold data on their stock and their customers. Figure 42.3 shows the worksheet tabs with appropriate names.

List the worksheets the Ria View Theatre Club might need in their spreadsheet model. What names might they choose for their worksheet tabs?

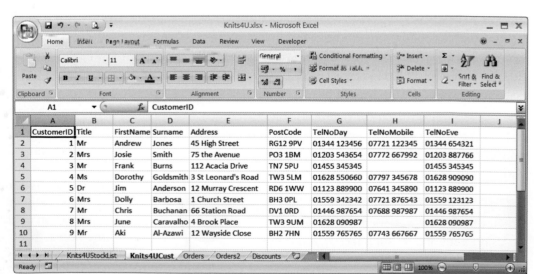

Figure 42.3: Named worksheet tabs

Each worksheet appears as a separate tab on the screen and the tabs can be labelled so you know what data is to be found where.

Labelling the worksheets in this way – and choosing sensible names – becomes more important when you need to use data from one worksheet in a formula on another worksheet. This is called cell linkage (see below).

Complex formulae

Formulae (see page 278) are the 'equations' that perform calculations on values in your worksheet.

- A formula can be as simple as =A5*17.5 or =SUM(A1:A20) and involve only one operation (*) or function (SUM).

- A formula can be as complex as =(-B7-SQRT(B7*B7-4*A7*C7))/(2*A7) which provides one of the roots of a quadratic equation with relevant values in A7, B7 and C7.

For the purposes of this unit, just two or more steps in a formula make it complex.

Case study: Knits4U (2)

Knits4U use complex formulae within their spreadsheet file. Figure 42.4 shows one example which calculates the price excluding VAT.

Give two examples of complex formulae that might be found in Ria View Theatre Club's spreadsheet model.

Large data sets

Processing a large data set might involve using a number of large and cumbersome worksheets. The reader will need help in interpreting this data.

- Using named ranges (page 295) within worksheets is one way of making formulae that rely on large amounts of data easier to understand.

- Summarising the data (page 300) and presenting the summary information on a single overview worksheet will help the reader to see the data more clearly.

- A summary could be in the form of a single representative value or graphical representation of the data (page 303).

Cell linkage

When data for a single spreadsheet model is held in a number of worksheets, it's inevitable that a formula in one worksheet will require data from a cell, or range of cells, in another worksheet.

Fortunately, there is a facility to link cells between worksheets which allows the user to create such complex formulae. Within the formula, a name preceded by an exclamation mark (!) indicates that the row and column numbers are on that (named) worksheet rather than within the worksheet where the formula is to be found.

Changes on one worksheet can then have an effect on the data on another worksheet, if the relevant cells are linked.

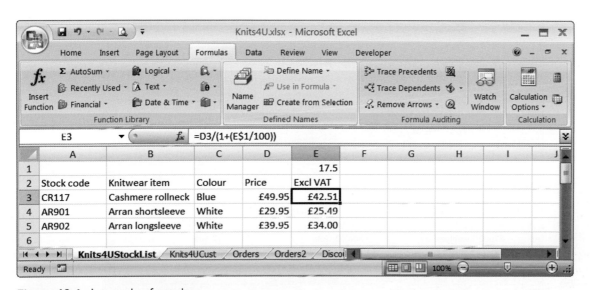

Figure 42.4: A complex formula

Did you know?

If you don't name your worksheet tabs, the formula will refer to the sheet by number: Sheet1 or Sheet2 say. It's far more user friendly to name the worksheets (see page 284).

Did you know?

The formulae with links to other workbooks are displayed in two ways, depending on whether the source workbook (the workbook that supplies data to a formula) is open or closed.

- When the source is open, the link will appear as, eg

  `=SUM([Turnover.xls]Annual!C12:C23)`

- When the source is not open, the link includes the entire path, eg

  `=SUM('C:\Accounts\[Turnover.xls] Annual'!C12:C23)`

Excel® provides options for controlling the updating of the links. All linked objects are updated automatically every time you open a file and at any time that the original data file changes while your file is open. When you open a workbook, a start-up prompt automatically asks if you want to update the links – it makes sense to do so at this time. You can also manually update the links if you wish.

Case study: Knits4U (3)

Knits4U use formulae which link cells between worksheets in their spreadsheet file. Figure 42.5 shows one example.

Look at your list of worksheets the Ria View Theatre Club might need in their spreadsheet model. How might these worksheets be linked?

Data entry forms

Spreadsheets can be used to record historical data but they become far more useful if they can be programmed to accept current data and to show the effect of inputting this new data.

Data entry forms may be designed as part of a user-friendly interface, providing a safe way for users to input such data to the model without risk to the design. They can include **form controls** such as **list boxes** and **drop-down menus** which force users to enter valid data.

In Excel®, the controls you need to create your own form are available on the Developer tab (see Figure 42.6).

The first forms that you might design are those which will serve as a **menu system** for the user.

A complex spreadsheet model can be set up to allow a number of tasks to be performed such as 'add new stock item', 'delete stock item', 'record stock order', 'record delivery of stock', 'record sale of stock' and so on. When a user opens the spreadsheet application, being presented with the various choices – in the form of a menu – serves to guide the user to the appropriate data within the spreadsheet. From

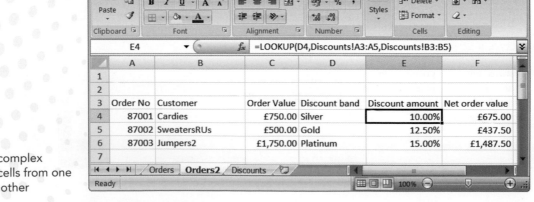

Figure 42.5: A complex formula linking cells from one worksheet to another

one STOCK menu (offering SALES, PURCHASES, REPORTS and EXIT), a user may then be presented with a second menu within the menu system with more choices to make, such as which REPORT is wanted today.

Controls can also respond to events, such as mouse clicks, by running **VBA** code (see page 306).

Key terms

Form controls – the original controls (label, group box, button, check box, option button, list box, combo box, scroll bar, spin button) that were provided with early versions of Excel ®.For more recently introduced controls, see ActiveX® Controls on page 306.

List box – displays one or more items of text from which a user can choose. The user might highlight the item or click on a radio button to indicate a choice.

Drop-down menu – for a particular data entry field, a list of valid entries that is compiled from cells elsewhere in the workbook, used to make data entry easier, or to limit entries to certain items that you define.

Menu system – a user interface device that presents the user with a window of buttons, each one leading – via a mouse click – to another lower level menu or the data required.

VBA – stands for Visual Basic for Applications. It is a macro-language version of Microsoft® Visual Basic used to program Microsoft® Windows®-based applications.

Did you know?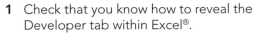

A combo box is like a list box except the user has to click on a down arrow to reveal the list of options. It's therefore more compact on the screen.

Activity: The Developer tab

1 Check that you know how to reveal the Developer tab within Excel®.

2 Explore the form controls (label, group box, button, check box, option button, list box, combo box, scroll bar, spin button) and create one or more sample forms to illustrate each example of form control.

3 Create a menu system for Ria View Theatre Club with options such as create a new venue, add a new event at a venue, book a coach for an event, take a booking for an event.

Data validation

It is important that the data that goes into a worksheet is accurate. Otherwise, the information gleaned from that worksheet is compromised.

Data validation begins when you first design your spreadsheet model and decide what data goes where, in which cell and on which worksheet. Excel® provides a wide range of validation options that can be applied to a cell or range of cells. You may:

- set upper and lower limits for numeric data entries (eg a month number must be between 1 and 12)

- compare the entry against items in a list (eg to make sure there is a stock item with that particular code)

- specify a time range and/or a date range (eg to make sure that the age of a person is within a sensible range)

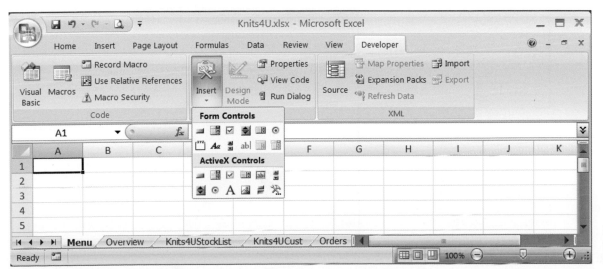

Figure 42.6: Forms toolbar from the Developer tab

- limit the number of characters accepted in a text string to prevent strings that are too long ruining a layout elsewhere on your spreadsheet
- calculate what is allowed, according to the contents of another cell – for example, if the cell contains an amount of credit available, then a loan for anything higher than that should be rejected
- use a formula to calculate what is allowed – in the Formula box (see Figure 42.7), the formula will have a `TRUE` (valid) or `FALSE` (invalid) value according to the data that is entered.

For some data, it may be necessary to insist that an entry is made before the entire form is accepted. For example, if an entry is zero, you may insist that the user enters the number 0, rather than just leave the entry blank.

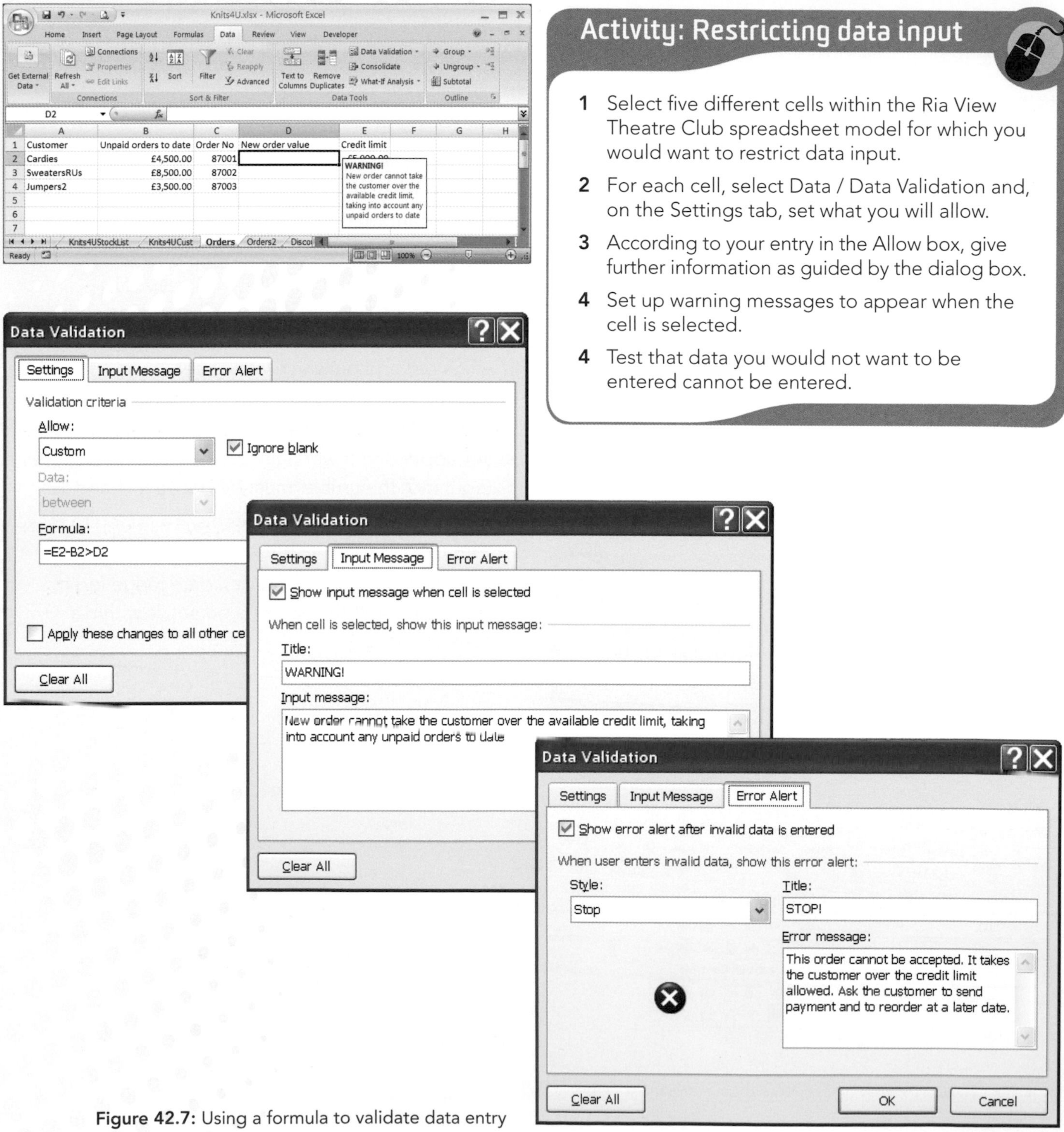

Figure 42.7: Using a formula to validate data entry

Activity: Restricting data input

1. Select five different cells within the Ria View Theatre Club spreadsheet model for which you would want to restrict data input.
2. For each cell, select Data / Data Validation and, on the Settings tab, set what you will allow.
3. According to your entry in the Allow box, give further information as guided by the dialog box.
4. Set up warning messages to appear when the cell is selected.
4. Test that data you would not want to be entered cannot be entered.

Error trapping

If you are using data entry forms, the design of the form – the order of fields to be completed – will guide the user through the correct order of entry but you may also need to provide prompts to remind the user what is expected. If a mistake is made – data which is considered to be invalid is input – it needs to be trapped and an error message displayed, explaining what is wrong and giving guidance so that the user might retry and enter the correct data.

Activity: Data validation and error

1 Select five different fields within the Ria View Theatre Club spreadsheet model that would give rise to a range of types of validation. Define the data validation that you would impose on data entry.

2 For each of the five fields, decide what warning and error message you would display if invalid data had been entered.

Lookup tables

A table can be used to store a range of values that apply according to some specified criteria. Rather than embed this data within formulae, the criteria and their matching values can be stored in a lookup table and then referred to using LOOKUP functions.

Case study: Knits4U (4)

Knits4U have differing discount rates according to the volume of business a customer places with them: Silver, Gold or Platinum. At a given time, these translate into percentages, eg 10%, 12.5% and 15% (see Figure 42.8).

Identify an application for lookup tables within the Ria View Theatre Club spreadsheet model. [Hint: consider their transport options.]

If, at a later date, the values need to be changed, they only need changing in the lookup table, not everywhere they are mentioned within a table. So, Knits4U can increase or decrease individual percentage discounts applicable to particular bands of customers.

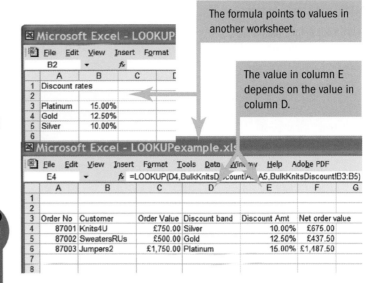

The formula points to values in another worksheet.

The value in column E depends on the value in column D.

Figure 42.8: Lookup table

Nested IF functions

An IF function sets a criterion (a condition being TRUE or FALSE) and, depending on the outcome (TRUE or FALSE), one of two values are returned. More complex problems can require nested IF functions, one within another, so that there are a greater number of values, any one of which might be returned.

The syntax for nesting the IF function is:

IF(condition1, value_if_true1, IF(condition2, value_if_true2, value_if_false2))

This would be equivalent to the following IF THEN ELSE statement:

IF condition1 THEN value_if_true1

ELSEIF condition2 THEN value_if_true2

ELSE value_if_false2

END IF

In this example there are three possible values: value_if_true1, value_if_true2 and value_if_false2. Note that the second and third options only apply if condition1 is FALSE.

Templates

Templates can be set up in many applications, and spreadsheet software is no exception. The benefits are the same: a model that you know works that you can apply to a new situation and time saved in laying out worksheets and setting up formulae.

Cell protection

Cells can be protected, either by hiding them from view or by locking them (see page 304) so that the user cannot gain access to them.

Activity: Spreadsheet complexity

1 Identify which of the complex features you might need to develop for the Ria View Theatre Club spreadsheet model. Make notes on where they might best be utilised.

2 Check that you are familiar with the processes involved, eg hiding cells or locking them, setting up a template or writing nested IF statements.

3 Prepare sample worksheets to demonstrate how these complex features work.

2.2 Formulae

The main benefit of a spreadsheet is that the software can do the calculations for you. Formulae are the 'equations' that perform calculations on values in your worksheet.

A formula starts with an equals sign (=) and is followed by the expression that describes the calculation you want to perform. Within the expression, you can use:

- numerical values, including decimal numbers with a decimal point and negative values indicated by a minus sign

- operators, + for addition, – for subtraction, * for multiplication and / for division, and logical operators (see page 291) such as AND, OR and NOT

- brackets, to indicate the order in which you want the calculation to be done – otherwise the evaluation is performed in accordance with the **BODMAS** principle

- functions such as SUM and logical functions such as SUMIF (page 292)

- cell references, relative and absolute as described next, to indicate what data, located in other cells, is to be used in the calculation for this cell.

Relative references and absolute references

When setting up a formula that includes a reference to another cell, you have two options: **relative** or **absolute cell referencing**. By default, new formulae use relative references.

Key terms

BODMAS – order of execution of evaluation: brackets, order (that means powers!), division and multiplication (working left to right) and addition and subtraction (working left to right).

Relative cell referencing – allows you to copy a formula across rows (or down columns) with any cell reference in the formula being changed automatically, relative to its original position.

Absolute cell referencing – allows you to copy or move a formula without the cell reference changing. By inserting a dollar symbol ($) before the letter and/or number of a cell reference you can make all or part of a cell reference absolute.

Case study: Knits4U (5)

Knits4U sells high-quality knitwear. Tourists may buy the jumpers without paying the VAT, provided the purchase is for export.

A stock list shows the price without VAT and, in a separate column, the price including VAT. The VAT rate is currently 17.5% but may change, and so absolute addressing (see Figure 42.9) is used for the VAT rate, rather than embedding the value in the formulae.

1 Experiment with the inclusion of the dollar symbol to check how necessary each one is, according to whether you replicate across rows or across columns.

2 Identify situations where you might need to use absolute addressing in the Ria View Theatre Club spreadsheet model.

If you don't use named ranges (page 295), the formula in cell E3 has to include absolute.

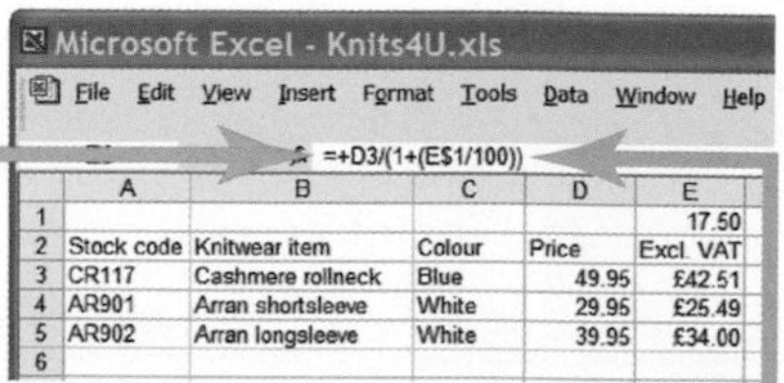

The dollar symbol before the row number means that the row number for E1 will remain the same when E2 is copied to E3 and E4, and so on. The reference to D3 will change relative to the row. So the formula in E4 is =+D4/(1+(E$1/100)).

Figure 42.9: Absolute addressing

Logical functions

A **function** is not the same as a formula; but it forms an important part of the formula.

Let's start with operators first which form the 'glue' in an expression, another building block of a formula.

- The usual **mathematical operators** (+, −, *, /) and many others, such as the percent sign (%) and the caret (^) for exponentiation, can be used within any expression for a formula to perform an arithmetical calculation.

- For decision-making purposes, there are also three **logical operators** AND, OR, NOT (see Table 42.1) and, instead of writing the operator between two expressions (such as A4+B7 or H9*17.5), the **arguments** appear within rounded brackets after the logical operator – and there can also be more than two of them. Notice also that, within the definitions for a function, triangular brackets (<>) are used to indicate the arguments of the function.

Key terms

Function – a command that results in a value being returned, such as SUM.

Mathematical operators – return the result of the calculation, eg 3+4 returns 7, 3*4 returns 12.

Logical operators – return a value of True or False, depending on the logical values in the argument.

Argument – a value or expression used within a function. It specifies what data is to be acted upon, the criteria that are to be applied or the resulting value that is required.

Logical functions – functions that return a value of True or False, depending on the conditions that you set up.

Logical operator	What it does	Syntax	Notes
AND	Returns TRUE if all arguments are TRUE. Returns FALSE if one or more argument is FALSE.	`AND(<logical1>,<logical2>,...)`	
OR	Returns TRUE if any argument is TRUE. Returns FALSE if all arguments are FALSE.	`OR(<logical1>,<logical2>,...)`	You can use an OR array formula to see if a value occurs in an array. (To enter an array formula, press CTRL+SHIFT+ENTER.)
NOT	Reverses the value of the argument.	`NOT(<logical>)`	If logical is FALSE, NOT returns TRUE; if logical is TRUE, NOT returns FALSE. NOT can be used when you want to make sure a value is not equal to one particular value.

Table 42.1: Logical operators

For the logical operators, the arguments should evaluate to logical values such as TRUE or FALSE, or the arguments could be arrays or references that contain logical values. If the array or reference argument contains text or empty cells, those values are ignored. If the specified range contains no logical values, the operator returns the error value: #VALUE!

Now, having covered operators in full – back to functions. We have straightforward functions like COUNT, SUM and AVERAGE (Table 42.2) and there are several options as to what you might use for the arguments:

- cell references (such as A5 and Overview!B7 or a named range)
- numbers
- strings
- expressions.

For example: COUNT(40,60,70) or SUM(A1:A7)

However, as well as the straightforward functions, you can incorporate logical functions (see Table 42.3) into expressions for your formula.

Function	Description
COUNT(<value1>, <value2>, ...)	Counts the number of cells that contain the value(s) listed
SUM(<cellref1>:<cellref2>)	Adds up the cells within the stated range
AVERAGE(<cellref1>,<cellref2>, ...)	Adds up the contents of the cells and divides by the number of cells listed

Table 42.2: Functions

Logical function	What it does	Syntax
IF	Checks the condition of the logical test and returns one of the two values accordingly.	IF (<logical_test>,<value_if_true>,<value_ if_ false>)
SUMIF	Tests the cells in cellrange1 against the criteria, and sums the corresponding cells within cellrange2.	SUMIF(<cellrange1>, "<criteria>",<cellrange2>)
IS	Checks the type of value and returns TRUE or FALSE, depending on the outcome. For example, the ISBLANK function returns the logical value TRUE if value is a reference to an empty cell; otherwise it returns FALSE.	ISBLANK(<value>) ISERR(<value>) ISERROR(<value>) ISLOGICAL(<value>) ISNA(<value>) ISNONTEXT(<value>) ISNUMBER(<value>) ISREF(<value>) ISTEXT(<value>)

Table 42.3: Logical functions

Correct operators

The different sets of operators can only be used with the appropriate functions and cell references. What can be used is defined by the syntax of expressions and formulae and if you make a mistake the formula will be rejected when you try to enter it.

Activity: Logical operators and functions

1 Experiment with logical operators and logical functions. Check that you understand the results that you are getting from your formulae.

2 Review your Ria View spreadsheet model. Where have you used formulae? Have you used logical operators and logical functions? Extend your model to include more complex formulae.

2.3 Structure and fitness for purpose

A worksheet is essentially a set of cells arranged in rows and columns but, within that format, you can create a structure. You can also set up a number of worksheets and link these.

To make it crystal clear what the data in your spreadsheet represents, you should include a title (to describe the whole spreadsheet and individual worksheets), column headings (to describe the data in each column) and row labels (to describe the data in each row).

Your overall aim should be to create an organised spreadsheet that is fit for purpose. This means, for example, making sure the size of font is legible enough for the intended audience, and that the layout of the data is as straightforward as possible.

Formatting

Each cell in your spreadsheet needs to be formatted and the format that you apply should depend on the contents – the type of data the cell holds (see Figure 42.10).

- For cells that contain numeric data, you need to specify the type of number: integer (ie whole number), the number of decimal places, percentage, currency or date/time.

- For cells that contain text, you can set the font, style, size and alignment. You should aim for consistency, using a minimal number of different fonts and sparing use of colour and shading, italics and bold.

- For cells that contain a formula, the format will depend on the type of data that the formula creates – for formulae that display a number, you can set the format of the cell as for numeric data; for formulae that display text, you can set the format of the cell as for text data.

Styling

To make the title, column headings and row labels stand out, it is a good idea to style them differently. For example, to draw attention to the data in particular cells and to create interest in your layouts, you can use colour for the font and/or background shading. You

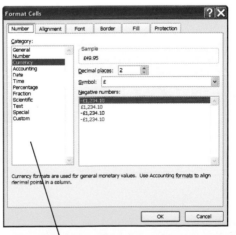

For numeric data, you have lots of choices of format... and the same goes for text.

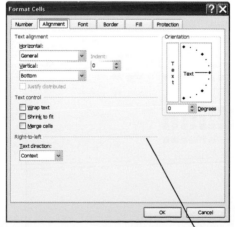

Whatever the data type, you can choose a font to suit.

Figure 42.10: Formatting options

might also outline a cell or range of cells – a border draws the eye to the cells and creates a focal point of the screen (see Figure 42.11). Similarly, shading can be used to make some cells (such as headings) stand out.

Column alignment is also important.

- Text is usually aligned left, but might be centred if the text is a column heading or even right-aligned, as the title in Column E of the Knits4UStockList worksheet (see Figure 42.11).

- Numbers, including currency and percentages, are usually aligned on the decimal point, or where it would be if one were displayed.

- Dates could be left, right or centre-aligned.

The most important consideration when styling is to be consistent. If you use bold and centred for your column headings, make sure all column headings are bold and centred. Inconsistent styling results in a messy-looking spreadsheet display.

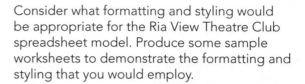

Activity: Formatting and styling

Consider what formatting and styling would be appropriate for the Ria View Theatre Club spreadsheet model. Produce some sample worksheets to demonstrate the formatting and styling that you would employ.

Context

A spreadsheet that is just rows and rows of numbers will not be fit for purpose if the reader cannot work out the context of the data. Appropriate column headings and row titles will assist the reader but each worksheet should also have an informative heading and the tabs should be renamed so that it is clear what data is stored on that particular worksheet.

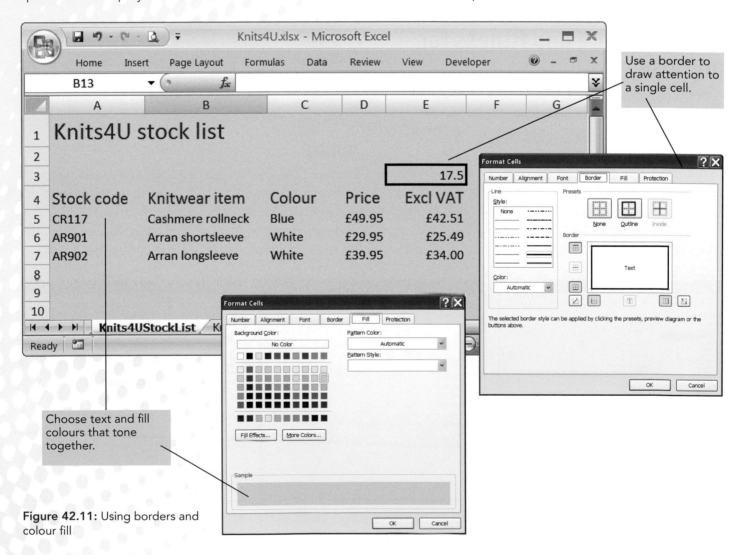

Figure 42.11: Using borders and colour fill

2.4 Features and functions

The more complex a spreadsheet becomes, the more likely it is that more than one user will need to have access to it – during development and/or during use. This section focuses on a range of features and functions that will be of particular use if more than one user is involved in the creation and/or editing of a workbook.

Named ranges

Each cell can be referred to by its column letter and row number, eg A7 or B9. A range of cells can also be referred to by the cell references, separated by a colon, eg A3:B7.

Cell references are fine and work well enough but named ranges provide a more meaningful way of referring to cells and ranges of cells within formulae (see Figure 42.12). You can even name non-adjacent cells as a named range if you wish, and you can also create 3D names that represent the same cell or range of cells across multiple worksheets.

Using named ranges is particularly important when a team of users are developing a complex spreadsheet, as it serves as documentation of the data.

File sharing

Sharing of files and data is possible, with restrictions. Having created a workbook that you want to make available for multi-user editing, you can enter any

Make the cell active by clicking on it and then enter the name for that cell in the Name field.

Formulae make more sense (and can be copied without worrying about absolute/relative addressing) if you use named cells.

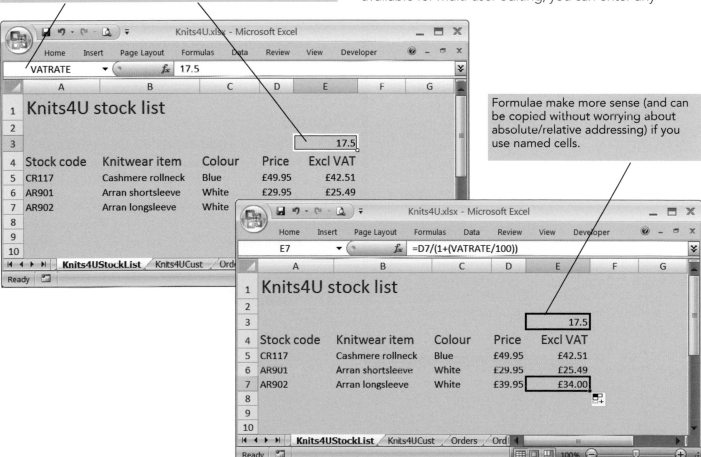

Figure 42.12: Naming cells and using named cells in formulae

data that you want to provide. Some features (such as merged cells, conditional formats and data validation) need to be incorporated prior to sharing because you cannot make changes to these features after you share the workbook.

Once you have set up the workbook for sharing, all users with access to the network will then have full access to the shared workbook, unless you use the Protect Sheet command (Tools / Protection / Protect Sheet) to restrict access.

Tracking changes

Track Changes is an option that logs any changes that are made to a shared workbook. Each user who has access to the file can view these changes. They can see when the change was made and who made the change. A user can then accept or reject the changes made.

Activity: Protecting your spreadsheet

1 Use the Help function provided with your spreadsheet software to find out how to protect or unprotect individual cells, row or columns of your spreadsheet and how you might prevent users from viewing certain rows or columns or certain formulae. Consider which cells, rows or columns of your Ria View spreadsheet model you need to protect, and apply that protection.

2 Find out how to prevent users from making changes to items that are part of a chart, such as the data series, axes and legends. Consider where you might include a chart in your Ria View spreadsheet model, include a chart and apply protection to it.

3 Find out how to control the size and position of the windows and prevent users from moving, resizing or closing the windows. Consider where you might want to exercise such window control within your Ria View spreadsheet model.

Security issues

Giving access to a workbook to other users introduces security issues.

- Who should have access?
- What level of access should they be given?
- What particular elements of the spreadsheet model need to be protected from change by other users?

Excel® offers a wide range of protection options.

User interface

The design of the user interface must take into account the needs of your intended user(s) and include appropriate user interface features such as data entry forms (page 286) and error trapping (page 289) via prompts and error messages.

Activity: Security and the user interface

1 Review the user interface for your Ria View spreadsheet model. Is it straightforward for a user to enter the data without error?

2 Produce some sample worksheets to demonstrate the error trapping techniques that you have employed.

Add-ins

Excel® offers many **add-in** programs (see Figure 42.13). Some are available when you install Excel® and others are available from the Microsoft® Office website.

The add-in is installed on your computer (as a .xla file) and then loaded into Excel®. Once loaded into Excel®, it becomes a feature and can be used like any other

Key term

Add-in – installed functionality that adds custom commands and new features to an application such as Excel®.

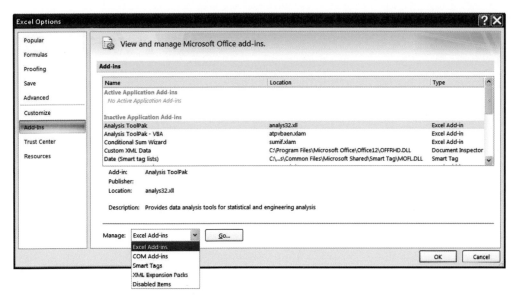

Figure 42.13: Excel® add-ins

The LOOKUP function is useful when:

- you have a table of values that may change at some later date, and which you therefore do not want to embed within a formula
- the value you want depends on the contents of a cell, and this also varies.

The values that you want to look up might be in the same worksheet or in a completely different worksheet within the same spreadsheet.

feature. Any commands that are associated with the add-in appear automatically on appropriate toolbars and menus.

Why not have all available add-ins present, all the time? The reason is that they take up space. So, to conserve memory and improve performance, it is wise to unload add-ins that you don't use or use only rarely. Unloading an add-in removes its features and commands from Excel® (although the add-in program remains on your computer so you can easily reload it when you next need it).

Built-in functions

Excel® provides many built-in functions and these can be sub-grouped by type, for example: cell functions (such as SUM; see Table 42.2 on page 292) and logical functions (such as SUMIF; see Table 42.3 on page 292), LOOKUP functions (see below), text functions (see Table 42.4) or statistical functions (such as AVERAGE; see Table 42.5 on page 298).

LOOKUP function

The LOOKUP function – to be used with a lookup table – has two syntax forms: vector and array. The vector form of LOOKUP looks in a vector for a value and returns a value from the same position in a second vector.

The array form of LOOKUP looks in the first row or column of an array for the specified value and returns a value from the same position in the last row or column of the array.

Text functions

Text functions act on the textual content of cells and can be used, for example, to change the case of text.

Table 42.4 shows how the text string 'jenny Lawson' (in cell A1) is displayed according to the text function that is used in another cell (A2).

In A1	Text function in A2	Result displayed in A2
jenny Lawson	=UPPER(A1)	JENNY LAWSON
	=LOWER(A1)	jenny lawson
	=PROPER(A1)	Jenny Lawson

Table 42.4: Example text functions

If you are not sure which function you need, Excel® provides help. Select Formulas / Insert Function and type a brief description or look through the lists of functions available.

Statistical functions

The usual mathematical operators (+, −, *, /) and many others, such as the percent sign (%) and the caret (^) for exponentiation, can be used within any expression for a formula to perform an arithmetical calculation.

In addition, Excel® offers many statistical functions some of which are listed in Table 42.5.

Statistical function	What it does	Syntax
AVERAGE	Returns the average of its arguments	=AVERAGE(number1,[number2],...)
COUNT	Counts how many numbers are in the list of arguments	=COUNT(value1,[value2],...)
FORECAST	Returns a value along a linear trend	FORECAST(x,known_y,known_x) Where x = the data point for which you want to predict a value, known_y = the dependent array or range of data and known_x = the independent array or range of data.
INTERCEPT	Returns the intercept of the linear regression line	INTERCEPT(known_y,known_x)
MEDIAN	Returns the median of the given numbers	MEDIAN(number1,number2,...)
SLOPE	Returns the slope of the linear regression line	SLOPE(known_y,known_x)
STDEV	Estimates standard deviation based on a sample	STDEV(number1,number2,...)
TREND	Returns values along a linear trend	TREND(known_y,known_x,new_x,const)

Table 42.5: Statistical functions

Finding data

The Find&Select function within Excel® is more powerful than that offered in, for example, Word®. Instead of simply searching on a match of a string of text, you can search for cells which contain a formula, for those that have comments attached or those for which validation has been specified.

Key term

Shortcut – an icon which, when double clicked, opens an application

Activity: Functions

1 Find out which add-ins are available and experiment with installing an add-in and using it.

2 Review your understanding of the built-in functions, in particular the LOOKUP function, some text functions and some statistical functions.

3 Consider how you might use built-in functions within your Ria View spreadsheet model. Prepare sample worksheets to show what your built-in functions do.

2.5 Refine

Having designed a spreadsheet model, the final stage is to consider refinements.

Improving efficiency

Efficiency could be improved by including **shortcuts** or aiding navigation.

Users of Microsoft® software have the option to set up a Quick Access Toolbar and to include the most frequently used commands on that toolbar, such as Save and Print. This saves the user clicking several times on various drop-down menus to achieve a particular outcome. If a shortcut saves just one click whenever the user wants to do something, over time the user will work more quickly.

Similarly, by grouping commands in a way that makes sense to the user's needs, such aids to navigation improve efficiency.

Formatting

While you may have already decided on the formatting of data within cells, what have you decided about the formatting of output?

- What fonts will you use for reports?
- What page orientation provides the best view for the reader?
- What headers and footers will you include on reports?
- How much of the spreadsheet is to be printed, ie what is the print area?
- Have you made good use of colour?
- Have you considered conditional formatting so, for example, 'bad' news appears in red?

Assessment activity 42.2

P2 P3 P4 M1 M2

BTEC

1 Develop a complex spreadsheet model to meet the needs of the Ria View Theatre Club (or some other organisation) P2. This will involve the use of formulae, features and functions to process information P3 and refining the complex spreadsheet model by changing rules and values. M1

2 Use appropriate tools to present data from your chosen spreadsheet model (or another that your tutor gives to you) P4 and analyse and interpret data from the spreadsheet model. M2

Grading tips

- Make sure that your spreadsheet model meets the 'complex' criteria and exhibits some aspects of complexity such as multiple worksheets (with links), complex formulae (for example at least two-step process), large data sets, cells linkage, data entry forms (for example menu systems, list boxes, drop-down boxes, event controls), data validation, error trapping, lookup tables, nested IF functions, templates and cell protection. P2

- Check that you have incorporated some of the required range: relative references, absolute references, logical functions (eg, IF, AND, OR, NOT, SUMIF) correct operators, named ranges, file sharing, track changes, security issues, user interface, add-ins, built-in functions, for example cell functions, LOOKUP functions, text functions, statistical functions and finding data. P3

- You will create charts and graphs from numeric data sets. This can be either the same data used in different graphical images or a number of different charts or graphs created from different data. Make sure your charts and graphs are fit for purpose, ie are of the appropriate type according to the type of data being presented, that they include appropriate titles, labels and axis scales and that you choose suitable colouration. P4

- Think about refinements such as introducing shortcuts or other methods to aid navigation, and improving the presentation by applying different styles and formatting techniques – all of which should make the spreadsheet model more presentable and user friendly. M1

- You might use sub-totals or pivot tables, data sorting and data comparison techniques (trends for example) to interpret a complex spreadsheet model. M2

PLTS

When you are identifying questions and creating a spreadsheet to resolve a problem using formulae and functions, you are demonstrating your skills as an **independent enquirer**.

When you are generating ideas and exploring possibilities to customise part of a spreadsheet to meet a given need, you are demonstrating your skills as a **creative thinker**.

Functional skills

When you are developing a complex spreadsheet model to meet particular needs, you are demonstrating that you can select, interact with and use **ICT** systems safely and securely for a complex task in no-routine and unfamiliar contexts.

When you are using formulae, features and functions to process information, you are demonstrating that you can enter, develop and refine information using appropriate software to meet the requirements of a complex task.

When you are using appropriate tools to present data, you are demonstrating that you can combine and present information in ways that are fit for purpose and audience.

3 Be able to automate and customise spreadsheet models

One of the main advantages of spreadsheet software is that it can be customised to meet the needs of the intended user as closely as possible and parts can also be automated.

3.1 Sorting and summarising data

Sorting will show the same data in different ways, enabling easy analysis and interpretation of the data within a spreadsheet model.

It is possible to sort the data in one column of a spreadsheet while leaving the rest of the data in place. However, if each row represents a record and each column a field, then sorting in this way destroys the integrity of the data. So, if the cells contain material that needs to be kept together in rows (or columns, depending on your design), it is important to expand the selection.

Sorting allows you to identify the smallest and largest items (at the start and end) and, provided some sensible ordering has been used, when it is graphed sorted data may indicate a trend.

Use of sub-totals

Faced with a lot of data, statisticians tend to try to find representative data, such as an average, which can be used to describe all the data using just one item of data. Such single numbers can give a lot of information to the reader.

Another type of single number that can inform the reader is the **sub-total**.

When presented with the sales figures (say) for every day in the year, it can become difficult to spot a trend. However, if the data is summed so that sub-totals of sales (for example weekly, monthly, for particular days of the week or according to lines of stock) are presented within the spreadsheet model, a trend can be established.

Case study: Knits4U (6)

The revenue figures for sales of particular garments are presented to the management every month so that the most popular stock lines can be identified and any lines for which sales have dropped to an unacceptably low figure are reviewed. Questions are asked:

- Is the style now so out of date that the line should be discontinued?
- Might sales increase if a different range of colours – but in the same style – were offered?
- If stock remains, should it be offered at a reduced price in the next brochure mailing?

1 Review your Ria View spreadsheet model. Where might you include sub-totals?

2 Having included sub-totals, what questions might be raised from the additional information provided by these sub-totals?

Pivot tables

A **pivot table** report is most useful when you want to analyse related totals. Each row and column (or field) in your source data becomes a pivot table field that summarises multiple rows of information as shown in Figure 42.14.

Key terms

Sorting – rearranges the data (eg in one column of a spreadsheet) into a sequence such as alphabetical or numerical, ascending or descending.

Sub-total – the sum of some data, which together with other sub-totals makes a grand total.

Pivot table – an interactive table that combines and compares data. The rows and columns can be rotated (pivoted on a cell) to produce different summaries of the source data.

Filtering – extracting data according to some criteria, eg all the data relating to one particular sales person or product.

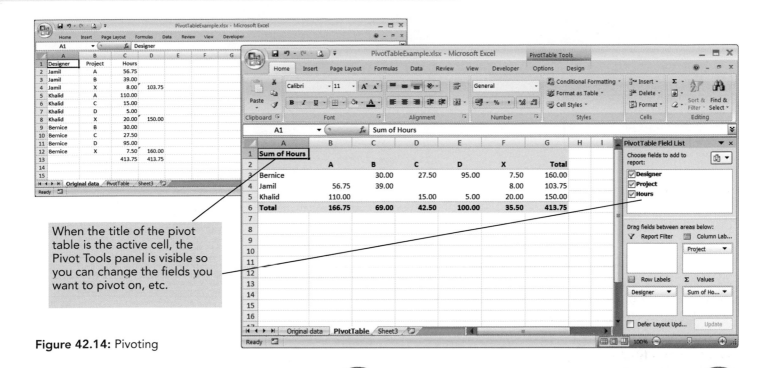

When the title of the pivot table is the active cell, the Pivot Tools panel is visible so you can change the fields you want to pivot on, etc.

Figure 42.14: Pivoting

Activity: Pivot tables

1 Choose a spreadsheet that has six or more columns/fields and at least ten rows of data and choose fields on which you might pivot the data.

2 Experiment with creating pivot tables – but use separate worksheets so that you also demonstrate your skills in linking data between worksheets.

Activity: Sorting on multiple fields

1 Choose a spreadsheet that has six or more columns/fields and at least ten rows of data.

2 Decide on three 'important' fields and experiment with sorting the data according to these three fields.

3 Compare the results which you get by changing which field is sorted first, second and third.

Sorting data on multiple fields

Having learnt how to sort on one field, for more complex data you might need to sort on multiple fields. The order in which you sort the fields can affect the outcome though.

Filtering data sets

Filtering is one way of finding a subset of data from a list. It focuses on one aspect of the data and allows the user to ignore data which does not meet some criteria. The filter can therefore be used to extract information to meet a specific user need (see Figure 42.15).

The filtered list displays only those rows of the list that match the criteria that you specify for a particular column. None of the data is lost – it is just hidden from view while the filter is on. To remove the effect of filtering, deselect Data / Filter.

3.2 Tools

Numeric data is harder to interpret than graphical representations of the same data. Statisticians rely on graphical representation of data because the shape of a graph can say a lot about the general trend of the data.

Fortunately, spreadsheet tools are available to present data graphically – as charts and graphs.

To show the before and after effects of filtering, the first step is to copy the original data from one place to another, using the Advanced Filter option on the Data menu.

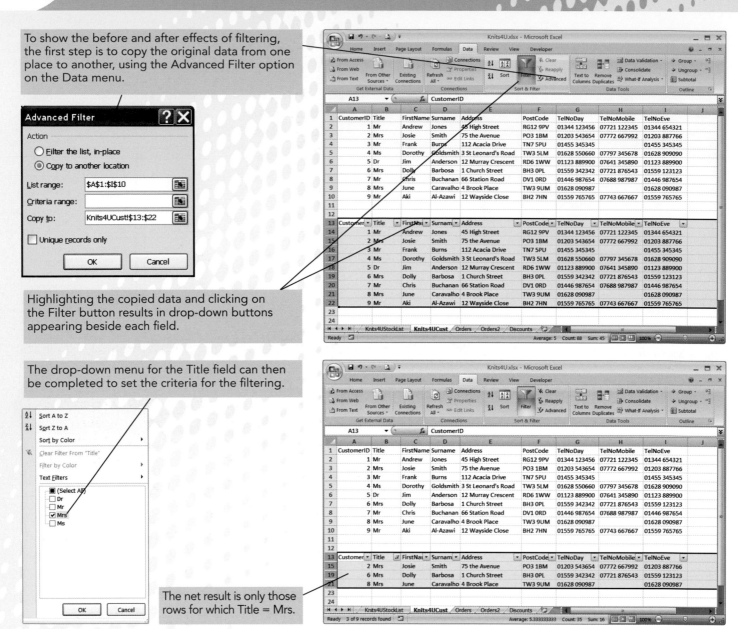

Highlighting the copied data and clicking on the Filter button results in drop-down buttons appearing beside each field.

The drop-down menu for the Title field can then be completed to set the criteria for the filtering.

The net result is only those rows for which Title = Mrs.

Figure 42.15: Filtering

Titles

Although the chart or graph may give an instant impression of the data used to generate it, the audience also need to know, in a condensed way, what data is being represented.

A title is therefore essential and should include a description (such as 'sales figures') and an indication of the date or time period to which the data relates (for example, 'for the year to 28 February 2011').

Labels

Within the chart or graph there will be axes that need careful labelling so that, for example, the axes scales are immediately clear to the reader. By clever choice

of colours and annotation of any **legend**, you can also increase the accessibility of the chart or graph.

Select appropriate type

Excel® provides a wide range of graphical representations (see Figure 42.16) and wizards for each one to help you to enter all the relevant parameters.

It makes sense to use the wizard to set up a chart or graph and then fine tune it so it shows exactly what you want. However, to create output that suits the requirements of the user and/or the audience, you must take care to use the type of chart that matches the data: **categorical** or **ordinal**, **discrete** or **continuous**.

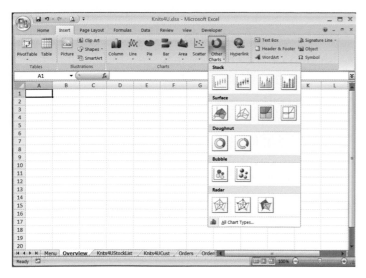

Figure 42.16: Graphical options available in Excel®

Key terms

Legend – (also called a key) an explanatory box that identifies the patterns or colours that are assigned to the data series or categories in a chart.

Categorical data – data that has separate categories, and that has no natural ordering.

Ordinal data – data that has a definite ordering, eg from smallest to largest, or oldest to newest.

Discrete data – data that takes values, but not the values between them. For example, shoes sizes are 4, 4½, 5, 5½, 6, 6½, 7 and so on. There is no shoe size between a 4 and a 4½.

Continuous data – data that can take a value anywhere on a number line. For example, time is a continuous variable, as are height, length and weight.

Here are some basic rules as to which charts suit which types of data.

- **Line graphs**: useful to display trends in continuous data. If a graph is used for discrete data (such as shoe sizes), the points should not really be joined, because the values between the discrete values are unachievable – but often the points are joined to show some trend.
- **Bar/column charts**: best for discrete ordinal data, such as shoe sizes. For discrete data, the bars should not touch. If a bar chart is used for continuous data, the bars should touch and the chart is then called a histogram.

- **Pie charts**: best for categorical data, such as colour of front door or make of car.
- **xy (scatter) graphs**: used to plot instances of a pair of variables such as height against weight of a class of learners. None of the points should be joined to any other but any cluster effects with points close to each other or lying along a general trend line show that there is some correlation between the two variables.

3.3 Presenting

This section focuses on two aspects of presentation: combining information and maintaining data.

Combining information

Often, a single source of data is not sufficient to inform the reader or to support an argument. Instead, you may need to bring together two or more sources of information. For example, you may show the results of a survey presented as the numerical data and totals, together with a pie chart of relevant results, to present the reader with the full picture. Such combining of information is an essential part of presenting complex data.

Maintaining data

Sometimes, it is not practical to keep large worksheet models together in the same workbook. Instead, you can set up several worksheets and link them.

For example: in a spreadsheet, one worksheet contains the current selling prices of products and another worksheet shows a forecast of turnover based on those prices. Unless suitable links are set up between the two worksheets, a change in the prices of products would mean that someone has to make a change to the data in the turnover worksheet too. Two sets of changes double the risk of input error and the time delay between the two entries means that the data is inconsistent for that period of time.

If, however, the data is held in a number of worksheets (or workbooks or software packages) that have been linked, any changes to one sheet will automatically impact on the data on other sheets. This will maintain the currency of all the data so you can be sure of an accurate and up-to-date forecast of turnover.

3.4 Analysing and interpreting data

Having presented the data in a more meaningful way (in a sensible order, with subtotals as appropriate), you can help your readers if you go one step further in analysing and interpreting the data for them.

- Converting data to charts or graphs instantly reveals trends in the data and is more meaningful to the reader (see above).

- With lists of data, techniques such as filtering and sorting (see page 301) serve to focus attention on relevant data and to present it in a sensible order to the reader.

- Trends are more easily noticed if data has been presented as a graph and trend analysis is then possible too (see page 303).

- Patterns in the data are also most easily spotted if the data is presented graphically.

- Data analysis is achievable using statistical formulae, calculating sub-totals (see page 300) and averages and so on.

- Results that you discover during the analysis stage need to be pulled together in the presentation so that the reader can see, at a glance, what the data tells you.

- Conclusions are also necessary to summarise what has been achieved, what the data proves or demonstrates and to draw to a close the report.

3.5   Customisation

Software applications are designed to suit everyone and yet every problem is different and every user has differing needs. So, tools are provided to allow you to customise the spreadsheet model to solve the user's specific problem and to meet their particular needs. In this section, we look at two types of tools: those which allow you to apply some security measures to restrict access and some others which allow you to create a relevant user interface with appropriate validation and the best working environment for the user.

Restricting data entry

Some cells on a worksheet – and perhaps entire worksheets – may contain material that you do not want the end user to access and/or change. If that is the case, you might want to restrict data entry. There are two main methods open to you:

- **locking cells** so the user can view them but not change the contents of them

- **hiding cells** (also rows and columns) so that the user is not even aware they are there.

The method of locking cells involves unlocking the cells that you want them to be able to change and then protecting the whole sheet using a password.

Modifying toolbars and menus

The software that you use to develop a spreadsheet model provides all the tools that you need to change the structure of the worksheet, to format the data and to present the data graphically. These features appear in toolbars and menus.

The end user of your spreadsheet model does not need all these tools. Indeed, you may prefer to restrict the user's actions by reducing the number of features available within the software. For example, to prevent users from copying and filling data by dragging and dropping cells, clear the Enable fill handle and cell drag-and-drop check box (Excel® Options dialog box, Advanced options), and then protect the worksheet.

The Ribbon, which is part of the Microsoft® Office Fluent user interface, is designed to help users quickly find the commands needed to complete a task. Commands are organised in logical groups that are collected together under tabs. It is not possible to customise the Ribbon without using XML and programming code but you can customise the Quick Access Toolbar to add buttons that represent the commands that you frequently use.

Checking data

To make a spreadsheet robust, the designer needs to incorporate methods of data validation (see page 287) which will prevent the user entering data – or omitting to enter essential data – either of which could adversely impact on the design or content of the spreadsheet model.

Data validation establishes limits on data so that the user is limited to entering data within some range or matching an entry in a list. In Excel® this is accessed through the Excel® Options dialog box, Advanced options.

If you want to insist the user enters something into a cell, ie to reject handle blank (null) values, you need to clear the Ignore blank check box (see Figure 42.7 on page 288).

Did you know?

Data validation is designed to show messages and prevent invalid entries only when users type data directly in a cell. When data is copied or filled, the messages do not appear. So, for validation to work, you need to customise the menus to prevent Copy or Fill being used.

Error messages

Error messages should give sufficient information to guide the user towards entering correct data. Simply displaying 'INVALID DATA' will not be useful! Instead, explain what is expected and invite the user to try again. See, for example, Figure 42.7 on page 288.

Activity: Customisation

1 Identify cells within your Ria View spreadsheet model that ought to be locked and other cells that ought to be hidden from the user's view. Consider also whole rows and columns that should be protected.

2 Check that you are confident with locking and unlocking cells so as to protect your spreadsheet.

3 Decide what options you would not want the end user to have and disable these options.

4 Experiment with customising the Quick Access Toolbar.

5 Review the validation that you have put in place for the Ria View spreadsheet model. Is it robust enough?

6 Revise the Ria View spreadsheet model so that at least one data entry field requires data to be entered.

7 Review the error messages that you have incorporated within the Ria View spreadsheet model. Are they informative to guide the user towards entering correct data?

3.6 Automation

The end user of a spreadsheet may be proficient in using the software, but the more that you automate processes, the easier it should be for the user.

Macros

If a task is to be repeated, it can be automated with a **macro**.

When you record a macro, Excel® remembers data about each step you take (what menu options you choose, what values you select, and so on) and stores this information about the macro in a new module attached to your workbook. When you run the macro later, it plays back the commands – including any mistakes you might have made when recording it!

Within the user interface, you can automate procedures by providing buttons for the user to press. The event of a particular button being pressed then initiates the appropriate procedure.

For the procedure to happen when the user clicks on the button, you first have to create a macro and then assign the macro to the button. The same macro could be assigned to more than one button in your spreadsheet model, so if there are actions that are used frequently, plan your macros carefully.

Did you know?

Microsoft® Excel® provides safeguards that help to protect your computer against viruses that can be transmitted by macros. If you need to share macros, they can be certified with a digital signature so that other users can verify that each macro is from a trustworthy source.

Key terms

Locking cells – restricting access to a cell so that it can be viewed but not changed by particular users.

Hiding cells – a protection mechanism that prevents the user from seeing a cell. As long as there is no option to unhide it, the cell is protected. You can hide entire spreadsheets from the user.

Macro – a series of commands and functions that are stored in a Microsoft® Visual Basic module and can be run whenever the user needs to perform the task.

ActiveX® control

Within your spreadsheet design, you may decide to include command buttons (on a menu page), list boxes (as part of your validation) and dialog boxes (to communicate prompts and error messages to the user). These are all examples of ActiveX® controls – small program building blocks – which were designed so that applications could work over the Internet through web browsers. ActiveX® control can be written in Visual Basic® but Excel® provides some via the Toolbox.

Did you know?

ActiveX controls are similar to Java applets in that programmers designed both mechanisms so that web browsers could download and execute them. However, they differ in that Java applets can run on nearly any platform, while ActiveX components officially operate only with Microsoft®'s Internet Explorer® web browser and the Microsoft® Windows® operating system.

Control Toolbox

Every component on a form is a control and the Control Toolbox offers both ActiveX® controls and others which cannot be viewed using a browser. See Data entry forms on page 286.

Visual Basic®

After you have recorded a macro, you can use the Visual Basic® Editor to view the code you have generated and to correct errors or change what the macro does. The Visual Basic® Editor is designed to make writing and editing macro code easy – plenty of online help is provided so it is not necessary to learn how to program or use the Visual Basic® language to make simple changes to your macros.

Did you know?

As well as editing the macro code, the Visual Basic Editor also allows you to copy a macro – such as printing or formatting – from one module to another. You could even copy macros between different workbooks. If you need to, you can rename the modules that store the macros or rename your macros.

Assessment activity 42.3

1 You are to customise a spreadsheet model to a given requirement. Your tutor will guide you as to what spreadsheet model to customise and brief you on the requirements of the end user. **P5**

2 You are to use automated features in a spreadsheet model to meet a given requirement. Your tutor will guide you as to what spreadsheet model to automate and brief you on the requirements of the end user. **P6**

3 Your end user is pleased with what you have done to automate the spreadsheet model but would like to understand more about the methods of automation that you have used and those you chose not to use. Prepare a presentation for such an end user comparing the different automation methods. **M3**

Grading tips

* Examples of customisation include restricting data entry, for example hiding information, protecting worksheets and cells, modifying toolbars and menus, checking data, for example data validation, range checking, not NULL and display error messages. **P5**

* Develop the spreadsheet model further by implementing automated features, such as macros, ActiveX® control, Control Toolbox or Visual Basic®. **P6**

* In the presentation define and explain by examples a range of different automation methods, ie macros, ActiveX® control, Control Toolbox and Visual Basic®. **M3**

4   Be able to test and document spreadsheet models

4.1 Test

A spreadsheet model is only useful if it meets the needs of the intended end user(s) – and works! Testing your spreadsheet model is therefore an essential part of the development process.

Your testing of the spreadsheet model

There is a lot to be considered during the process of testing your spreadsheet model.

- As a belt-and-braces check, you would be advised to perform manual calculations of all formulae in your spreadsheet model, paying special attention to those that involve functions.
- You should trial every data entry form, making sure that every field within that form has been set up with appropriate validation checks.
- You could build in **cross-cast checks** to help test the calculations within worksheets. For example, calculating the total sales for a team of salespeople over twelve months, with one calculation by month and another by salesperson; the two totals should tally.

Key term

Cross-cast check – doing a calculation in two different ways and checking that the two totals are the same.

- To make sure you have the correct outcomes in terms of layout and displayed values, check that your data is displayed at the appropriate level of detail: for example, to the nearest penny for currency or to the nearest £1000 for larger amounts of money.

Case study: Knits4U (7)

Apart from manually checking each calculation, or using a calculator, the developer of the Knits4U spreadsheet model built in checks to make sure the calculations are correct. Figure 42.14 on page 301 shows intermediate values in column D of the Original data worksheet, plus a total of those intermediate values in cell D13. This tallies with the value in cell C13.

1 In your Ria View spreadsheet model, identify at least one place where intermediate values might be displayed and where a cross cast could be used to verify calculations.

2 Consider situations that might cause the checking values not to match. Ask yourself: What could you do to prevent this happening?

- Last but not least, you must bear in mind that the spreadsheet model has been developed for an end user – a client with particular needs – and you must ask yourself whether your model meets the 'suitability for client' check.

User testing

Ideally you, the designer, will have created a sound spreadsheet model with correct calculations so that whatever data is entered, the correct results should be produced. Once the design is complete though, the user also needs to test that the results are as expected.

Test plans

Whether it's the designer or the end user who is testing a spreadsheet model, a test plan should be drawn up listing precisely what will be tested and then, during the testing, what happened (see Table 42.6).

WORKSHEET LEVEL TESTING	Date tested	Notes	Issues to be investigated further

Check layout and content of each worksheet
    Sheet 1
    Sheet 2
    …			

Check formulae within each worksheet
    Sheet 1
    Sheet 2
    …			

Check formulae that link worksheets
    Sheet 1
    Sheet 2
    …			

MENU LEVEL TESTING	Date tested	Notes	Issues to be investigated further

Check layout and content of each menu
    Main menu
    New customer menu
    New product menu
…			

Check links from each menu
    Main menu
    New customer menu
    New product menu
…			

Check formulae that link worksheets
    Main menu
    New customer menu
    New product menu
…			

Table 42.6: Example test plan

The material put through the system should include normal data, **extreme data** and **erroneous data**, so that all situations are properly tested.

Key terms

Extreme data – data at the upper and lower acceptable limits.

Erroneous data – data that is not valid.

Activity: Testing

1 Identify the tests you should carry out on the Ria View spreadsheet model to make sure it works.

2 Invent examples of normal, extreme and erroneous data that can be used for testing purposes.

3 Carry out testing and record what happens on your test plan.

4.2 Feedback

Feedback on the success, or otherwise, of your spreadsheet model will help to inform future designs. Depending on the circumstances, there are various approaches to obtaining feedback:

- For a project with a large number of end users, you might conduct a survey. This could be online and the request to complete this survey might pop up when they start to use the application.

- The survey might be presented as a questionnaire, which the end user completes after using the application for a while.

- If there are not many end users, you might conduct one-on-one interviews or group interviews, possibly using the questions within your questionnaire as a prompt to the discussion.

Having gathered the feedback, the next stage is to analyse the results, take on board all criticisms of the developed spreadsheet model and then to make recommendations as to how – going forward – the model might be refined to better meet the needs of the end user. Such refinements take time, may delay the implementation of the spreadsheet system and may also involve additional costs to the end user. All this has to be negotiated and agreed before further development commences.

Activity: Feedback

Your tutor will supply you with a spreadsheet model and your task is to evaluate the spreadsheet and to give feedback.

With others in your group, collate this feedback, analyse the results and make recommendations as to how the spreadsheet model could be improved.

4.3 Alternative formats

Spreadsheets can be saved in a number of different formats, such as:

- xls (Excel® spreadsheet)
- csv (comma-separated variable)
- txt (text)
- xms (extended memory specification)
- html (hypertext markup language, as used for web pages).

CSV is one of the most useful formats – it can be read by many applications, so data created in one type of spreadsheet software can easily be exported to other programs.

Activity: Alternative formats

1 Experiment with exporting from Excel® to alternative formats and then retrieving the data from other applications.

2 Make notes on any limitations that you discover and share these with others in your class.

4.4 Documentation

As with all IT projects, documentation is essential so that those coming to the project after the designer has moved on can see what was done and why. If further development is to be undertaken, it can be done without upsetting what is already in place.

Documentation falls into two distinct types.

- **User documentation**: This provides instructions to those who have to use the system and may be provided in the form of a guide, which can be used for troubleshooting.

- **Technical documentation**: This focuses on the hardware and software resources and is written for the benefit of future IT professionals who might have to amend the spreadsheet model or develop it in some way.

With technical documentation particularly and user documentation to a lesser extent, there should be instructions as to how the systems can be worked, details of all calculations (the formulae and functions used within worksheets) and the validation procedures that have been put into place.

Assessment activity 42.4

1 Your tutor will provide you with a spreadsheet model that is to be tested to ensure it is fit for purpose. You will check the accuracy of the spreadsheet model and present your evidence in the form of a test plan. **P7**

2 Select a spreadsheet model – or use one provided by your tutor – and export the contents of the model to an alternative format. **P8**

3 Document your spreadsheet model by producing both user documentation and technical documentation. **P9 M4**

4 Your tutor will advise you which of your spreadsheet model designs you are to evaluate. You will incorporate feedback from others and make recommendations for improvements. **D2**

Grading tips

- Make sure the functionality works as required and that the calculations are accurate. Check the data validation, and that data has been displayed to appropriate levels of detail (for example, currency to two decimal places). Record what you tested and the results on your test plan. **P7**

- Your conversion to an alternative format could be evidenced through an observation and witness statement. You might, for example, convert to an alternative format and then import the converted file into some other relevant software. **P8**

- Your user documentation should include instructions on how to use the spreadsheet model, especially when navigating with user interfaces. Your technical documentation should include the required hardware and software resources, instructions and an explanation of calculations used in the spreadsheet model. **P9 M4**

- Reflect on your performance in building a spreadsheet model and what hurdles you have had to overcome to achieve the desired result. Did the spreadsheet model meet the given requirements? What did other people think of the spreadsheet model? Make sure your recommendations are sensible. **D2**

PLTS

When you are anticipating, taking and managing risks when testing a spreadsheet model, you are demonstrating your skills as a **self-manager**.

When you are inviting feedback from users when evaluating a spreadsheet model, you are demonstrating your skills as a **reflective learner**.

Functional skills

When you are evaluating a spreadsheet model, incorporating feedback from others and making recommendations for improvements, you are demonstrating that you can evaluate the selection, use and effectiveness of **ICT** tools and facilities used to present information.

Khalid
Spreadsheet designer

Khalid works for Solutions UK Limited and his specialism is cost-benefit analysis, a relatively simple and widely used technique for deciding whether to make a change.

Part of Khalid's job is to identify the benefits of a course of action, add up the value of these benefits and subtract any costs associated with it. If the benefits outweigh the costs, the client is recommended to go ahead with the project. Simple!

Khalid knows that costs may be one-off or ongoing. Benefits, however, he realises are most often received over a period of time. So, in designing the spreadsheet model for a particular client, Khalid tries to build the effect of time into any analysis and he does this by calculating a payback period.

For most projects, the companies are willing to invest monies to get the project off the ground but will be looking for payback over a specified period of time – say, five years.

In its simplest form, the type of cost-benefit analysis that Khalid designs is carried out using only financial costs and financial benefits. For example, a simple cost-benefit analysis of a road scheme would measure the cost of building the road and subtract this from the economic benefit of improving transport links. It would not measure either the cost of environmental damage or the benefit of quicker and easier travel to work.

A more sophisticated approach to cost-benefit analysis – and one that Khalid aims to provide – is to try to put a financial value on these intangible costs and benefits. This can be highly subjective.

How do you put a price on the environmental importance of a copse that is home to butterflies but lies in the way of a planned motorway?

For the motorist, what value can be put on stress-free travel to work in the morning?

For those that live near the proposed route, what price do you put on air and noise pollution?

Think about it!

1 Identify a cost-benefit issue that is important to you.

2 List the costs and list the benefits. Try to put a value on each item.

3 Produce a simple spreadsheet model to show the payback period for your project.

Just checking

1. Explain the four main types of content that you may place in any one cell. What other content options does your spreadsheet software offer?

2. What is an active cell?

3. Explain these terms: categorical data, ordinal data, histogram, discrete, continuous.

4. Give two examples of spreadsheet models that forecast the future.

5. Why are spreadsheets useful for statistical analysis?

6. What is a representative value?

7. Explain these terms: ordering, sorting, filtering, hide, lock.

8. What is a pivot table? What does it mean to pivot a table?

9. Explain how you can protect the integrity of data during a sort.

10. What kind of data is best presented using a pie chart? Under what circumstances might you display data as a scatter graph?

11. What is a macro? How can macros be used to customise a spreadsheet solution?

edexcel

Assignment tips

- When looking at the kinds of problems spreadsheets are used to solve, focus on the simple tasks that can be done before thinking through the more complex options. Work from the bottom up.

- When developing your own complex spreadsheet model, don't forget to pay attention to the small details: the layout of a worksheet, the detailed validation of every data entry, the design of your charts and graphs.

- Aim for automation which saves the user time – rather than just demonstrating your skills in automating. Ditto for customisation. Ask yourself: What does the user really need?

- Be thorough in your testing and write down everything that you spot during the testing process. Systematic discovery of problems and then, later, systematic solving of the faults will result in a fully working system.

Glossary

8-bit – where a single byte is used for each item of data. A byte has 8 bits, each of which can be set to a one or zero. This gives 256 different combinations of bit patterns.

A

Absolute cell referencing – allows you to copy or move a formula without the cell reference changing. By inserting a dollar symbol ($) before the letter and/or number of a cell reference you can make all or part of a cell reference absolute.

Acessibility – the ease with which websites can be accessed by users, especially referring to those with particular technologies or special needs.

ActionScript – a language used in Flash animations, for example to create buttons.

Add-in – installed functionality that adds custom commands and new features to an application such as Excel.

Administrator account – a user account that has total access rights and permissions. This allows total unrestricted access to all hardware and software resources.

Argument – a value or expression used within a function. It specifies what data is to be acted upon, the criteria that are to be applied or the resulting value that is required.

Array – a collection of variables that have a single name.

Artifacts – unwanted visible elements in a picture or animation.

Asset – any type of object within a multimedia product, such as an image, movie clip or sound file.

Autocrop – a function that trims unwanted edges from an image or animation.

Auto-increment – means adding a value (normally one) automatically and is used to describe the process of automatically assigning a value to the primary key of a new record which is the last primary key plus one. It is used where no naturally occurring primary key is available.

B

Back-out procedure – restoring the system to the state it was in before the installation took place.

Back up – to copy computer work to another place so that it is kept safe in case of emergency such as file corruption, fire, flood or theft. Many users back up to CD-ROM, then store these somewhere secure, such as a fireproof safe or off-site in another location.

Bandwidth – the capacity a network connection can conduct at one time.

Bitmap format – saves the image as a map of pixels.

Bitmap graphics – also called raster graphics, they are made from lots of pixels, each with a colour.

Black box testing – focuses on the testing of functional requirements. The test designer develops a series of valid and invalid inputs and checks for each combination to see if the output is as expected.

Blu-ray discs – a form of DVD that can store more data than other discs and allows for more detailed games.

BODMAS – order of execution of evaluation: brackets, order (that means powers!), division and multiplication (working left to right), addition and subtraction (working left to right).

Body – the part of the code where all the elements that are visible on the web page are coded.

Bureau – an organisation that carries out services, such as printing, for other businesses or clients. A design studio may not have expensive specialist printing facilities, so sends work to a bureau to make use of their printing equipment.

Business case – a proposal stating the objectives, costs and benefits of a project.

C

Cache memory – very fast electronic memory between RAM and another device, used to make the system run faster.

Call – to access a function from wherever it is stored and execute it.

Categorical data – data that has separate categories, and that has no natural ordering.

CCD – stands for charge-coupled device. It is an image sensor used in digital cameras and other devices that converts the image to digital signals.

Cel – a piece of transparent film that can be drawn on then overlaid with other cels to create a composite image.

Certificate-based authentication – a method of coding information so the people at either end are identified by a digital certificate, coupled with a digital signature. These can confirm the identity of the sender or recipient.

CGI – stands for computer generated imagery and is where computers are used to create animation to be integrated into the live action in a movie.

Checkpoints – points between milestones where progress can be checked.

Cinematograph – invented by the Lumière brothers in 1895, it used 35mm celluloid film.

Claymation – where models or puppets are moved frame by frame to create an animation.

CLE – stands for command line editor. It enables you to edit text files using the command line.

Client side scripting – when the script is executed on the user's computer. This is the opposite of server side scripting, which is executed on the web server. Server side scripting is used for more advanced interactive features such as connecting to a database.

Colorimeter – a light-sensitive instrument that can be used to calibrate a computer screen to match the colours produced by a printer.

Colour depth – the number of bits used by the graphics system to hold the colour of each pixel on the screen. A 24-bit colour depth means the number of colours available on a computer system will be 16.7 million.

Comment – an uninterrupted line of code which describes what is happening and helps developers understand how it works.

Compression – where a mathematical calculation is performed on a file in order to 'squash' it and make it smaller.

Concept artist – a individual who will sketch or paint scenes from the game before it is made.

Concept designing – outlining the overall design of the product. This gives the general feel of it and the effect it should have on the users.

Concept keyboard – also called an overlay keyboard. It has keys that have been preset to specific functions. The keys often have images or symbols to guide the user. A concept keyboard can do anything a QWERTY keyboard and/or mouse can do. For example, it can be used to access the Internet, run programs, play movies and music.

Connectedness – the ease with which users move from one location to another, such as between software applications which appear familiar and therefore less threatening.

Constant – data that is stored that cannot be changed.

Container – a device for storing data that is used in games.

Continuous data – data that can take a value anywhere on a number line. For example, time is a continuous variable, as are height, length and weight.

Cookies – packets of data exchanged between the client computer and web server for authentication or personalisation of a website.

CPU – stands for central processing unit, another name for the processor. This is a chip that fits into a socket on the motherboard. Modern CPUs are often made by AMD or Intel. The AMD family of CPUs include Athlon and Opteron. Intel processors include Pentium and Celeron.

Crash – when a computer program stops working and communicating with other parts of the computer system altogether.

Cross-cast check – doing a calculation in two different ways and checking that the two totals are the same.

CRT – stands for cathode ray tube. CRT is a screen technology that uses a phosphor-coated glass tube to display images. The tube makes the unit quite deep, especially for large screens, as electron rays need to be fired at the display from the back of the tube, with room to spread out to the size of the display. This technology uses a lot of electricity and older models can produce some radiation, which concerns many users.

CSS – stands for cascading style sheets. It is a form of web language which standardises the layout throughout a website.

Cut-out animation – where shapes are laid against a background and moved for each shot of the camera.

D

DAB – stands for digital audio broadcasting. DAB radios require no tuning and provide a clearer, crisper sound than traditional radios.

Data mining – the extraction of large amounts of information, often about customers of businesses.

Data mining tools – tools that involve the automatic collection of large amounts of data and then analyse the data for trends and patterns.

Delimiter – a character used to separate fields when data is stored as plain text. The delimiter most often used is the comma, hence the term comma-delimited file.

Deliverable – a product or service that a project aims to produce.

Device driver – a program that tells a computer system how to communicate with a hardware device.

Dialog box – a window that responds to a command and allows you to make choices. In Office® applications, clicking on a menu item with three dots (…) after it will open a dialog box.

Discrete data – data that takes values, but not the values between them. For example, shoes sizes are 4, 4½, 5, 5½, 6, 6½, 7, and so on. There is no shoe size between a 4 and a 4½.

Dithering – uses in-between colours to reduce the harsh contrast of two colours.

DIV – a method of defining a style for a block of HTML (hypertext markup language). It includes an automatic paragraph break.

DMA – stands for direct memory addressing. DMA is the name given to circuits on the motherboard which are used to move large amounts of data from one part of the system to another.

DOM – stands for document object model. It is used to integrate styles, content and formatting for web pages.

Drawn animation – where animators draw each frame of the film.

Drop-down menu – for a particular data entry field, a list of valid entries that is compiled from cells elsewhere in the workbook, used to make data entry easier, or to limit entries to certain items that you define.

Dynamic website – one which is updated live online. Usually, there are scripting languages and/or databases.

E

Ease – (also known as the fairing) the speed at which a tween is performed.

E-D – stands for eDimensional. E-D glasses make computer games appear more vividly 3D.

Entity – a real world object of importance about which data must be captured in a system under investigation. Examples are employees, learners, stock, orders and so on.

Erroneous data – data that is not valid.

Event – an action which can cause a reaction in the code.

Extreme data – data at the upper and lower acceptable limits.

F

FAT – stands for file allocation table. The FAT is held on the disk to connect names of files and folders to where they actually are on the disk. When a file is opened or saved, the disk address needs to be looked up in the FAT before the file can be found. FAT can be likened to a phone book holding the addresses of files on the disk.

Filtering – extracting data according to some criteria, eg all the data relating to one particular sales person or product.

Firewall – a piece of software that protects the system from unauthorised access. This is especially important for web servers.

Flipbook – a very simple type of animation where drawings are put on separate pages and then flicked through to animate.

Form controls – the original controls (label, group box, button, check box, option button, list box, combo box, scroll bar, spin button) that were provided with early versions of Excel.

Formula – (plural 'formulae') an expression written in terms of cell references and operators, which specifies a calculation that is to be done. The result of the calculation appears in the cell in which the formula is stored.

Fps – stands for frames per second (fps), or the number of individual images that are shown every second.

FPS – stands for first person shooter in gaming. This is a game where the player sees through the eyes of the character.

Frame – a section of a web page which, when used with other frames, can make up a page of independently functioning sections.

Frame (animation) – a single section of film that contains one image of the animation.

FTP – stands for file transfer protocol. It is the protocol used to upload web pages on to a web server. Unusually, the term is used as both a noun and a verb.

Full image backup – a single file that stores all contents from a storage device such as a hard drive.

Function – a command that results in a value being returned.

G

Games designer – the person who decides how the game is going to play, what it is going to look like, how many levels it will have, etc.

Games developer – a company or an individual who develops computer game software.

Gaming platform – a physical or software device that allows the playing of games.

Gantt chart – a wall chart showing how long the tasks should take with when they start and finish.

Geons – 2D images that are quickly recognisable by the user from almost any angle.

GB/s – stands for gigabytes per second. It is a data transfer rate measured in 1,000,000,000 bytes per second.

GIF – stands for graphics interchange format. It is a bitmap image format that can support animations.

Goal seeking – working from a known numerical goal back to whatever data entries are needed to achieve that goal.

'Go live' – when a website is uploaded to be viewed on the Internet.

H

Hang – when a computer program or an entire system stops responding to input.

Handles – markers on a shape that show where a shape can be adjusted.

Haptic technology – technology that enables the user to interact with the device using their sense of touch. For example, ticket machines, cash points, computer games, mobile phones and other such devices, all use haptic (touch screen) technology.

Hardware – the physical part of a computer system, including components inside the system unit, peripherals such as monitor and printer, as well as specialised devices such as a digital camera.

Head – the head of the web page, the part of the code where all the styling and other invisible parts are written.

Head-up display – a device worn on the head like glasses that can be used to watch DVDs or to experience a virtual activity.

Hiding cells – a protection mechanism that prevents the user from seeing a cell. As long as there is no option to unhide it, the cell is protected. You can hide entire spreadsheets from the user.

House style – a design theme carried throughout a website or even a business, eg letters, faxes, emails, web pages, etc.

HTML – stands for hypertext markup language. It is the language used as a basis for all web pages.

Hyperlinks – originally called hypertext, these are words that are interactive and, when clicked, open a web page or file.

I

IDE – stands for integrated development environment, software which helps write programming code.

If statement – a control structure in programming which decides the direction of code.

Input mask – used to control what users are allowed to enter in as input in a text box. The key purpose is to improve the quality of the input data.

Interactive whiteboard – a screen that has a touch-sensitive display and can connect to the Internet, file servers and computer applications. Information can be written on the screen with a special marker pen and changes can be made and stored in the same way as when working on a computer.

Interactivity – two-way communication between user and computer.

Interpret – to convert HTML, which the developer can understand, to a language the computer understands.

Input/output statement – a statement that either brings data into the current code block or sends it out. If, for example, a block of code deals with the amount of damage a sword attack will have on an opponent, the input statement may contain data about the power level of the sword and the output statement may contain the amount of damage that will be dealt.

IP address – a unique number which identifies a computer on a network, in the format of four numbers separated by full stops eg 127.0.0.1

Iteration loops – a control structure in programming which repeats code for a set amount of time.

J

JPEG – stands for joint photographics expert group. It is a bitmap image format that can hold more than 16 million colours in an image.

Joystick – an input device that can be used for playing video games.

K

KB/s – stands for kilobytes per second. It is a data transfer rate measured in 1000 bytes per second.

Kinetoscope – invented by Thomas Edison, it was an early projector using perforated film.

L

LCD – stands for liquid crystal display. This type of visual system is used, for example, in cash machines and mobile phones.

LED – stands for light emitting diode. This system is the same as LCD but with a different form of backlighting, usually resulting in a much slimmer model.

Legend – (also called a key) an explanatory box that identifies the patterns or colours that are assigned to the data series or categories in a chart.

License key – a software key certifies that the copy of a program is original and has not been illegally copied.

Limited animation – where the same cels are used over and over again.

List box – displays one or more items of text from which a user can choose. The user might highlight the item or click on a radio button to indicate a choice.

Locking cells – restricting access to a cell so that it can be viewed but not changed by particular users.

Logical construct – terms which allow data and instructions to be linked together such as AND, OR and NOT.

Logical functions – functions that return a value of True or False, depending on the conditions that you set up.

Logical operators – return a value of True or False, depending on the logical values in the argument.

Loop – a piece of code which is executed over and over again until it fulfils a preset criterion.

Lossless compression – allows the original image to be rebuilt from the compressed (reduced-size) image.

Lossy compression – does not allow the original image to be rebuilt from the compressed (reduced-size) image.

M

Macro – a series of commands and functions that are stored in a Microsoft® Visual Basic module and can be run whenever the user needs to perform the task.

Man hour – the amount of work a person can be expected to do in one hour.

Mask – a tool you can use to select a certain area of an image to protect it from changes, such as applying colour, filters or other effects.

Mathematical operators – return the result of the calculation, eg 3+4 returns 7, 3*4 returns 12.

MB/s – stands for megabytes per second. It is a data transfer rate measured in 1,000,000 bytes per second.

Megapixel – a million pixels. It is a unit of image-sensing capacity in a digital camera.

Memo – short for memorandum. It is a short note between colleagues.

Menu system – a user interface device that presents the user with a window of buttons, each one leading – via a mouse click – to another lower level menu or the data required.

Method – an action which can be performed by an object.

Milestones – major points in the project where a number of activities should have been completed.

MMORPG – stands for massive multiplayer online role playing game.

Mood boards – a collage of images, textures and other items, aimed at providing an idea of the look and feel of a product. They are usually A3 size.

N

Navigation diagram – a diagram that shows how the different parts of a project will combine. In web design, it shows how different pages will interrelate.

Non-disclosure – an agreement used to protect the confidentiality of information when it is shared with a third party.

NPCs – stands for non-player characters.

O

Object – a special type of data which has properties and methods or a game element that has characteristics and abilities such as the main character, an enemy or an item.

Operator – a mathematical symbol used in a calculation or comparison.

Ordinal data – data that has a definite ordering, eg from smallest to largest, or oldest to newest.

P

Parallel processes – processes that can run side by side, at the same time.

Parameter – a value passed to or from a function to use in its execution.

Parameter query – a query that prompts the user of a database to set specific criteria for the fields selected for that query by the database designer.

Path – a pre-determined route through the room that an object can take.

Payback period – during a project, this is the length of time taken before the cash benefits exceed the cost.

PDA – stands for personal digital assistant. This small handheld device offers a calendar, contact list and other useful programs.

Performance capture – where human acting is 'captured' by a computer and then used by animators to create the images.

Persistence of vision – refers to the ability of the human eye to preserve the image it has just seen for a brief instant. Therefore, when the eye sees a series of images that follow each other, it retains each image and the brain processes it as a continuous image.

PERT chart – PERT stands for program evaluation and review technique. The chart shows all the tasks in a project, with their durations and dependency information, identifying which other tasks need to be completed before a task can be started.

Phonograph – invented by Thomas Edison in 1877 to record the spoken word.

Pivot table – an interactive table that combines and compares data. The rows and columns can be rotated (pivoted on a cell) to produce different summaries of the source data.

Pixel – short for picture element. It is a dot of colour on a screen or other output device.

Pixel perfect – a term used in the design field where graphics are accurate down to the very last pixel.

Plug-in – software which will play specific types of files. For example, modern versions of browsers like Internet Explorer® come with Flash Player® which is a plug-in to allow the user to play Flash animation. Most browsers have a range of plug-ins automatically installed or available for download.

Power-up – a collectible item in a game that improves the abilities of the player.

Predictive model – an equation or calculation used to forecast an event.

Primary key – aims to uniquely identify every record preferably using only one attribute. Sometimes more than one field in a record could act as a primary key.

Producer – the individual responsible for overseeing the development cycle of the game.

Programmer – the individual who writes the code that eventually becomes a game. A programmer may also be referred to as a developer.

Program structures – different ways in which the code runs. There are three main types: sequential structures run one line after another, selection lets code be run only under certain conditions, and iteration lets you repeat lines of code whenever necessary to save time and computer memory.

Project methodology – a standard, documented way of tackling a business project.

Property – what is being changed.

Proprietary – owned, often by a company. In computing, proprietary often refers to the way a document file is structured, eg CorelDRAW® uses a CDR format for its vector files, which are structured so that CorelDRAW® can open them.

Proxy server – a server that acts as a connector to other servers, either for security, speed or more dubious reasons, such as circumventing restrictions.

Pseudoclass – a section of CSS code which controls certain behaviours of HTML, for example a:hover.

Public key encryption – a method of coding information so only the people with the right key at both ends of the communication can decode it.

Q

Qualitative research – involves collecting information about people's opinions, views and preferences about something. It allows you to make 'quality' judgements about your findings (based on fact, not on your own opinions).

Quantitative research – involves collecting data that can be measured and counted. The data collected can usually be presented in the form of graphs, tables and charts. It is important to use a large enough sample to ensure that you have used sufficient 'quantity' for the results to be valid and not guesswork.

R

RAM – stands for random access memory. It is the name given to the electronic memory plugged into the main motherboard inside the system unit. RAM is often 1 GB or more in a modern computer system. This component is often replaced when a PC has a memory upgrade.

Range – defines a rectangular shape within a worksheet, for example the range A3:B7 includes columns A and B, and rows 3 to 7.

Real time – where audio and video signals are transmitted almost instantaneously.

Regression – type of analysis that estimates the relationship between variables so that a given variable can be predicted from one or more other variables.

Relational database – contains a set of tables which are linked together by the relationships between the tables. It is for this reason such a database is called relational.

Relative cell reference – allows you to copy a formula across rows (or down columns) with any cell reference in the formula being changed automatically, relative to its original position.

Rendering – the process combining audio and visual elements with any applied effects to produce a file that can be played in real time.

Representative values – single values that represent many items of data. They include mean, mode and median, as well as other statistical values.

Reserved word – a word which is already used in the programming language and therefore cannot be used as a variable name.

Resolution – short for display resolution. This is the number of pixels or lines to the inch on the screen or output device. It is usually written as two numbers: the number of pixels across then the number down. So a 1024x768 display resolution has 1024 pixels across and 786 down, giving 786,432 dots on the screen.

Review points – points where the project manager and others meet to review the progress of the project.

Risk – any event, foreseen or not, that may happen and that puts the success of the project in jeopardy.

Risk assessment – an analysis of a task against each of the steps that could be taken to achieve the task.

Risk mitigation – the actions taken to reduce the effect of a risk if it should happen.

Rollover buttons – work as normal buttons on a web page, but when the mouse hovers over them, the image or text changes.

Router – a network device which can direct data traffic to the correct destination.

RSI – stands for repetitive strain injury. This can result from overuse of a computer mouse.

S

Scenario – a set of values that you can substitute automatically on your worksheet.

Screen design – depicts the layout of a web page and should be drawn before starting to build it.

Search engine visibility – getting a website listed as highly as possible on a search engine. This will increase the number of visitors to a site.

Selector – similar to the title of the style.

Select query – a query that selects the data from the fields that you specify and with the criteria that you set for those fields.

Sequential processes – processes that need to run in sequence, ie the next process cannot start before the previous process has completed.

Shortcut – an icon which, when double clicked, opens an application.

Software – the collection of programs installed on the computer.

Solid state device – a device that has no moving parts. USB pen drives are solid state because they store data onto electronic circuits which hold their values even when unplugged. USB hard drives are not solid state because the hard disk spins (moves) when used.

Sorting – rearranges the data (eg in one column of a spreadsheet) into a sequence such as alphabetical or numerical, ascending or descending.

SPAN – a method of defining a style for a block of HTML (hypertext markup language).

Spider – a type of bot (short for robot – a computer program that runs automatically) used by search engines to find websites for search engines.

Sprite – the graphical image that represents a game element.

Stakeholder – a person or organisation that is actively involved in a project or whose interests the project may affect.

Static website – one which has only fixed information on it and is usually just a presentation of information. If it is to be altered, the designer needs to change the code and then upload the amended page to the web server; a laborious task.

Storyboard – shows the sequence of a project. In web design, it shows how different pages will interrelate.

Storyboarding – In animation, a storyboard shows how different frames and scenes will interrelate.

Streaming – feeding the video file to the user's computer in a continuous smaller volume of data, buffered by temporarily storing it and feeding to the player gradually so it is displayed steadily on the screen.

Structured walk-through – a review by one or more developers who manually go through the main paths of a program or system, simulating how the computer executes them.

Style – a group of formatting decisions to be applied together as defined in the CSS. For example, to have text display as red and centred could be a style.

Syntax – the grammar of a programming language, prescribing the order in which words can be used.

Sub-total – the sum of some data, which together with other sub-totals makes a grand total.

T

Table – a collection of cells placed on a page and data (text, images, etc) can each be placed in separate cells, which is a very good way of controlling layout.

Tags – elements of web page code, either in HTML or CSS. Usually they are written between angle brackets, < and >, to indicate that they are code words.

Tester – an individual who usually works in a team to make sure that there are no defects or glitches in the game.

Text reader – software that translates text into speech.

Trace – the individual pixels of a bitmap converted into the mathematical algorithm of a vector.

Trichromatic system – uses combinations of three colours that are the basis of 3D vision: red, blue and green.

Tweening – short for 'in betweening'. This is where the animator states where point A and B are and the computer fills in the intermediary movement.

U

Uncanny Valley – the theory that if animation looks too real, audiences will feel uncomfortable.

Uploading – the process of putting a website on to a web server so it can be distributed across the Internet.

USB – stands for universal serial bus. It is a connection method that enables files to be transferred and stored.

User acceptance testing – a process carried out by the user that involves completing a series of tests on the newly installed software. Each feature of the software is individually tested to ensure that it is in fact a working application. This helps the user to confirm that the installation has been completed effectively.

V

Validation – the process of checking that data entered into a system is reasonable and in the correct format.

Value – the amount the property is being changed.

Variable – used to store data and is given a name, eg the data 'Fred' might be stored in variable 'firstname'.

VBA – stands for Visual Basic for Applications. It is a macrolanguage version of Microsoft® Visual Basic used to program Microsoft® Windows®-based applications.

Vector – an image which is saved as a mathematical algorithm. Each line is saved as co-ordinates of each point and details of colour, width, etc.

Vector format – saves the image as a mathematical algorithm.

Vector graphics – define objects as coordinate points and use mathematics inside the software to calculate how to display the image onto the screen or printer.

Verification – is a method of checking that the data entered on to the system is correct and the same as that on the original source.

W

Web server – a server which distributes web pages on to the Internet.

What-if questions – situations where the result depends on a number of input variables and you want to know the effect on the result if you were to change one or more of the input variables.

White box testing – tests internal structures or workings of an application. It uncovers coding errors and other software problems but cannot identify if the overall system meets the requirements specification.

WiFi – an increasingly popular standard for wireless networking and connection of PCs and other devices such as printers. WiFi is based on the 802.11 standard for wireless transmissions.

WIMP – stands for windows, icons, menus and pointers. WIMP refers to a number of ways to interact with an interface.

Wire-framing – used to draw an image of a 3D object that shows only the edges of the object.

Wizard – a program that enables a user to carry out a complex task by following a series of simple steps using dialog boxes.

WUI – stands for web user interface. This is a series of processes and guidance for writing in a single language.

Z

Zoetrope – originally known as the daedalum, a machine invented by William Horner in 1834. It spun a strip of images at high speed in order to show movement.

Zoopraxiscope – invented by Eadweard Muybridge, it was a development of the zoetrope. It used light which was shone through images on glass.

Index